Zope

web application construction kit

Martina Brockmann
Katrin Kirchner
Sebastian Lühnsdorf
Mark Pratt

SAMS
201 West 103rd Street, Indianapolis, Indiana 46290

Zope Web Application Construction Kit

International Standard Book Number: 0-672-32133-5

Library of Congress Catalog Card Number: 00-111264

Printed in the United States of America

First Printing: October 2001

04 03 02 01 4 3 2 1

Trademarks

All terms mentioned in this book that are known to be trademarks or service marks have been appropriately capitalized. Sams Publishing cannot attest to the accuracy of this information. Use of a term in this book should not be regarded as affecting the validity of any trademark or service mark.

Warning and Disclaimer

Every effort has been made to make this book as complete and as accurate as possible, but no warranty or fitness is implied. The information provided is on an "as is" basis. The authors and the publisher shall have neither liability nor responsibility to any person or entity with respect to any loss or damages arising from the information contained in this book or from the use of the CD or programs accompanying it.

Acquisitions Editors
Shelley Johnston Markanday
Jennifer Kost-Barker

Development Editor
Scott D. Meyers

Managing Editor
Charlotte Clapp

Project Editor
Carol Bowers

Copy Editor
Pat Kinyon

Indexer
Eric Schroeder

Proofreaders
Jessica McCarty
Plan-It Publishing

Technical Editor
Tom Deprez
Tino Wildenhain

Team Coordinator
Amy Patton

Media Developer
Dan Scherf

Interior Designer
Gary Adair

Cover Designer
Alan Clements

Cover Art
Brendan Davis

Contents at a Glance

Table of Contents

About the Authors

Martina Brockmann was born in 1978 in Eastern Germany. She finished school in 1998 and moved to Berlin, where she started studying History and Computer Science at the Technical University of Berlin. When she started working at beehive two years later, Martina made first contact with Zope. At beehive she wrote documentation and user manuals for beehive's own projects and for projects of beehive's customers. Earlier this year Martina worked as a co-writer for *Zope: Content Management and Web Application Server*, which is the first German Zope book.

K. Kirchner was born in Berlin in 1977 and finished school in 1996. After getting a degree in Commercial Correspondence, Kirchner started studying Computer Science at the Technical University of Berlin and began working at beehive GmbH. Since then, Kirchner has been writing e-books on Zope and documentation for projects of beehive's customers, and has co-authored the first German Zope book *Zope: Content Management and Web Application Server*.

Mark Pratt is the managing director of beehive GmbH. He co-wrote the CMF chapter as well as Chapter 1 with K. Kirchner.

Sebastian Lühnsdorf has been working for beehive GmbH since June 1995. He is responsible for planning, designing, and implementing Web applications based on Zope. He is the co-author of the free Zope product the MetaPublisher and created the CMFMetaPublisher especially for this book.

Acknowledgments

There were so many wonderful people who helped us make this book great that we could probably spend three pages just listing all the names.

Foremost, there are the people from Sams Publishing:

Shelley Johnston Markanday, who helped in the beginning with coordinating everything, and Jennifer Kost, who took over after Shelley had gone on maternity leave (Congratulations, Shelley!).

Pat Kinyon, who worked on making this book something that doesn't read like it was written by a dyslexic (you should really appreciate her efforts).

Carol Bowers, who took over for the author review phase and coordinated everything with the technical editors and the copy editors.

Scott Meyers, who found Chapter 4 so fascinating that we didn't get it back for months, and who left a few comments throughout the book for us.

Now that we've got past the Sams people, we'd like to thank technical editors Chris Withers, Tino Wildenhain, and Tom Deprez for their hard work on their respective chapters and for proofreading all the code.

We would also like to thank the people from Zope Corporation, formerly known as Digital Creations, especially Tres Seaver for the CMF and for explaining it to us, and John Platten for his review.

Speaking of reviews: After we put Chapter 5, "The Content Management Framework (CMF)," online, we got a lot of responses. Some people sent information about typos that we overlooked and some even sent suggestions on how we could improve the chapter. Unfortunately we weren't able to implement as many of those suggestions that we would have liked. But nevertheless we thank everyone who took the time to read through the chapter and e-mail us, especially Tom Deprez, Norman Khine, Dave Lehman, Greg McCall, and Jean-Louis Berliet.

Of course, we also thank beehive GmbH and our colleagues there who provided us with background and technical information for some of the chapters.

There might be more we could list here, for example, the authors of all the products used in this book without whom this book wouldn't be half as good, and family and friends who kept us sane during our hard work. To all of them, a big thank you for your help and support.

Personal Acknowledgments

Martina Brockmann:

Besides all the persons mentioned above I'd like to thank my parents for giving me food, all their love, and my first computer. And of course I need to thank my friends Heike, Steffi, Franziska, Antje, Matthias, Sascha, and even Christoph because they have always been there for me and helped me get through the dark ages of adolescence, without going gaga. I dedicate this book to my good friend Sandra, who has always encouraged me to be all myself and who is one of the best persons to talk to on the phone, endlessly.

K. Kirchner:

I'd like to thank my parents and my best friend, Sonja, who listened to me rant whenever I was stuck in a chapter or stressed out from working all night, even though they didn't understand half of what I was talking about. I'd like to thank my sister and brother-in-law who also listened from time to time. This book is dedicated to my beautiful niece, Marlena, who has just turned four months and whom I love very much.

Tell Us What You Think!

As the reader of this book, *you* are our most important critic and commentator. We value your opinion and want to know what we're doing right, what we could do better, what areas you'd like to see us publish in, and any other words of wisdom you're willing to pass our way.

You can e-mail or write me directly to let me know what you did or didn't like about this book—as well as what we can do to make our books stronger.

Please note that I cannot help you with technical problems related to the topic of this book, and that due to the high volume of mail I receive, I might not be able to reply to every message.

When you write, please be sure to include this book's title and author as well as your name and phone or fax number. I will carefully review your comments and share them with the author and editors who worked on the book.

Email: `webdev@samspublishing.com`
Mail: Mark Taber
Associate Publisher
Sams Publishing
201 West 103rd Street
Indianapolis, IN 46290 USA

INTRODUCTION

Who Should Use This Book

This book is designed for any developer who wants to build next generation Web applications using the popular Open Source Web Application Server—Zope.

We hope that this book will help you appreciate how Zope can significantly reduce the time it takes to build complex Web applications.

If you've never downloaded Zope, you'll be surprised to find how small the standard distribution of Zope is (at the time of writing, the .tgz archive or self-extracting Zip archive is less than 5MB). However, when you unzip and/or untar your Zope installation, you'll be pleased to find that it comes with everything you need to start your first experiments, such as an object-oriented database and Web server.

Whether you're a seasoned Zope developer looking to learn new tricks or an aspiring Web application developer interested in acquiring some Zope Zen, we trust you'll find what you're looking for in this book. We assume that you have already mastered a programming or scripting language, such as Python (the language in which much of Zope was written) as well as some Structured Query Language (SQL). Building on what you already know, we'll teach you how to use ZClasses and DTML for basic prototyping, introduce you to several great Zope Products that can be easily customized, and how to use some of the hundreds of available Python modules that cover everything related to the generation of dynamic graphs and PDF documents.

How to Use This Book

After we've covered basics, such as the installation of Zope, we'll explain how to compile a database adapter so that you can hook a relational database to Zope. If you're not interested in working with a relational database but prefer to use Zope's built-in database (ZODB) instead, feel free to skip Chapter 3, "Connecting Zope to External Relational Databases."

Of course, you always use the ZODB when working with Zope because the objects you create are stored within it. In Chapter 3, you will find a section dedicated to the ZODB.

If you're interested in learning how to generate dynamic PDF files and how to deliver them via Zope, feel free to jump to Chapter 12, "Generating Dynamic PDFs." However, please be aware that throughout the book we are gradually trying to impart some Zope Zen; if you skip and jump all around the book, you might miss some important connections.

We do encourage you to find the pace you feel comfortable with and to experiment. After you've got Zope installed, its Web management interface is surprisingly versatile, allowing you to control almost all of Zope's functions and code. As a result, getting into Zope is surprisingly easy and addictive!

Section I: Introduction and Review

Section I of this book introduces Zope and the philosophy behind it—the so-called Zope Zen. It describes what project Zope is best used for, how to install and configure Zope, and how to connect it to your database. The last part of the section describes Zope's own programming language.

Chapter 1, "The Zope Web Application Construction Kit," explains what Zope is and basic Zope concepts. It also introduces Zope products and Python modules that can be used to expand Zope's functions and can be modified to fit your needs.

In Chapter 2, "Installation and Configuration," you learn how to install Zope on the Windows and UNIX platforms, using Linux as an example. It also explains what the ZServer is and how to run Zope with it or Apache.

Chapter 3, "Connecting Zope to External Relational Databases," describes how to connect external relational databases to Zope via database adapters that already exist for the most common databases, such as Oracle, Sybase, MySQL, and Postgres. It explains how to send information from and to the database by using SQL statements.

Chapter 4, "Building a Prototype," explores Zope's Document Template Markup Language (DTML), Zope's Undo System, and ZClasses that make for a great prototyping combination. It shows how to create a message board with a ZClass and how the board's entries are stored in a database.

Section II: Building a Portal and Adding Services

In Section II, you learn how to create a portal where members can interact with each other and how a content management system helps you to more easily maintain a Web site. All this is done by taking existing Zope products and modifying them to your own needs.

Chapter 5, "The Content Management Framework (CMF)," introduces the free, open-source Zope product CMF. The CMF provides a basic portal where logged-in members can publish contents and interact with each other. This chapter explains how to install the CMF and how to change its design and create new content types.

Chapter 6, "The MetaPublisher," introduces the Metapublisher, a free Zope product that helps you to easily create things like guestbooks or photo galleries. This chapter explains the basic usage of the MetaPublisher and shows how it can be used in conjunction with the CMF portal to allow the portal member to add entries.

Chapter 7, "Creating a Threaded Discussion Group," shows how to integrate an existing discussion product into a CMF portal and how to modify it for your own needs.

Chapter 8, "Creating Polls and Surveys," describes different Zope products that, when modified properly, can help you find out how well your site and Web applications are received by its users.

Section III: More Cool Web Applications

Section III offers an overview of other Web applications that help you make your Web site more accessible for visitors and shows you the best way to add a search engine. We also cover more advanced Python modules and how to integrate them into Zope to generate dynamic graphs and PDFs.

In Chapter 9, "Automatically Building Sitemaps," you learn why sitemaps are useful and how to create a dynamic sitemap using Zope's integrated Tree- and In-Tag. The chapter also introduces an existing sitemap product NFGnav and shows you how to modify them to meet your needs.

Chapter 10, "Adding Search Capabilities," teaches you how to effectively add a search engine to your Web site or portal by using the ZCatalog, a search engine that comes with Zope.

In Chapter 11, "Creating Dynamic Graphs in Zope," you learn how to use the Python Image Library (PIL) and the occasional Zope product to create dynamic graphs in Zope that show, for example, the results of a survey or poll in the form of a pie chart or bar graph.

Chapter 12, "Generating Dynamic PDFs," shows you how to use The ReportLab Library, a very powerful system to create dynamic Adobe Acrobat (PDF) files for documents, such as reports or contracts that can then be delivered in a customized form via Zope.

PART I

INTRODUCTION AND REVIEW

CHAPTER

CHAPTER 1

THE ZOPE WEB APPLICATION CONSTRUCTION KIT

Welcome to the Zope Web Application Construction Kit (WACK). In this chapter, we will answer the question "What is Zope?" and explain the most common ways of interacting and programming in Zope. In the next chapter, we'll install a Zope server so you can try out the examples that are included in this book.

What Is Zope?

Zope is the leading open source Web application server.

In this book, we define Web applications as applications that don't have to be installed on your local PC to run. The only requirement is a Web browser that acts as a (thin) client between you and the (Web) server that actually runs the applications. In a way, a Web application server fills a role similar to an operating system in that it provides several common services, such as user authentication, that a developer can easily access through API calls.

As you become comfortable with the various built-in tools and services that are included in the standard distribution of Zope, you'll notice a steady decrease in the time required to build complex Web applications.

Because Zope is open source, any part of the source code can be changed to reflect the needs of the individual Web application developer. Zope is also royalty free, so you could, for example, build a Zope-based application and sell it on a CD-ROM or DVD 100 million times without having to pay a single cent in royalties.

Zope has won many converts in the last two years, and a vibrant development community has developed all over the world. This community works with Digital Creations, the original developers of Zope, to add new features and plan its future growth.

Joining and participating in Zope's growth is easy. There are several mailing lists, the Zope.org community Web site, and plenty of ways to contribute.

On Zope.org, you can submit tips, how-tos, news items, and code or Zope products you've written. If you find or develop something useful, share it with the community!

Working with Zope

DTML, ZClasses, Z SQL methods, Python products, and Python scripts, are all different ways of working with Zope. It's up to a developer to chose the method he or she prefers.

DTML

The Document Template Markup Language (DTML) is Zope's built-in scripting language, which is similar to the PHP scripting language. DTML tags are embedded in a Web page and, when this Web page is called by a Web browser, are executed.

Unlike PHP3 and 4, DTML is not designed to be the primary language for the development of Zope applications, although some programmers (mis)use DTML for this purpose. DTML should be used as "superglue" connecting dynamic data—regardless of whether it is held within Zope or an external relational database—and templates that define the visual appearance of the Web site and how dynamic data should be represented visually.

ZClasses

With ZClasses, a developer can define new objects. These objects can be based on common Zope objects, such as a folder or DTML document, but they can be extended any way the developer sees fit. What makes ZClasses unique is that they can be created and managed solely via Zope's Web interface, so there is no need to open a shell or learn Python to work ZClass magic. Figure 1.1 shows a ZClass Configuration screen.

Using nothing but DTML, ZClasses, and the ZODB, a developer can build Web applications within a short period of time. This makes ZClasses great for prototyping because they can usually be created faster than a comparable Zope (Python) product.

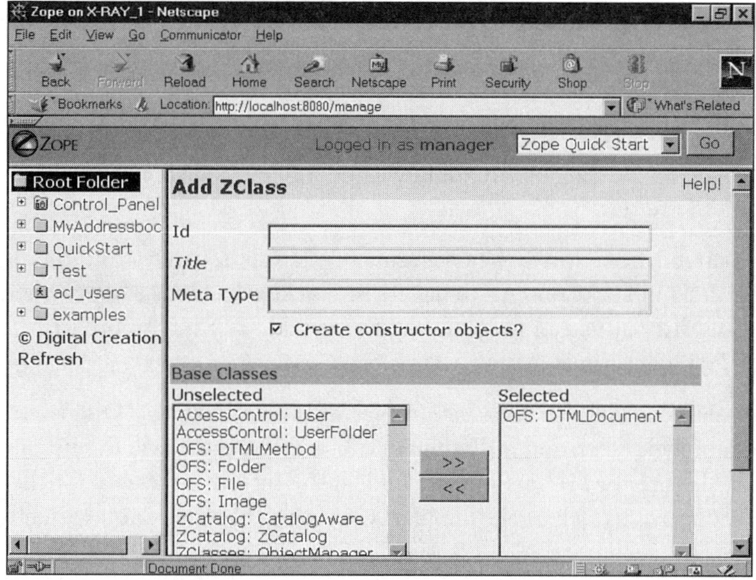

Figure 1.1
ZClass Configuration screen showing inheritance of classes.

Z SQL Methods

Zope SQL methods allow database developers to program directly via Zope's Web interface. Z SQL methods become available to the developer when he has compiled a Database Adapter (DA) for which the database Zope is supposed to open a connection.

DAs currently exist for MySQL, Postgres, Oracle, Sybase, the ODBC, and Interbase.

Z SQL methods make it very easy for a database developer to feel right at home because Zope has wizards that can generate templates for the display of data as well as create simple search interfaces.

Moreover, due to the database connection objects, it is easy to switch from working with a development database to the actual database. You create the Z SQL methods using the database connection object for the test database and later change the database connection object so that it connects Zope with the actual working database.

As is the case with ZClasses, DTML, such as `<dtml-sqlvar ...>`, is used to tie the dynamic data coming from the database into templates.

(Python) Zope Products

Zope products are applications written specifically for Zope.

Thanks to a wizard-like approach, adding a new instance of a Zope product is as simple as giving the new instance an idea and selecting the appropriate options. Zope takes care of the rest.

When written true to form, the program code is kept separate from the templates, allowing designers or Content Managers to quickly change the appearance of an application without having to know any Python and anything more than the most basic DTML commands.

A good example would be a discussion forum product such as ZDiscussion/Confera. Its program logic is written in Python and is only accessible via the file system. But a Content Manager or Webmaster will find all the screens necessary for the creation of discussion boards as well as the templates for visual customization within the Zope Web interface.

When properly implemented, Zope products give regular users who are not blessed with software development skills the control they need to roll out services to particular areas of the Web site as they see fit.

Figure 1.2 shows the Options view of a Squishdot instance. Squishdot is a free Zope product that works as a message board. In this view, the site manager can decide, for example, whether postings to the Squishdot site are moderated and when or if they expire.

There are several hundred free Zope products available for download via the Internet. These products cover a wide range of tools for building everything from news systems, Weblogs, polls and surveys, and sitemaps.

One thing a Zope Web applications developer needs to learn is how to take existing Zope products and quickly change them to fit a particular project's needs. Sometimes, all it takes is a little DTML; other times, it will take a few lines of Python code. Regardless of the approach, Zope products are a Web applications programmer's best resource to learn from and improve on.

Python Modules

Python is an interpreted, object-oriented programming language and has been around for a decade. It is an easy-to-learn language and is frequently compared to programming languages, such as Perl or Java.

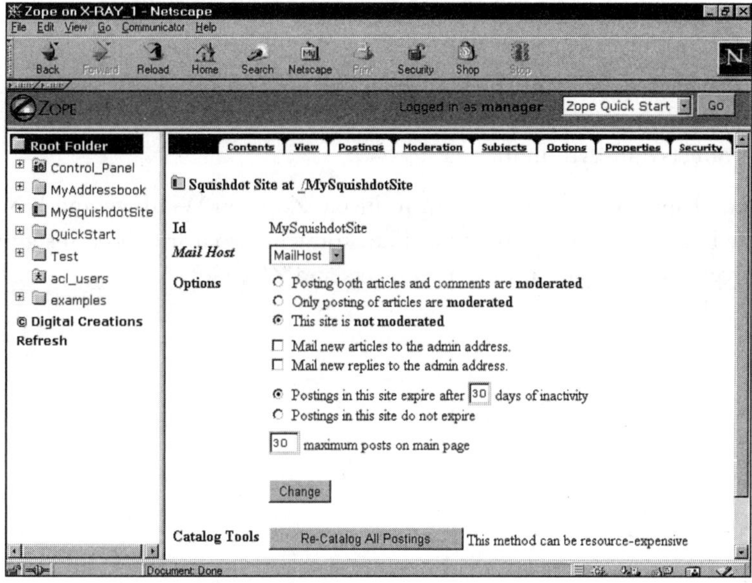

Figure 1.2

Configuration options of the Squishdot Zope product.

Python has a very clear syntax and has all the features one would expect from a modern object-oriented language. Modules, classes, exceptions, high-level dynamic data types, as well as dynamic typing, have brought many recent converts to Python.

Because Zope was mostly written in Python and, therefore, is object-oriented, it is very easy to use existing Python modules to augment or enhance your Web applications.

Python has been around for over a decade, so smart Zope programmers should visit `http://www.python.org` on a regular basis to find out about new Python modules or enhancements. Chances are that some of your next project requirements have already been met by a Python library. In this book, we hope to introduce two very valuable Python modules to you and explain how to tie them into Zope.

In this book, we will work with two Python modules:

- *The Python Image Library PIL*—Written by the Swedish company Pythonworks
- *The ReportLab Library by ReportLab*—Capable of creating dynamic Adobe Acrobat PDF files

Both libraries are free, and both are tools with which a Zope Web application programmer should be comfortable.

Summary

This chapter has given you an overview of what Zope is and short explanations of DTML (Zope's own markup language), ZClasses, and Z SQL. You also learned about Zope products and Python modules.

The next chapter will show you how to install Zope on Windows and UNIX systems and how to access Zope for the first time. You will also learn about installing new Zope products and about importing objects and ZClasses.

CHAPTER 2

INSTALLATION AND CONFIGURATION

Before Starting the Installation Process

Before installing Zope, you will need to decide on which platform you want to use it. Currently, there are Windows, Linux, Solaris, and source downloads available at the Zope.org Web site (`http://www.zope.org`). Follow the Download link to get to the newest Zope version available.

For each of the platforms, there is a setup file for new installations as well as for upgrading from an earlier version of Zope. Should you already have a Zope installation on your computer, you might want to use an upgrade instead of having to install a completely new Zope instance. You should visit the Zope.org Web site frequently to ensure that you have the newest version.

Sometimes, you will find a hotfix for the current and earlier Zope versions. Hotfixes provide you with an easy way to get rid of known bugs without having to upgrade a running installation. If you are using a Zope version that has known bugs or security risks, you need to install a hotfix. See Zope.org's download page for the latest hotfix.

Hardware and Software Requirements

Zope does not require any special hardware, so a standard working machine should do. However, you may want to make sure to have at least 50MB free disk space, depending on how much you will be working with Zope. The size of the data file does not solely depend on how many objects you create in Zope but also on how many actions you execute.

Also, the more memory you have, the faster Zope will work.

Unless you use Zope on a Windows machine, you need to install Python 1.5.2 or higher on your machine. The Windows version of Zope comes with its own Python version that will be installed and compiled during the Zope setup.

What Is the ZServer?

Every Zope distribution comes with the so-called ZServer. This is a Web server written in C. It allows you to run Zope without having a Web server, such as Apache. In addition to the Web server, the ZServer provides an FTP server and a PCGI server. This allows a create in Zope but also on how many actions you execute. user to transfer data from and to Zope via FTP.

Sometimes, you may want to use Zope with Apache rather than the ZServer because Apache provides more services than the ZServer or because you have a Web site only partly managed in Zope. For the installation instructions, see the "Installation Using Apache" section later in this chapter.

There is a How To on `zope.org` that gives a step-by-step explanation of running your ZServer with SSL support. It can be found at `http://www.zope.org/Members/Ioan/ZopeSSL`.

Installation on Windows

Installing Zope on Windows, no matter whether you use Windows 95/98, Windows NT, Windows Me, or Windows 2000, is an easy process. To use Zope with Windows, you need to download the respective setup file that is called something similar to this: `Zope-2.3.0-win32-x86.exe`.

After you have downloaded create in Zope but also on how many actions you execute. the setup file to your computer, start the installation process by either clicking the file in the Windows Explorer or by selecting Execute from the Windows Start menu and browsing for the file.

The installation mainly runs automatically, but you will need to give some information during the process.

First, you will be prompted to choose a path where Zope is to be installed (see Figure 2.1).

Next, create an initial manager for Zope by entering a name and password (see Figure 2.2). You will need the initial manager's name and password later to access the Zope management screen for the first time (see "Accessing the Zope Management Interface for the First Time" later in this chapter).

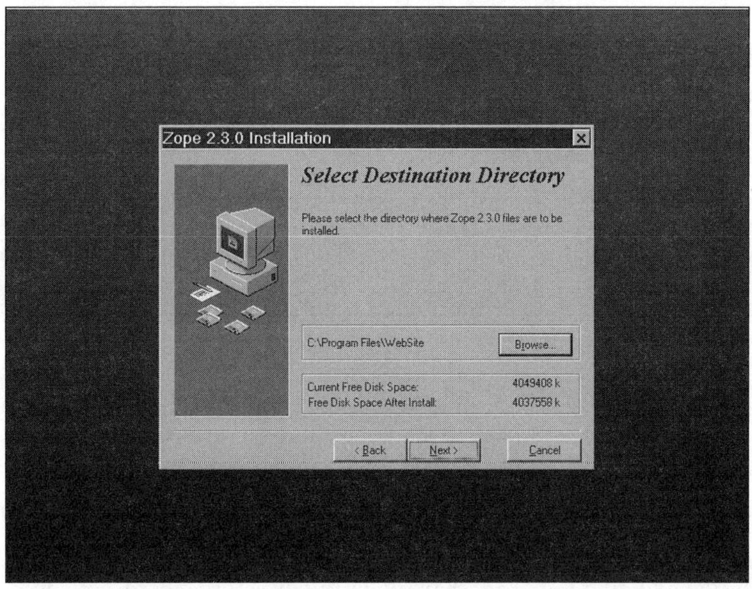

Figure 2.1
The Select Destination Directory screen.

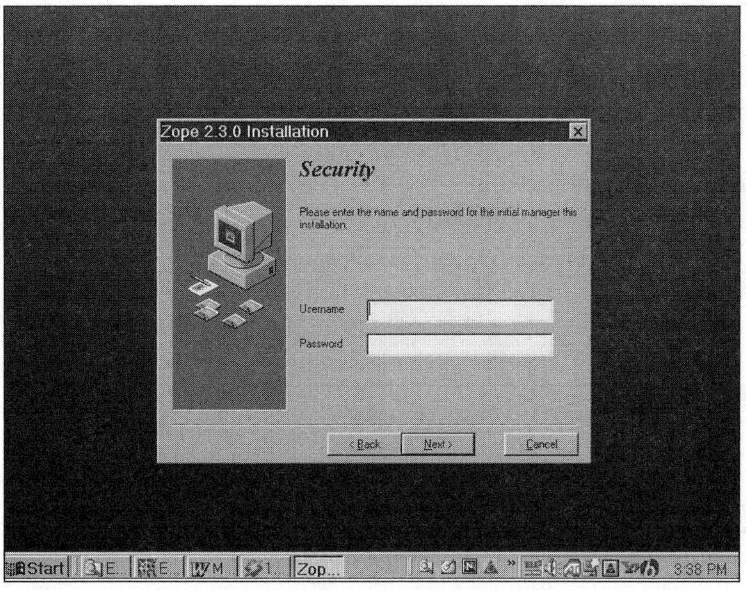

Figure 2.2
Select a name and password for the initial manager.

If you use Windows NT or Windows 2000, you may choose to run Zope as a Win32 service. This means that the Zope server will start automatically on booting Windows so you won't need to start it manually whenever you want to work with Zope. If you decide to run Zope as a service, select Run as a Win32 Service when given the choice.

> **Note**
> Installing Zope on Windows NT (or Windows 2000) may require you to be logged in as administrator.

If you are not working with Windows NT or Windows 2000, or you decide not to run Zope as a service, you will have to start the Zope server manually by executing the `start.bat` file in the Zope installation folder each time you want to work with Zope.

This completes your interaction with the setup program, and the setup will now continue on automatically. After the setup program is completed, you can start the ZServer by executing the `start.bat` file in the directory where Zope was installed. Now you can start working with Zope, so you can skip to the "Accessing the Zope Management Interface for the First Time" section later in this chapter.

Installation on Linux

In this section, we will explain the "normal" installation of Zope on a Linux machine, as well as how to use Apache with your Zope server.

Using the Linux Installation File

Download the Linux installation file `Zope-2.3.0-linux2-x86.tgz` from the Zope download page at `www.zope.org` and save it to the directory `/usr/local/`. If you think you will have more than one Zope installation on your machine, you might want to create a special folder exclusively for Zope. In this case, create a new folder in `/usr/local/` possibly called ZopePark. The following description, however, assumes you do not have this special folder.

> **Note**
> The Linux installation file for Zope contains the precompiled code files. If complications occur using this file, try installing Zope with the source codes (see the next section, "Installation Using the Source Codes").

Go to the `/usr/local/` directory and extract the installation file with the following command:

```
tar -xvfz Zope-2.3.0-linux2-x86.tgz
```

This will create a new folder, `Zope-2.3.0-linux2-x86`, in `/usr/local/`. Change to this new directory and run the install script as follows:

```
./install -u nobody -g nobody
```

The options `-u` and `-g` stand for user and group. If you do not run the installation with the user and group options set to nobody, the unpacked files will be owned by a specific user—for example, the user that created the `tgz` file. This may cause problems later with some files and directories that need to be accessible by everyone. Setting the user and group options to nobody makes sure that the files access, start, and stop `Zope.cgi`, and the `var` directory will be owned by nobody. At the end of the installation process, you will be given the initial manager's password. Write down this password and keep it from unauthorized persons. This password is necessary to access the Zope management interface later.

Now, you only need to start the ZServer with the following command:

```
./start &
```

This will start the ZServer with the default ports:

HTTP Server:	8080
FTP Server:	8021
PCGI Server:	8099

You can change these ports if they conflict with existing ports. The ports can be changed using the `-w` (for HTTP port), `-f` (for FTP port), and `-m` (for PCGI port). For more information on the options with which the ZServer can be started, type in

```
start -h
```

This will show you all possible options and their meanings.

If you want to stop the ZServer, run the stop script by typing

```
./stop
```

You can go on to the "Accessing the Zope Management Interface for the First Time" section later in this chapter now.

Installation Using the Source Codes

To install Zope on Linux using the source codes (the non-compiled files), download the source codes file called `Zope-2.3.0-src.tgz`. Also, make sure that Python 1.5.2 is correctly installed on your machine. For the latest version of Python, see the download page at `www.python.org`.

> **Note**
> The following installation was done on a SuSe Linux 6.4 server, but the process with RedHat is similar and may only differ in pathnames.

To install Zope, you need to be logged in as `root`. If you want to run more than one Zope instance on your machine, you may want to create a superfolder (for example, ZopePark) that will house your different Zope instances. Move to the `/usr/local/` directory and create the new folder `ZopePark`.

Now copy the installation file to the new folder and unpack the file with the following command:

```
tar xvzf Zope-2.3.0-src.tgz
```

The unpacking process will create a new folder, `Zope-2.3.0-src`, with all files and subfolders for the Zope instance.

Now you can change the folder name `Zope-2.3.0-src` to a Webserver name with the following command:

```
mv Zope-2.3.0-src Webserver
```

The next step is to compile the ZServer. Change into the Webserver directory and start the compiling process as follows:

```
python wo_pcgi.py
```

The Python modules will now be compiled without the pcgi wrapper (wo means without). Compilation with the pcgi wrapper were only necessary for Zope versions earlier than version 2.2.0. The newer versions do not need the wrapper anymore.

After the compilation process is completed, you will see the following message onscreen:

```
creating default database
chmod 0600 /usr/local/ZopePark/Webserver/var/Data.fs
------------------------------------------------------------------
```

```
creating default access file
Note:
        The super user name and password are 'superuser'
        and 'qODQClkW'.

        You can change the superuser name and password with the
        zpasswd script.  To find out more, type:

        /usr/bin/python zpasswd.py
```

Write down the superuser name and password!

If the Webserver directory and all the files and subdirectories in it do not belong to `root`, you will now need to change the permissions. To do this, go to the `/usr/local/ZopePark/` directory and enter the following command:

```
chown -R root.root Webserver
```

The subdirectories `var` and `access` need to be given different permissions because they need to be accessible by anyone. Change to the Webserver directory and use the following commands to change the permissions:

```
chown -R nobody.nogroup var

    chown -R nobody.nogroup access
```

You may not need to change the permissions, depending on the role the ZServer is running as. If your ZServer runs as `root`, you do not need to change permissions because it will be able to access `var` and `access` anyway.

The following part of the installation is only necessary if you want to access Zope via the Internet.

You need to assign an IP address to the ZServer. In our example, we will use the following data:

www address:	`www.mycompany.com`
IP address:	`212.11.222.333`

To assign the IP address, you need to edit the start script file `start` that can be found in the Webserver directory. At this point, this file should look like Listing 2.1.

Listing 2.1
Original start

```
#! /bin/sh
reldir=`dirname $0`
PYTHONHOME=`cd $reldir; pwd`
Export PYTHONHOME
Exec /usr/bin/python \
      $PYTHONHOME/z2.py \
      -D "$@"
```

Change the last line, as shown in Listing 2.2.

Listing 2.2
Modified start

```
#! /bin/sh
reldir=`dirname $0`
PYTHONHOME=`cd $reldir; pwd`
Export PYTHONHOME
Exec /usr/bin/python \
      $PYTHONHOME/z2.py \
      -D "$@" -a 212.11.222.333 -f 8021 -u nobody -w 80 -m -
```

Table 2.1 explains the options you have just entered in the last line of the start script file.

Table 2.1
ZServer Options

Option	Explanation
`-a 212.11.222.333`	IP-Adresse = 212.11.222.333
`-f 8021`	FTP auf Port 8021
`-u nobody`	Username = nobody
`-w 8080`	HTTP-Server auf Port 8080
`-m -`	Monitor-Server ist ausgeschaltet

You will find more information on the different options in the `z2.py` file in your Zope server directory (`/usr/local/ZopePark/Webserver/`).

Now, your Zope server is ready to be accessed via the Internet after you have started the ZServer.

To start the ZServer, execute the start script file in your Zope server directory with the following command:

```
./start &
```

You should see something similar to the following on your screen:

```
[1] 3001
        root@linuxserver:/usr/local/ZopePark/Webserver > ------
2000-08-30T12:46:28 INFO(0) ZServer Medusa (V1.16.4.2) started at Wed Aug 30
➥14:46:28 2000
        Hostname: linuxserver.mycompany.com
        Port:8080

------
2000-08-30T12:46:28 INFO(0) ZServer FTP server started at Wed Aug 30 14:46:28
➥2000
        Authorizer:None
        Hostname: linuxserver
        Port: 8021
```

Note that `linuxserver` in these lines will be replaced by the name of your Linux server on your screen.

The installation of Zope on your Linux machine is now completed. Go to "Accessing the Zope Management Interface for the First Time," later in this chapter.

Installation Using Apache

If you want to build SSL-secured Web sites, you need to use Zope with Apache or you need to install the SSL support for the ZServer. We will explain two ways to use Zope with Apache.

Using Zope with Apache

This installation process was done on a RedHat 6.1 machine with Apache 1.3.9. The default configuration has `httpd.conf` in the `/etc/httpd/conf` directory, port 80, and the startup/shutdown script in the `/etc/rc.d/init.d/httpd` directory.

Install Zope as described in "Using the Linux Installation File" earlier in this chapter. However, before starting the ZServer, copy the `Zope.cgi` file into the `/home/httpd/cgi-bin/` directory with the following command:

```
cp -p Zope.cgi /home/httpd/cgi-bin
```

The option `-p` is very important because this will preserve the file's attributes if possible. This means that the user and group will be preserved for this file. This is necessary because `Zope.cgi` should be owned by nobody, even in the `/home/httpd/cgi-bin/` directory.

Now, you need to edit the `/etc/httpd/conf/httpd.conf` file to assure that Apache transfers authentication data to `Zope.cgi`. To do this, open the `Zope.cgi` file in a text editor. Make sure to be logged in as `root` or you will not be able to save the changes to the file. Now, add the lines in Listing 2.3 to the end of the file.

Listing 2.3

Rewrite Rule

```
1: RewriteEngine on
2: RewriteCond %{HTTP:Authorization} ^(.*)
3: RewriteRule ^/Zope(.*) /home/httpd/cgi-bin/Zope.cgi$1
4: ➥ [e=HTTP_CGI_AUTHORIZATION:%1,t=application/x-httpd-cgi,l]
```

> **Note**
> The RewriteRule (lines 3 and 4) need to be on one single line—not as it is here—or it will not work correctly.

The ExecCGI option must be specified for the `/home/httpd/cgi-bin/` directory. If you are not sure where it is, go to the `/etc/httpd/conf/` directory and open the `access.conf` file. If you do not see the line

```
Options ExecCGI
```

somewhere between the lines

```
<directory /home/httpd/cgi-bin
```

and

```
</directory
```

add it in there.

> **Note**
> In later versions of Apache, all configuration options can be found in the `httpd.conf` file.

With the following command, restart Apache still logged in as `root`:

```
/etc/rc.d/init.d/httpd restart
```

The configuration is now complete, and you will now be able to access your Zope server via Apache. Open your browser and type in the following URL:

```
http://localhost/Zope/manage
```

The browser will ask for a name and password. Use the superuser's name and password that you wrote down during the Zope installation process. Note that Zope's `root` folder is named `Zope` now. If you access the management screen by connecting to the ZServer directly (by typing the URL)

```
http://localhost:8080/manage,
```

the `root` folder will be unnamed.

Using Zope as a Front End to the ZServer

In some cases, you have an existing Web site where only a part is hosted on Zope. This can be done with Apache's `ProxyPass` and `ProxyPassReserve` directives and the Zope product SiteAccess that is already installed in Zope 2.3.0.

The `ProxyPass` directive is constructed as follows:

```
ProxyPass /visible_path http://backserver:port/path...
```

The `ProxyPassReverse` directive looks the same but has `ProxyPassReverse` where it says `ProxyPass` in the previous line.

When `Proxypass` is used, if there is a request to the `/visible_path` location, it is intercepted. The part up to and including `/visible_path` is taken from the URL and is replaced with `http://backserver:port/path...`. The request is then sent to this new URL and waits for an answer.

The `ProxyPassReverse` does the same thing, but the other way around. Requests starting with `http://backserver:port/path...` are translated back to begin with `/visible_path`.

This process makes believe that everything is happening on the front server, although part of the requests are redirected to somewhere else.

> **Note**
> The `ProxyPass` directive and the `ProxyPassReverse` directive must be in one line.

Example

Let's say you have an existing Web site `http://www.mycompany.com/` and now you want to add a discussion forum that will be hosted on Zope. Install the Zope server as previously described and have it listen to port 8080—the default port. Now, you need to make sure that Apache's `mod_proxy` is activated. To do so, check whether the `httpd.conf` file contains the lines in Listing 2.4.

Listing 2.4

Lines that Show Apache's `mod_proxy` Is Activated

```
LoadModule proxy_module
libexec/apache/libproxy.so
AddModule mod_proxy.c
```

You can now define the `ProxyPass` and `ProxyPassReverse` directives in the main server's `<Directory` section. To do so, add the lines in Listing 2.5.

Listing 2.5

`ProxyPass` *and* `ProxyPassReverse` *Directives*

```
ProxyPass /DiscussionForum/ http://www.mycompany.com:8080/
ProxyPassReverse /DiscussionForum/ http://www.mycompany.com:8080/
```

You will also need to add the lines in Listing 2.6.

Listing 2.6

`ProxyPass` *Directives for Zope Images*

```
ProxyPass /misc_ http://www.mycompany.com:8080/misc_
ProxyPass /p_ http://www.mycompany.com:8080/p_
```

These lines will make sure that the Zope image and the object icons in Zope will load correctly.

Save the changes and restart Apache. Now, every request to the `http://www.mycompany.com/DiscussionForum/*` URL is automatically redirected to the ZServer at `http://www.mycompany.com:8080/`.

However, most URLs in Zope are absolute URLs that are constructed with variables defined in Zope containing the URL and port number on which Zope believes it is running. Therefore, they are not compliant with the URL that is set in the `ProxyPassReverse` directive and cannot be translated back. This means that the circle is broken and most or all of your Zope pages and images will not load.

You can use the SiteAccess product to work around this problem. Since Zope 2.3, the SiteAccess product is part of the Zope distribution and does not need to be installed. Go to the Zope management interface (see the section, "Accessing the Zope Management Interface for the First Time") and create a new `SiteAccess` object in the Zope `root` folder by selecting SiteRoot from the drop-down menu. Fill out the following form shown in Figure 2.3 with data concerning Base and Path.

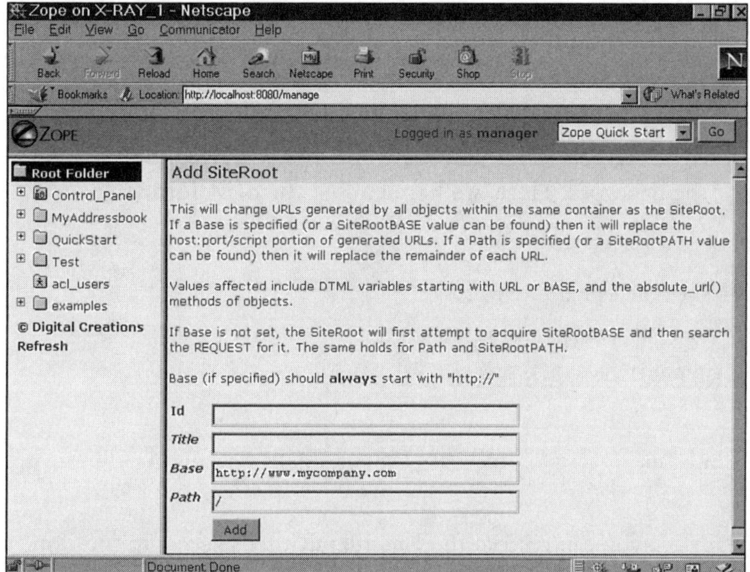

Figure 2.3
The `SiteRoot` object.

Now click Add and everything is set.

If you want to use Zope on a virtual host, you need to define the `ProxyPass` and `ProxyPassReverse` directives in the definition of your virtual host of the `httpd.conf` file.

Creating and Changing the Emergency User Password

The Emergency user is not created by default during the Zope installation. Whereas the initial manager is created as an object within Zope, the Emergency user is not an actual object in the ZODB. The Emergency user was known as superuser during earlier Zope versions, and is used for emergencies if, for example, other users are deleted accidentally.

If you want to create an Emergency user or change the Emergency user's name or password at any given time, type the following command:

```
python zpasswd.py access
```

This will prompt you to enter a new Emergency user name, password, and a confirmation of the password as follows:

Username: **superuser**

Password: **12345**

Verify password: **12345**

After you have entered a name and password, you will need to decide on an encoding format for the password. Here, we have chosen the SHA format.

Please choose a format from

SHA—SHA-1 hashed password
CRYPT—UNIX-style crypt password
CLEARTEXT—No protection

Encoding: **SHA**

In the next step, you can restrict the Emergency user's access to the Zope instance by naming the domains from which access is to be allowed:

```
Domain restrictions:
```

If you do not want to restrict access, do not enter anything here. This will give the superuser access to Zope from anywhere.

The Emergency user's name and password has now been changed or the user was created.

Accessing the Zope Management Interface for the First Time

To start working in Zope, open your browser and type

```
http://localhost:8080/
```

or type the respective URL that you have defined for your Zope server.

This will get you to the Zope Quick Start screen. There you have a few options for continuing. For example, you can start by reading the Zope Manual or you can start working in the management screen by clicking the Zope management interface link. Zope will ask for a name and password. Use the superuser's name and password that you entered during the setup.

You can also access the management screen directly by adding `/manage` to Zope's URL, as follows:

```
http://localhost:8080/manage
```

> **Note**
> The addition of `/manage` can be used on every object you create in Zope. This will get you to the management interface of the respective object, provided that you are allowed to access the object's management interface.

Installing New Zope Products

Zope products are components written in Python that can be installed to be used in Zope. After installing a new Zope product, you can create instances of this product. Creating an instance of a product means creating a new object in Zope. An object, for example, can be a folder, a DTML method, or a whole application depending on the product installed.

The Zope community provides hundreds of free Zope products that are divided into categories such as External Access, User Management, or Navigational. The products are free to download either from the download page at `www.zope.org`, or you may want to check `www.zope-treasures.com`.

Installing new Zope products is a simple process. Download the file and save and move it to the directory of your Zope installation, for example:

```
/usr/local/Zope-2.3.0-src/       (Unix systems)

C:\Program Files\Website\        (Windows systems)
```

On UNIX systems, you again use the `tar` command to unpack the file:

```
tar xzvf product_name.tgz
```

On Windows machines, use WinZip or a similar pack program to extract the file.

Sometimes, the files contained in the packed file already have the correct path that will be created during the unpacking process. The correct path is

```
/lib/python/Products/product_name
```

However, sometimes the path is not correct. You will then have to move the product_name directory from wherever it was unpacked to the `/lib/python/Products` directory. It is essential that the `product_name` directory is in the `Products` directory; otherwise, Zope will be unable to recognize the new product and will not install it. If you know or notice beforehand that the files only have the product_name directory as a path, change the directory to `Zope_installation/lib/python/Products` before starting the unpacking process.

After you have unpacked the file, restart the Zope server. On startup, Zope will check every product in the `Products` directory and compile or re-compile it if necessary. Re-compiling only happens if there are no compiled versions of Python files in any of the subfolders of the `Products` directory or if the compiled versions are older than the non-compiled versions. If the non-compiled version of a file is newer than the existing compiled version, this means that there were changes made to the file (non-compiled) and that the file needs to be compiled again so the latest version is being used.

If the new product was installed correctly, you will find an entry in the drop-down menu in Zope's management interface that will allow you to add instances of this new product. This completes the installation of a new Zope product.

Importing Objects into Zope

Zope has an Import/Export function that allows you to import or export single objects or entire parts—containing hundreds of objects—to or from Zope. This comes in handy if you create an entire project in Zope that you then want to transfer to another Zope installation to be used there.

In the Zope management interface, there is an Import/Export button. To export objects from Zope, check the check box on the left to the object you want to export and then click the Import/Export button (see Figure 2.4).

You have two choices to determine where to save the exported file:

- *Download to local machine*—You get to choose where on your machine you want to save the file.
- *Save to file on server*—The file is saved to the `/var` directory of the Zope installation.

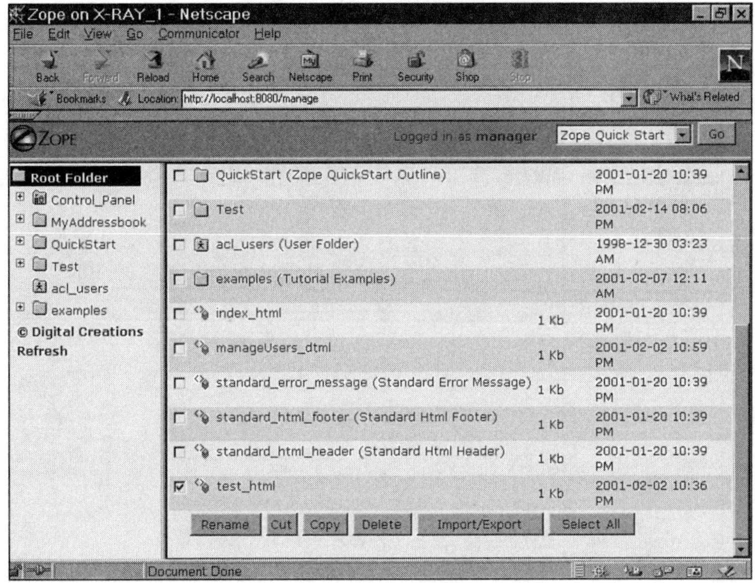

Figure 2.4
The selected object `test_html`.

This will bring up the page shown in Figure 2.5.

Moreover, you can choose whether the file should be saved in XML format. If you choose not to use the XML format, the file will be saved in a Zope-specific format, `zexp`.

To import a file again, make sure to put the file in the `/import` directory of the Zope installation. You cannot choose where Zope should import the file from, so if it is not in the `/import` directory, Zope will be unable to find the file and will give you an error message.

After you have put the file in the `/import` directory, go to the Zope management interface and click the Import/Export button in the folder or subfolder to which you want to import the file. The page you will be brought to is the same as the page used for exporting objects. The lower part of the page is used for the import (see Figure 2.6).

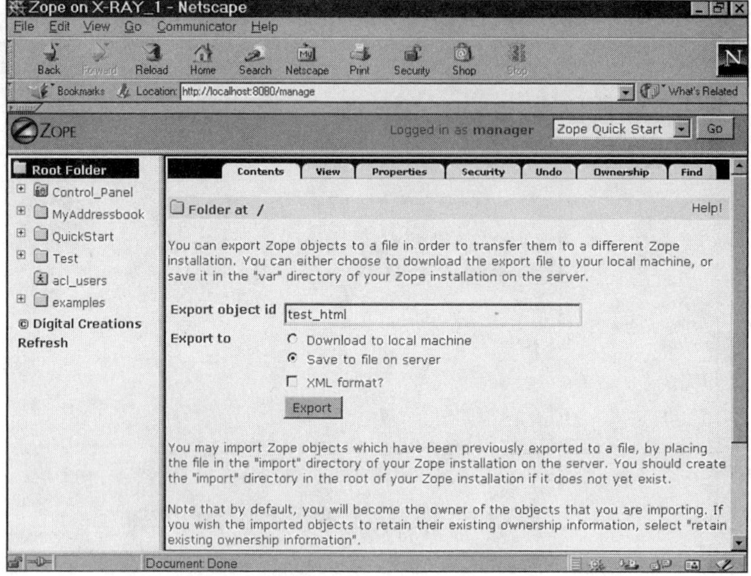

Figure 2.5

Exporting the object `test_html`.

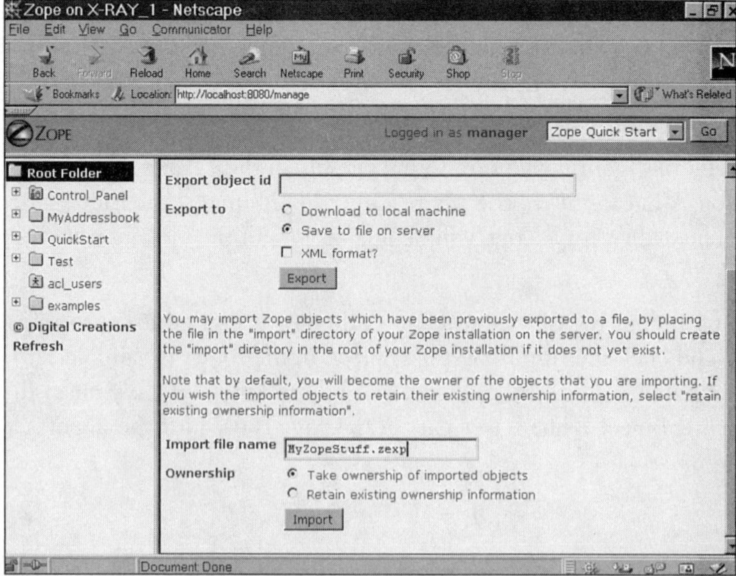

Figure 2.6

Importing an object.

Enter the name of the file you want to import in the Import File Name text field. You can now choose whether you want to take the ownership of the imported objects or if the objects should keep the owner they had when they were exported. Ownership will be explained later in the book.

> **Note**
> When importing a file, you must enter its full name with extension. The name is also case sensitive on all platforms except Win32.

Now click the Import button. If everything was all right, Zope will tell you that the import was successful, and you can return to working with Zope.

Importing ZClasses

ZClasses are Zope's way of providing extensible, sharable, persistent objects. They allow you to produce entire Internet applications without having to program in Python. Also, you can do things with ZClasses that you cannot do with DTML and Python scripts, such as access the file system. This is made possible by basing your ZClasses on existing Python classes that allow those actions.

You can use ZClasses to describe specific classes in Zope, such as `car`, `job`, `CD-ROM`, and `book`. These objects can have certain attributes, such as `price`, `description`, and `title`. This way, ZClasses can be used to easily create an online shop where all articles are objects in Zope.

ZClasses can also be exported. However, importing a ZClass is slightly different than importing a normal object in Zope, but only in that the place where you import the ZClass is a specific place and cannot freely be chosen.

To import a ZClass, put the exported ZClass file into the `/import` directory. Now, go to the `/Control_Panel/Products` folder in the Zope management interface. Click the Import/Export button and enter the complete filename into the Import File Name text field. After you click the Import button, the ZClass will be ready for you to use.

Transferring Files to Zope Via FTP

The ZServer provides its own FTP port. This way, you can transfer data directly into the Zope's ZODB. To be able to use this feature, you need an FTP client on your machine. A free FTP client for Windows, for example, is `WS_FTP`.

On Windows

In this section, we will show how to connect to Zope's FTP port using the FTP program WS_FTP. You can also follow the instructions in the Linux section later to connect. However, using WS_FTP gives you a graphic user interface whereas the Linux way works strictly in the shell.

After you have downloaded and installed `WS_FTP`, start the program. You will see the window shown in Figure 2.7.

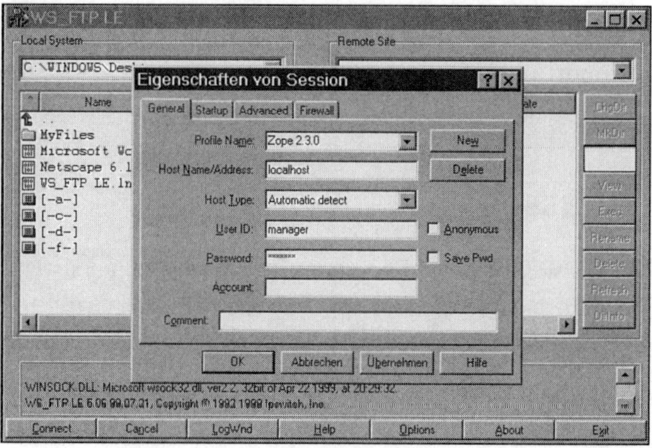

Figure 2.7
Creating a connection to Zope.

The fields, of course, are empty at first. Enter the data according to which Zope server you want to connect.

Profile Name:	This is just a name that you can choose so that you can recognize the connection.
Host Name/Address:	Here, you enter the hostname or IP address of the respective Zope server. In the previous example, it is the Zope server installed on the local machine.
User ID:	This is your Zope username.
Password:	The password that belongs to your Zope username.

If you are certain that no one else will be accessing your computer, you may want to check the Save pwd check box so you don't have to enter the password every time you connect to the Zope server.

Because a normal FTP port is :21 but the ZServer's FTP port is :8021, you need to change the default value for the FTP port in WS_FTP for this connection. This is done by clicking the Advanced tab at the top of the window. Now change the Remote Port from `21` to `8021` (see Figure 2.8). If you have started your ZServer FTP service with a different port number, enter that number instead.

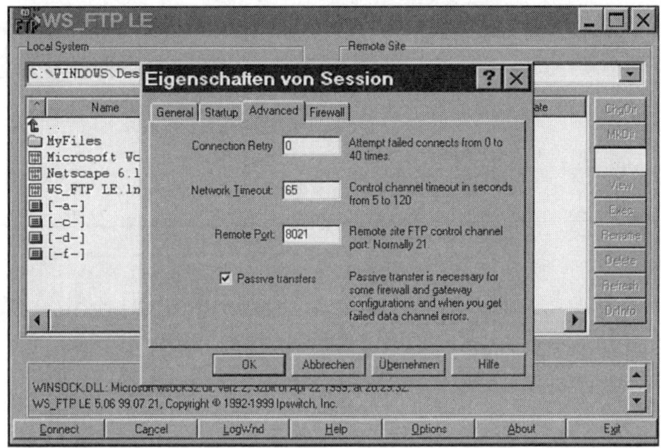

Figure 2.8
Setting the correct FTP port.

Now you can click the OK button and WS_FTP will connect you to the Zope server. The window you will see contains your file system on the left side and the Zope structure (everything that is in the ZODB) on the left side (see Figure 2.9).

Now you can transfer the files by selecting them in the left frame (your local machine) or the right frame (Zope server) and clicking the respective little arrow button in the middle (-> or <-).

You can also create new folders on your Zope server by clicking the MkDir button on the right side.

Moving through your Zope server folders is done by double-clicking the respective folder, or, if you want to move a folder up in the hierarchy, by clicking the two dots (..) at the top of the list of objects (right side).

To close the connection to the Zope server, click the Close button at the lower-left of the window.

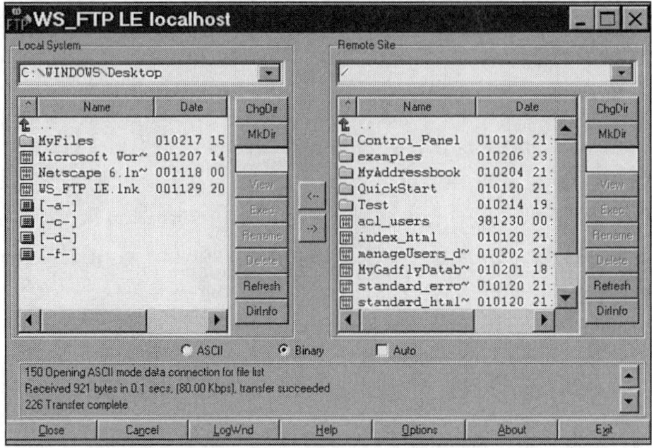

Figure 2.9
Transferring data to Zope.

On Linux

To use FTP on Linux, start the FTP program by entering the word **ftp** in the shell. Your prompt will change to something similar to the following:

```
ftp>
```

Now, open a connection to the Zope server using the following command:

```
ftp> open www.mycompany.com 8021
```

It is necessary to give the Zope server's FTP port because it differs from the usual port :21. If you started the Zope server with a different FTP port, enter the respective number instead of 8021. The command will open the connection and ask you for a username and a password. After you have successfully logged in, you can start transferring data from your local machine to the ZODB and vice versa.

To transfer data from your local machine to the ZODB, use the command put, as follows:

```
ftp> put local_file_name remote_file_name
```

`remote_file_name` is optional if you want the file to keep the same name. The local file must be in the same directory where you are. To change your local directory, use the `lcd` command. For example, if you want to change to the local directory MyZopeDirectory, enter the following command:

```
ftp> lcd MyZopeDirectory
```

To change the remote directory (the directory on the Zope server), use the normal `cd` command.

You can also transfer data from the Zope server to your local machine. This is done by using the command get as follows:

```
ftp> get remote_file_name local_file_name
```

This time, `local_file_name` is optional if you want the filename to remain the same.

To get a list of the objects that are in the current remote directory, type in the following command:

```
ftp> dir
```

or

```
ftp> ls
```

depending on how much information you want to receive about the respective files. Unfortunately, it is not possible to get a list of objects on your local machine. Consequently, you need to know which file you want to transfer and where to find it.

It might be a good idea to enter the `hash` command before starting to transfer files. This way, you get a sign marking every 1024 bytes or 2048 bytes, which will help you see how much of your file has been transferred.

Summary

In this chapter, you learned how to get your Zope server up and running, both on Windows and on UNIX machines. We also showed you two ways to use Zope with Apache. Additionally, you learned how to install new Zope products to enhance your Zope installation and how to transfer files from and to Zope using FTP.

The next chapter deals with Zope and databases. It will show you how to connect Zope to your database management system using database adapters and how to use SQL and Z SQL methods to work with your database.

CHAPTER 3

CONNECTING ZOPE TO EXTERNAL RELATIONAL DATABASES

Introduction

In this chapter, we will talk about relational databases and how they can be used with Zope. We start with an introduction to relational databases and then go on to the databases that are part of the Zope distribution, namely ZODB and Gadfly. Gadfly is a simple database that should only be used for demonstration purposes or to learn how to use Zope with a database.

After an introduction to the ZODB and relational database management systems (RDBMS), we will go through a step-by-step explanation of how to install the MySQL database adapter for Zope and how the connection between Zope and a MySQL table is established. Then we will show you how to use Zope's integrated demonstration database (Gadfly) to start working with SQL statements.

What Is the ZODB?

The ZODB (Z Object Database) is a database integrated in Zope. The ZODB's main function is to ensure that the objects created in Zope are persistent and are not deleted after shutting down the Zope process. Therefore, when working in Zope, every object is stored in the ZODB. But not only does the object get stored, its current state, information about it, and how it is used is stored as well, that meaning the user's actions are stored. This allows the user to undo those actions. This means that the ZODB is a transactional, object-oriented, persistence mechanism.

However, the ZODB is no alternative for a relational database. For one thing, it is not possible to send complex SQL queries to the ZODB. Moreover, you may already have a consisting database. If that is the case, you would not want to have to enter all the data again in another database or transfer it in another way. Another argument against using the ZODB instead of a Relational Database Management System (RDBMS) is that the ZODB is not suitable for storing large amounts of data.

Relational Database Management Systems (RDBMS)

Mainly, you can divide databases into two categories: commercial relational database management systems and open-source relational database management systems.

The leading commercial RDBMSs are Oracle (`www.oracle.com`) and Sybase (`www.sybase.com`).

However, these databases are not suitable for home users or small businesses because of the cost factor. The price for a license for one of these databases varies from a few thousand up to a few hundred thousand dollars which, for some companies, may be too expensive. They also are much more resource intensive. But both Oracle and Sybase are worth their money because they come with many more features and possibilities than their open-source counterparts.

The most important open-source RDBMSs are

MySQL (`www.mysql.com`)

PostgreSQL (`www.postgresql.com`)

Interbase (`www.interbase.com`)

In this chapter, we are going to describe how to connect a MySQL database to Zope. This procedure only differs from say, Oracle or Sybase, in that you need to use the respective database adapter for those databases.

> **Note**
>
> Most of the previously mentioned databases are transactional databases. However, out-of-the-box MySQL is not transaction aware.
>
> Zope does work best with transactional databases. Inconsistency problems can arise when a ZODB transaction is aborted if the RDBMS is not transactional.

Why Are Database Adapters Necessary?

Database adapters are links between Zope and the respective external relational databases. Through this link, data is sent between the two entities. Zope sends SQL statements that are then analyzed within the database and then the database sends the requested information. Without this link, Zope does not know where to send the SQL statements a user wants to have processed.

Which Database Adapter Do I Need?

Because there are differences between the interfaces of the various RDBMS by which applications can connect to the database, each database needs a special database adapter. Therefore, you cannot use a MySQL database adapter for Zope if you want to connect to a Sybase database.

The Zope community already provides you with database adapters for the most-used databases. You can find those adapters on the download page of `Zope.org` under the category External Access.

For example, if you have a MySQL database, you need to download the MySQL database adapter, which is called something like `ZMySQLDA-1.1.4-nonbin.tar.gz`. If you want to connect Zope to an Oracle database, you will have to download the appropriate file (for example, `ZOracleDA-2.2.0b1-src.tgz`).

Connecting MySQL and Zope

In this section, you will learn how to install the MySQL database adapter for Zope and how to establish the connection between MySQL and Zope. We have used the following software:

Operating System:	SuSe Linux 6.4
MySQL Database Version:	MySQL 3.22.32
Python Version:	Python 1.5.2.
Database Adapter:	`ZMySQLDA-1.1.4-nonbin.tar.gz`
Database Driver:	`MySQL-python-0.3.2.tar.gz`

We assume that you already have an existing MySQL database and will not describe how to create such a database in MySQL.

The database adapter, as well as the database driver, can be downloaded under the category External Access on the Download page of `www.zope.org`. The database driver file is a MySQL database module that contains newer drivers for the database adapter.

> **Tip**
> Visit `Zope.org` frequently for the latest database adapters for your database.

Installing the MySQL Database Adapter and the Latest Drivers

Suppose your Zope directory is `/usr/local/ZopePark/Zope-2.3.0-src/` and that you downloaded the database adapter file for the MySQL database (`ZMySQLDA-1.1.4-nonbin.tar.gz`). The files within the packed file already contain the correct paths within the Zope directory.

As a result, you only need to copy the database adapter file to your Zope directory

```
cp ZMySQLDA-1.1.4-nonbin.tar.gz /usr/local/ZopePark/Zope-2.3.0-src/
```

or you can move the file with the following command:

```
mv ZMySQLDA-1.1.4-nonbin.tar.gz /usr/local/ZopePark/Zope-2.3.0-src/
ZMySQLDA-1.1.4-nonbin.tar.gz
```

Now go to the Zope directory

```
cd /usr/local/ZopePark/Zope-2.3.0-src/
```

and enter the following command to unpack the database adapter file:

```
tar -xzvf ZMySQLDA-1.1.4-nonbin.tar.gz
```

The files will now be unpacked to the `/lib/python/Products/ZMySQLDA/` directory within your Zope directory. Now move the database driver file to the `/lib/python/Products/` directory and unpack it using the same `tar` command used previously.

Next, you need to edit the `setup.py` file in the `/lib/python/Products/MySQL-python-0.3.2` directory or at least make sure that the paths to the `include` and `library` directories in your MySQL installation are correct.

The next step is to compile the drivers files because they come in a non-binary version. It is necessary to first compile the drivers because the database adapter cannot be compiled without a compiled version of the drivers. To compile the drivers, go to the `/lib/python/Products/MySQL-python-0.3.2` directory, which was created during the unpacking process by the database drivers file. Enter the following commands:

```
python setup.py build <ENTER>

python setup.py install <ENTER>
```

Now that the drivers are set up correctly, you can compile the actual database adapter. Change to the source directory in the database adapter directory (`/lib/python/Products/ZMySQLDA/src/`) and enter the following commands:

```
make -f Makefile.pre.in boot <ENTER>

make <ENTER>
```

In case you run Python with a command other than Python (python1.5.2, for example), you need to add the command that will call Python to the first of the previous lines as follows:

```
make -f Makefile.pre.in boot PYTHON=python1.5.2
```

The `make` command should create a `MySQLModule.so` file in the source directory. Now you just need to copy or move the `MySQLModule.so` file to the `ZMySQLDA` directory and restart your Zope server. The Z MySQL Database Connection should then appear in the drop-down menu on your Zope Management screen.

> **Tip**
> Try to find someone with a similar machine and configuration as yours and who has a binary (compiled) version of the database adapter. This will make the installation process much easier because then you just need to copy the respective directories into your Zope installation.

> **Note**
> Although there is a Windows version of MySQL and the `setup.py` file of the database drivers can be changed so that it can be used on Windows, it is *not* advisable to use MySQL with Zope on a Windows machine. However, if you do want to use MySQL on Windows, try to find someone who can give you the binary version of the database adapter and the database drivers, but make sure it was compiled on a Windows machine. This will save you from having to compile the files yourself, which is the main problem on a Windows machine.

Establishing a Connection

A database connection in Zope means a direct link between Zope and an existing database file—not between MySQL in general and Zope. Therefore, you need to create such a connection for every database you want to access from Zope.

To create such a connection, start your Zope server (see Chapter 2, "Installation and Configuration"), open your browser, and enter the Zope management screen.

If the installation of the database adapter was successful, the Available Objects menu below the list of objects contained in the current folder (right frame) now contains a new object—Z MySQL Database Connection. To create the connection, select Z MySQL Database Connection from the menu. The browser is being directed to a new page, the Add page for creating the database connection.

The Id and Title fields have default values that you can change to make different connections easier to distinguish. In the Database Connection String field, you enter the data Zope needs to find the database:

```
name_of_the_database_file[@host] username password
```

The optional parameter `@host` is necessary only if your database is on a different machine than your Zope installation.

> **Note**
> When creating a new database connection, you should do so directly in the folder where you will be using it, or somewhere higher up in the folder hierarchy. You cannot use a connection that is below the Z SQL methods in the Zope hierarchy.

The connection will be established after you click the Add button.

Example

Let's assume that you have a MySQL database called `Addressbook` and that you want to access this database file via Zope. If necessary, start the Zope process and go to the Management screen. Create a new folder by selecting Folder from the drop-down menu atop the list of objects in the `root` folder. Fill out the form with the information shown in Figure 3.1.

Now change into the newly created folder and add a Z MySQL database connection object. Fill out the form as follows (assuming that you have a user John with the password 123):

ID:	**`MyAddressbookConnection`**
Title:	**`MySQL Database Addressbook`**
Database Connection String:	**`Addressbook John 123`**
Connect Immediately:	**`Checked`**

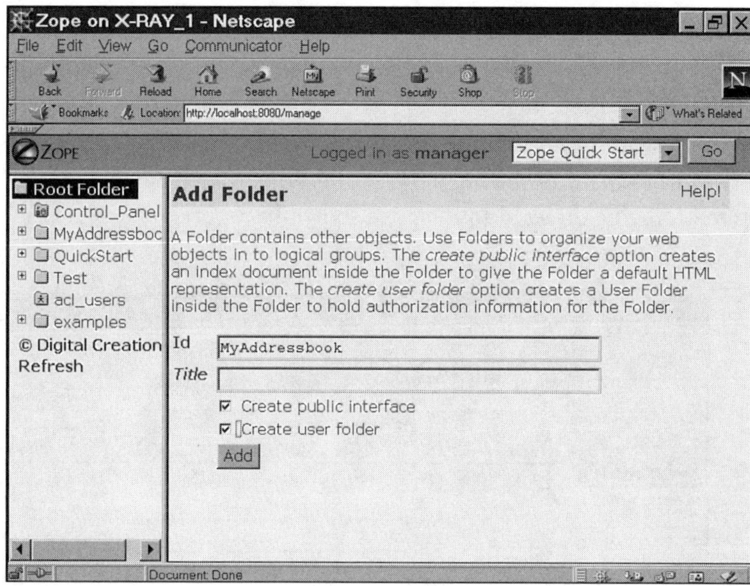

Figure 3.1
Adding the `MyAddressbook` *folder.*

After you have clicked the Add button, the database connection object will appear in the list of objects in the MyAddressbook folder. You have established a link between the Addressbook database and Zope now, and you can start sending queries to and receive data from the `Addressbook` database. You can test this via the Test View that will be explained later in the chapter (see "The Different Views of the Database Connection").

Gadfly—Zope's Integrated Demo Relational Database

Gadfly is a simple RDBMS that comes with Zope. Its features and possibilities cannot compete with any of the previously mentioned RDBMSs, but it is sufficient for testing purposes. This RDBMS is written entirely in Python and supports the basic RDBMS Structured Query Language (SQL).

Gadfly can be run on any machine where Python is installed and is independent from the platform on which you are working. That allows you to copy the Gadfly directory via a binary stream from a Windows machine to a Linux machine.

Because Gadfly supports log-based recovery protocols, you can recover actions made in the database even if the database was not shut down properly.

Establishing a Gadfly Database Connection

Before you can use the Gadfly database, a database connection needs to be established. This is done by creating an instance of the database adapter in Zope.

To create an instance of the Gadfly Database Connection, choose Z Gadfly Database Connection from the drop-down menu in the Zope Management screen. Your browser will automatically be directed to the page shown in Figure 3.2.

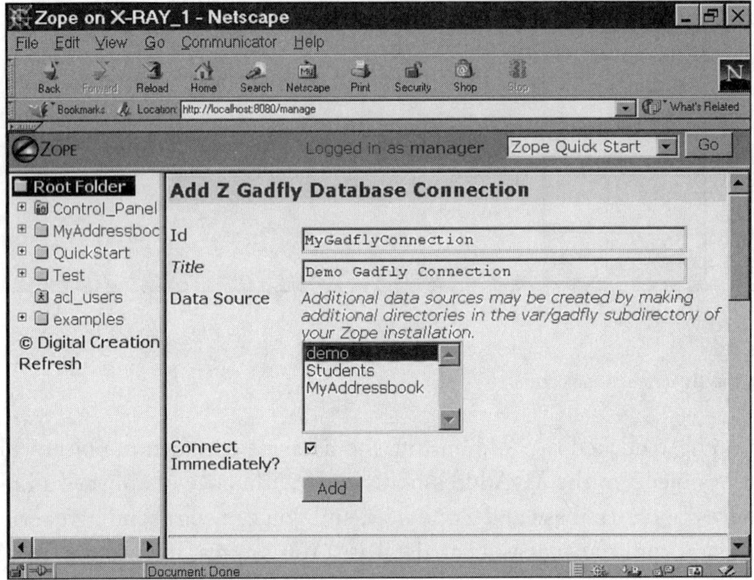

Figure 3.2

Add a Z Gadfly Database Connection.

Fill out the form with the following data:

ID:	**`MyGadflyDatabaseConnection`**
Title:	**`Demo Z Gadfly Database`**

Now, select Demo from the list of data sources, make sure the box to the right of Connect Immediately? is checked, and press the Add button. The database connection is created and the connection to the database is automatically opened. Your browser is now directed back to the Content view of your `root` folder where you can see the new instance of the database connection, as shown in Figure 3.3.

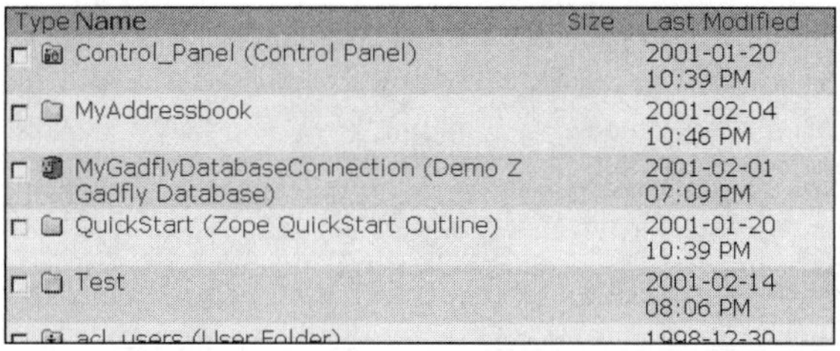

Type	Name	Size	Last Modified
	Control_Panel (Control Panel)		2001-01-20 10:39 PM
	MyAddressbook		2001-02-04 10:46 PM
	MyGadflyDatabaseConnection (Demo Z Gadfly Database)		2001-02-01 07:09 PM
	QuickStart (Zope QuickStart Outline)		2001-01-20 10:39 PM
	Test		2001-02-14 08:06 PM
	acl_users (User Folder)		1998-12-30

Figure 3.3
The instance of the Z Gadfly Database Connection.

> **Note**
> Whenever you create objects in Zope, you have to give the object an ID. This ID cannot contain spaces or special characters that are invalid in URLs because the ID is used as an URL to the respective object. You need not choose a title for a new object, but it sometimes makes it easier to have a short description for a title.

The Different Views of the Database Connection

If you click MyGadflyDatabaseConnection, you are directed to the Status View of the database connection. This is the default view for this type of object.

Status View

This view shows you the status of the respective database connection. For example, it tells you whether the database connection is open or closed, as seen in Figure 3.4. You can also change that status by clicking Close Connection or Open Connection. The name of the button changes depending on the status of the connection.

Properties View

The Properties View (see Figure 3.5) allows you to change the properties of the database connection. The properties include the title, the source for the connection, and whether the connection is to be established immediately.

You can use one instance of the Z Gadfly Database Connection to connect to different databases, but only one database at a time. If you want to create a new database called something other than Demo, see the "How to Create Different Z Gadfly Databases" section later in this chapter.

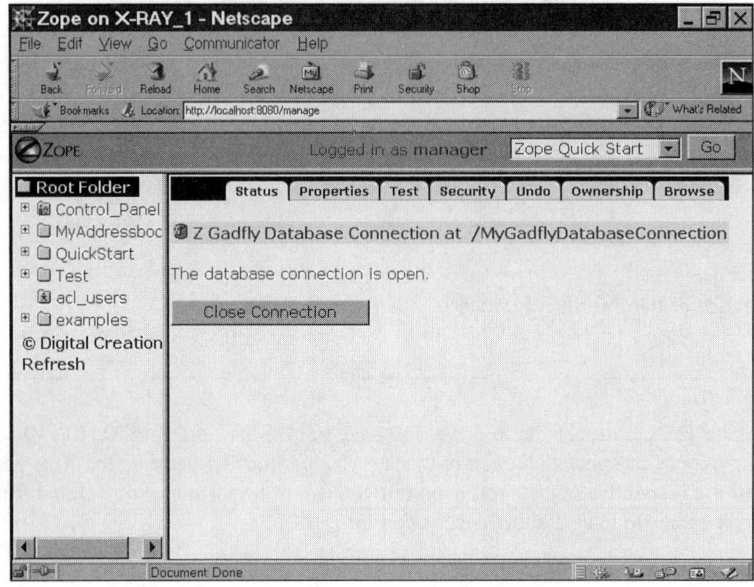

Figure 3.4

Status View of the database connection.

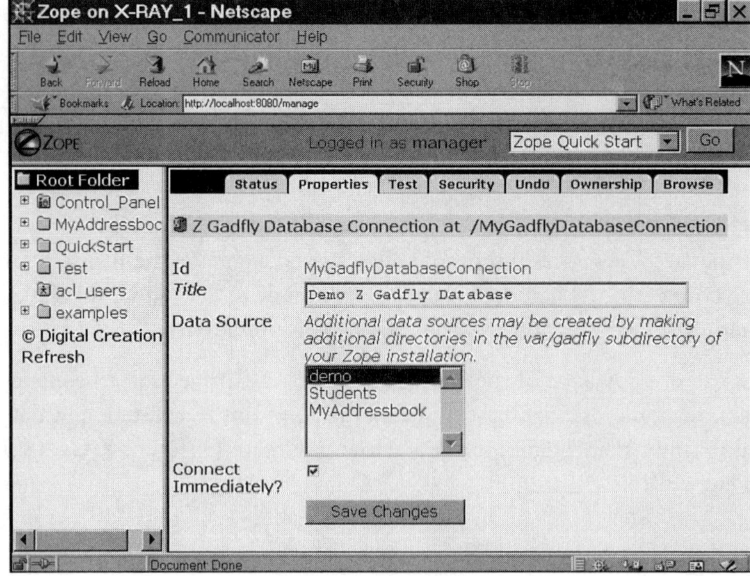

Figure 3.5

Properties View of the database connection.

Test View

This view allows you to test SQL statements. Enter the SQL query in the text area and click the Submit Query button (see Figure 3.6). The query will be sent to the database and executed. In this way, you can test SQL statements without creating Z SQL methods.

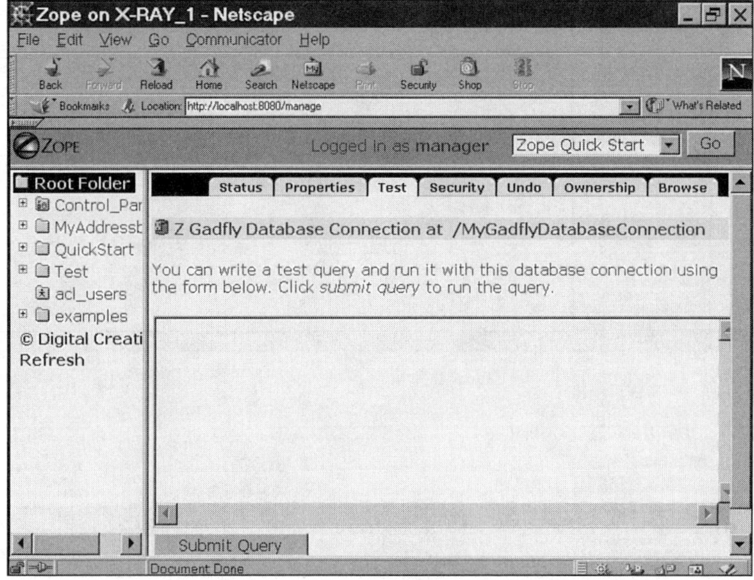

Figure 3.6
Test View of the database connection.

Figure 3.7 shows the result of your query—if there is any. Below the result, the view shows the statement used.

Security View

The Security View (see Figure 3.8) exists in most objects in Zope. It is used to create new roles or change the permission settings for the existing roles. It also contains a link to another page where local roles can be set. The list of permissions depend on whether you look at the Security View of a folder or of a non-folder object. Folder objects such as a folder or a Z Discussion can contain other objects.

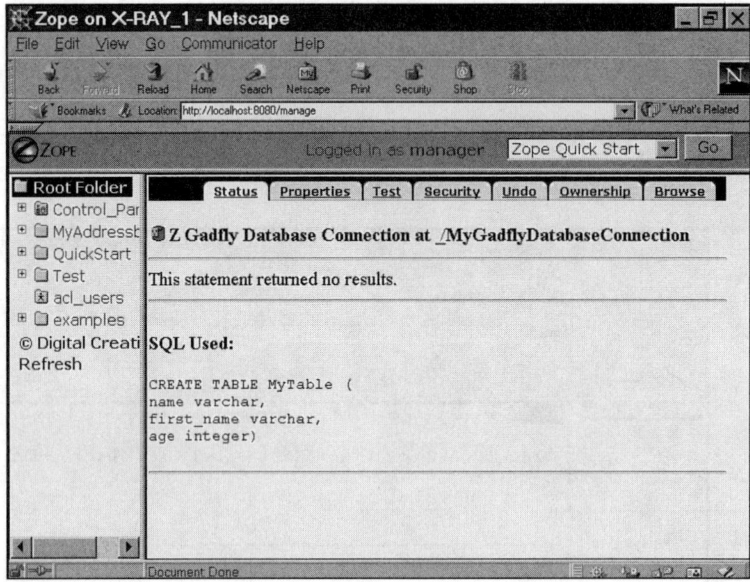

Figure 3.7

Result of a submitted SQL query.

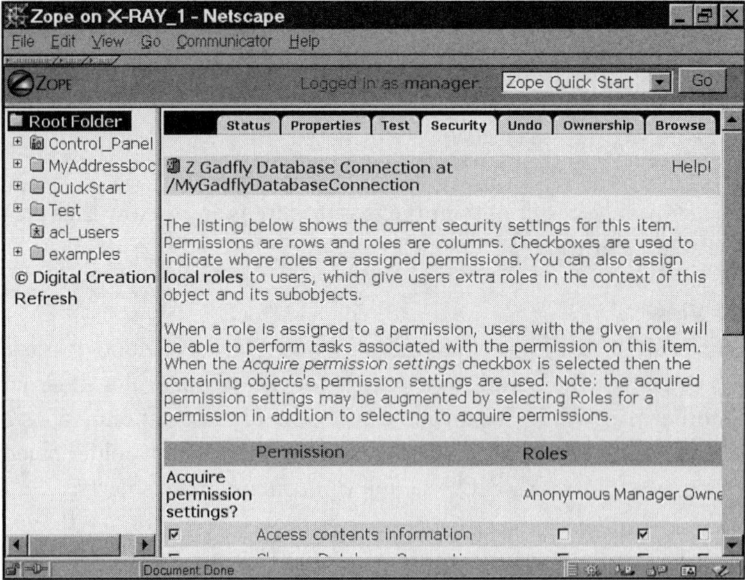

Figure 3.8

Security View of the database connection.

Undo View

The Undo View (see Figure 3.9) is another view that is common with most Zope objects. Here, you can undo actions made in the current folder or one of its subfolders. Select the actions you want to undo and then click the Undo button below the list of actions.

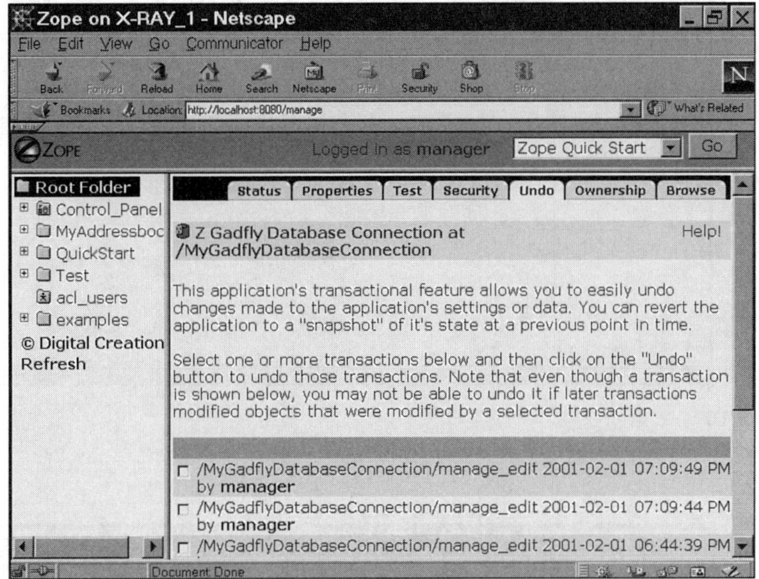

Figure 3.9

Undo View of the database connection.

Ownership View

The Ownership View is also a common view in Zope (see Figure 3.10). It states either who created the current object or who took over the ownership of the object. When you create a new object in Zope, Zope registers you as the owner of this object.

However, any Zope user who has the role Owner, or whose role has the permission Take Ownership, can take over ownership of any object in Zope. Taking over ownership is done via the Ownership View. If you are allowed to take ownership, the Ownership View will look like Figure 3.11.

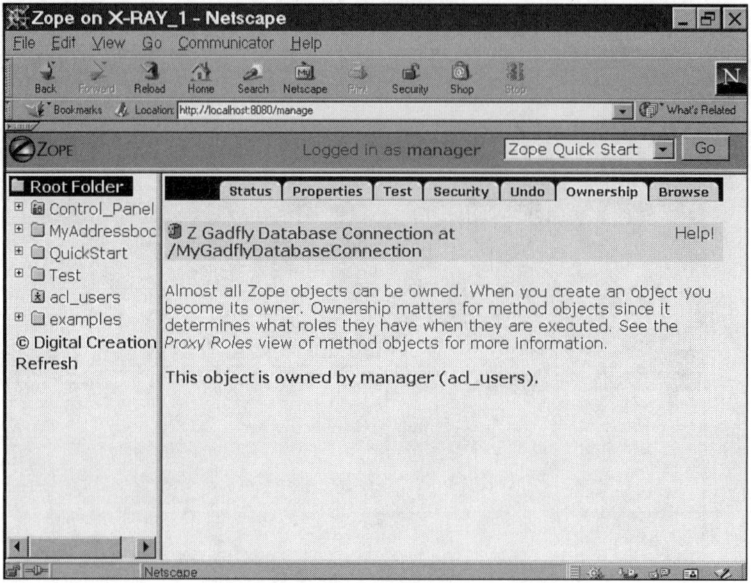

Figure 3.10

The Ownership View where the object is owned by the manager.

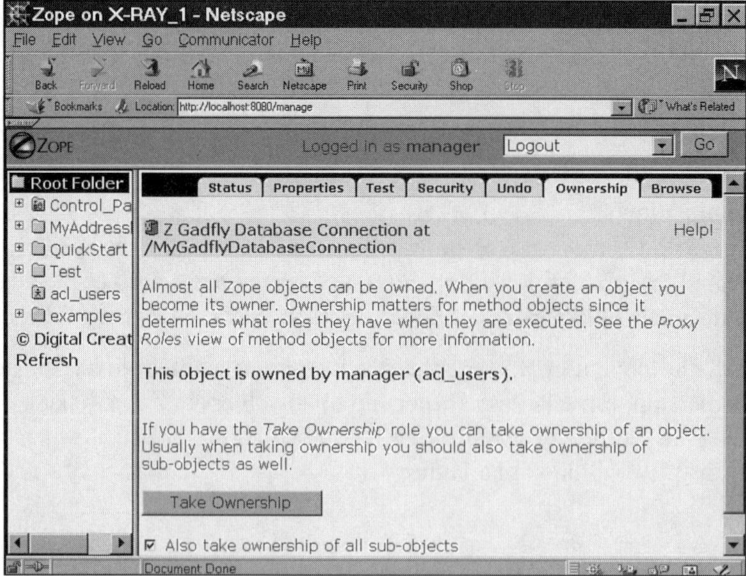

Figure 3.11

The Ownership View with the Take Ownership button.

Having ownership of an object can be important when executing methods in Zope.

Browse View

In the Browse View, you can see—and browse through—the content of the tables and rows that exist in the database that the Z Gadfly Database Connection is currently connected to (the data source of the connection). The view shows the name of the tables and the rows in the tables. It also shows the type of the rows. Figure 3.12 shows the `Testtable` table that contains three rows: `Name`, `First_name`, and `Age`. The types are shown by the images in front of the row names and the type names after the row names.

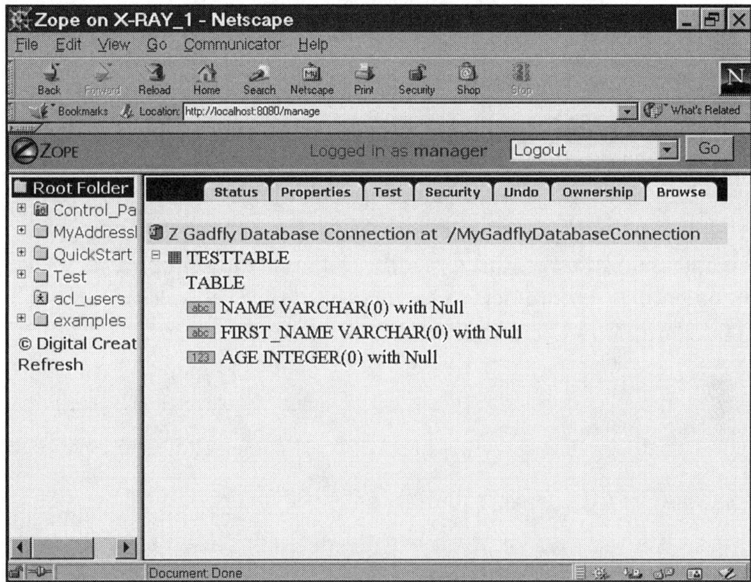

Figure 3.12

Browse View of the database connection.

> **Note**
>
> At the time of writing, the Z Gadfly Database only supports the `VARCHAR`, `INTEGER`, and `FLOAT` field types. This is another reason why the Z Gadfly Database is only suitable for test purposes.

How to Create Different Z Gadfly Databases

When you created the Z Gadfly Database Connection earlier in the chapter, you selected the Demo database to be used with this connection. As mentioned before, you can use more than one database with a connection, but only one database at a time.

To create a new database that you can use with any Z Gadfly Database Connection, go to the `/var/gadfly` folder in your Zope installation folder. There you will find a subfolder `/demo`, which is where anything you have done so far with the `demo` database is being stored. Now, you just need to create a new folder in the `/gadfly` folder, and you can start creating tables in the new database.

You can either create a new Z Gadfly Database Connection for the new database and select the name of the new folder instead of Demo, or you can use the existing Z Gadfly Database Connection and change the data source in the Properties View.

Introduction to SQL

The following pages will give you an overview of some of the most important SQL statements that will get you started with SQL. For the given examples, we use the Z Gadfly Database. However, the Z Gadfly Database only supports some of the actual SQL statements. For more detailed information on SQL, please refer to an SQL book. There are also some good tutorials on the Internet at

`http://www.w3scripts.com/sql/`

or

`http://w3.one.net/~jhoffman/sqltut.htm`

or

`http://sqlcourse.com/`

After introducing the statements, you will learn how to use Z SQL methods to interact with your database via a Web page.

Example: Creating an `Addressbook` Database

For this example, we want to create a database using the Z Gadfly Database that is to function as an address book. Consequently, we need certain data to be stored in this database:

Last Name
First Name
Address
City
ZIP Code
Phone Number

First, we need to create a new folder on the file system in the `/var/gadfly/` directory so that we can store the addresses in a separate database. We will call this folder `MyAddressbook`. The `/var/gadfly/` directory now contains two folders—`demo` and `MyAddressbook`. For this example, we will use the database connection that we created earlier in the chapter.

Go to the Properties View of the `MyGadflyDatabaseConnection` and change the data source from `demo` to `MyAddressbook`. The connection is now established and we can start creating tables in the database and fill those tables with data.

The `CREATE TABLE` Statement

Next, we create a table via the Test View. Enter the following SQL statement into the text area in the view:

```
CREATE TABLE Addressbook (
     Name varchar,
     FirstName varchar,
     Address varchar,
     City varchar,
     ZIP integer,
     Phone varchar)
```

After you have clicked the Submit Query button, you can see the new table in the Browse View. You need to click the plus sign next to ADDRESSBOOK to see all names of the table columns, as shown in Figure 3.13.

The `INSERT INTO` Statement

The first step in creating an address book is done. Now we need to fill the table with data. This is done with the `INSERT INTO` statement. The statement's syntax is as follows:

```
     INSERT INTO table_name (first_row_name,...,last_row_name)
     VALUES (first_value, second_value, ... , last_value)
```

In this example, if we want to enter the address

John Smith
249 9th Ave
New York, NY 10001
(212)987-1234

into the `Addressbook` table, we need to send the following SQL statement to the `MyAddressbook` database:

```
INSERT INTO Addressbook
(Name, FirstName, Address, City, ZIP, Phone)
VALUES
('Smith', 'John', '249 9th Ave', 'New York, NY', 10001, '(212)987-1234')
```

This SQL statement will return the result shown in Figure 3.14.

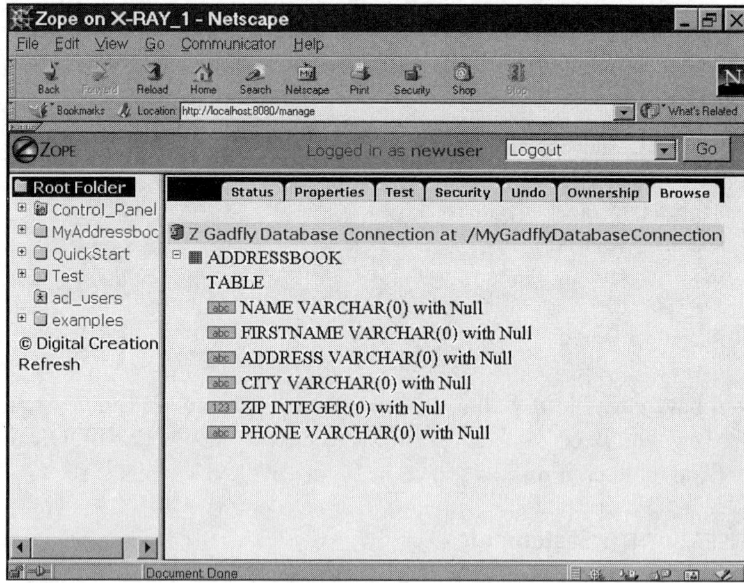

Figure 3.13
Browse View of the created table.

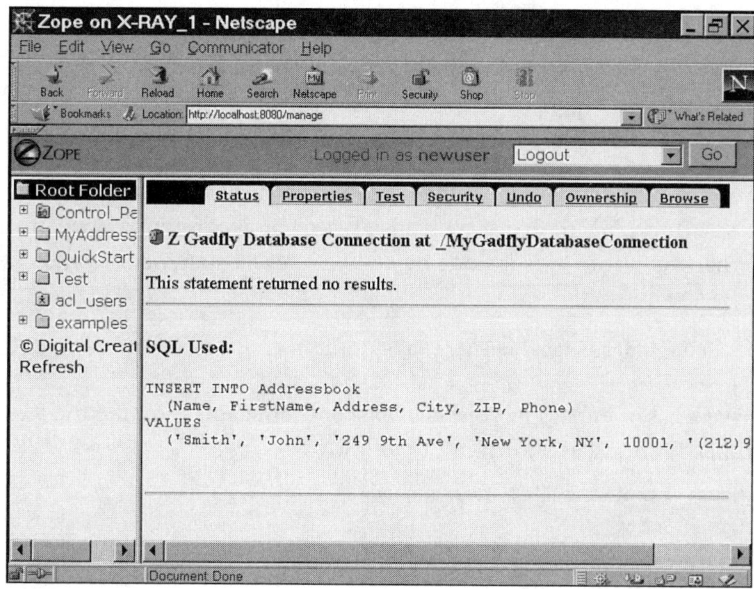

Figure 3.14

A data record was successfully inserted.

Although this page looks like an error, it is actually the standard result page if an SQL statement does not return data.

The `SELECT...FROM...` Statement

To see the new data entered in the table, we need the `SELECT...FROM...` statement. This statement can be used to get a certain kind of data from a table or the entire table. To see the entire table, you use a wildcard `*`, as shown in the following:

```
SELECT * FROM Addressbook
```

The result of this statement is

ADDRESS	NAME	FIRST NAME	PHONE	CITY	ZIP
249 9th Ave	Smith	John	(212)987-1234	New York, NY	10001

To select certain rows from the table, you use the names of the table rows instead of the wildcard, as shown in the following:

```
SELECT Name, FirstName FROM Addressbook
```

This statement will give you the following result:

NAME	FIRSTNAME
Smith	John

If you want to get certain records from a table, perhaps the name of everyone who lives in New York, NY or everyone whose last name is Smith, you need to specify exactly what you want. This is done by adding a `WHERE` statement to the `SELECT...FROM...` statement:

```
SELECT * FROM Addressbook WHERE (Name='Smith')
```

If you have a list of entries in your `Addressbook` table and combine the row and column specifications, as shown in the following:

```
SELECT Name, FirstName FROM Addressbook
WHERE (Name='Smith')
```

you might get something like

NAME	FIRSTNAME
Smith	Jane
Smith	John
Smith	Ellen

The UPDATE Statement

It is often necessary to change records in an address book because some of the information has changed, perhaps the phone number and/or the address of a person. This is done with the `UPDATE` statement. The `UPDATE` statement has the following form:

```
UPDATE table_name SET col_name = new_value
```

Using this statement on a table would change the values of the entire `col_name` column. Therefore, you need to specify which row you want to change. Again, this is done with the `WHERE` specification:

```
UPDATE table_name SET col_name = new_value
WHERE col_name = certain_value
```

The following is an example of how to change the last name of Jane Smith to Williams:

```
UPDATE Addressbook SET Name='Williams'
WHERE Name='Smith' AND FirstName='John'
```

The `DELETE FROM` Statement

To delete records from a table, you use the `DELETE FROM` statement. Again you need the `WHERE` statement to specify what you want to delete. For example, if you want to delete the John Smith record from the `Addressbook` table, the necessary command will be

```
DELETE FROM Addressbook
WHERE Name='Smith' AND FirstName='John'
```

Using Z SQL Methods to Submit SQL Statements

Using the Test View is not a very comfortable way to send SQL statements if you frequently want to add new records to the database or want to search the database. An easier way to do this is to make use of Z SQL methods and DTML methods. The DTML methods will contain forms where you can enter a new record or a search query. They then send the entered data to Z SQL methods that build a complete SQL statement and send it via the connection to the database. You need a Z SQL method for each type of SQL statement you want to use. However, because you can give arguments to the Z SQL method, it is possible to create a Z SQL method in such a way that it can be used for different varieties of an SQL statement. In this way, you can create templates for your SQL statements.

> **Note**
> Before creating a Z SQL method, you need to make sure that there is a database connection either in the same folder or in a folder above.

Creating a Z SQL Method

To create a Z SQL method, go to the folder where you want to use the Z SQL method and select the Z SQL method option from the drop-down menu. Your browser is automatically directed to the form shown in Figure 3.15.

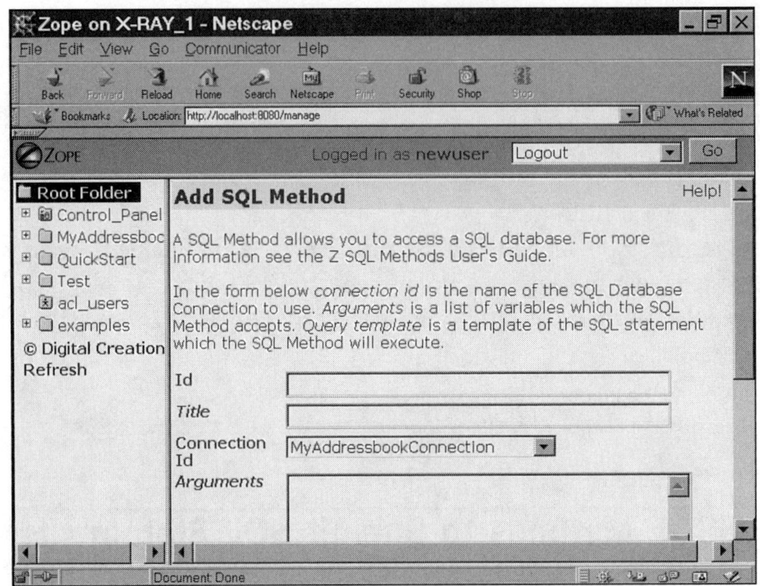

Figure 3.15
Adding a Z SQL method.

Choose an ID and a Title for that particular Z SQL method, for example

ID: **`addRecord`**
Title: **`Adds a New Record`**

Now you need to choose which of the accessible database connections the Z SQL method is to use. Select the respective connection from the drop-down Connection ID menu. Next come the arguments—or parameters—that the SQL statement will need to be complete. For example, if you want to enter a new record in the `Addressbook` database that we created a few pages ago, you need the following arguments:

```
Name FirstName Address City ZIP Phone
```

Note that there are no commas between the arguments. You can also leave the Arguments text area empty if you do not need any arguments for the desired SQL statement.

Now that you have entered the parameters, you can define the SQL statement for this specific Z SQL method. When defining the statement, you will need `<dtml>` commands to insert arguments into the statement. To finish creating the Z SQL method, enter the code in Listing 3.1 into the Query Template text area:

Listing 3.1

Query Template

```
INSERT INTO Addressbook
(Name, FirstName, Address, City, ZIP, Phone)
VALUES
('<dtml-sqlvar Name type=string>',
'<dtml-sqlvar FirstName type=string>',
'<dtml-sqlvar Address type=string>',
'<dtml-sqlvar City type=string>',
<dtml-sqlvar ZIP type=int>,
'<dtml-sqlvar Phone type=string>')
```

Note that because ZIP needs to be an integer, there are no quotes around <dtml-sqlvar ZIP type=int>.

There are three ways to finish this Z SQL method:

- By clicking the Add button, which will return you to the Contents View of the folder
- By clicking the Add and Edit button, which will take you directly to the Edit View of the new Z SQL method
- By clicking the Add and Test button, which will take you directly to the Test View of the Z SQL method

After you click one of the buttons, the Z SQL method is created and can be called from DTML methods.

Calling the Z SQL Method from a DTML Method

You will need two DTML methods to use the Z SQL method you just created

- One for the form where the data for a new record can be entered
- One that calls the Z SQL method and sends the data from the form to it

Create a new DTML method called addnewRecordForm_html in the MyAddressbook folder and enter the code in Listing 3.2.

Listing 3.2

addNewRecordForm_html *(DTML Method)*

```
 1: <dtml-var standard_html_header>
 2: <h1>Add a New Record</h1>
 3: <form action="result_html" method=post>
 4:   <table bgcolor="#CCCCCC" width="100%">
 5:   <tr>
 6:     <td><b>Name:</b></td>
 7:     <td><input type="text" name="name" size=20></td>
 8:   </tr>
 9:   <tr>
10:     <td><b>First Name:</b></td>
11:     <td><input type="text" name="first_name" size=20></td>
12:   </tr>
13:   <tr>
14:     <td><b>Address:</b></td>
15:     <td><input type="text" name="address" size=40></td>
16:   </tr>
17:   <tr>
18:     <td><b>City:</b></td>
19:     <td><input type="text" name="city" size=15></td>
20:   </tr>
21:   <tr>
22:     <td><b>ZIP Code:</b></td>
23:     <td><input type="text" name="zip:int" size=5></td>
24:   </tr>
25:   <tr>
26:     <td><b>Phone:</b></td>
27:     <td><input type="text" name="phone" size=15></td>
28:   </tr>
29:   <tr>
30:     <td colspan=2><input type="submit" value="Add Record"></td>
31:   </tr>
32:   </table>
33: </form>
34: <dtml-var standard_html_footer>
```

As you can see in the `<form>` tag (line 3), this form calls the DTML method `result_html`. This DTML method is the one that actually calls the Z SQL method and then tells the user whether the new record was entered successfully. Create another DTML method using the code in Listing 3.3.

Listing 3.3

`result_html` *(DTML Method)*

```
 1: <dtml-var standard_html_header>
 2: <dtml-try>
 3:   <dtml-call "addRecord(Name=_['name'],
 4: FirstName=_['first_name'],
 5: Address=_['address'],
 6: City=_['city'],
 7: ZIP=_['zip'],
 8: Phone=_['phone'])">
 9:   <dtml-call "REQUEST.set('status', 'ok')">
10: <dtml-except>
11:   <dtml-call "REQUEST.set('status', 'failed')">
12: </dtml-try>
13: <dtml-if "_['status']=='ok'">
14:   <h1>New record was successfully added.</h1>
15:   <form action="index_html">
16:     <input type="submit" value="OK">
17:   </form>
18: <dtml-else>
19:   <h1>Adding the new record failed. No record was added.</h1>
20:   <table>
21:     <tr>
22:       <td>
23:         <form action="addNewRecordForm_html">
24:           <input type="submit" value="Try again">
25:         </form>
26:       </td>
27:       <td>
28:         <form action="index_html">
29:           <input type="submit" value="OK">
30:         </form>
31:       </td>
32:     </tr>
33:   </table>
34: </dtml-if>
35: <dtml-var standard_html_footer>
```

In this DTML method, the Z SQL method is called in a `<dtml-call>` tag (line 3). After the name of the Z SQL method, you declare the parameters in parentheses. First, you name the name of the argument as it is declared in the Z SQL method, and then you give the name of the variable as it is defined in the entry form.

The <dtml-try> tag (line 2) is used here to set the 'status' variable, depending on whether the insertion was successful (line 9) or not (line 11). If the 'status' variable has the value 'ok', the user is informed of the successful insertion and can go on to the index_html page by clicking a Submit button (lines 15–17). If the insertion failed for any reason, the 'status' variable will contain the value 'failed'. In that case, the user is informed that there was an error and he or she can either try again to enter the data (lines 23–25) or go on to the index_html page (lines 28–30).

Creating a Search Form and a Result Page

You can also create a search form for your database. Again, you need a Z SQL method and two DTML methods. You need

- A Z SQL method that contains the SELECT...FROM... statement
- A DTML method that contains a search form
- A DTML method that shows the search results

First, create a new Z SQL method with the following data:

ID:	**searchAddressbook**
Title:	**Search the Addressbook Table**
Database Connection ID:	**MyAddressbookConnection**
Arguments:	**Name FirstName Address City_ZIP Phone**

Query Template:

```
SELECT *FROM Addressbook
WHERE
(Name='<dtml-sqlvar Name type=string>' OR
 FirstName='<dtml-sqlvar FirstName type=string>' OR
 Address='<dtml-sqlvar Address type=string>' OR
 City='<dtml-sqlvar City type=string>' OR
 ZIP=<dtml-sqlvar ZIP type=int> OR
 Phone='<dtml-sqlvar Phone type=string>')
```

Now create a DTML method called searchAddressbookForm_html with the code in Listing 3.4.

Listing 3.4

searchAddressbookForm_html

```
 1: <dtml-var standard_html_header>
 2: <h2><dtml-var title_or_id> <dtml-var document_title></h2>
 3: <form action="searchResults_html" method=post>
 4:   <table width="100%">
 5:   <tr>
 6:     <td><b>Name:</b></td>
 7:     <td><input type="text" name="name" size=20></td>
 8:   </tr>
 9:   <tr>
10:     <td><b>First Name:</b></td>
11:     <td><input type="text" name="first_name" size=20></td>
12:   </tr>
13:   <tr>
14:     <td><b>Address:</b></td>
15:     <td><input type="text" name="address" size=40></td>
16:   </tr>
17:   <tr>
18:     <td><b>City:</b></td>
19:     <td><input type="text" name="city" size=15></td>
20:   </tr>
21:   <tr>
22:     <td><b>ZIP Code:</b></td>
23:     <td><input type="text" name="zip:int" value="00000" size=5></td>
24:   </tr>
25:   <tr>
26:     <td><b>Phone:</b></td>
27:     <td><input type="text" name="phone" size=15></td>
28:   </tr>
29:   <tr>
30:     <td colspan=2><input type="submit" value="Search Addressbook"></td>
31:   </tr>
32:   </table>
33: </form>
34: <dtml-var standard_html_footer>
```

Note the 'value' declaration in the <input> tag for the ZIP code (line 23). It is important to define a default value here because the SQL statement will return an error if you don't. This is only necessary for integer and float values because there are no quotation marks surrounding the <dtml-sqlvar> tag in the SQL statement.

As you can see from the `<form>` tag (line 3), you need another object—`"searchResults_html"`. This is the second DTML method you need that will call the Z SQL method and show the results of the search. Create this second DTML method with the code in Listing 3.5.

Listing 3.5

searchResults_html *(DTML Method)*

```
 1: <dtml-var standard_html_header>
 2: <h2><dtml-var title_or_id> <dtml-var document_title></h2>
 3: <table width="100%" border=2>
 4:   <tr>
 5:     <th>Name</th>
 6:     <th>First Name</th>
 7:     <th>Address</th>
 8:     <th>City</th>
 9:     <th>ZIP Code</th>
10:     <th>Phone</th>
11:   </tr>
12:   <dtml-in "searchAddressbook(Name=name,
13:                        FirstName=first_name,
14:                        Address=address,
15:                        City=city,
16:                        ZIP=zip,
17:                        Phone=phone)">
18:   <tr>
19:     <td><dtml-var name></td>
20:     <td><dtml-var firstname></td>
21:     <td><dtml-var address></td>
22:     <td><dtml-var city></td>
23:     <td><dtml-var zip></td>
24:     <td><dtml-var phone></td>
25:   </tr>
26:   </dtml-in>
27: </table>
28: <dtml-var standard_html_footer>
```

The important part of this DTML method is the `<dtml-in>` loop (lines 12–26). It is necessary to call the Z SQL method within a `<dtml-in>` tag and not just a `<dtml-var>` tag so that you can go through the list of records the database sends back and show the information from each record that you want to show.

The <dtml-in> tag calls the Z SQL method searchAddressbook (line 12). The parameters are given within the parentheses after the name of the Z SQL method: first, the name of the argument as it is declared in the Z SQL method and then, after the equals sign, the name of the variable as it is defined in the search form. Within the loop, you can then show the results by calling the column names of the table (lines 19–24). However, the column names have to be given with lowercase characters, even if you declared a column with a capital first letter. The database is not case sensitive and returns the table entries with the columns in lowercase characters. Zope, however, is case sensitive and so you must use lowercase characters to call the columns or Zope will not know the variables.

Updating a Record

Writing a dynamic SQL statement to update a record in a table is more complex because there are so many varieties on what you want to update and in which record. For example, you may want to change the last name of a certain person from Smith to Jones. However, you only want to change Ellen Smith's name and not John Smith's. The easiest way to so this is to update the whole record. That way, you just have to hand over all columns of the old record as well as all of the new one.

Create a new Z SQL method with the following data:

ID: **updateRecord**

Arguments: **Name FirstName Address City ZIP Phone**

NewName NewFirstName NewAddress NewCity NewZIP NewPhone

Query Template:

```
UPDATE Addressbook
SET
Name='<dtml-sqlvar NewName type=string>',
FirstName='<dtml-sqlvar NewFirstName type=string>',
Address='<dtml-sqlvar NewAddress type=string>',
City='<dtml-sqlvar NewCity type=string>',
ZIP=<dtml-sqlvar NewZIP type=int>,
Phone='<dtml-sqlvar NewPhone type=string>'
WHERE
Name='<dtml-sqlvar Name type=string>' AND
FirstName='<dtml-sqlvar FirstName type=string>' AND
Address='<dtml-sqlvar Address type=string>' AND
City='<dtml-sqlvar City type=string>' AND
ZIP=<dtml-sqlvar ZIP type=int> AND
Phone='<dtml-sqlvar Phone type=string>'
```

As you can see, there are ten arguments because the `Addressbook` table has five columns and you need both the old entry and the new one.

To update a record, you need a form similar to the one you need to add a new entry. However, it needs to be modified so that the old entry can be seen in the text fields of the form and can also be handed over hidden to the Z SQL method. Create a new DTML method with the code in Listing 3.6.

Listing 3.6

`updateEntryForm_html` *(DTML Method)*

```
<dtml-var standard_html_header>
<h1>Update the Record</h1>
<form action="updateRecord_html" method=post>
<input type=hidden name="name" value="<dtml-var name>">
<input type=hidden name="firstname" value="<dtml-var firstname>">
<input type=hidden name="address" value="<dtml-var address>">
<input type=hidden name="city" value="<dtml-var city>">
<input type=hidden name="zip:int" value="<dtml-var zip>">
<input type=hidden name="phone" value="<dtml-var phone>">
<table bgcolor="#CCCCCC" width="100%">
<tr>
   <td><b>Name:</b></td>
   <td><input type="text" name="newname" value="<dtml-var name>
➥ "size=20></td>
</tr>
<tr>
   <td><b>First Name:</b></td>
   <td><input type="text" name="newfirst_name"
➥ value="<dtml-var firstname>" size=20></td>
</tr>
<tr>
   <td><b>Address:</b></td>
   <td><input type="text" name="newaddress"
➥ value="<dtml-var address>" size=40></td>
</tr>
<tr>
   <td><b>City:</b></td>
   <td><input type="text" name="newcity"
➥ value="<dtml-var city>" size=15></td>
</tr>
<tr>
   <td><b>ZIP Code:</b></td>
```

Listing 3.6

Continued

```
29:    <td><input type="text" name="newzip:int"
➥ value="<dtml-var zip>" size=5 maxsize=5></td>
30: </tr>
31: <tr>
32:    <td><b>Phone:</b></td>
33:    <td><input type="text" name="newphone"
➥ value="<dtml-var phone>" size=15></td>
34: </tr>
35: <tr>
36:    <td colspan=2><input type="submit" value="Update Record"></td>
37: </tr>
38: </table>
39: </form>
40: <dtml-var standard_html_footer>
```

The old entry values are handed over to this update form from a different DTML method (`index_html`) that we will create a little later. In lines 4–9, the old entry values are given as hidden so that they can be transferred together with the new values to the Z SQL method later. In lines 11–34, the part of the form that can be seen and filled out is defined. The old entry values are put into the text fields so that the user can see what he or she is about to change and also because this way he or she does not need to re-enter the values that don't need to be changed.

Now there is one question: From where do you get the old record entry? You could create an `index_html` page that shows all entries of the `Addressbook` table and also gives the user a button with which he or she can update an existing entry. This button will give the old entry over to the update form. Listing 3.7 contains the code for the `index_html` page.

Listing 3.7

`index_html` *(DTML Method)*

```
<dtml-var standard_html_header>
<h2><dtml-var title_or_id></h2>
<table>
<tr>
   <th>Name</th>
   <th>First Name</th>
   <th>Address</th>
   <th>City</th>
```

Listing 3.7

Continued

```
 9:    <th>Zip code</th>
10:    <th>Phone</th>
11:    <th></th>
12: </tr>
13: <dtml-in "getAll()">
14: <tr>
15: <form action="." method=post>
16:    <td><dtml-var name>
➥ <input type=hidden name="name" value="<dtml-var name>"></td>
17:    <td><dtml-var firstname>
➥ <input type=hidden name="firstname" value="<dtml-var firstname>"></td>
18:    <td><dtml-var address>
➥ <input type=hidden name="address" value="<dtml-var address>"></td>
19:    <td><dtml-var city>
➥ <input type=hidden name="city" value="<dtml-var city>"></td>
20:    <td><dtml-var zip>
➥ <input type=hidden name="zip" value="<dtml-var zip>"></td>
21:    <td><dtml-var phone>
➥ <input type=hidden name="phone" value="<dtml-var phone>"></td>
22:    <td>
23:       <input type="submit" name="updateEntryForm_html:method" value="Update">
24:       <input type="submit" name="deleteEntry:method" value="Delete">
25:    </td>
26: </form>
27: </tr>
28: </dtml-in>
29: </table>
30: <dtml-var standard_html_footer>
```

This DTML method shows a table with the column names of the `Addressbook` table as headlines (lines 4–12). The rest of the table is created by using the Z SQL method `getAll` (line 13) that consists of a simple `'SELECT * FROM Addressbook'` without any arguments. Going through the result of this Z SQL method, you can create the table rows and enter the different entries of the `Addressbook` (lines 14–21). In the last table cell of each row, there needs to be an Update button that sends the entries' contents to the `updateEntryForm_html` (the code will be given shortly) and there is also a Delete button that will be needed later (lines 23 and 24). You may have noticed that there is no real value for the action of the form (line 15). This is a Zope-specific feature. You can have different actions using one single form. In our case, we have two different actions—update and delete. The action is given as the name in the declaration of the respective button (lines 23 and 24). Note that you need to add **:method** to the name value as follows:

```
name="updateEntryForm_html:method".
```

The action value in your form must be "." or Zope will not recognize this special kind of action.

Now you only need the DTML method that calls the Z SQL method. Therefore, create a new DTML method called `updateRecord_html` with the code in Listing 3.8.

Listing 3.8

`updateRecord_html` *(DTML Method)*

```
 1: <dtml-var standard_html_header>
 2: <dtml-try>
 3: <dtml-call "updateRecord(Name=_['name'],
 4:                          FirstName=_['firstname'],
 5:                          Address=_['address'],
 6:                          City=_['city'],
 7:                          ZIP=_['zip'],
 8:                          Phone=_['phone'],
 9:                          NewName=_['newname'],
10:                          NewFirstName=_['newfirst_name'],
11:                          NewAddress=_['newaddress'],
12:                          NewCity=_['newcity'],
13:                          NewZIP=_['newzip'],
14:                          NewPhone=_['newphone'])">
15: Entry has been successfully updated.
16: <form action="index_html" method=post>
17: <input type="submit" value="OK">
18: </form>
19: <dtml-except>
20: Error while updating. Entry was <b>NOT</b> updated.
21: <form action="." method=post>
22:   <input type=hidden name="name" value="<dtml-var name>">
23:     <input type=hidden name="firstname" value="<dtml-var firstname>">
24:     <input type=hidden name="address" value="<dtml-var address>">
25:     <input type=hidden name="city" value="<dtml-var city>">
26:     <input type=hidden name="zip" value="<dtml-var zip>">
27:     <input type=hidden name="phone" value="<dtml-var phone>">
```

Listing 3.8

Continued

```
28:      <input type="submit" name="updateEntryForm_html:method"
➥ value="Try Again">
29:      <input type="submit" name="index_html:method" value="Return to Index">
30: </form>
31: </dtml-try>
32: <dtml-var standard_html_footer>
```

This DTML method works like the DTML method `result_html` that we used when adding a new entry. It calls the Z SQL method `updateRecord` and hands over the ten arguments the Z SQL method expects. Should there be an error, the DTML method will inform the user (line 20) and give him or her the choice of trying again (line 28) or returning to `index_html` (line 29).

Deleting a Record

To delete a record from the `Addressbook` table, create a new Z SQL method using the following data:

ID: **`deleteRecord`**

Arguments: **`Name FirstName Address City ZIP Phone`**

Query Template:

```
DELETE FROM Addressbook
WHERE
Name='<dtml-sqlvar Name type=string>' AND
FirstName='<dtml-sqlvar FirstName type=string>' AND
Address='<dtml-sqlvar Address type=string>' AND
City='<dtml-sqlvar City type=string>' AND
ZIP=<dtml-sqlvar ZIP type=int> AND
Phone='<dtml-sqlvar Phone type=string>'
```

Again, you need a DTML method that calls this Z SQL method and hands over the necessary information, such as `Name`, `FirstName`, and so on. Create a DTML method called `deleteEntry` using the code in Listing 3.9.

Listing 3.9

`deleteEntry` *(DTML Method)*

```
 1: <dtml-var standard_html_header>
 2: <h2><dtml-var title_or_id> <dtml-var document_title></h2>
 3: <dtml-try>
 4:   <dtml-call "deleteRecord(Name=_['name'],
 5:                    FirstName=_['firstname'],
 6:                    Address=_['address'],
 7:                    City=_['city'],
 8:                    ZIP=_['zip'],
 9:                    Phone=_['phone'])">
10:   Entry was successfully deleted.
11: <dtml-except>
12:   An error occurred. Entry was <b>NOT</b> deleted.
13: </dtml-try>
14: <form action="index_html" method=post>
15:   <input type="submit" value="OK">
16: </form>
17: <dtml-var standard_html_footer>
```

The DTML method `index_html` we used in the section before contains a Delete button. This button can be used now when deleting an entry from the `Addressbook` table. The Delete button in `index_html` calls the DTML method `deleteEntry` and hands over the entry's values. The DTML method then calls the Z SQL method `deleteRecord` and either tells the user that the entry was deleted successfully (line 10) or that an error occurred (line 12). A Submit button (line 15) takes the user back to the DTML method `index_html`.

Summary

You have now learned how easy it is to connect Zope to a database and should also be proficient in creating and using a database connection and changing the data source of such a connection. The short introduction to SQL, as well as the examples, should have helped you get some practice with SQL and SQL statements. The next chapter will show you how to create a prototype in Zope. Because the prototype we will create in that chapter uses a database, you will be able to use the knowledge you gathered in this chapter.

CHAPTER 4

BUILDING A PROTOTYPE

Introduction

You made it through the previous chapters and have finally arrived at chapter four. Up to this point, you have learned about the general ideas behind Zope and have gotten used to the famous Zope Zen. You can set up and configure your own Zope servers on your machine properly, and you know how to connect Zope to any database.

At this time, we will start showing you how to effectively accomplish tasks with Zope's own scripting language, the so-called DTML. Additionally, we will introduce you to Zope's built-in undo system and Zope's ZClasses. Last but not least, we will make up a simple but useful prototype using a combination of DTML and ZClasses.

The Basics

There are still some things to clear up. Because we know that you are already experienced with Zope, we will keep our explanations brief and precise. But if your Zope experience has not been that intense so far, we recommend that you look at the next sections, because we will refer to these expressions later in the book.

During the next sections, we will discuss the following terms:

- The Zope Management screen
- First view, second view, and third view
- Acquisition
- Templates
- Zope versions
- Users, roles, and permissions
- Zope's Undo System/Packing the Database

The Zope Management Screen and Its Components

When you are working on a Zope server via a Web browser, such as Netscape Communicator, Microsoft Internet Explorer, or Opera, you are situated in the Zope Management screen.

Figure 4.1 shows a Management screen as displayed by Netscape Navigator.

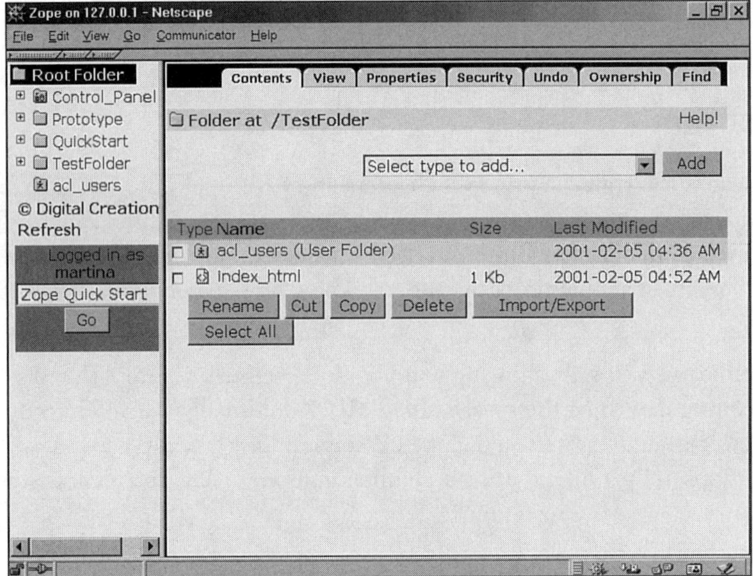

Figure 4.1

The Management screen as it is seen via Netscape Navigator.

> **Note**
> Depending on the version of your Zope server, the appearance of the Management screen differs. The Help link and the user ID are not shown if your Zope server is older than version 2.0.

- *User ID*—The name of the user who is working at this screen at the moment is shown here.
- *Available Objects Menu*—This drop-down menu enables you to add any of the contained objects to a folder.
- *Path Information*—Shows the path inside the Zope server where you are.
- *Zope Tab Bar*—Contains several tabs you can click to activate miscellaneous functions. Note that the tabs that are included in the tab bar depend on the object that you selected.

- *Button Bar*—Contains the buttons that you can use to copy, rename, export, delete, and move objects.
- *Help Link*—When clicked, this button activates the Zope Help System and shows various help texts.

First View, Second View, and Third View

While accomplishing tasks with Zope, you are constantly editing DTML scripts, typing Python code, working within the Zope Management screen, or watching the results of your efforts by means of a Web browser. Each of these activities takes place in a special interface. These interfaces are also called *views*.

First view is the Zope interface itself and shows the whole source code that implements Zope. There is not a unique interface in which to "see" the first view. Every time you are working with the Zope source code, you are in the first view—no matter which text editor you are using.

The *second view* of an object means its appearance in the Zope Management screen. As long as you modify an object via the Management screen, you are in the second view. Figure 4.2 presents the `index_html` document in the second view.

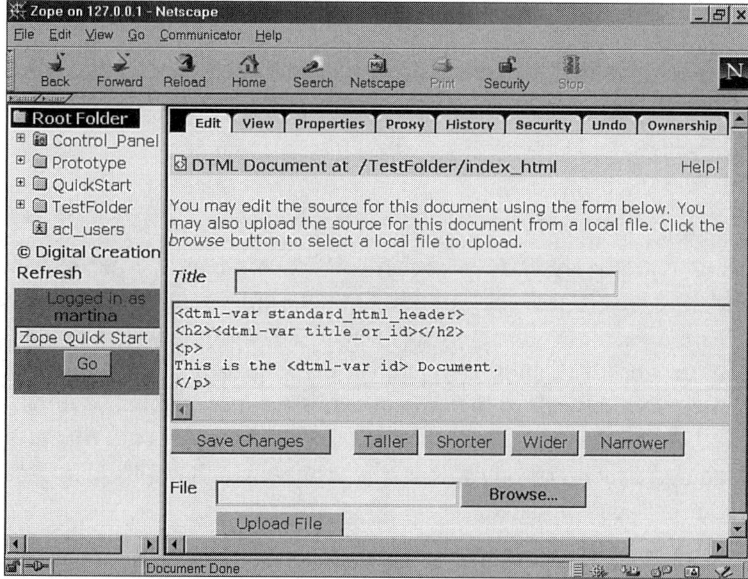

Figure 4.2
The second view.

The result of your efforts that can be viewed by you or the visitors of the appropriate Web site, respectively, is called the third view. Even if the programmed Web site contains elements that are based on Zope functionalities, such as database management, you are still in the third view. Figure 4.3 shows the `index_html` document in the third view.

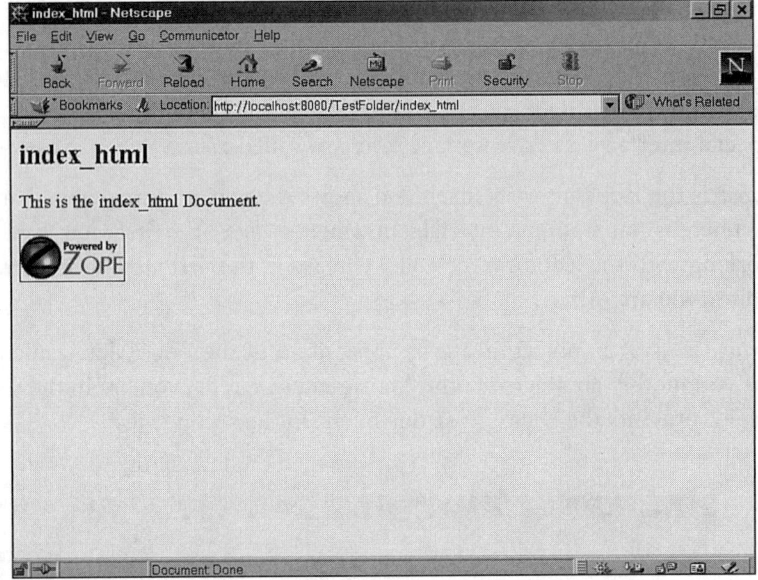

Figure 4.3
The third view.

Zope Versions

Zope Versions are a very useful tool that will come in handy, especially with large projects that require a great deal of development time and maintenance. Zope's version feature enables you to have an "active" variant of a project publicly accessible while you can work with another version at the same time. The public variant is not affected by any modifications that are done in the other version, so it will remain stable even if everything else has fallen apart. When you are sure that everything will work to your satisfaction, you can save the changes you have made in the new version so that your project is updated.

To work with Zope Versions effectively, there are some things to consider:

1. First of all, a version has to be created. You can simply add one with the available objects menu.

2. To start working in a version, you have to "enter" it. To do so, click the name of your new version and choose the Join/Leave tab from the tab bar. Use the Start Working in Version button to enter your version.

> **Note**
> You can only work in one version at a time. Zope will constantly show a message that tells you in which version you are working (see Figure 4.4).

You are currently working in version /TestFolder/TestVersion

Figure 4.4
This message tells you that you are currently working in the TestVersion version.

3. From now on, Zope "knows" that you are working in a version and you can start making your modifications. As you are doing this inside a version, your work will not affect the original objects.

4. Objects that have been modified with a version are locked. That means that no one can edit the original objects until the modifications from within a version are saved or discarded. When an object is locked, Zope marks it with a small lock in the content screen (see Figure 4.5).

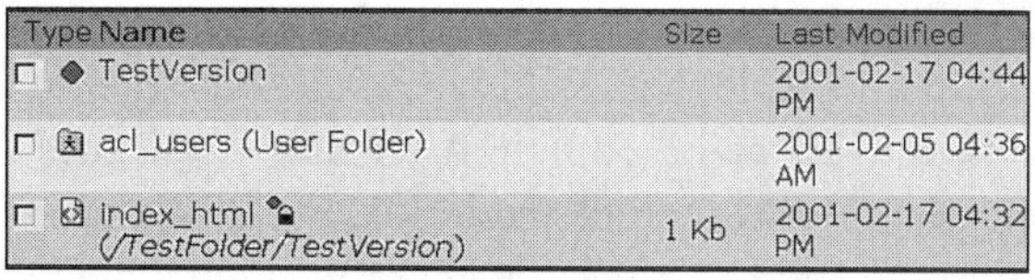

Type Name	Size	Last Modified
TestVersion		2001-02-17 04:44 PM
acl_users (User Folder)		2001-02-05 04:36 AM
index_html (/TestFolder/TestVersion)	1 Kb	2001-02-17 04:32 PM

Figure 4.5
The `index_html` object is locked.

> **Note**
> If you should add new objects or delete objects while working in a version, the folder will be blocked as well, so be careful when making changes in the root folder. Blocking the root folder means that the contained objects become inaccessible for each user working on the Zope server.

5. To save or discard changes, click the name of the version you are working in and choose the Save/Discard tab from the tab bar. To save, click the Save button; to discard, click the Discard button.

6. To quit working in a version, you need to choose the Join/Leave tab from the tab bar. Click the Quit button to stop working in a version.

Acquisition

Acquisition is one of Zope's crucial concepts that describes the way in which Zope objects acquire data from other objects and on which the object hierarchy of a Zope server is built.

> **Note**
> The Zope developers are in the process of rethinking the Acquisition concept. That means that Acquisition will change in future versions of Zope.

By means of acquisition, you can call any kind of objects, such as DTML methods, images, or external methods, from within another Zope object and Zope will find the called object for you. That means that you call an object by its name and Zope will look up an object with this name along the acquisition path. The first object found is called.

The acquisition path starts within the actual object and winds through each folder that lies above. The path ends with the root folder. Imagine the following folder structure:

```
root/ Folder1/Subfolder1
             /Subfolder2
```

When you try to call a variable from within a DTML method in Subfolder1, the contents of that method are searched first. After that, Zope goes through the other objects inside Subfolder1, and then through Folder1, until the root folder is reached. If Zope doesn't find the appropriate variable at this point, an error message is returned.

Note that Subfolder2 is not searched because it is a parallel folder of Subfolder1 and does not belong to the acquisition path.

> **Note**
> The root folder is always at the end of an acquisition path, so its objects can be acquired by any object in a Zope server.

In this way, acquisition can make your programming efforts much easier because you don't have to do the same things over and over again. You can have one method that does some useful stuff inside the root folder, and then you can call it from any other object.

Overriding variables is very easy. Simply put the object with the same ID as the object you want to override one step upwards in the object hierarchy. Imagine that you want to use a modified version of the `standard_html_header` in a folder. All you have to do is add a `standard_html_header` object to the folder that contains the object that calls it. Then Zope will find the modified version first and won't go down to the original header.

> **Note**
> When you override a folder, you cannot access any objects from the folder that is overridden.

As useful as the concept of acquisition is, there will be situations when you do not want to use it, and you are not required to. When using the DTML `with` and `let` tags, you can ignore the usual acquisition rules. For details, see "The `<dtml-with>` Tag" and "The `<dtml-let>` Tag" sections later in this chapter.

Templates

Because of acquisition, it's easy to create simple and even complex template structures with Zope.

A *template* is something like a skeleton or a scheme that defines the basic structure of Web pages and gives these pages a common appearance.

In the next paragraphs, we will show you how to build a prototype of a simple Content Management System. This prototype has a template structure as well. Each single page of the CMS will appear in the same design (see Figure 4.6).

The content of the following pages will change, but the general design will not. Each visible page that belongs to the prototype will have a *main table*, which is khaki and where the major functions are executed.

The *navigation bar* contains links that lead the user to the corresponding pages.

The user's role is always shown in the upper-left corner of the screen, right beside the user's name.

This template structure can easily be created by modifying the two DTML methods `standard_html_header` and `standard_html_footer`. These methods are called at the end and at the beginning of the objects that appear inside the main table. The main table is embraced by the `standard_html_footer` and the `standard_html_header`. In the

"Creating the Template Structure" section later in this chapter, we will explain the creation of our template structure in detail.

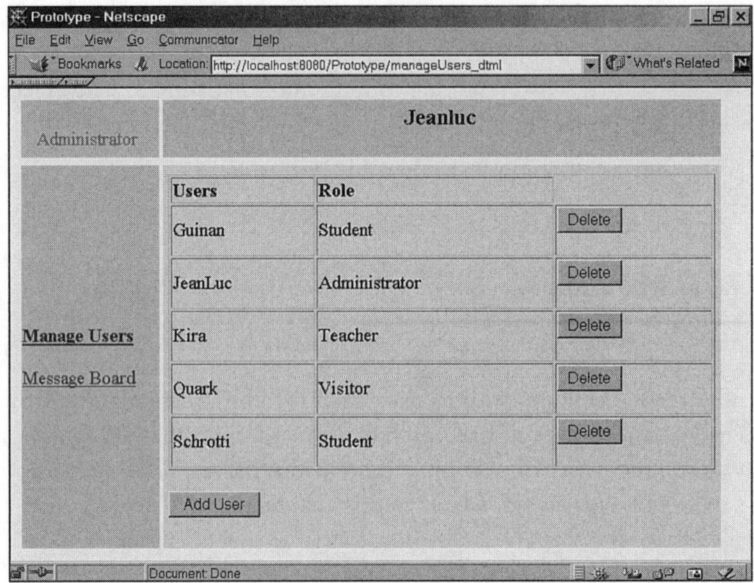

Figure 4.6

The User Management area of the prototype.

Users, Roles, and Permissions

Another important element of Zope is its user system. It enables you to administer authentification permissions for your projects in an easy way. First, we will briefly explain the terms user, role, and permission:

- *User*—Users are objects with one or more roles. That means, a visitor of a Web site who is given the ID and the password of an existing user can act as this user and can do everything the user is allowed to do. This, of course, depends on the give role.
- *Role*—A role is a bundle of permissions.
- *Permission*—A permission means a right that allows the user who is given the role to do something. For example, a user can only add a MailHost object to a folder if he has been given the Add MailHost Object permission.

Users can only be added in an object called `acl_users`. This object is automatically created when you create a folder and activate the Create User Folder check box.

The second way to create a user folder is to use the available objects menu and choose User Folder.

> **Note**
> There can be only one user folder inside a folder. To avoid security leaks, you cannot copy or move a User Folder.

To create a user, do the following:

1. Click the ID link of the user folder into which you want to put the user.
2. Fill out the form (see Figure 4.7):
   - *Name*—Give the user a name. A Web site visitor who wants to act as this user has to log in with this name.
   - *Password*—The password that is assigned to the user. The name and password authenticate a Web site visitor as an authenticated user.
   - *Confirm*—Type the password again.
   - *Roles*—Choose at least one role for the user.
3. Click the Add button.

After you have created a user, you can make your Web page accessible for this user only, or you can restrict access for anonymous users. Additionally, you have the opportunity to define your own roles and permissions.

During this chapter, we will show in detail how we made use of the rather complex user system.

The DTML Namespace

Namespace is another term for what you might know as *scope the name where variables live*.

The namespace is a dictionary of dictionaries where you can find all the variables that are valid for the duration of a certain time. The namespace is not static but changes dynamically. If you call a variable by its name, Zope will look it up in the namespace and return the appropriate value.

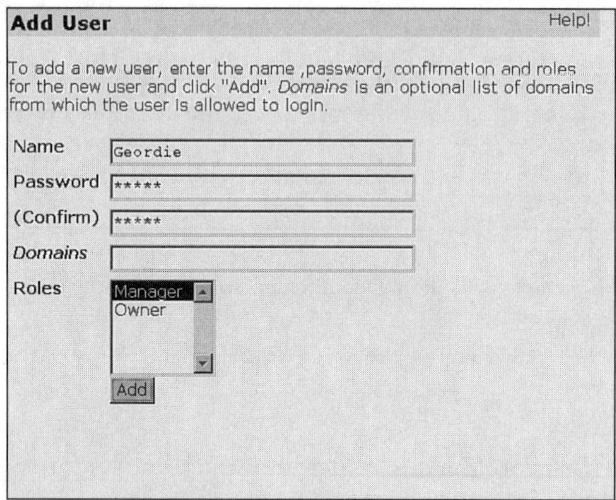

Figure 4.7.
Fill in the form to create a new user.

This works like a stack, which means that the variables that were put in last will be looked up first. In using the DTML `let` and `with` tags, you can add variables to the namespace that will exist only as long as the tag is computed. On the other side, variables that are defined in a DTML object using the DTML `var` or `call` tags are in the namespace as long as the whole object is computed.

Zope's Undo System

Another useful feature that comes with Zope is its built-in Undo system. It allows a user to undo recently executed actions, such as deleting or modifying a DTML method. That means that a previously performed action is cancelled and the former state of the corresponding object is restored.

The Undo function is accessible via the Undo tab. Click the Undo tab and a table is shown that contains all the undoable actions within the actual folder (see Figure 4.8).

This figure shows three actions that can be undone in a folder. The table gives you the name of the object that is concerned and the method that was used to modify the object. You can see the name of the user who modified the object printed in bold letters. The object's modification time is given on the right side.

To undo an action, simply activate the corresponding check box and click the Undo button. Imagine you want to undo the action that was executed at 05:15:58 p.m. (see Figure 4.9).

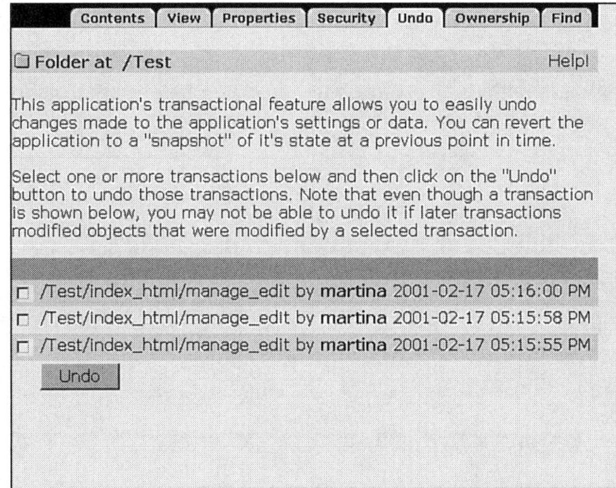

Figure 4.8

There are three undoable actions inside this folder.

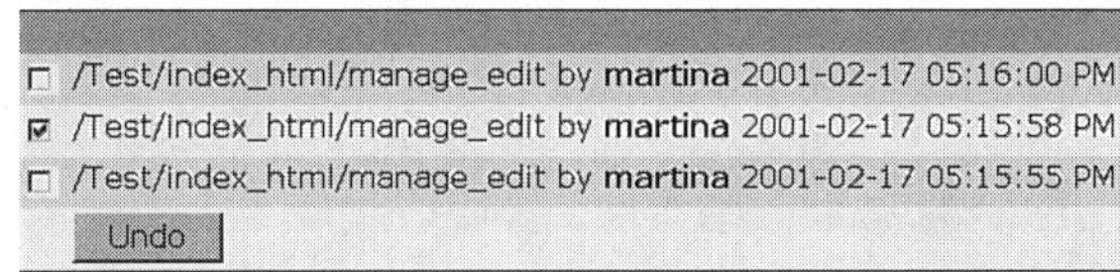

Figure 4.9

Select the action in the middle of the table.

After activating the check box and clicking the Undo button, you will find out that you cannot undo this action. You are shown an error message (see Figure 4.10).

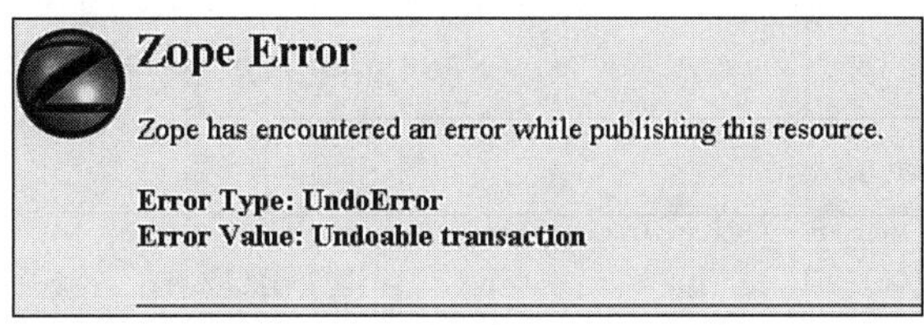

Figure 4.10

Undoing has failed.

Zope tells you that the action is undoable. The reason is that another action was executed after the action you wanted to undo had been executed. Consequently, you have to undo the latest done action first.

> **Note**
> This error appears only if there is a possible conflict between different executed actions. Of course, you can undo actions that have been executed before other actions as long as they do not affect one another.

You have two possibilities. First, you can undo the single actions step by step. But a more effective way is to undo all the actions at the same time by activating every needed check box and then clicking the Undo button. The result for our example looks like Figure 4.11.

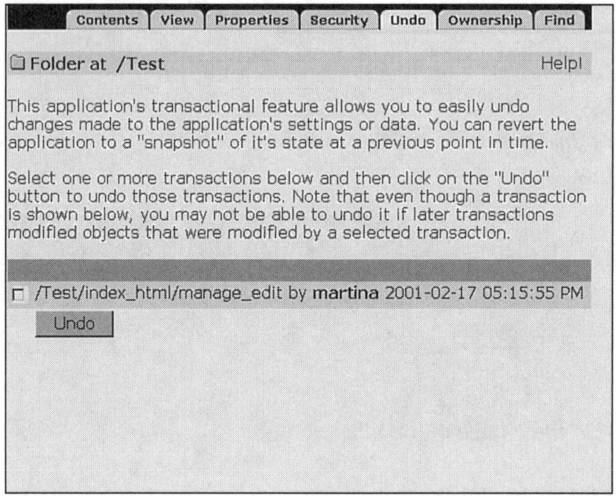

Figure 4.11
The two actions are undone.

The two latest actions are undone while one undoable action is still remaining.

Packing the Database

As you certainly know, each object on a Zope server is stored inside the Zope Object Database—the ZODB. In the file system, the ZODB is stored in a file called `data.fs`.

This file also contains "snapshots" of each object that has been modified. When an action is undone, Zope simply restores this old version of the objects from the ZODB. This is also the reason why the size of `data.fs` is constantly increasing as long as someone is working on a Zope server.

Imagine that somebody wants to upload a rather large file of about 30MB to a Zope server—by the way, this would not be a very good idea. Of course, `data.fs` will then get 30MB larger. But, because of the Undo system, the file will not decrease when the user deletes the uploaded file from his or her Zope server. Thus, it is necessary to "pack" a Zope server's database from time to time. *Packing the database* means that older revisions of objects are removed. Undoable actions will disappear as well.

> **Note**
> You cannot undo the packing of the database.

To do so, go to the Control Panel, found at the root folder, and click the Database Management link. In the following page, you will find the Pack button (see Figure 4.12). Simply click it, and all undoable actions will be removed.

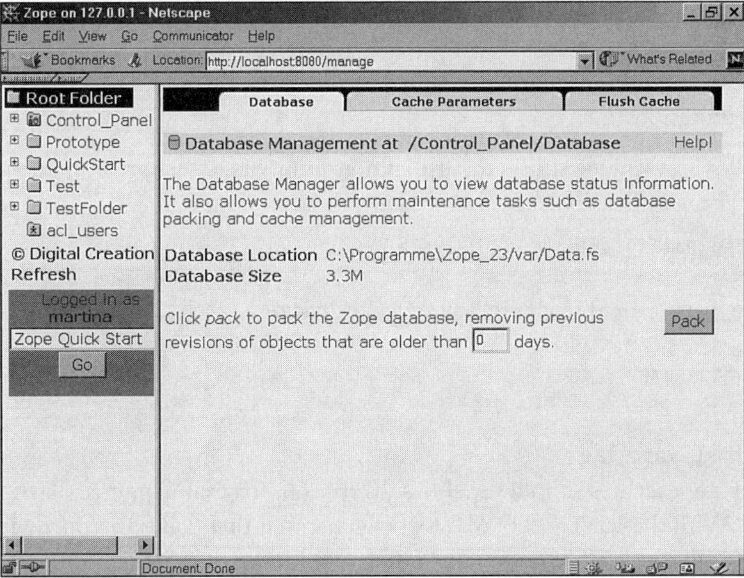

Figure 4.12

The database screen.

This tab provides some additional information:

- *Database Location*—The full path where `data.fs` is stored
- *Database Size*—The actual size of `data.fs`

In the small input field beside the Pack button, you can define how old an undoable action must be to be removed from the database. The default value 0 deletes every revision. If you want to delete those actions that have taken place one day ago, simply type `1` into the input field.

DTML

During this chapter, we will deal with Zope's own scripting language—DTML. First, we will explain the DTML syntax in general, and then we will describe each DTML tag.

DTML Syntax

DTML syntax works quite similar to HTML syntax. DTML uses tags that are enclosed in square brackets. The following scheme shows the use of non-empty DTML tags:

```
<dtml-tag name attribute = "value">
```

There can be more than one attribute, but there are also some tags that do not accept any attributes.

The following scheme shows the use of non-empty tags that are also known as container tags:

```
<dtml-tag name attribute = "value">

    tag body, might contain any kind of code

</dtml-tag name>
```

The `<dtml-var>` tag

The `var` tag executes simple variable substitution, for example, it replaces variable data by text. With the `var` tag, HTML text is generated that codes the third view. So text is always produced, even if it contains other variables such as images or sound files, with the `var` tag.

Imagine that you would like to insert an additional Zope logo somewhere into a document. You could do that with the following statement:

```
<dtml-var Zope AttributionButton>
```

In the third view, the Zope logo will appear in the desired place. However, the browser used by you alone is responsible for the representation of the third view. Zope generates only the source text.

The `name` *Attribute*

The `name` attribute is used to receive data from the DTML namespace. With its name, a variable is looked up and its value is displayed and transferred to the appropriate tag. For example, an `Image` object can be looked up and displayed as follows:

```
<dtml-var imageObject>
```

There are some rules for the creation of variable names. Zope variables can contain special characters, such as hyphens. But because this is not supported by the syntax of Python, we recommend not using special characters inside variable names.

The `expr` *Attribute*

Complex statements are computed with the `expr` attribute. The attribute's value—the statement that can be analyzed—must be enclosed in double stating lines. The statement syntax will be the Python syntax

```
<dtml-var expr="REQUEST.AUTHENTICATED_USER">
```

This code displays the ID of the user of the current object.

Look at `www.python.org` to find detailed information about Python syntax.

The `namespace` *Variable*

With the `namespace` variable variables, which do not correspond to the usual rules of name forming, can be looked up directly from the namespace:

```
<dtml-if "_['foo-bar'] == 'hallo'">
```

As you can see, the variable `foo-bar` contains an `-`, which would be interpreted as a minus sign inside the expression variable. But in using the namespace variable, the variable can be looked up and no error is raised.

The `<dtml-raise>` Tag

You can use this tag to cause and generate your own Zope error messages. You can define your own name for your error message and the error message that is to be displayed. The `raise` tag is a container tag.

The error message's name has to be put in the starting tag, the error message text itself is located in the tag body:

```
<dtml-raise error_message>
error message text
</dtml-raise>
```

The error message name must consist of a single word. You can define the actual text of your error message in the tag's body.

The following example produces a simple error message:

```
<dtml-raise myError>
Here is the Problem.
</dtml-raise>
```

The error output is shown in Figure 4.13.

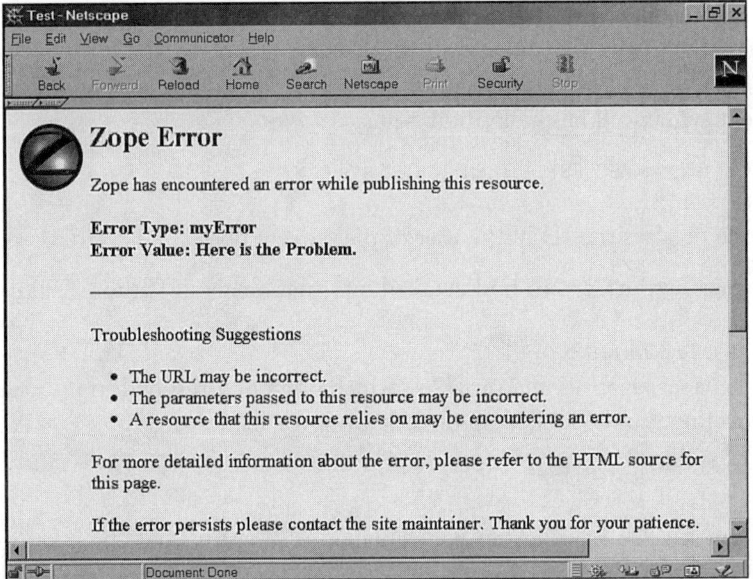

Figure 4.13
The third view of your self-induced Zope error.

The `<dtml-try>` and `<dtml-except>` Tags

It is possible that sometimes you will try to access variables without knowing whether they are defined or can be looked up. If you should try to look up a non-existing variable, Zope will generate an error message. The same will occur when you call incorrect statement expressions. Sometimes that can be a problem, because due to the error message, the representation of the document is not possible in the third view.

With the help of the `try` and `except` tags, error messages can be avoided. The `try` tag is a container tag that does not accept any attributes. It contains the statements that are to be executed, but these can possibly cause an error message.

Additionally, a try tag contains one except tag that can contain the statements that can be executed alternatively.

> **Note**
> There must be an except tag inside the try tag.

The <dtml-except> tag is an empty tag that does not accept any attributes.

Look at the following scheme:

```
<dtml-try>
      statements, which might cause an error
<dtml-except>
statements, which do not cause errors, like e.g. a message about the error.
</dtml-try>
```

Imagine that you want to call a variable my_Var and you don't know whether it exists in the namespace in a statement expression.

To avoid a Zope error message, you must use the try tag as follows:

```
<dtml-try>
    <dtml-var my_Var>
<dtml-except>
          the variable my_Var is not defined.
</dtml-try>
```

The error message is avoided, the remainder of the document can be represented, and the viewer of the third view is informed of the fact that my_Var does not exist.

The <dtml-finally> Tag

The finally tag can be used only within try tags. It defines a block statement that is executed independently of whether an error message must be avoided or not.

The finally tag is used instead of except tags.

```
<dtml-try>
        <dtml-var my_Var>
<dtml-finally>

    <dtml-var title_or_id>
</dtml-try>
```

The <dtml-with> Tag

The with tag is very useful in the following cases:

- When variables with the same name but different values are to be looked up
- When new variables are to be defined in the namespace of Zope
- When objects, which are situated in the hierarchy below the current object, are to be accessed

Particularly if user informations are called via a form, it can occur that there is already a variable with the same name as a form variable in the namespace of a document. This is farther down in the namespace batch than the already existing variable and cannot be called easily.

The variable ID is determined for the identifier of an object in Zope. If you insert a variable ID over a form into the namespace, when you have built a portal where users are supposed to log in giving their user ID and their password, for example, and then try to call it with

```
<dtml-var id>
```

Zope will display the ID of the current object and not the input ID from the form.

You can prevent that by using with tags:

```
<dtml-with REQUEST> Your Id is:
     <dtml-var id>
</dtml-with>
```

Now the value from the form is displayed and not the current object identifier.

The with tag adds another namespace batch to the namespace of the current object, which is set above on the current batch.

The object, whose namespace batch is to be added, is defined in the starting tag. The statement to be executed is in the tag body. Also, the tag body can contain additional <dtml-with> tags.

```
<dtml-with object>
statements
</dtml-with>
```

Variables from sub-objects can be accessed:

```
<dtml-with subfolder>
 the Id of the subfolder is: <dtml-var id>
</dtml-with>
```

Additionally, a new variable inclusive value can be set on the top of the current namespace with the help of the namespace variable. That means that you can define a variable with a certain value that is valid only as long as the body of the `with` tag is computed.

In the following example, a `costs` function that executes a cost calculation is to be called.

A variable `price`, which is transferred as an argument to the function, could already be defined. Let's say it has the value 500, but now the calculation is to be executed with another value, perhaps 100.

```
<dtml-with "_(price=100)">
 <dtml-var "costs(price)" >
</dtml-with>
```

The cost calculation can be executed with the new price of 100. Outside the `with` tags, the namespace is in the initial status again. That means that whenever a `price` is called before or after the `with` tag, its value will be 500.

The `only` Attribute

Within `with` tags, the `only` attribute can be used to limit the namespace. With this attribute, objects are defined such that specific variables are to be looked up, so the acquisition path can be ignored.

In the following example, only the variable ID that was required over a form is to be represented:

```
<dtml-with REQUEST only>
<dtml-if id> the Id is: <dtml-var id>
<dtml-else>No Id specified.
</dtml-if>
</dtml-with>
```

> **Note**
> If the desired variable is not contained in the `attribute` object, a Zope error will be displayed.

The `<dtml-let>` Tag

The `let` tag operates in a similar way as the `with` tag and is, among other things, especially helpful to keep your source code short and simple.

The `let` tag is a container tag.

A new namespace batch is set on the current batch, which is then populated with the variables that are defined in the starting tag.

Among other things, the `let` tag functions exactly the same as if the `with` tag and the namespace variable had been used.

Consequently, the following code lines are equivalent:

```
<dtml-let price=100>
<dtml-var "costs(price)">
</dtml-let>

<dtml-with "_(price=100)">
< dtml-var "costs(price)" >
</dtml-with>
```

Additionally, several variables can be set up within one single `let` tag.

Each new variable allocation must take place in a new line. The statements and name are successively analyzed or looked up, so allocations can refer to one or the other:

```
<dtml-let x="5" y="10" z="y" result="x*y*z">
<dtml-var result>
</dtml-let>
```

In this example, `x`, `y`, `z`, and `result` are successively analyzed. The output value will be the result, which is now 500.

The `<dtml-comment>` Tag

The `comment` tag indicates text that is not to be considered by Zope. The `comment` tag is a container tag that includes the text you want ignored:

```
<dtml-comment>
text to be ignored
 </dtml-comment>
```

Zope ignores all text that is in the body of the `comment` tag, so you can insert comments that describe your source code.

The `comment` tag is especially useful for the elimination of errors. You de-comment code fragments to find the code section that contains an error.

It is also possible to write nested comments.

De-commented text does not appear as comment in the source text of the third view. If you require that, you need to use normal HTML comments for the indication of comments.

The `comment` tag does not accept any attributes.

The <dtml-return> Tag

The return tag lets DTML methods return data instead of text. This data can then be acquired by other objects.

The following example returns the 25; all text is ignored:

```
<dtml-var id>
<dtml-call "REQUEST.set('x',25)">
<dtml-return "x">
```

We will explain the use of the call tag in the "The <dtml-call> Tag" section later in this chapter.

The <dtml-if> Tag

The if tag is used when source code is to be generated, depending on a certain condition. That is, DTML source text is only translated by Zope if a certain condition is fulfilled.

Conditions are not fulfilled if the expression that defines the condition is an empty string, an empty list, or an empty Dictionary, which then supplies zero or false.

The if tag is a container tag.

The starting tag contains the condition that is stated either in the name or the expr attribute.

The following is a simple example:

```
<dtml-if title>
<dtml-var title>
</dtml-if>
```

The starting tag checks whether a title exists. If this is the case, the text the tag body is analyzed. Here, the title of the object is looked up and displayed. If the condition is not fulfilled, nothing occurs.

The <dtml-else> Tag Within the <dtml-if> Tag

The else tag, when inserted into an if tag, initiates the text that Zope is to process if a condition is not fulfilled.

Consequently, alternative expressions can be executed. The else tag is an empty tag. The previous example can be easily optimized:

```
<dtml-if title>
Title: <dtml-var title>
<dtml-else>
    The object does not have a title
</dtml-if>
```

The <dtml-call> Tag

The call tag operates similar to the var tag. Variables are also looked up, methods are executed, and so on. But the call tag does not generate text; no text substitution is executed.

The <dtml-call AUTHENTICATED_USER> call will not cause any visible output via the screen. The user is looked up, but is not displayed.

That seems to make little sense. However, the call tag is very practical if methods are executed whose result is not to be displayed.

Many Python methods return a None as a sign that their execution worked without errors. Usually, a mysterious None is not satisfactory.

Consequently, the call tag is frequently used to define its own variables. Imagine that you want to create a list within a DTML method. You can do that as follows:

```
<dtml-var " REQUEST.set('list', ['Paul', 'John'])">
```

This will return a None in the third view. To avoid that, use the following statement:

```
<dtml-call "REQUEST.set('list', ['Paul', 'John'])">
```

> **Note**
> Use the call tag if you want an action to be executed. If you are interested in the result of an action, use the var tag.

The <dtml-in> Tag

With the in tag, sequences, such as lists, tuples, and dictionaries, can be traversed through in a loop.

In the starting tag, the sequence that will be traversed is determined, and the tag body contains the statements that are to be applied to individual elements of a list.

```
<dtml in sequence of attributes>
  statements
</dtml-in>
```

With the help of in tags, you can, for example, pass through the items of a list to represent it in a table.

```
<dtml-call "REQUEST.set('list', ['Paul', 'John'])">

<dtml-in list>
<dtml-if sequence-start>
        <table border=1>
          <tr><th>sequence-start?</th>
              <th>sequence-end? </th>
              <th>sequence-key</th>
              <th>sequence-item</th>
          </tr>
</dtml-if>
     <tr>
          <td><dtml-var sequence-start></td>
          <td><dtml-var sequence-end></td>
          <td><dtml-var sequence-index></td>
          <td><dtml-var sequence-item></td>
     </tr>
<dtml-if sequence-end>
        </table>
</dtml-if>
<dtml-else>
     The sequence is empty.
</dtml-in>
```

First, the list is checked to determine whether it is empty. If that is the case, the code from the `else` tag is computed. Otherwise, a table heading is defined. Thereafter, the list is passed through, and the values are entered, into the table cells.

Counter Loops with the `in` *Tag*

Another useful function of the `in` tag is the capability of producing counter loops. A *counter loop* executes statements with a certain number of repetitions.

The `in` tag uses the Python method `range()`. It accepts three arguments:

```
range(start value, final value, incrementation)
```

So `range(1,10,2)` would create the list `[1,3,5,7,9]`.

The `<dtml-tree>` Tag

The `tree` tag works much the same as the `in` tag. Here, Zope objects are traversed and displayed in dependence of their hierarchy. They are then shown as a tree with branches and sub-branches.

```
<dtml-tree ZopeObject>
    <dtml-var id>
</dtml-tree>
```

The DTML `tree` tag accepts a lot of useful attributes. As we will deal with this tag in detail in Chapter 9, you should look at those pages for further information.

The `<dtml-sendmail>` Tag

The `sendmail` tag enables you to send electronic mail via the Standard Mail Transport Protocol (SMTP). The following scheme shows the tag's usage:

```
<dtml-sendmail smtphost=name of the smtphost>
To:the receiver's email address
From:the sender's email address
Subject:a subject

The text of the mail.
</dtml-sendmail>
```

> **Note**
> To get this working, you need to have a `MailHost` object created.

The `<dtml-mime>` and `<dtml-boundary>` Tags

Whenever you want to send attachments via an e-mail, you have to use the `mime` tag. This tag will enclose the boundary tags that contain the file objects to be sent:

```
<dtml-sendmail smtphost= name of smtphost>
To:
From:
Subject:

Message
<dtml-mime>
<dtml-boundary name="Name of the attached file" disposition=attachment>
<dtml-var "Id of the file to be attached">
</dtml-mime>
</dtml-sendmail>
```

> **Note**
> Each attached file needs its own boundary tag.

Our Prototype—Goals and Preconditions

In the next sections, we will demonstrate how to build a simple Content Management System. This CMS is a prototype of a larger and more sophisticated project, such as the real life example we will program in a later chapter.

Prototypes are often used for demonstration purposes. They can help a programmer show the possibilities of Zope to an undecided customer, and they can help customers decide what features they would like to be programmed.

Because a prototype is mainly used to demonstrate something, it does not have the full functionality of the whole project. As a result, it can be created in a simpler way that saves a lot of time. An effective way to build prototypes that are simple but nevertheless useful is to use DTML code along with ZClasses. We will start working with ZClasses in the "Creating an `ArticleClass` ZClass" section later in this chapter. No Python code will be needed. During this chapter, we will do just that.

An Outline of the Prototype

Our prototype simulates something like a moderated message board for students. Students can write articles and visitors can view these articles after they are moderated. The moderator of this board is a teacher who will decide whether an article should be made live (visible) or deleted. There will also be an administrator who manages the prototype's users.

We want to allow four different user groups to have access and execute various actions on the message board. They will have to log in on the message board via a login screen. There will be four different roles with the corresponding permissions. Table 4.1 shows these roles and gives an overview over their permissions.

Table 4.1

Roles and Permissions for Our Message Board

Roles	Permissions
Student	Writes articles
	Views the live article database
Teacher	Views the student's non-live articles
	Submits articles to the live article database
	Deletes the student's non-live articles
	Views the live article database
Administrator	Adds users—students, teachers, administrators, and visitors
	Deletes users
	Views the live article database
Visitor	Views the live article database

> **Note**
>
> Users without these roles, such as anonymous users, do not have any permissions. They are not allowed to view anything but the login screen.
>
> But there is one exception—users with the Manager role are not restricted in anything. They have full access. This is done to give a Manager the ability to maintain the prototype and to create the first administrator. Additionally, as the Message Board's programmer, the Manager has the opportunity to test each single function. The Manager role is one of those roles that are automatically created by Zope.

As long as an article has not been made live, it is stored just as a usual Zope object. When the teacher decides to make it a live article, it will be submitted to an article database. We will use Zope's Gadfly database for this purpose. For information about Gadfly, see `http://www.chordate.com/gadfly.html`. Students, teachers, administrators, and visitors can view the entries of this database.

An article will be an instance of a class called `Article` that is to be made up as a ZClass. `Article` objects will consist of a headline, the name of the article's author, and the contents.

An administration interface will be needed on which the different users can work. Additionally, this interface will have a template structure to easily give the single pages a common appearance.

Figure 4.14 shows the User Management Area of the prototype that is, at the moment, accessed by a user with the name Admin and the Administrator role.

As the outline shows, there are five major tasks to be done:

- Make up the template structure.
- Organize the user authentification.
- Create a ZClass article.
- Build an administration interface.
- Connect the message board to a ZGadfly database.

In the next section, we will start dealing with the template structure.

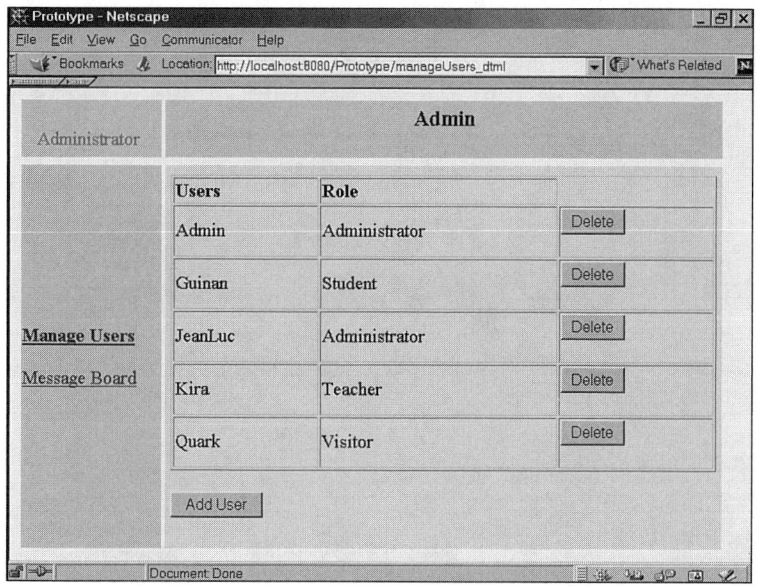

Figure 4.14
The Prototype's User Management Area.

Creating the Template Structure

In this chapter you will not only build the template structure for the prototype, but you will create a login screen as well.

We want our prototype to have a common appearance. Because we want to define the message board's appearance just one time, not again and again, we will now make up a template structure.

Consequently, we need to create a folder that will contain all the objects needed for the message board and then create three DTML methods—`standard_html_header`, `standard_html_footer`, and `links_html`. Two more DTML objects, that we will call `index_html` and `login_html`, are needed for the login screen.

You could also use DTML methods for all those objects.

> **Note**
> We decided to keep this example as simple as possible. For a more complex project, it would make sense to store those objects in different folders, so you could create a login folder.

If you want to follow our example, add the objects just mentioned. Add them to a folder called `Prototype`. Your `Prototype` folder will then look like Figure 4.15.

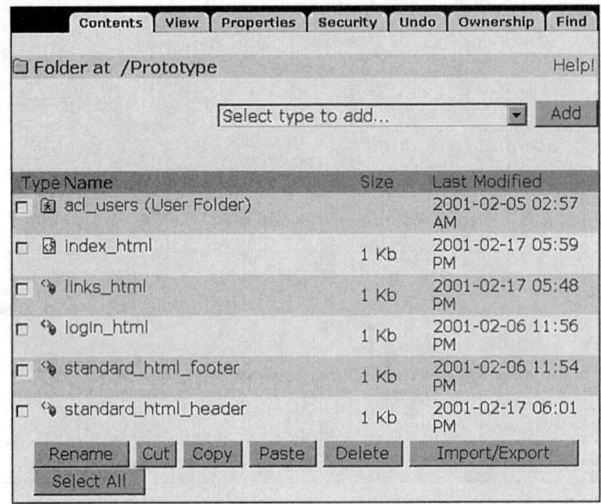

Figure 4.15

The contents of the Prototype folder.

Remember how the prototype is supposed to look. Figure 4.16 shows the login screen of the Message Board. This screen is the result displayed when you call `index_html`.

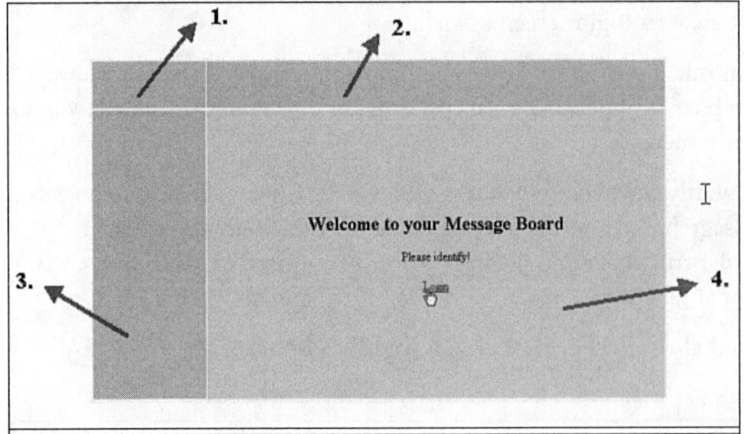

Figure 4.16

The login screen.

1. After the correct login, the authenticated user's role is shown here.
2. The authenticated user's name.
3. The Navigation bar. Depending on the authenticated user's role, various links will lead him or her through the Message Board.
4. The Main Area. This is where any content is shown and the various actions will take place.

Now, click the Edit tab of the `index_html` object and replace any text with the code in Listing 4.1.

Listing 4.1

index_html

```
1: <dtml-var standard_html_header>
2: <center>
3: <dtml-if "AUTHENTICATED_USER.has_role('Anonymous')">
4: <h2>Welcome to your Message Board</h2>
5:<p>
6: Please identify!
7:<p>
8: <a href="login_html">Login</a>
9: </dtml-if>
10: </center>
11: <dtml-var standard_html_footer>
```

The `standard_html_header` object is called in line 1.

The code in lines 2–10 computes the content of the main table. We will look at this fragment later.

The `standard_html_footer` is called in line 11.

As you can see, the parts that are outside the main table, which define the Main Area, must be defined inside the `standard_html_header` and the `standard_html_footer`. We will look at the header object first in Listing 4.2.

Listing 4.2

standard_html_header

```
<html>
<head><title><dtml-var title_or_id></title></head>
<body>
```

Listing 4.2

Continued

```
 4: <table width=100% height=15%>
 5:    <tr>
 6:           <td align=center width=20% bgcolor=lightgreen>
 7:             <dtml-unless "AUTHENTICATED_USER.has_role('Anonymous')">  <br>
 8:              <font color=red><dtml-var "AUTHENTICATED_USER.getRoles()[0]">
</font>
 9:             </dtml-unless>
10:           </td>
11:           <td align=center width=80% bgcolor=lightgreen>
12:             <dtml-unless "AUTHENTICATED_USER.has_role('Anonymous')">
13:             <h3><dtml-var AUTHENTICATED_USER capitalize></h3>
14:             </dtml-unless>
15:   </td>
16:    </tr>
17: </table>
18: <table valign="top" width=100% height=88%>
19:     <tr>
20:           <td width=20% bgcolor=lightgreen><dtml-var links_html> </td>
21:           <td bgcolor=khaki width=100% height=100%>
22:             <table width=100%>
23:               <tr><td>
```

A common HTML header is defined in lines 1–3.

Lines 4–17 define the top of the Prototype screen where username and user role are shown.

The table that defines the bottom of the page is opened in line 18.

The Navigation bar is defined in lines 20 and 21. The `links_html` object is called, which contains the contents of the Navigation bar.

In line 22, the second table row opens another table, but the table is not closed at the end of the method. That means that whatever object is calling the `standard_html_header` will be shown inside this table.

Because you have already seen the code of `index_html`, you know that the tables are not closed in that document, so the `end` tags have to be inside the `standard_html_footer` (see Listing 4.3).

Listing 4.3

standard_html_footer

```
1: </td>
2: </tr>
3: </table>
4: </tr>
5: </table>
6: </body>
7: </html>
```

All the tables that were opened inside the `standard_html_header` are closed in lines 1–5.

A common HTML footer is defined in lines 6 and 7.

In Listing 4.4, we will have a look at the `links_html` that is responsible for the contents of the Navigation bar:

Listing 4.4

links_html

```
<dtml-if "AUTHENTICATED_USER.has_role('Teacher')">
<a href="http://localhost:8080/Prototype/Articles/admin_html">
➥ <b>Manage Articles</b></a> <br>
<a href="http://localhost:8080/Prototype/Article_DB_archive/searchReport">
➥ Message Board</a>
<dtml-elif "AUTHENTICATED_USER.has_role('Student')">
    <a href="http://localhost:8080/Prototype/Articles/addForm_html">
➥ <b>Add Article</b></a><br><p>
<a href="http://localhost:8080/Prototype/Article_DB_archive/searchReport">
➥ Message Board</a>
<dtml-elif "AUTHENTICATED_USER.has_role('Administrator')">
    <a href="http://localhost:8080/Prototype/manageUsers_dtml">
➥  <b>Manage Users</b></a> <br><p>
<a href="http://localhost:8080/Prototype/Article_DB_archive/searchReport">
➥ Message Board</a>
<dtml-elif "AUTHENTICATED_USER.has_role('Visitor')">
<a href="http://localhost:8080/Prototype/Article_DB_archive/searchReport">
➥ <b>Message Board</b></a>
<dtml-elif "AUTHENTICATED_USER.has_role('Manager')">
    <a href="http://localhost:8080/Prototype/addUserForm_dtml">
➥  Add User </a> <br>
    <a href="http://localhost:8080/Prototype/manageUsers_dtml">
➥  Manage Users </a> <br>
```

Listing 4.4

Continued

```
     <a href="http://localhost:8080/Prototype/Articles/admin_html">
➥ View Articles </a> <br>
     <a href="http://localhost:8080/Prototype/Articles/addForm_html">
➥  Add Article </a> <br>
     <a href="http://localhost:8080/Prototype/
Article_DB_archive/searchReport">
➥ Message Board</a>
</dtml-if>
```

The various links that will lead to different objects are coded here. The DTML `if` construct controls which user can be linked to which objects.

You can simply use the code in Listing 4.4 for your object, but the `links_html` and the login will not work because the appropriate documents have not been added yet.

The template structure is done now. You just need to call `standard_html_header` and `standard_html_header` within each object of the prototype that shows any result. This ensures that those objects will automatically appear inside the table between the two DTML objects.

The Login Procedure/Password Verification

Now we will have a closer look at the `index_html`. The code that you have already seen only works together with the code inside the `login_html` (see Listing 4.5).

Listing 4.5

Code Fragment from `index_html`

```
<dtml-if "AUTHENTICATED_USER.has_role('Anonymous')">
<h2>Welcome to your Message Board</h2>
       <p>
Please identify!
       <p>
<a href="login_html">Login</a>
</dtml-if>
```

In this fragment, you can see that a link that leads to the `login_html` is only shown if the user has the Anonymous role. An anonymous user will click the Login link and will be directed to the `login_html`.

This object contains only one code line:

```
<dtml-call "RESPONSE.redirect('index_html')">
```

With this line, the user is instantly redirected to the `index_html`. This does not seem to make much sense, and it does not work yet either. To make the login procedure work and to raise a password verification window, you have to change the security settings of `login_html` and you have to add a few new roles. Up to now, even anonymous users are allowed to view the `login_html`, but we want to deny access for them so that Zope asks for authentication.

To create a `login_html` just like in our example, simply substitute everything `inside` `login_html` with the previous code line.

Adding New Roles

To add a new role, go to the folder where you want to make the role valid and click the Security tab. In our example, go to the `Prototype` folder. A table is shown that contains an overview of existing roles and their permissions.

You will find an input field at the bottom of the page. Type the name of the new role and click the Add Role button (see Figure 4.17).

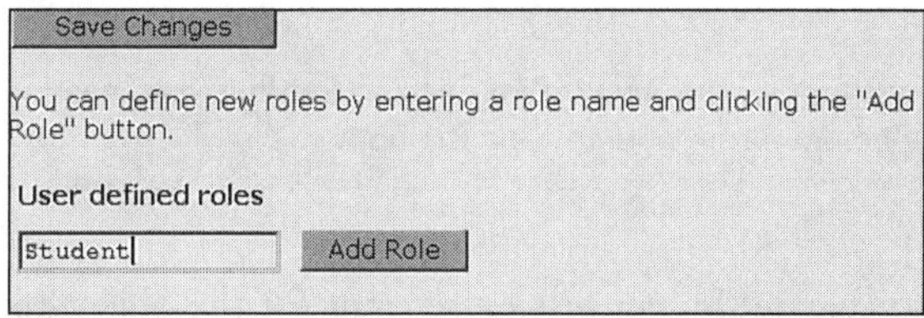

Figure 4.17
Type in the role's ID: Student.

First add the new `Student` role. After you have done that, you can see the new role inside a select menu where it can be deleted again (see Figure 4.18).

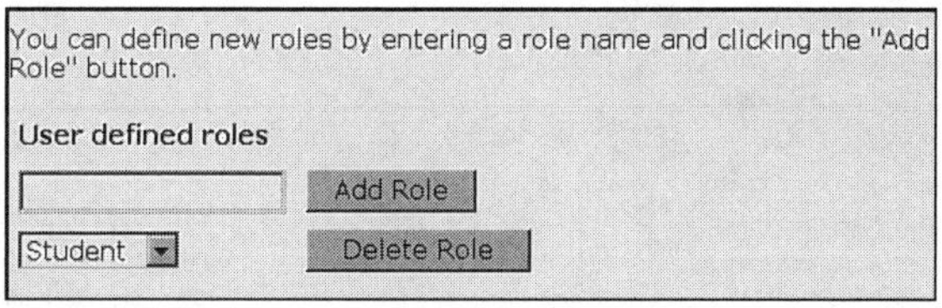

Figure 4.18
The Student role has just been created and can now be deleted as well.

Add the Administrator, Teacher, and Visitor roles in the same way. When you are finished, these roles will appear in the roles overview as well.

This table shows the Zope Permissions to which a role is assigned. If a permission is checked under a certain role, this permission is assigned to the role.

On the left side of the screen is a column with the name Acquire Permission Settings?. The check boxes in this column are activated by default. This means that the permission settings for this object are defined via acquisition. That means it does not matter what check box is checked under a role; the permission settings are acquired by the folders above.

If you want to change the permission settings, you can uncheck the check box under Acquire Permission Settings? and the new settings will become valid.

> **Note**
> Be careful when you try to change the permission of the Manager role. When you are working on a Zope server, you will be a user with the role of Manager most of the time. It would be extremely annoying if you took your own permissions away and you might not be able to continue to work.
>
> Note also that unchecking the Acquire Permission Settings box means that any role with the unchecked view box won't be able to view the object.

Now we want to change the permission settings for the object `login_html`. Go to that object and click the Security tab. You will see the table shown in Figure 4.19.

	Permission	Roles						
Acquire permission settings?		Administrator	Anonymous	Manager	Owner	Student	Teacher	Visitor
☑	Access contents information	☐	☐	☑	☐	☐	☐	☐
☑	Change DTML Methods	☐	☐	☑	☐	☐	☐	☐
☑	Change cache settings	☐	☐	☑	☐	☐	☐	☐
☑	Change permissions	☐	☐	☑	☐	☐	☐	☐
☑	Change proxy roles	☐	☐	☑	☐	☐	☐	☐
☑	Delete objects	☐	☐	☑	☐	☐	☐	☐
☑	FTP access	☐	☐	☑	☐	☐	☐	☐
☑	Manage properties	☐	☐	☑	☐	☐	☐	☐
☑	Take ownership	☐	☐	☑	☐	☐	☐	☐
☑	Undo changes	☐	☐	☑	☐	☐	☐	☐
☑	View	☐	☐	☑	☐	☐	☐	☐
☑	View History	☐	☐	☑	☐	☐	☐	☐
☑	View management screens	☐	☐	☑	☐	☐	☐	☐

Save Changes

Figure 4.19
The Permission settings for `login_html`.

We want to take the View permission away from the anonymous user. Until now, each user has the View permission via acquisition.

Remember that the `index_html` calls the `login_html`, which redirects the user back to the `index_html`. Users who do not have the permission to view the `login_html`, such as an anonymous user, cannot be redirected. As a result, they will be shown an error message and denied access to our Message Board.

Make the changes shown in Figure 4.20 and click the Save Changes button.

> **Note**
> Again, remember not to deny permissions for the Manager role, such as the View permission, because you still need to work with this role.

Undo changes	☐	☐	☑	☐	☐	☐	☐
View	☑	☐	☑	☐	☑	☑	☑
View History	☐	☐	☑	☐	☐	☐	☐

Figure 4.20
Modify the View permission to deny anonymous users permission to view the `login_html` *page.*

Now an anonymous user does not have the View permission for the `login_html`.

To control the effect of your modifications, close your browser windows and open them again, or simply use the logout feature of Zope. As long as you are still logged in as Manager, Zope will not ask you for authentication.

Now, when you try to log in with the `index_html`, Zope will ask you for your username and password (see Figure 4.21).

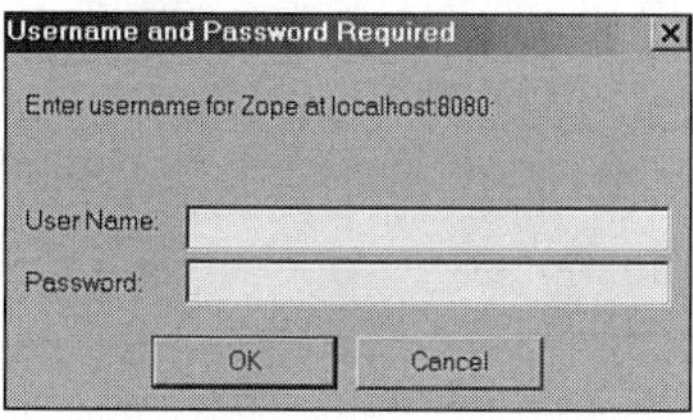

Figure 4.21
Zope asks for authentication.

A user with a role other than anonymous is now able to log in to the Message Board. When they are redirected to the `index_html`, their roles won't be anonymous and so they will have access to the prototype.

Anonymous users will be shown a Zope error message.

Creating an `ArticleClass` ZClass

A ZClass is a special class that can be added and used within Zope. You, as the Zope user, can make your own ZClasses, but you do not have to program in Python. After a ZClass is added and installed properly, you can instantiate it—you can add ZClass objects via the available objects menu. ZClasses can be exported and imported as well.

ZClasses are a very powerful tool with which you can even set up complex Content Management Systems. But they are especially interesting for Zope beginners and non-programmers because they do not require any programming knowledge. Of course, you will have to use some DTML scripts, but those are not very complicated.

ZClasses work much like classes you might already know from object-oriented languages, such as Java or Python.

ZClasses have methods and properties. They are instantiated from base classes and they can contain sub-objects. Additionally, a ZClass always has a `Meta` type that will be the name of the ZClasses objects.

When setting up a ZClass throughout the remainder of this chapter, we will go through five steps:

1. We will add a product that will contain the ZClass.
2. We will add a ZClass in this product.
3. We will define some information for the ZClass.
4. We will make up a Property sheet.
5. We will define views.

Adding a New Product

We will now create a new `Prototype` Zope product step-by-step.

1. Go to the Control Panel of your Zope server and click Product Management (see Figure 4.22).
2. Click the Add Product button (see Figure 4.23).
3. Type the ID **`Prototype`** and then click Generate (see Figure 4.24).

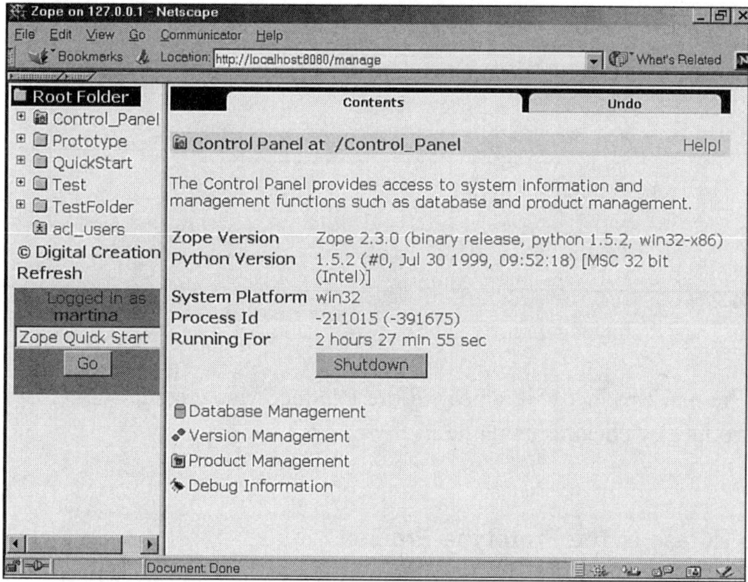

Figure 4.22

Go to the Product Management screen.

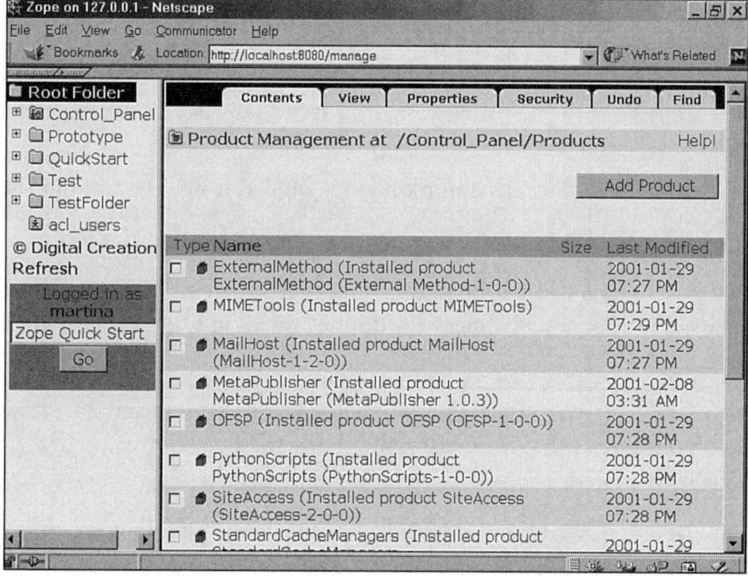

Figure 4.23

You want to add a new product.

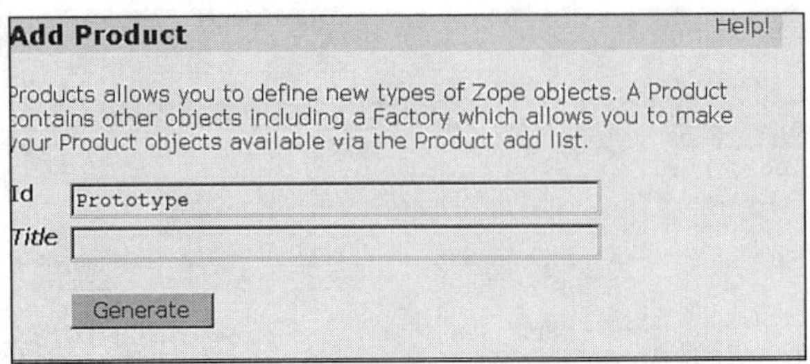

Figure 4.24
Generate a new Prototype product.

4. The new product will appear in the Product Management table. Enter the product by clicking its name in the table.

Adding a ZClass to the Prototype Product

Now we need a new ZClass for our `Prototype` product and we will place the new ZClass directly into the product.

1. When you are inside the new product, choose ZClass from the Available Objects menu.
2. A ZClass configuration form appears. Please fill in the data as shown in Figure 4.25. Base classes are chosen in clicking the desired base class in the left combo box and then clicking the arrow that points to the right.

The input fields might need some explanation:

- *Id*—Because a ZClass is a common Zope object, it needs a unique ID.
- *Title*—This field is optional. Simply give your ZClass a title.
- *Meta Type*—This will be the name of an object that will be instantiated from this ZClass. This name will appear inside the Available Object menu after the ZClass is created.
- *Base Classes*—As you already know, each ZClass is instantiated from another base class. That means that a ZClass will inherit the behavior of the class from which it was instantiated.

  If you have followed our suggestions, have added the following two base classes:

  - *ZCatalog: Catalog Aware*—This enables you to catalog your ZClass objects. For example, you could sort them by name.

- *ZClasses: Object Manager*—This allows your object to contain sub-objects. Suppose that you wanted to set up an online catalog using a ZClass. This ZClass will define book objects. These objects could contain an image that might show the book's cover and that could be viewed by the customers of the online shop.

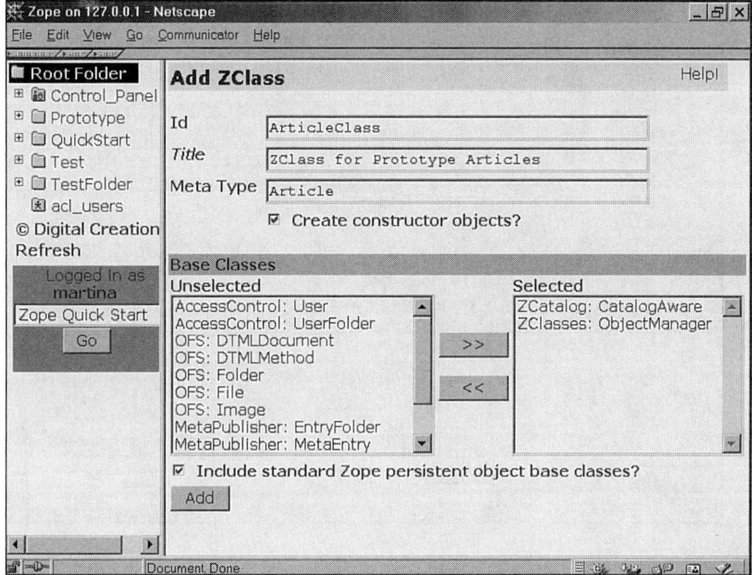

Figure 4.25
Adding a ZClass.

> **Note**
> Once chosen, the base classes cannot be changed. To choose another base class, you have to create a new ZClass.

- *Create constructor objects*—Check this option and Zope will create the following useful objects in the folder of your product:
  - The `ArticleClass_add` DTML method
  - The `ArticleClass_addForm` DTML method
  - A Zope permission with the name `ArticleClass_add_permission`
  - An `ArticleClass_factory` object

We will work with these objects later in this chapter.

- Click the Add button. The Prototype folder will now contain the objects shown in Figure 4.26.

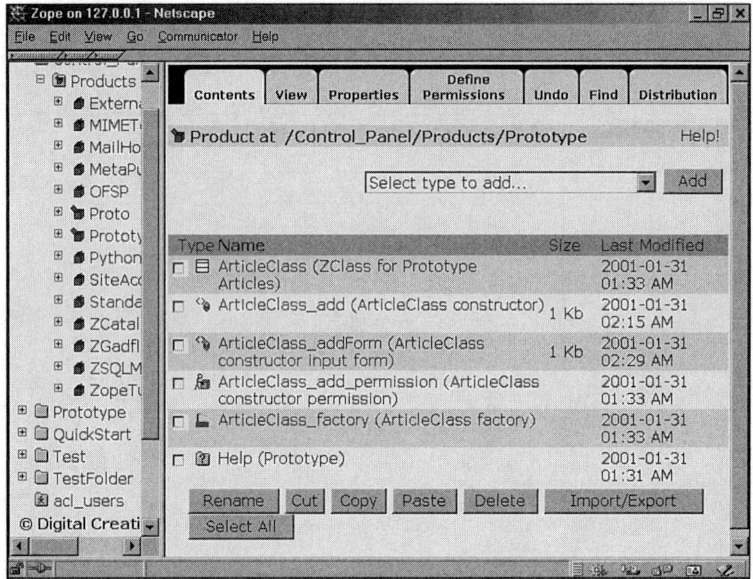

Figure 4.26

The contents of the Prototype folder.

> **Note**
> You can see that your ZClass also contains a `Help folder`. The folder is used to contain objects that can be used to provide online help for the product.

The ZClass is added.

- Open the Available Objects menu, and you will see that an `Article` object is already available (see Figure 4.27).

But, before we can add useful articles, we will have to modify the `Article` ZClass by defining its properties.

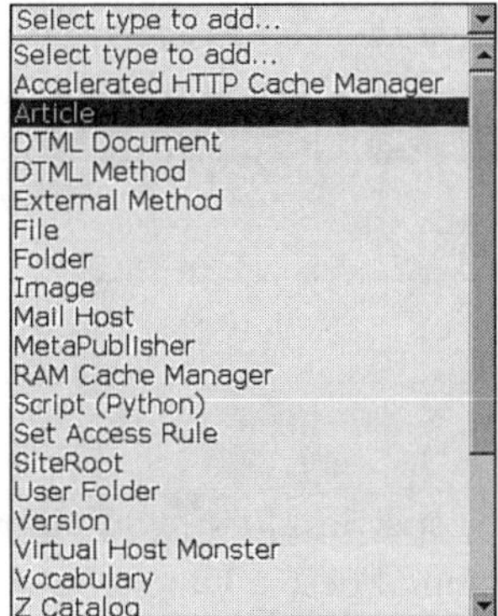

Figure 4.27

Articles can now be added via the Available Objects menu.

Properties

Enter the ZClass object by clicking its ID inside the Contents view of the Prototype product. This ID would normally be `ArticleClass`. Then click the Property Sheets tab (see Figure 4.28).

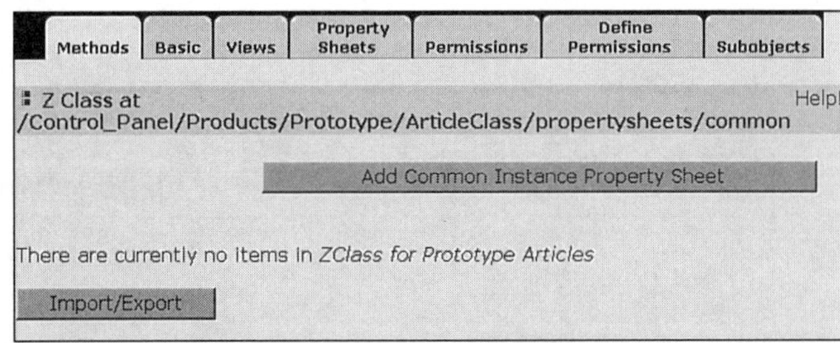

Figure 4.28

The Property Sheets screen.

As you can see, there are no property sheets defined yet. A property sheet consists of all the properties that are defined for the ZClass. You could call the properties the ZClasses attributes as well. Each instantiated object of a ZClass will have the properties defined in the property sheet. One ZClass can have more than one property sheet.

Click the Add Common Instance Property Sheet button to add a new property sheet. Insert the data shown in Figure 4.29.

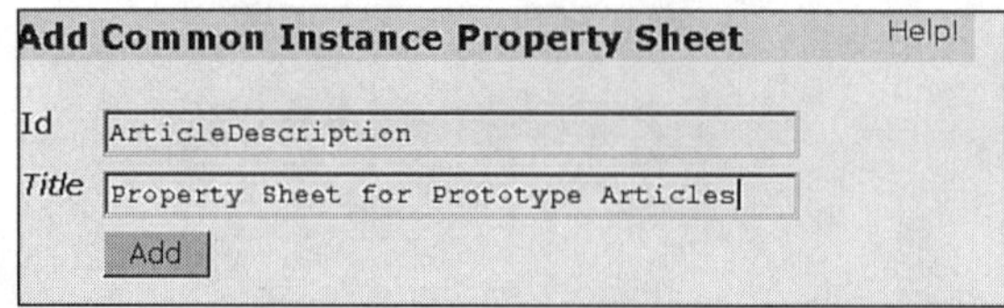

Figure 4.29
Add a new property sheet.

Now it's time to define the properties. First, you should think about what an article on the Message Board will contain. These components will become the properties of the ZClass.

A Message Board article needs

- A headline
- The author's name
- The message text or contents.

Properties consist of a Name/ID, the corresponding value, and a property type (see Figure 4.30).

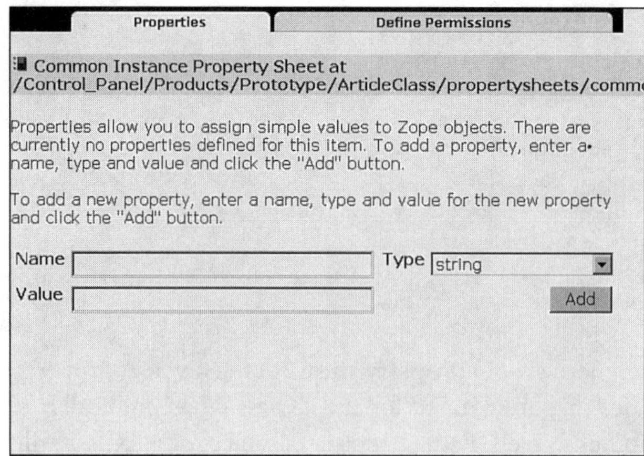

Figure 4.30
The Properties tab.

You can choose from the following property types:

- `boolean` Properties of the type `boolean` can have the value `0` or `1`, or False or True, respectively. `boolean` property types are displayed as a check box. The default value is `0`. When a value other than `0` is assigned, the check box becomes checked.
- `date` The value of a `date` property is a date value. Do not leave the input field empty. An empty string will cause an error. A date example would be 2001/08/21.
- `float` Properties whose values are floating-point numbers. They can have up to nine numbers after the point. Do not leave the input field empty. A standard value, such as `0`, must be entered.
- `int` Numbers of the data type `integer`.
- `lines` Provides a selection field. Add the property, and then add the selections into the `textarea` field. This type is needed for the `selection` and the `multiple selection` property type.
- `long` Really big numbers. Their size is only limited by the RAM of the currently used machine. Zope will add a l behind the value.
- `string` State strings of any length and combination of characters. The input field can be left empty.
- `text` Works almost like string, but will provide a text field.
- `tokens` Generates a list from an input string. The string's elements are divided by empty. Consequently, `"John George Paul Ringo"` becomes `['John', 'George', 'Paul', 'Ringo']`.
- `selection` A property of the type `lines` is needed for this property type. Type in the value field the name of the `lines` property from which you want to select items.

  `selection` will create a pull-down menu from which to choose the assigned lines property type. One element can be chosen.
- `multiple Selection` A property of the type `lines` is needed for this property type. Type in the value field the name of the `lines` property from which you want to select items.

  `Multiple selection` works like `selection`. More than one element can be chosen.

Now you should add a property sheet for Article. Please create the following properties with the given property types:

- Author: `string`
- Headline: `string`
- Contents: `text`

See the results in Figure 4.31.

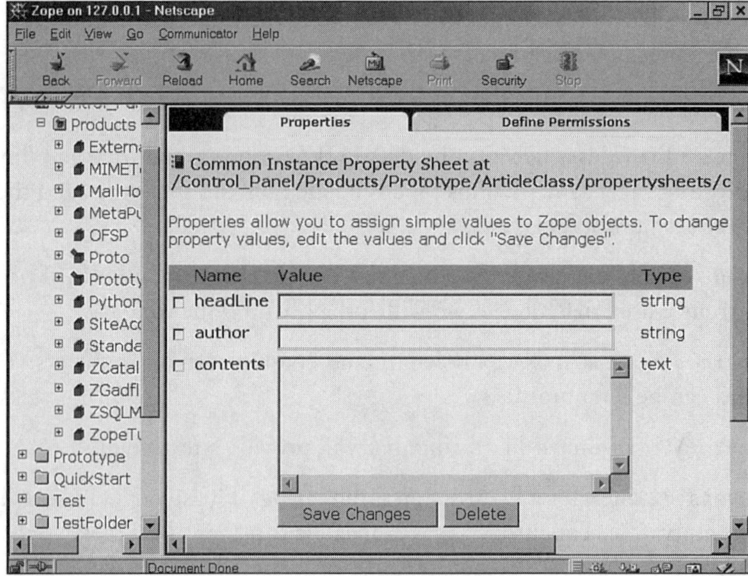

Figure 4.31
The property sheet for `ArticleClass` *is added.*

At this point, you have set up a new product, you have added a ZClass, and you have assigned the appropriate properties to the ZClass.

In the next section, we will define the views for the ZClass.

Defining the Views

To manage the properties of the ZClass's objects via the Management screen, you need to define its views.

Click the Views tab while you are inside the Property Sheets page of the ZClass (see Figure 4.32).

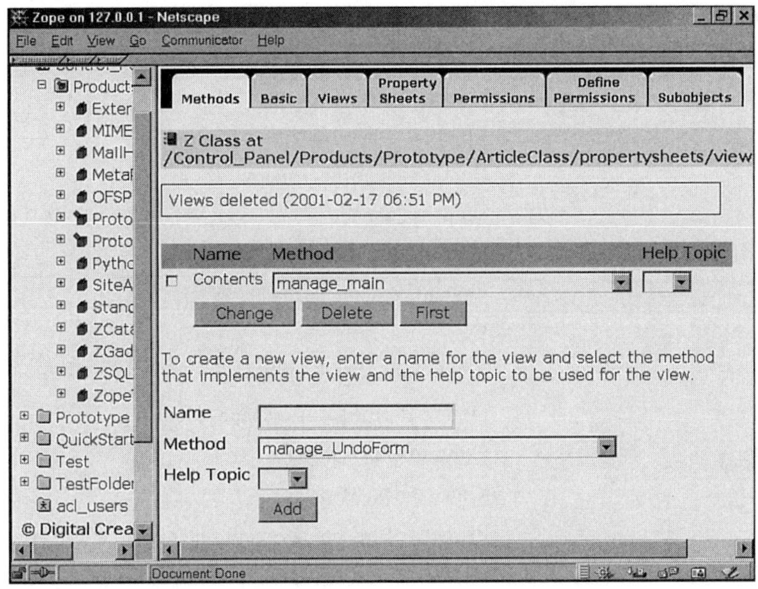

Figure 4.32

The Views tab.

As you can see, there is one view already defined that calls the Python `manage_main` method. The reason is that you have chosen the base ZClass—Object Manager. With this class, the object is able to contain sub-objects, and this view will define a tab for an Article object that will show the contained sub-objects.

Depending on the chosen base classes, Zope will make up the views shown in Table 4.2.

Table 4.2

Base Classes and Their Corresponding Methods

Base Class	Views: Corresponding Methods
No base class	Security: `manage_main`
User	Security: `manage_main`
User Folder	Contents: `manage_main`
	Security: `manage_access`
	Undo: `manage_UndoForm`
DTML document	Edit: `manage_main`
	Upload: `manage_uploadForm`
	Properties: `manage_propertiesForm`

Table 4.2
Continued

Base Class	Views: Corresponding Methods
	View:
	Proxy: manage_proxyForm
	Security: manage_access
DTML method	Edit: manage_main
	Upload: manage_uploadForm
	View:
	Proxy: manage_proxyForm
	Define Permissions: manage_access
Folder	Contents: manage_main
	View: index_html
	Properties: manage_propertiesForm
	Import/Exprt: manage_importExportForm
	Security: manage_access
	Undo: manage_UndoForm
	Find: manage_findFrame
File	Edit: manage_main
	Upload: manage_uploadForm
	Properties: manage_propertiesForm
	View:
	Security: manage_access
Image	Edit: manage_main
	Upload: manage_uploadForm
	Properties: manage_propertiesForm
	View: view_image_or_file
	Security: manage_access
Generic user folder	Contents: manage_main
	User List: manage_listUsers
	Cache: manage_chache
	User Info: manage_userInfo
	Properties: manage_properties
	Security: manage_access
	Undo: manage_UndoForm
XlogAware	Security: manage_access

Table 4.2
Continued

Base Class	Views: Corresponding Methods
CatalogAware	Security: `manage_access`
ZCatalog	Contents: `manage_main`
	Catalog: `manage_catalogView`
	Find Objects: `manage_catalogFind`
	MetaData: `manage_catalogSchema`
	Indexes: `manage_catalogIndexes`
	Status: `manage_catalogStatus`
Object Manager	Contents: `manage_main`

We will now create two useful views that we want to appear as tabs inside the Zope tab bar for the `Article` objects:

The Edit view will enable you to edit an `Article` object's contents.

Go to the button of the page and look at the form. Fill in the data shown in Figure 4.33.

To create a new view, enter a name for the view and select the method that implements the view and the help topic to be used for the view.

Name: Edit Properties
Method: propertysheets/ArticleDescription/manage
Help Topic:
Add

Figure 4.33
Fill in the data shown.

An `Article` object will now have the Tab Edit properties that will enable you to edit it. When clicked, the tab calls the Python `manage` method.

The View tab will show the contents of an object's properties. To add this view, there will be a little more work to do because there is no predefined Python method we can use. Consequently, we have to create this method. Leave the Views tab and click the Methods tab.

Add a new DTML method via the available Objects menu and give it the ID `showArticle_dtml` (see Figure 4.34).

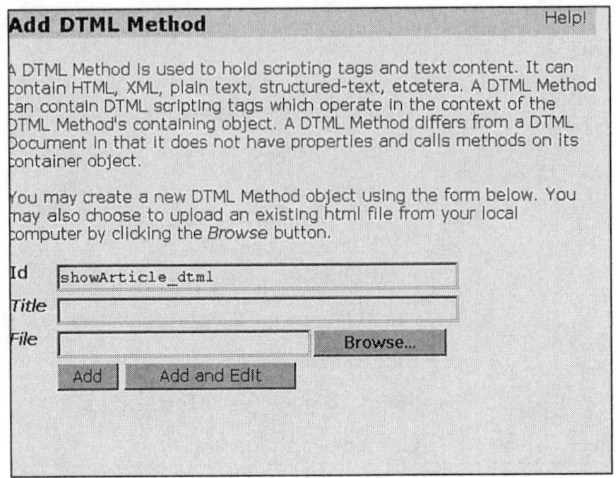

Figure 4.34

Create the `showArticle_dtml` *DTML method.*

Enter the method, and replace the standard code with the code in Listing 4.6.

Listing 4.6

showArticle_dtml

```
<table align="left"><tr>
<p>
<tr><th>Head Line</th>
      <td><dtml-var headLine></td>
</tr>
<tr><th>Author</th>
      <td><dtml-var author></td>
</tr>
<tr><th>Contents</th>
      <td><dtml-var contents></td>
</tr>
</table>
</html>
```

A simple table is coded that will contain the object's properties. A property can be accessed via the DTML `var` tag as follows:

```
<dtml-var propertyName>
```

See "The `<dtml-var>` Tag" section earlier in this chapter for details.

Now that the method is added, you can go back to the Views tab. Enter the **`the name View`** and choose `showArticle_dtml` from the pull-down menu.

The Views screen should look like Figure 4.35.

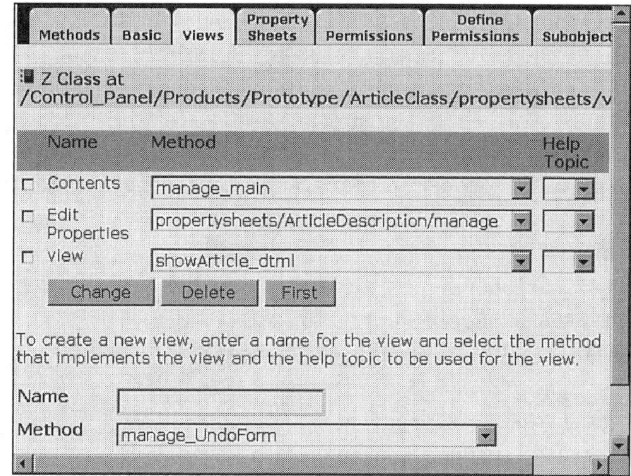

Figure 4.35

The Views screen after the needed views have been created.

At this point, your work concerning the `Article` ZClass is done. You can now try to add an article in the Prototype folder that you have already created.

You will be shown the screen in Figure 4.36.

Add Article

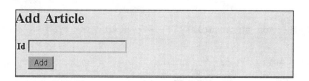

Id

Add

Figure 4.36

The form with which to add an article.

This is not very satisfying, because you cannot insert values for the properties that are contained in an article.

The method that is used to add a ZClass instance has not been adapted to the properties of the `Article` ZClass yet. We have to modify the DTML object

ArticleClass_add, which can be found inside the Prototype product folder (see Listing 4.7).

Listing 4.7

ArticleClass_add

```
<HTML>
<HEAD><TITLE>Add ArticleClass</TITLE></HEAD>
<BODY BGCOLOR="#FFFFFF" LINK="#000099" VLINK="#555555">
<dtml-with "ArticleClass.createInObjectManager(REQUEST['headLine'],
➥REQUEST)">
        <dtml-call "propertysheets.ArticleDescription.manage_editProperties(
                    REQUEST)">
</dtml-with>
<dtml-if DestinationURL>
 <dtml-call "RESPONSE.redirect(
        DestinationURL+'/manage_workspace')">
<dtml-else>
    <dtml-call "RESPONSE.redirect(
            URL2+'/manage_workspace')">
</dtml-if>
</body></html>
```

We have to modify the ArticleClass_addForm method as well. The method provides the form with which an ArticleClass instance can be created (see Listing 4.8).

Listing 4.8

ArticleClass_addForm

```
<HTML>
<HEAD><TITLE>Add an Article</TITLE></HEAD>
<BODY>
<H2>Add an Article</H2>
<form action="ArticleClass_add"><table>
<tr><th>Head Line:</th>
    <td><input type=text name=headLine size="40"></td>
</tr>
<tr><th>Author:</th>
    <td><input type=text name=author size="40"></td>
</tr>
<tr><th>Contents:</th>
    <td><textarea name=contents cols="40" rows="10"></textarea></td>
</tr>
<tr>
```

Listing 4.8

Continued

```
16: <center><td><input type=submit value="Add">
17: </td></center></tr>
18: </table></form>
19: </body></html>
```

This simple method provides the form where the data is typed in that will be passed to `ArticleClass_add`, line 5, where the article is created.

Lines 6–13 define the input fields for the headline, author, and contents.

Next, we are going to create a management interface for our Message Board.

Building an Administration Interface

In this section, we will build the administration interface for the Message Board. We will add and modify a few DTML objects and a folder `Articles`. This folder will contain the articles created by the students and DTML methods of the management interface as well.

Table 4.3 shows the Zope objects needed for the administration interface and a short description of each object's function.

Table 4.3

The Zope Objects for the Administration Interface

Zope Object	Function
Articles	The folder that will contain the students' non-live articles and a few DTML objects
`admin_html`	Displays the functions a teacher is allowed to execute
`addForm_html`	Creates an HTML form needed to add a new article
`addInstance_html`	Adds a new article
`viewEntry_html`	Enables a teacher to view the contents of an article
`delete_html`	Deletes an article
`requestDelete_html`	Creates an HTML form that asks a teacher whether he or she really wants to delete an object
`addUserForm_dtml`	Creates an HTML form needed to add a new user
`addUser_dtml`	Adds a new user
`deleteUser_dtml`	Deletes a user
`manageUsers_dtml`	Displays an overview of existing users

The following methods are stored in the Prototype folder:

- manageUsers_dtml
- addUser_dtml
- addUser_dtml

The Methods

In this section, we will describe each DTML object used to build the Administration interface. We will display and explain the source code.

We will start with addForm_html (see Listing 4.9).

Listing 4.9

addForm_html

```
<dtml-var standard_html_header>
<table align="center" valign="center" width=100% height=100%>
<tr align=center><h2>
      Add Article</h2>
</tr>
<form action="addInstance_html">
<tr><th>Head Line</th>
     <td><input type=text name="new_headLine" size="60"></td>
</tr>
<tr>
     <td><input type=hidden name="new_author"
➥value="<dtml-var "AUTHENTICATED_USER">"></td>
</tr>
<tr><th>Contents</th>
     <td><textarea name=new_contents cols="50" rows="10"> </textarea>
     </td>
</tr>
<tr><td>
      <input type=submit value="Add">
</form> </td>
<td>
<form action=index_html>
             <input type=submit value="Cancel">
      </form>
</td></tr>
</table>
<dtml-var standard_html_footer>
```

The method shown in Listing 4.10 organizes the creation of a user.

Listing 4.10

addUser_dtml

```
1: <dtml-call "REQUEST.set('name', _['Name'])">
2: <dtml-call "REQUEST.set('password', _['Password'])">
3: <dtml-call "REQUEST.set('confirm', _['Confirm'])">
4: <dtml-call "REQUEST.set('roles', _['Roles'])">
5: <dtml-call "REQUEST.set('domains', _['Domains'])">
6: <dtml-call "acl_users.manage_users('Add',REQUEST,RESPONSE)">
7: <dtml-call "RESPONSE.redirect('manageUsers_dtml')">
```

In lines 1–5, the user data is taken from `REQUEST` and passed to the method `manage_users`, which eventually creates the new user.

The input data of the created form is passed to the `addInstance_html` DTML method in line 6.

Lines 8 and 13 create the input fields for the headline and the contents of the new article.

In line 11, the author's name is passed hidden because we do not want a student to type in the wrong name.

In line 22, the Cancel button leads the student back to the `index_html`. See Figure 4.37 to view the `addForm_html`.

The next method we will look at is `addInstance_html`, the method that adds an article (see Listing 4.11).

Listing 4.11

addInstance_html

```
 1: <dtml-var standard_html_header>
 2: <dtml-try>
 3: <dtml-call
 4: "REQUEST.set('headLine',REQUEST.form['new_headLine'])">
 5:  <dtml-with "manage_addProduct['Prototype']">
 6:  <dtml-call "ArticleClass_add(_.None,_, NoRedir=1)">
 7: </dtml-with>
 8: <form action=admin_html>
 9: <dtml-in "objectValues(['Article'])">
10: <dtml-if "(_['sequence-item'].id ==
11:            REQUEST.form['new_headLine'])">
```

Listing 4.11
Continued

```
12: <dtml-call "REQUEST.set('new_headLine',_['sequence-item'])">
13: </dtml-if>
14: </dtml-in>
15: <dtml-call
16: "_['new_headLine'].propertysheets.ArticleDescription.manage_
➥ changeProperties({
17:     'headLine'                 : REQUEST.form['new_headLine'],
18:     'author'                 : REQUEST.form['new_author'],
19:     'contents'                : REQUEST.form['new_contents'],
20: })">
21: <table align=center valign=center>
22: <br><br><br>
23: <form action=admin_html">
24: <input type=submit value="Okay">
25: <dtml-call "RESPONSE.redirect('Article_DB_archive/searchReport')">
26: </form>
27: </table>
28: <dtml-except>
29: <table border align="center"><td align="center">
30: <h2>Sorry, Article cannot be added.</h2><br>
➥ The head line must be unique and mustn't contain any special characters.<p>
31: <form action="addForm_html"><input type=submit value="Okay"></form></td>
32: </table>
33: </dtml-try>
34: <dtml-var standard_html_footer>
```

The `try` tag is used in line 2 to avoid Zope error messages in case an error should occur.

An empty `Article` object is created in lines 5–7 using the `ArticleClass_add()` method. The method's first two parameters (`_.None` and `_`) are the current namespace so that the method can use the existing variables. The last parameter (`NoRedir`) states that the browser is not to be redirected after the object was created. If `NoRedir` is set to 0, the browser will be redirected. The empty `Article` object's ID will be the article's headline.

In lines 16–20, the property data the user has typed in are assigned to the new article by using the `manage_changeProperties` Python method.

For more information on this method and other methods, see the Zope API explanations. You can use the `Help!` link in the Zope Management screen to get there.

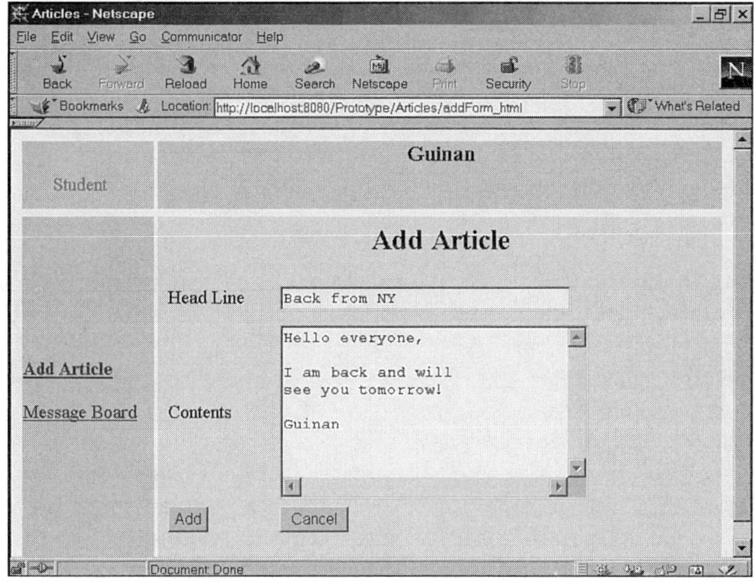

Figure 4.37

The third view of `addForm_html`.

Lines 28–32 provide that should an error occur, the message shown in Figure 4.38 is displayed.

Figure 4.38

This error message is shown when an article could not be added.

The `admin_html` method (see Listing 4.12) will be accessible only by users with the Teacher role. It will list the articles recently added by the students.

Listing 4.12

`admin_html`

```
<dtml-var standard_html_header>
<table border=1 width=100% height=100%>
```

Listing 4.12

Continued

```

<tr width="100%">
<td><b> Head Line</b></b></td>
<td><b> Author</b></b></td>
</tr>

<dtml-in "PARENTS[0].objectValues(['Article'])" sort=headLine>
<tr width="100%" >
<td><dtml-var headLine></td>
<td><dtml-var author></td>
<td><table><tr> <td>
<FORM ACTION="viewEntry_html">
            <input type=hidden name="headLine" value="<dtml-var headLine>">
             <input type=hidden name="author" value="<dtml-var author>">
            <input type=hidden name="contents" value="<dtml-var contents>">
            <input type=submit value="View">
   </FORM></td>
<td>
<FORM ACTION="http://localhost:8080/Prototype/Articles/addForm_DB_entry">
            <input type=hidden name="headLine" value="<dtml-var headLine>">
             <input type=hidden name="author" value="<dtml-var author>">
            <input type=hidden name="contents" value="<dtml-var contents>">
            <input type=submit value="live">
</FORM><td>
<td>
<FORM action="requestDelete_html">
          <input type=hidden name="deleteObject"
                            value="<dtml-var headLine>">
          <input type=hidden name="headLine" value="<dtml-var headLine>">
          <input type=submit value="Delete">
            </FORM>
</td></table>
</td>

</dtml-in>
</table>
</form><p>
<dtml-var standard_html_footer>
```

In lines 9–37, the `in` tag goes through the elements of the current folder with the meta type `Article`. The existing articles are listed in a table, sorted by headline.

In lines 14–19, a View button is defined that, when clicked, lets the user view the contents of an article. The `viewEntry_html` method will be needed for this.

A Live button is defined in lines 21–25. When the user clicks this button, he or she will be able to make the article a live article and submit it to the Article database. The `addForm_DB_Entry` method is called. We will explain this method in the section "Connecting the Prototype to a ZGadfly Database" later in this chapter.

A Delete button is defined in lines 28–33. It enables a user to delete an article. We will need the `requestDelete_html` method.

The article we just added will be listed as shown in Figure 4.39.

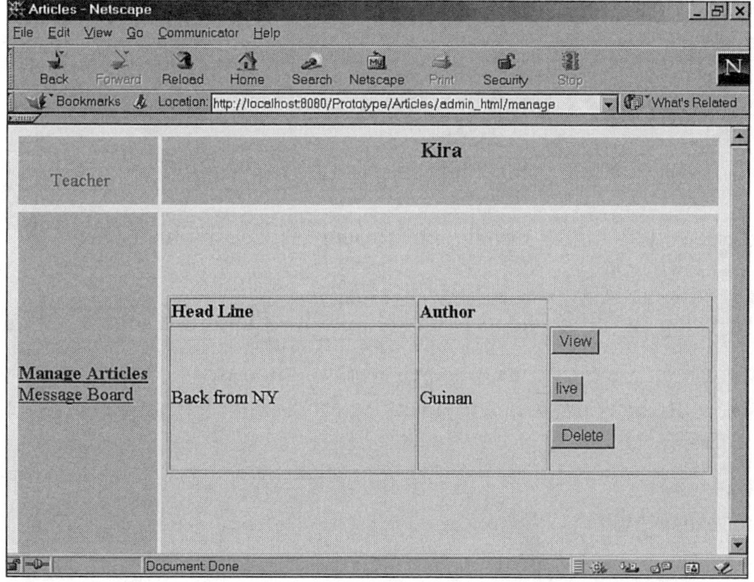

Figure 4.39
The Article table.

Now we will create a method that enables the user to view the contents of an article. Add a new DTML method with the `viewEntry_html` ID (see Listing 4.13).

Listing 4.13

viewEntry_html

```
<dtml-var standard_html_header>
<center><h2>View Entry</h2></center>
<table height=100% border>
  <tr><th>Head Line</th>
    <td width=100%><dtml-var headLine></td>
  </tr>
  <tr><th>Author</th>
    <td width=100%> <dtml-var author>
    </td>
</tr>
<tr><th>Contents</th>
    <td width=100%><dtml-var contents>
    </td>
</tr>
</table>
<br><p>
<center>
</center>
<dtml-var standard_html_footer>
```

The source code is rather simple. The properties are simply displayed by using the `<dtml-var>` tag.

The third view of the article just added looks like the screen shown in Figure 4.40.

Now we will create the `requestDelete_html` method that is displayed to ask the user whether he or she really wants to delete an article (see Listing 4.14).

Listing 4.14

requestDelete_html

```
<dtml-var standard_html_header>
<center><H2> Delete Article: </H2> <br><p><dtml-var headLine>
➥</center><br><p>
<table align=center><tr><td>
<form action="delete_html">
  <input type=hidden name="deleteObject"
            value="<dtml-var headLine>">
  <input type=submit value="Delete">
</form></td><td>
<form action="admin_html">
   <input type=submit value="Cancel">
```

Listing 4.14

Continued

```
11: </form></td></tr>
12: </table>
13: </center>
14: <dtml-var standard_html_footer>
```

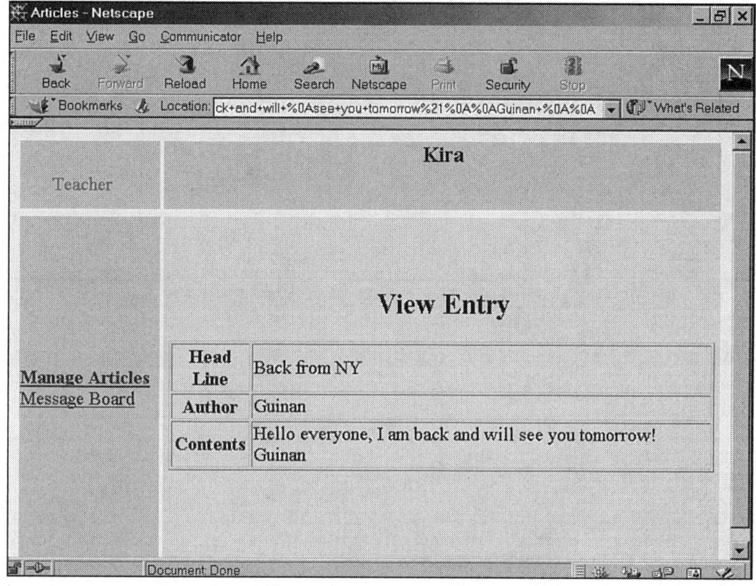

Figure 4.40

Viewing an article.

In lines 5 and 6, the headline of the current article is passed to `delete_html`, because the ID of an article is its headline.

In lines 9–11, the user can decide not to delete the article and can click the Cancel button (see Figure 4.41).

If the user decides to delete the article and clicks Delete, the article will be deleted via `delete_html` (see Listing 4.15).

The next method, `delete_html`, finally deletes an article.

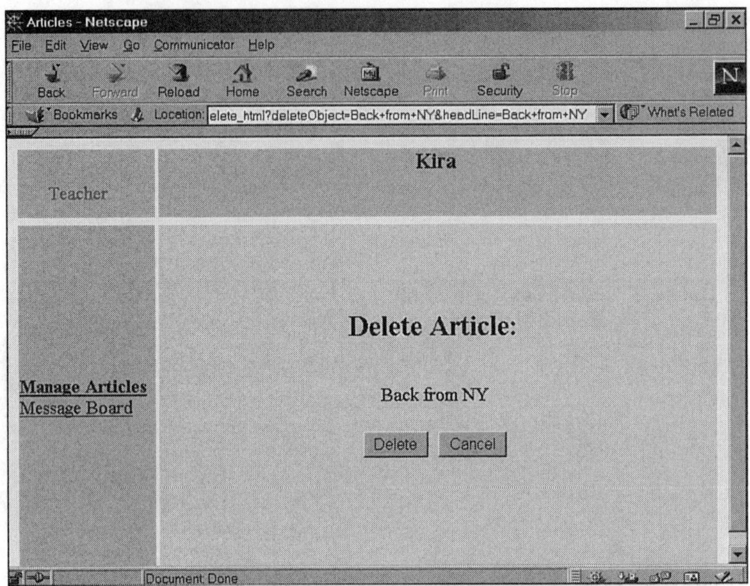

Figure 4.41
The third view of `requestDelete_html`.

Listing 4.15
`delete_html`

```
 1: <dtml-var standard_html_header>
 2: <dtml-call "manage_delObjects(ids=[deleteObject])">
 3: <p>
 4:  <center><dtml-var deleteObject>
 5: <br><p> <h2>Deleted!</h2>
 6: <form action="admin_html">
 7: <input type=submit value="Okay">
 8: </form>
 9: </center>
10: <dtml-var standard_html_footer>
```

In line 2, the `manage_delObjects` Python method is called. The ID of the article is given as its argument (`deleteObject`).

Again, see the Zope API for details on this method.

The user is informed about the process in line 5 (see Figure 4.42).

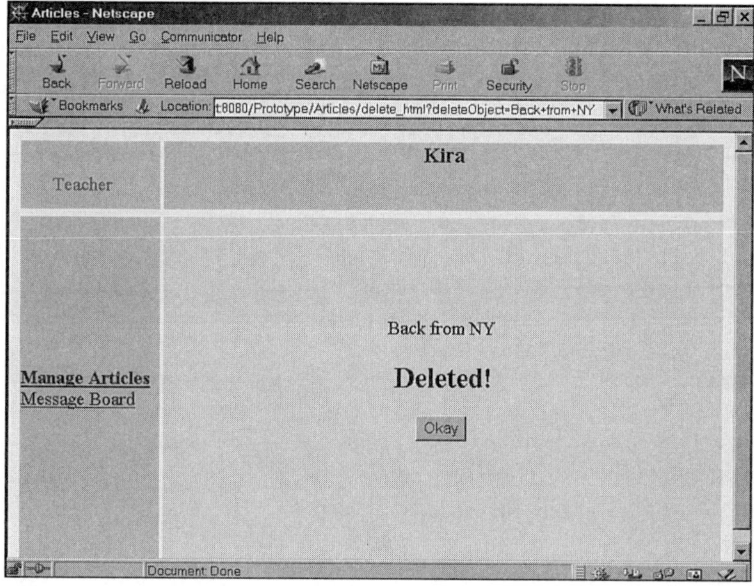

Figure 4.42

The user is informed that the article is deleted.

All the methods described in this section are inside the `Articles` folder. Next, we will explain the methods that are inside the `Prototype` folder. Those will make up the User Management Area of our Message Board.

The `manageUsers_dtml` DTML method computes a list of the valid users (see Listing 4.16). See Figure 4.43 for the third view of this method.

Listing 4.16

manageUsers_dtml

```
<dtml-var standard_html_header>
<table border=1 width="100%">
<tr>
<td><b>Users</b></td>
<td><b>Role</b></td>
<td></td>
</tr>
<dtml-in "acl_users.getUsers()">
<tr>
<td> <dtml-call "REQUEST.set('User',_.str(_['sequence-item']))">
<dtml-var sequence-item>
```

Listing 4.16

Continued

```
12: </td>
13: <td><dtml-var "acl_users.getUser(_['User']).getRoles()[0]">
14: </td>
15: <td>
16: <FORM action="delete_User" method=post>
17: <dtml-call "REQUEST.set('i',_['sequence-index'])">
18: <input type=hidden name="deleteUser"
➥value="<dtml-var "acl_users.getUsers()[i]">">
19: <input type=submit value="Delete">
20: </FORM>
21: </td>
22: </tr>
23: <dtml-else>
24: <center><h2>No users defined</h2></h2>
25: </dtml-in>
26: </table>
27: <p><form><input type=submit name="addUserForm_dtml:method"
➥ value="Add User"></form>
28: <dtml-var standard_html_footer>
```

In line 8, the `getUsers()` Python method returns a list of those users who are defined inside the `acl_users` folder. With the `in` tag, we go through the list's elements to list the users in a table.

A Delete button is defined in line 19. The user's ID is passed hidden to the `deleteUser_dtml` method.

Line 24 provides that if there aren't any users defined inside the `acl_users` folder, the user is informed about that fact.

The Add button calls the `addUserForm_dtml` method in line 27.

The form used to create a new user is coded in the addUserForm_dtml method (see Listing 4.17). Figure 4.44 shows the third view of this method.

Listing 4.17

`addUserForm_dtml`

```
<dtml-var standard_html_header>
<h2>Add User</h2>
<FORM>
<table>
<tr>
```

Listing 4.17

Continued

```
 6:    <td><b>Id (Name of the User):</b></td>
 7:    <td><input type=text size=20 name=Name></td>
 8: </tr>
 9: <tr>
10:    <td><b>Password:</b></td>
11:    <td><input type=password size=10 name=Password></td>
12: </tr>
13: <tr>
14:    <td><b>Confirm</b></td>
15:    <td><input type=password size=10 name=Confirm></td>
16: </tr>
17: <tr>
18:    <td><b>Domains:</b></td>
19:    <td><input type=text size=20 name=Domains:tokens></td>
20: </tr>
21: <tr>
22:    <td><b>Roles:</b></td>
23:    <td><select name=Roles:tokens>
24:        <option selected>Student</option>
25:        <option>Teacher</option>
26:        <option>Visitor</option>
27:        <option>Administrator</option>
28:        </select>
29:    </td>
30: </tr>
31: <tr>
32:    <td><input name="addUser_dtml:method" type=submit value="Add User"></td>
33:    <td><input type=reset value="Reset"></td>
34:    <td><input  name="manageUsers_dtml:method" type=submit value="Cancel">
35:      </td>
36: </tr>
37: </table>
38: </FORM>
39: <dtml-var standard_html_footer>
```

Lines 10–28 define the input fields for a user's ID, password, password confirmation, domains, and roles.

The Add button calls the `addUser_dtml` method in line 32.

In line 33, the Reset button resets any input.

In line 34, the Cancel button redirects the user to the User Management Area.

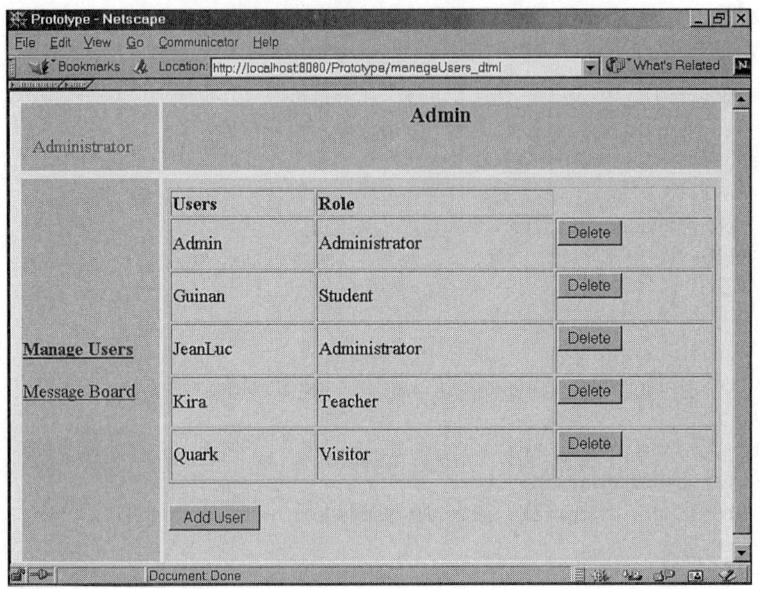

Figure 4.43
The User Management Area.

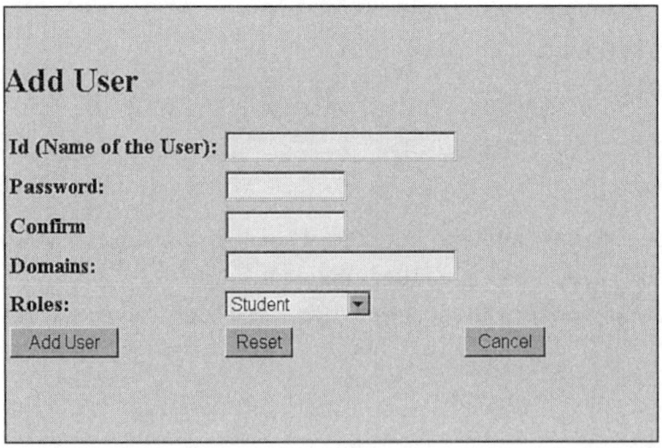

Add User
Id (Name of the User):
Password:
Confirm
Domains:
Roles: Student
Add User Reset Cancel

Figure 4.44
The User form.

The `delete_User` method (see Listing 4.18) deletes a user.

Listing 4.18

delete_User

```
1: <dtml-try>
2: <dtml-call "REQUEST.set('names', [_.str(REQUEST.form['deleteUser'])])">
3: <dtml-call "acl_users.manage_users('Delete', REQUEST, RESPONSE)">
4: <dtml-call "RESPONSE.redirect('manageUsers_dtml')">
5: <dtml-except>
6: sorry, an error occurred
7: </dtml-try>
```

To avoid any error messages, we are using the <dtml-try> tag again in line 1.

In line 2, a variable with the names ID is assigned to the deleteUser value that contains the ID of the user to be deleted.

The manage_users Python method is called to delete the user in line 3.

In line 4, you are redirected to the User Management Area.

Per line 6, if anything goes wrong, you are informed that an error occurred.

At this point, you have built an administration interface for the Message Board. However, there are some methods you still have to create that will accommodate dealing with the database.

In the next section, we will show you how to connect the Message Board to a ZGadfly database.

Connecting the Prototype to a ZGadfly Database

First, we will create a new Article_DB_archive folder within the Prototype folder. This folder will contain the methods for the database.

Go to the file system and switch to the var/gadfly subdirectory of your Zope installation. Create a prototypeArticles folder that will contain the ZGadfly database.

For more information about the Gadfly database, go to http://www.chordate.com/gadfly.html.

Now, enter the new folder, choose ZGadfly Database Connection from the Available Objects menu, and enter the required data as shown in Figure 4.45.

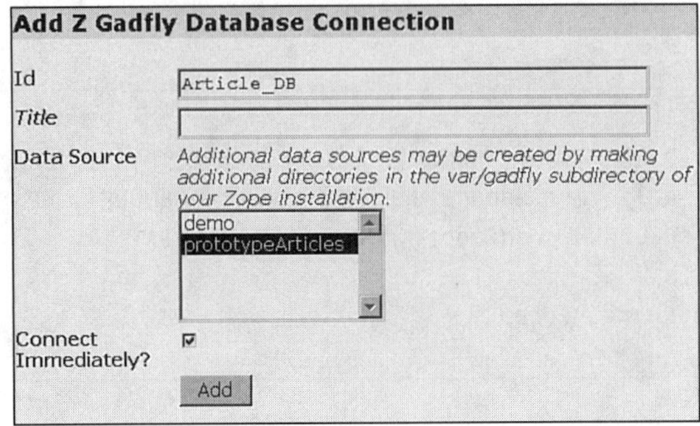

Figure 4.45

Creating a new database connection.

After the database connection is created, enter it by clicking its ID (see Figure 4.46).

Figure 4.46

Entering the database.

Now we can create the table that will contain the `Article` data. To do so, choose the Test tab and enter the following statements:

```
CREATE table Articles
   (headLine varchar,
    author varchar,
    contents varchar)
```

The table is created that will return the result shown in Figure 4.47.

Click the Browse tab and you can see the added table (see Figure 4.48).

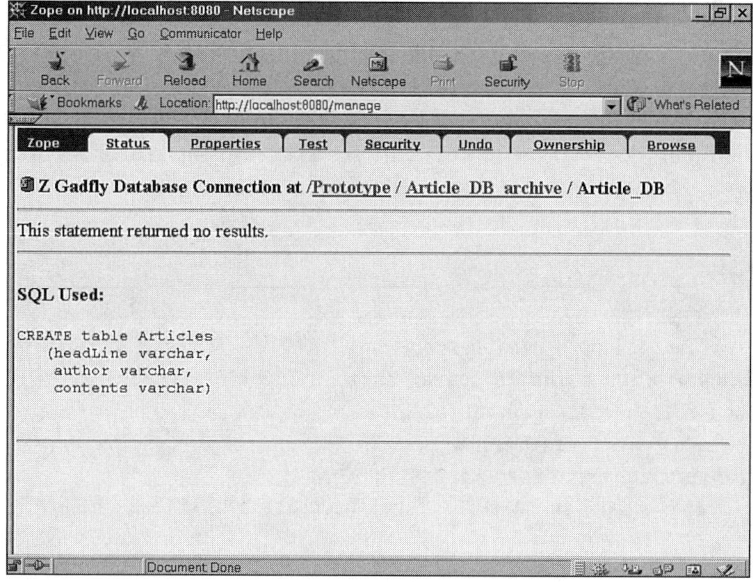

Figure 4.47

The database table is created.

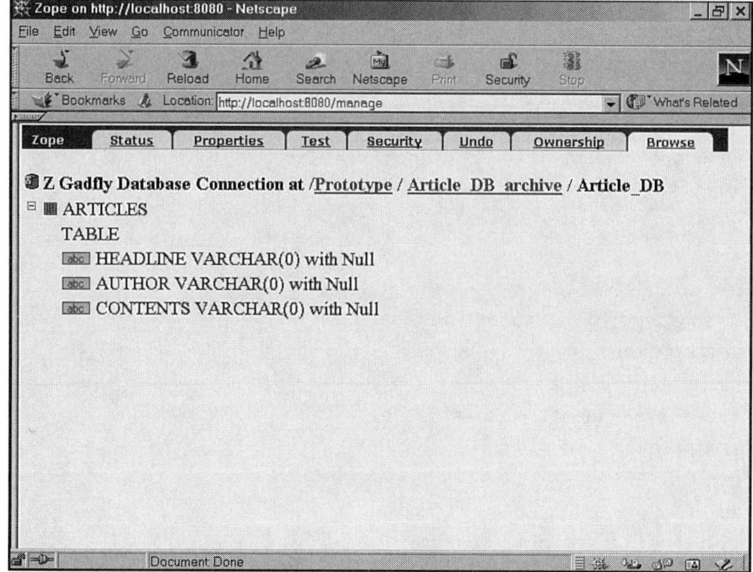

Figure 4.48

Browse the database table.

Now we need to fill the table with data. Because we want to receive the table data from our Message Board, we don't need to create an input form or anything like that. Instead, we will add the `addForm_DB_entry` DTML method (see Listing 4.19) that asks the Teacher whether he or she really wants to submit the selected article to the database (see Figure 4.49). If the teacher chooses to submit the article, its properties are passed to another DTML method—`callInsert_html`.

Listing 4.19

addForm_DB_entry

```
 1: <dtml-var standard_html_header>
 2: <center><h2>Make the following article live</h2></center><br> <p>
 3: <form action="callInsert_html">
 4: <table border=1 width=100%>
 5: <tr><th align=left>Head Line:</th>
 6:      <td> <dtml-var "REQUEST.form['headLine']"> </td>
 7: </tr>
 8: <tr><th align=left>Author:</th>
 9:      <td><dtml-var "REQUEST.form['author']"> </td>
10: </tr>
11: <tr><th align=left>Contents:</th>
12:      <td><dtml-var "REQUEST.form['contents']"> </td>
13: </tr>
14: <input type=hidden name="headLine" value="
➥<dtml-var "REQUEST.form['headLine']">">
15: <input type=hidden name="author" value="
➥<dtml-var "REQUEST.form['author']">">
16: <input type=hidden name="contents" value="
➥<dtml-var "REQUEST.form['contents']">">
17: </table>
18: <br>
19: <table align="center"><tr>
20:      <td><input type=submit value="Okay">
21: </form></td><td>
22: <form action="../">
23:    <input type=submit value="Cancel">
24: </form></td>
25: </tr>
26: </table>
27: <dtml-var standard_html_footer>
```

In lines 5–13, the data of the current article is shown.

The articles values for the headline, author, and contents are passed hidden in lines 14–16 because they are not to be modified.

When the `OK` button in line 20 is clicked, the data is passed to the `callInsert_html` in line 3.

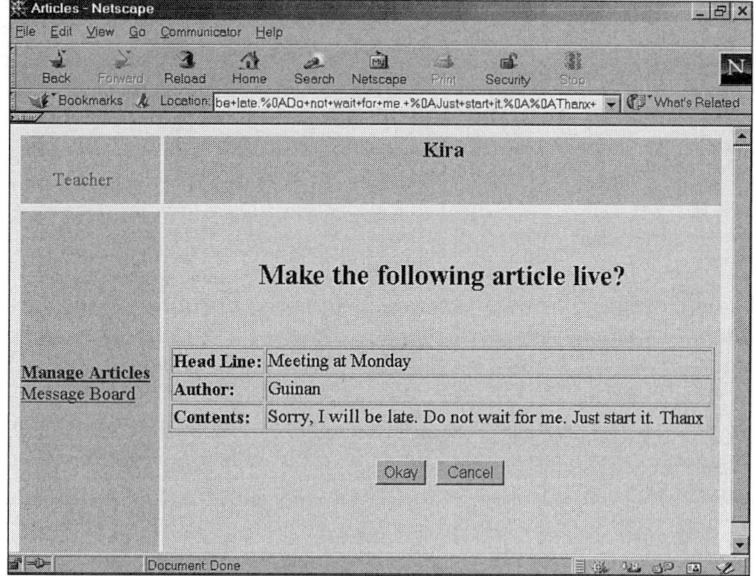

Figure 4.49

Making an article live means submitting it to the live article database.

The `callInsert_html` DTML method (see Listing 4.20) connects to the database by calling the `insertArticles` ZSQL method.

Listing 4.20

`callInsert_html`

```
<dtml-call "Article_DB_archive.insertArticles(
headLine=headLine,
author=author,
contents=contents)">
<dtml-call "manage_delObjects(ids=[headLine])">
<dtml-call "RESPONSE.redirect('admin_html')">
```

As you can see, the method does not only pass the article's properties to the ZSQL method. It also calls the `manage_delObjects` Python method and deletes the article from the list of non-live articles.

The `insertArticles` ZSQL method (see Listing 4.21) has to be added to the `Article_DB_archive` folder.

Listing 4.21

`insertArticles`

```
INSERT into Articles
   (headLine, author, contents)
VALUES
   ('<dtml-var headLine>','<dtml-var author>',
    '<dtml-var contents>')
```

Now we only need a method that shows us the contents of the whole database. This will be the method that creates the Message Board that can be accessed by every validated user.

We have to create a ZSQL method that will search the database. Create a `show_DB_entries` ZSQL method. The method contains only one statement (see Figure 4.50):

```
select * from Articles
```

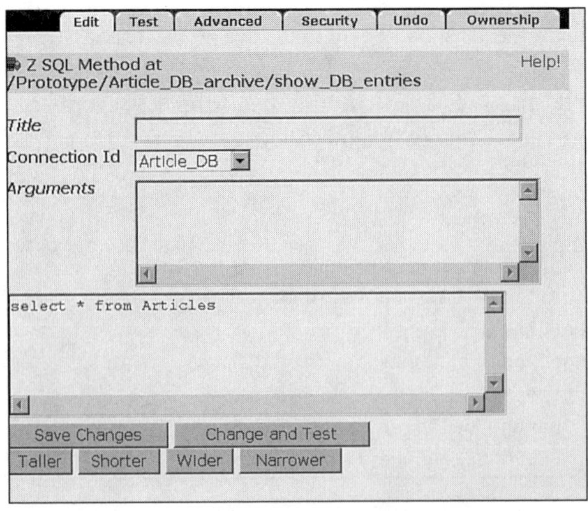

Figure 4.50

This SQL statement will show the contents of the whole database.

No arguments are needed because we don't really want to search the database; rather, we want to get the whole contents of the database table, so the used SQL statement is simple.

Next, we will create a Search Interface. It will generate a method that will show the result of the database search (see Figure 4.51).

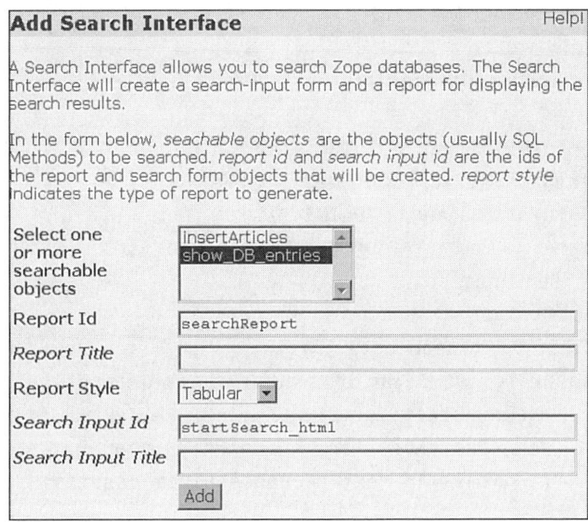

Figure 4.51

Creating a ZSearch interface.

As there aren't any arguments, the `startSearch_html` method is not needed. The method will only provide a button that, when clicked, will call the `searchReport` method. We changed the method's code as shown in Listing 4.22.

Listing 4.22

searchReport

```
<dtml-var standard_html_header>
<dtml-in show_DB_entries size=50 start=query_start>
   <dtml-if sequence-start>
      <dtml-if previous-sequence>
        <a href="<dtml-var URL><dtml-var sequence-query
                 >query_start=<dtml-var
                 previous-sequence-start-number>">
        (Previous <dtml-var previous-sequence-size> results)
        </a>
```

Listing 4.22
Continued

```
10:         </dtml-if previous-sequence>
11:         <table border width="100%" height="100%">
12:           <tr>
13:             <th>AUTHOR</th>
14:             <th>CONTENTS</th>
15:             <th>HEADLINE</th>
16:           </tr>
17:     </dtml-if sequence-start>
18:           <tr>
19:             <td><dtml-var AUTHOR></td>
20:             <td><dtml-var CONTENTS></td>
21:             <td><dtml-var HEADLINE></td>
22:           </tr>
23:     <dtml-if sequence-end>
24:         </table>
25:         <dtml-if next-sequence>
26:             <a href="<dtml-var URL><dtml-var sequence-query
27:                >query_start=<dtml-var
28:                next-sequence-start-number>">
29:             (Next <dtml-var next-sequence-size> results)
30:             </a>
31:         </dtml-if next-sequence>
32:     </dtml-if sequence-end>
33: <dtml-else>
34:   <center><h2>There are no Messages!<h2></center>
35: </dtml-in>
36: <dtml-var standard_html_footer>
```

We simply modified this object in line 34 so that we are shown the message There Are No Messages! if the database is empty.

At this point, the Prototype is almost ready. But we still have to set the security settings for the Prototype's objects.

Organizing the User Authentification

In this last step, we have to define the Prototype's security settings via the Security tabs of the single objects.

For the `Teacher` role, set the following permissions:

Access contents information and View for `index_html`, `links_html`, `login_html`, `standard_html_footer`, `standard_html_header`, `addForm_DB_entry`, `admin_html`, `requestDelete_html`, `viewEntry_html`, `insertArticles`. Access contents information for `callInsert_html`. Access contents information, View, and Delete objects for `delete_html` and `Articles`. Access contents information, View, Manage Properties, Use Database Methods for `Article_DB_archive`. Access contents information, View, Manage Properties, Use Database Methods, Delete objects for `fullSweep`.

For the `Visitor` role, set the following permissions:

Access contents information and View for `index_html`, `links_html`, `login_html`, `standard_html_footer`, `standard_html_header`, `Article_DB_archive`.

For the `Student` role, set the following permissions:

Access contents information and View for `index_html`, `links_html`, `login_html`, `standard_html_footer`, `standard_html_header`, `addForm_html`, and `Article_DB_archive`. Access contents information, View, Add Articles for `Articles`. Access contents information, View, Manage Properties for `addInstance_html`. Add Articles, Manage Properties for `Prototype`.

For the `Administrator` role, set the following permissions:

Access contents information, View for `addUserForm_dtml`, `index_html`, `links_html`, `login_html`, `standard_html_footer`, `standard_html_header`, `manageUsers_dtml`, `Article_DB_archive`. Manage Properties, View, Access Contents information for `deleteUser_html`. Manage Properties, View, Access Contents information for `addUser_dtml`.

PART II

BUILDING A PORTAL AND ADDING SERVICES

CHAPTER

CHAPTER 5

THE CONTENT MANAGEMENT FRAMEWORK (CMF)

The Content Management Framework (CMF) previously known as the Portal Toolkit (PTK) is part of Digital Creations' strategy to create a framework for building content management systems and portals.

This means that CMF-1.0, the product we refer to in this book, is an implementation or example of the CMF, but not the CMF itself. Why make this distinction? For portals and content management systems to be useful, they need to be customized so that they incorporate the workflow of the site based on its use. While the majority of core services in a portal or CMS are identical, it is the differences that typically take the most time to develop to a particular organization's needs.

The CMF core services as outlined in the *Introduction to CMF* (`http://cmf.zope.org/doc/introduction.txt`) and written by Paul Everitt are:

- MembershipServices (includes personalization)
- CatalogingServices (using Zope's ZCatalog)
- WorkflowServices
- BasicContentServices
- SiteDesignServices
- IntegrationServices
- DiscussionServices
- ArchivingServices
- SyndicationServices
- RatingServices
- TestingServices

We think the best way to visualize how the content management framework can help developers is by seeing it as a well-built foundation for the attachment of components. These components can be services in the form of software (such as a threaded Web discussion board) or components, such as "WorkflowServices," which define how users can interact with a Web site.

What Can the CMF Do for You?

The CMF is a great foundation for starting your portal. It anticipates particular needs but respects diversity. This means that the CMF includes several simple applications and workflows, but you will be able to selectively take components out and replace them with your own. A theme that you'll hear over and over again in this book is how using the Zope and, in this case, CMF infrastructure, can save you a lot of time.

People at Digital Creations (D.C.) and within the Zope community spend a lot of time thinking about how this portal and content infrastructure can be designed to accommodate more than one use. By using the CMF, you are essentially benefiting from the experience of hundreds of development hours by developers all over the world who have created more portals than you are likely to create in your lifetime.

For example, built into the CMF are things such as "Topics," which allow members to create custom views of data in the CMF, such as "All Press Releases about Achievers International within the last two weeks" and keep track of topics that interest them when they log in to their portal workspace. Additionally, members can use features similar to a bookmark in a browser to quickly jump to resources they find particularly useful within the portal via a feature called "Favorites."

If an online community is to thrive, members must be able to contribute. On `Zope.org`, for example, members can contribute content like how-tos, news articles, as well as set up their own personal homepage and upload any Zope products they may have created.

To address the growing needs of the Zope community, D.C. has recently launched two new portal Web sites:

- `dev.zope.org`
- `cmf.zope.org`

Each of these Web sites has a particular focus and, therefore, provides slightly different services to its users.

The portal at dev.zope.org is designed for the discussion and the management of new features in Zope, as well as products deemed important to the continued expansion of the Zope community. In contrast to Zope.org, it does not provide services such as personal homepages.

cmf.zope.org is the official Web site for developers interested in or working with the content management framework. It uses the latest version of the CMF software and, like Zope.org, allows users to join and upload their own files such as "skins" that they may want to contribute to the community. Users can also create custom views to data available on the portal including "Topics" as well as links called "Favorites" that allow the user to quickly jump to his or her favorite sections or pages on the portal.

Installation

Installing the CMF is as simple as any other Zope product.

1. Download the product file.
2. Unzip the file in either the Zope or product directory, depending on how the product was zipped.
3. Restart your Zope server.

These three steps are valid for installing any product you can find on Zope.org, ZopeTreasures.com, or any other site containing one or more Zope products.

The actual installation takes place in step three, when the Zope server is restarted. Every Zope product contains an initiation file (__init__.py) that is compiled on a restart. When compiled, this file causes the product to be acknowledged by and imported into Zope. If there is a problem during the compilation, the product will not be installed correctly, and you will not be able to use the product in your Zope installation. If there is a problem, go to Control_Panel/Product_Management/<NameOfTheProduct>/ in your Zope Management screen. The traceback shown there might tell you why the installation went wrong.

Download

You can download the latest version of the reference implementation via the CMF Web site at http://cmf.zope.org/download.

> **Note**
> For Internet Explorer users: When downloading the file, make sure the file extension is `tar.gz` before clicking OK in the download window. If necessary, change it to `tar.gz`. This will make it easier for you to use WinZip after download.

Make sure that you have the right version of Zope installed. All CMF examples within this book use Zope version 2.3.1. If you have an older Zope version, you will need to upgrade before you will be able to use the content management framework.

You should visit `Zope.org` and `cmf.zope.org` frequently to stay up-to-date about new products and latest versions of existing products.

Now that you have downloaded the appropriate file(s), we can move on with the installation.

Unzipping the Product File

Depending on your operating system, there are different ways to unpack the product file. With a Windows system, you will need WinZip or a similar program that can handle Zip files as well as `tar` and `gzip` files. With Linux or UNIX, use `tar` to unzip the file.

Windows System (Using WinZip)

If your WinZip was installed correctly, you should be able to unzip the CMF file by simply double-clicking it in the Windows Explorer. WinZip may tell you that there is one compressed file in the packed file and ask whether you want to decompress it. Answer with Yes and then extract the decompressed files to the directory of your Zope installation. WinZip creates a new directory (CMF-1.0beta, for example) containing three subdirectories in your Zope directory:

- CMFCore
- CMFDefault
- CMFTopic

Move those directories and their content to the `Zope-directory/lib/python/Products/` directory.

The last step of installing the CMF is to restart your Zope server. Go on to the "Restarting the Zope Server" section to see how to do this.

UNIX/Linux System

The first step to install the CMF is to copy or move the packed CMF file to your Zope directory. Now extract the file using the following command:

```
tar -xzvf CMF-1.0.tar.gz
```

> **Note**
> If this command does not work (for example, if you do not have `gnu tar` installed on your system), try the following command:
>
> ```
> gzip -c -d CMF-1.0.tar.gz | tar -xvf
> ```

This will create a directory CMF-1.0beta in your Zope directory. This directory contains three subdirectories:

- CMFCore
- CMFDefault
- CMFTopic

Copy or move these directories to the Products directory at `Zope-directory/lib/python/Products/`.

Now restart your Zope server and the installation is complete.

Restarting the Zope Server

To restart the Zope server, go to the Zope directory and execute the start script. On Windows, this start script is called `start.bat` and can be executed by simply double-clicking it in the Windows Explorer. If it is already running, shut it down before restarting. To shut the process down, use the Shutdown button in the `Control_Panel` of the Zope Management screen.

On a Linux machine the start script is just called `start`. To execute the script, type the following:

```
./start &
```

at the prompt. Make sure to shut down the Zope process before restarting it. You can do that by using the `stop` script as follows:

```
./stop
```

Achievers International—ZWACK Use Case

In this book, we will show how to solve the real-world needs of a non-profit organization, Achievers International, by building this organization both a portal using Zope and the content management framework. In later chapters, we will show how to roll out additional services to the members of the portals in the form of Zope products.

About Achievers International

Achievers International helps students form companies and learn how to become entrepreneurs by helping them slip into roles, such as CEO, VP Marketing, and so on. Achievers International then teams up different student companies worldwide. These schools then import and export various goods and try to sell them at a profit. If profits are made, students can decide how to spend the money.

Since its inception, 21 schools and 4,600 students on 5 continents have participated in the program. Because Achievers International promotes modern technologies, such as videoconferencing and Internet technologies, to prepare students for the challenges of a global marketplace, helping them build a portal using Zope and the new CMF seemed like a great idea.

To find out more about Achievers International and to see the Zope portal in action, visit `http://www.achieversinternational.org`.

Goals

Regardless of for whom you build Web applications, real value is created when technology can be woven to fit the needs of a real organization.

Because Achievers International members are all over the globe, the portal has to keep all members informed and up-to-date through a constant flow of pertinent information. So the goal is to provide the software infrastructure to students, and teachers must be able to publish articles and discuss information.

For this purpose, we will be using different products and features of the CMS to create the following services:

- A threaded Web discussion area based on ZDiscussions
- A content management system for news articles (using MetaPublisher)
- Polls (using the Poll Product)
- Surveys (using PMP Survey)
- Downloadable help files and starter kits for students (CMF)

To figure out what roles exist and which role needs to be able to do what, we spoke with Karen Kennedy and Norma Duncann of Achievers International. Two of the questions we asked were

- What kind of content do you foresee publishing?
- Who (which group) gets to decide when, for example, an article is displayed?

After we felt that we had understood the answers Karen and Norma had given us, we were able to define the following core roles:

- Administrators
- Teachers
- Students

We then created the following profiles to better understand how they would interact with the portal.

Administrators

Administrators are employees or volunteers of Achievers International who watch over and have the final decision about what content belongs on the Web site.

They are able to remove any content they don't deem acceptable and can approve articles or information via the portals Content Management System (CMS) from students and teachers. Additionally, AI employees will be able to create surveys and polls (see Chapter 8, "Creating Polls and Surveys").

They can also add, approve, and suspend users who sign onto the portal.

Teachers

Teachers or coordinators act as coaches, giving advice to the students. The AI portal will need to provide a section only for coordinators to share information on educational/training issues.

Students

Because the portal is essentially built to meet the needs of the students, students who live in different parts of the world, we will need to provide them with software-based services that will allow them to collaborate and exchange information online.

These software services will include a Web-threaded Web discussion forum (see Chapter 7, "Creating a Threaded Discussion Group"), a content management system (see Chapter 6, "The MetaPublisher"), and a repository of support files designed to help them with the program.

Additional Roles

At later stages of this project, we may decide to add additional roles, such as "Discussion Moderators" who could be real business experts who volunteer and share their knowledge with students via the Web discussion boards.

The permissions of these experts would have to be narrowly defined, which, thanks to the Zope management interface (ZMI), is just a series of clicks that create and define new roles.

Preconditions

The Achievers International Web site, like the majority of Web sites on the Internet, is made up of static pages and CGI scripts.

When importing an existing Web site into Zope, several options exist. The most straightforward is to use an FTP or WebDAV client.

If your ISP or System Administrator is running your Zope server with Apache instead of ZServer, you will not be able to access your installation via either FTP or WebDAV protocols, because ZServer is the only server capable of handling these protocols for Zope at this time.

One Zope product, "`load_site`" (`http://www.zope.org/Members/itamar/load_site`) will allow you to get around this problem by uploading multiple files via the HTTP protocol.

In this case, we chose to simply FTP the original Achievers International files via FTP using ZServer and Zope.

Rapid Application Development (RAD)

One of the greatest strengths of Zope is that with the development infrastructure it provides, as well as the over 250 Zope products that exist for Zope today, developers will find few reasons to reinvent the wheel.

With Zope products, you will likely be able to save several days of development time by modifying existing code instead of building an application from scratch.

Because Zope is also an application server, you'll also notice over time that the skills you learn to build one type of application will be useful to build a completely different type of application.

By the end of this book, we hope that you'll see what we mean and will be able to compare this to your previous experiences of learning and integrating various different vendor solutions.

Using the requirements of Achievers International, we hope to introduce you to some of the more interesting Zope products and how these can be modified to help a real-world organization.

Working with the CMF

This section will introduce you to the main functions of a CMF portal, such as the search and member pages. It will also describe the workflow of publishable objects and how it is managed in the portal.

Getting Started

Now that you have installed the CMF correctly to your Zope installation, you can start working with it. This is done by creating instances of this product in the Zope Management screen.

The first thing to do is enter the Management screen of your Zope installation. Open your browser and enter the URL **`http://localhost:8080/manage`**. Depending on the domain where you installed Zope, you may need to type in a different URL.

This leads directly to the Management screen. You can either add a new portal here in the `root` directory or create a folder first. A folder may be the better solution, if you intend to add more than one portal and want to keep them together.

After you have decided where to add the portal, choose CMF Site from the drop-down menu at the top of the list contained in the current folder. The following page consists of a form with the following text fields:

- ID
- Title
- Membership Source
- Description

ID and Title are typical for all objects in Zope. The ID is part of the URL that leads to an object, such as the portal. Therefore, the ID must not contain special characters, with the exception of the underscore (_) or hyphen (-). It can also contain spaces because Zope will replace all spaces with the string `%20` so that the ID can be used in the URL without causing problems.

The Membership Source is a select box. You can choose between letting the CMF create a new user folder or using your own existing user folder.

The Description field allows you to enter a short description of the purpose of the portal that will later appear on the portal's homepage.

Fill out the Add Portal form with the following data:

ID:	**`AchieversInternational`**
Title:	**`Portal`**
Membership Source:	**`Create a user folder in the portal`**
Description:	**`This portal is a means for students and teachers to interact with each other.`**

After you have clicked the Add button, the portal is created and the browser frame will display a Welcome page of the portal (see Figure 5.1).

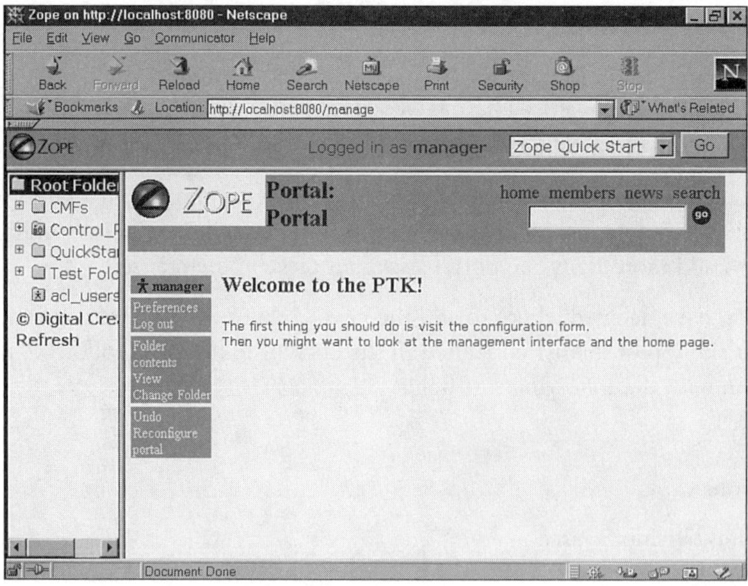

Figure 5.1
The CMF's Welcome page.

The Welcome page advises you to go first to the configuration form. This form is used to configure the portal's settings/options. It contains fields to change the portal's apparent e-mail information (Portal 'From' Name, Portal 'From' Address), the SMTP

Server, and some options concerning the portal's properties—Portal Title, Portal Description, as well as the Password Policy (see Figure 5.2).

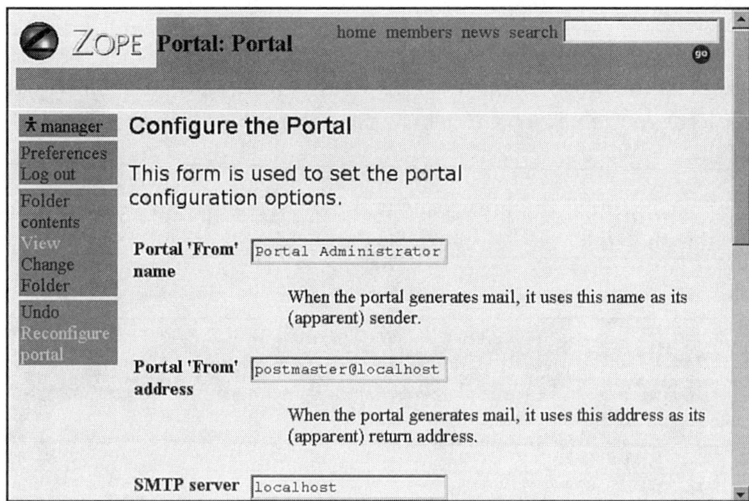

Figure 5.2
The portal's configuration options.

All the fields can be chosen freely, except for the SMTP Server field. You need to enter a valid SMTP server here, or e-mails sent by the portal will not be sent and can produce an error.

The Different Main Pages of the Portal

There are four major pages in the portal: the homepage, the Members page, the News page, and the Search page.

These four pages can always be reached by clicking the respective link in the top bar of the portal.

The Portal's Homepage

Click the Home link to go to the portal's homepage. You can find the link in the list of links at the top of the page on the right.

The homepage consists of four parts:

- The top bar contains the Zope logo, the list of links mentioned previously, and a search form.

- On the left, you find the so-called action box. The contents of this box varies from user to user, depending on the user's rights to execute actions and on the user's current position within the portal. However, the top of this box always shows the name of the user who is currently logged on.
- On the right is a news box. This box contains published news items sorted by date, with the most recent news item at the top. It also contains a More... link that leads to the news pages where the news articles are listed with their headlines.
- The fourth part of the homepage is the overview part. The description of the portal is shown here (see Figure 5.3).

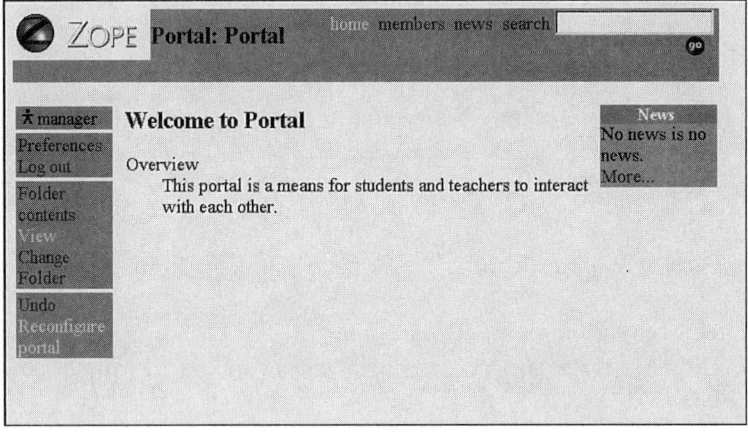

Figure 5.3
The portal's homepage.

The top bar and the action box are consistent throughout the portal. The overview and the news box are only on the homepage.

The Member Page

Go to the Members page by clicking the Members link in the top bar. This page lists the portal members who choose to be shown. You can move through the list of members by using the Previous and Next links if there are more members than the ones showing (see an example in Figure 5.4). The default number of listed members is 25, but you can change this number, press Enter, and the list will change accordingly.

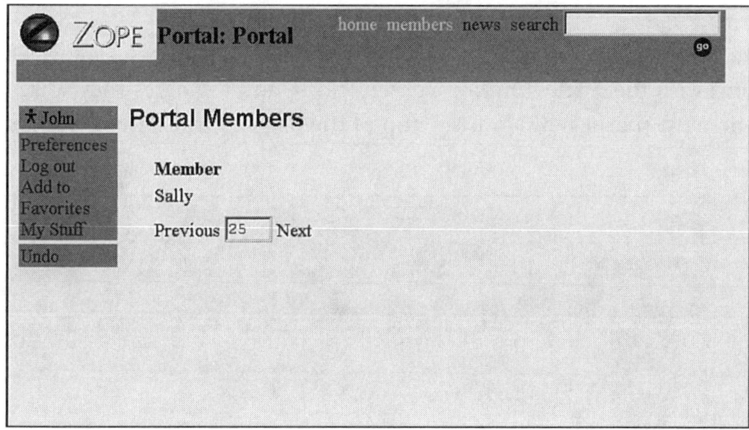

Figure 5.4
The portal's Member page.

As a portal administrator, you are able to see all member names, not just the ones who choose to be seen. After each member name, you can also see whether that member chose to be listed (see Figure 5.5).

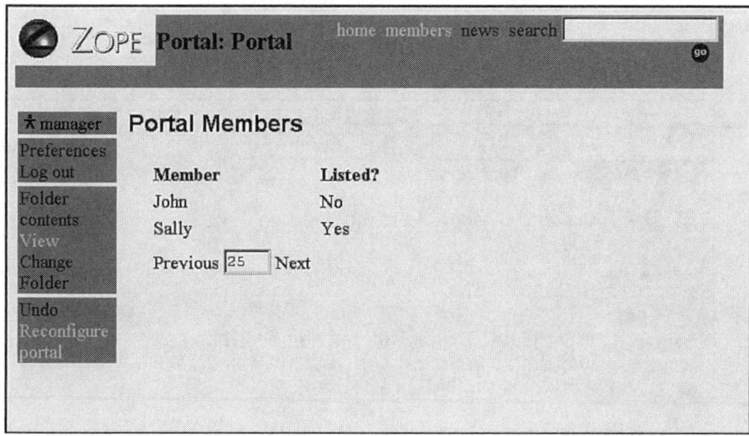

Figure 5.5
Administrator's view of the Member page.

To learn how a member can choose whether he or she wants to be listed on the Member page, see the "Preferences" section under the "The Actions Box" section later in this chapter.

The News Page

Click the News link in the top bar to go to the News page. This page lists all published news items with their titles, authors, descriptions, and the dates they were published. Again, the most recent news is at the top of the list (see an example in Figure 5.6).

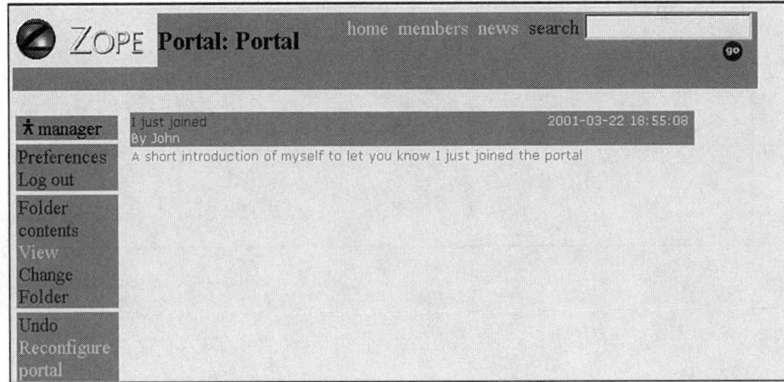

Figure 5.6

The portal's News page.

To read the full news item, click its title. The entire news item appears on the following page (see Figure 5.7).

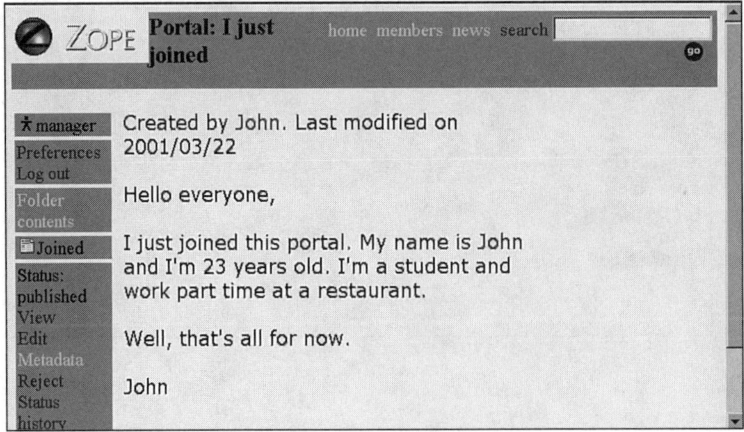

Figure 5.7

One news item.

The Search Page

There are two ways to search the portal: simple or advanced search. The simple way to search is typing the word(s) you are looking for into the Search field in the top bar and pressing Enter or clicking Go. This search will go through the titles, descriptions, and bodies of every accessible object.

To use the advanced search, click the Search link in the top bar and the Search page appears (see Figure 5.8).

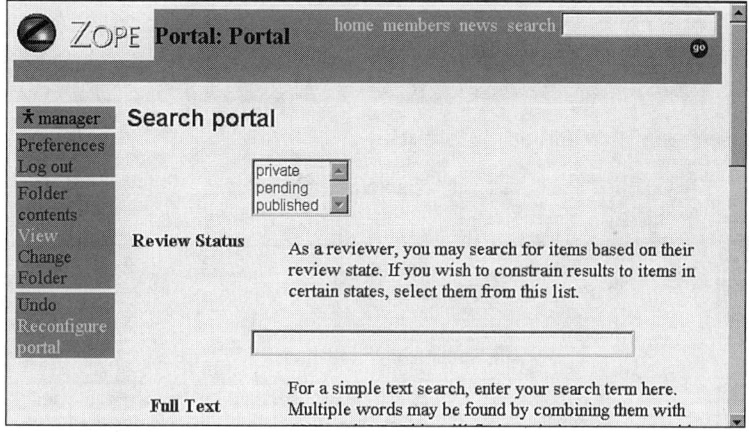

Figure 5.8
The portal's Search page.

A member has the following options narrowing his or her search:

- Full Text
- Title
- Description
- Find items since…
- Item type
- Creator

The administrator has an additional box, Review Status. That way, he can determine whether the objects he is looking for are to be private, pending, and/or published. For example, if the administrator chooses pending, the search will only return objects that are pending at that moment.

The Actions Box

As previously mentioned, the actions box contains different actions, depending on the user's permissions.

Preferences

Every user can choose whether he or she wants to be listed on the Members page. He or she does so on his or her Preferences page by clicking the Preferences link in the action box (see Figure 5.9).

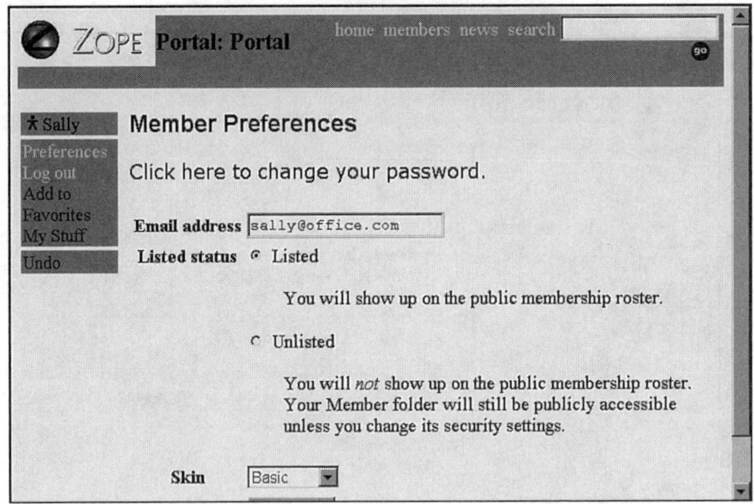

Figure 5.9
The Preferences page of a member.

On this page, a member can also change his or her e-mail address and which skin he or she wants the portal to have. Skins will be explained later in this chapter in the "Customizing the Portal's Design and Layout" section.

At the top of the form is a link to a page where the member can change his or her password.

Logout

The Logout link is used to log out of the portal. If you are also logged in to Zope, you may need to log out there as well to fully log out.

Add to Favorites

A member can create a Favorites list of published objects, such as news items, documents, and so on, so that those objects are more easily found later. A favorite is a link to a specific object. Its ID and title are automatically created. The ID and URL can be edited later.

My Favorites

If a member has at least one favorite, the actions box contains another link: My Favorites. With this link, the member has easy access to his or her favorites. The favorites can also be accessed via the Favorites folder in the member's folder.

My Stuff

The My Stuff link directs the browser to the uppermost folder of the current member. Here, as well as in all subfolders, the member can add any object type, such as documents, news, links, and so on. The existing objects are listed and can be viewed by clicking their names.

Actions When Viewing an Object

When viewing an object, the actions box contains certain actions that are the same for every object:

- View
- Edit
- Metadata
- Submit
- Status history

When an object is submitted, it is pending until a reviewer either publishes or rejects the object. A published object can also be retracted when it is published or pending.

Portal members are created when they join the portal, and reviewers need to be created in the Zope Management screen. There is a special Reviewer group that is created when adding a CMF to your Zope installation. The reviewer can be the site's administrator, but because administrating a site is enough work for a person, you might want to give the Reviewer role to different people.

The status of all objects is part of the staging process:

- Submitted
- Pending

- Published
- Rejected
- Retracted

Consequently, an object needs more actions than those just listed, depending on its current status and if the current user is a reviewer:

- Publish
- Retract
- Reject

View The View link shows the current object in the third view. The third view, for example, is the way an HTML page looks in a browser—not the code that makes up the HTML page. The actions box shows the current status of the object below its name (see Figure 5.10).

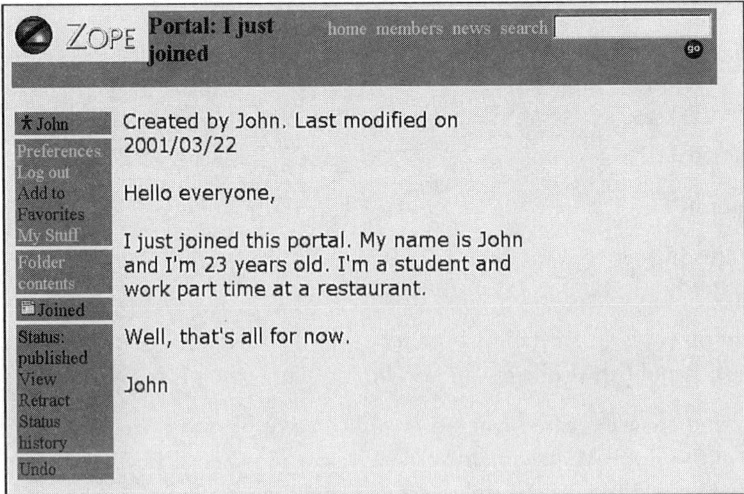

Figure 5.10

The third view of an object.

Edit Click the Edit link to change the object—for example, to upload a new file if the current object is of the `File` type or change the lead-in of a news object. The data that can be edited depends on the object's type.

Metadata The metadata is the title, description, subject, and format of an object (see Figure 5.11). There is more metadata that can be edited by clicking the Edit All Metadata link at the right top of the metadata edit form.

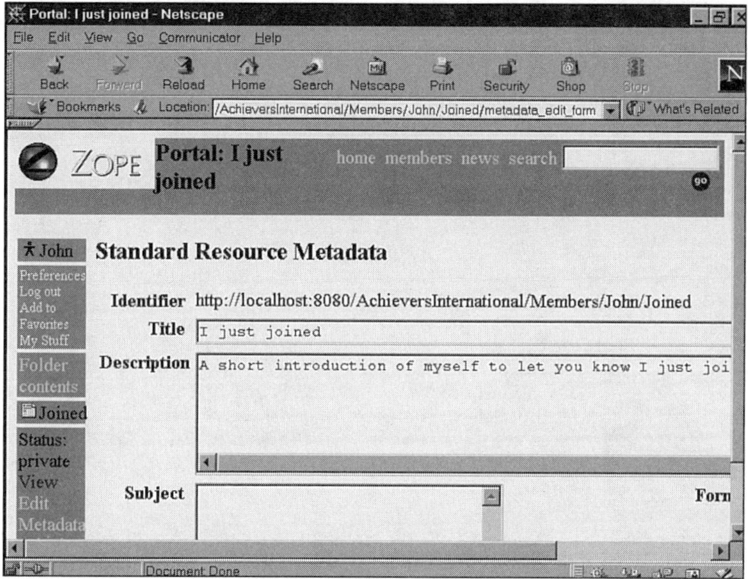

Figure 5.11
The form to edit metadata.

Submit Submitting an object is part of the staging process. If a member wants to publish an object so that it can be seen by other members of the portal, he or she has to submit it. In the Submit page, the member can enter a comment concerning the object (see Figure 5.12).

Status History The status history gives an overview of the object's different statuses, such as private, pending, published, and so on. It also states the dates when the status changed and who changed it (see Figure 5.13).

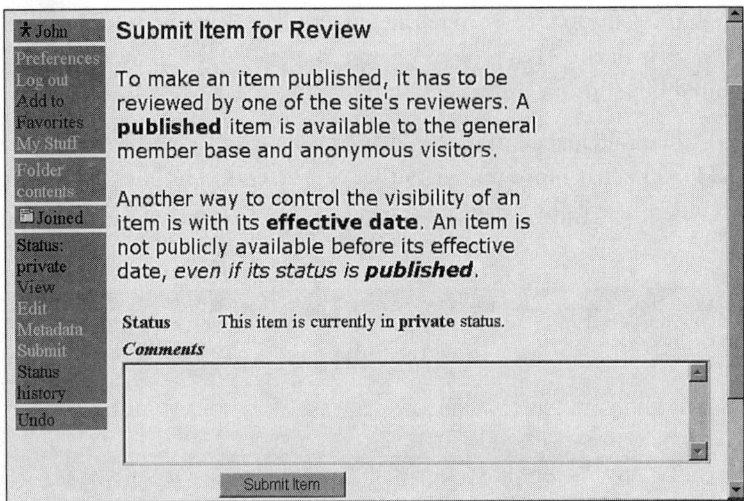

Figure 5.12
Submitting an object.

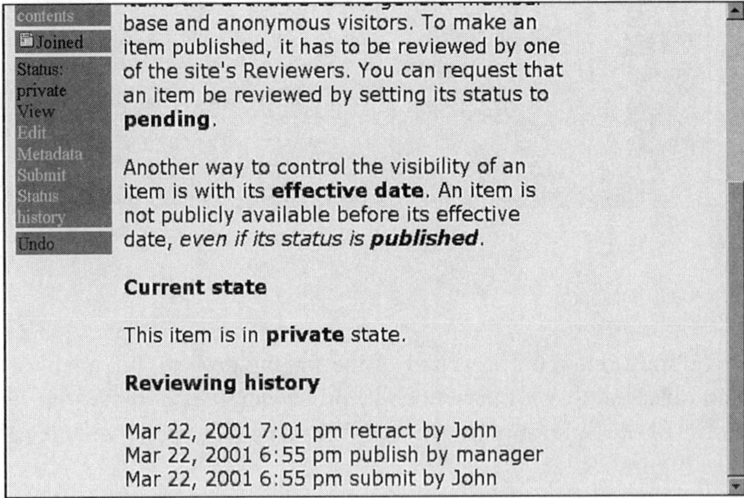

Figure 5.13
The status history of an object.

For example, if a comment was given at the submission or publishing of an object, this comment is listed below the corresponding status change.

Publish If the current object is pending and the current user is a reviewer, the actions box contains the Publish link. If the reviewer has looked at or read through an object, he or she can deem it fit for the public and publish it.

After submitting the published form, the object's status changes to published and it is now visible to all members of the portal.

Retract A member might decide to retract a published or pending object for any reason (for revision, for example). Clicking the Retract link leads to the retract form. The member may enter a comment concerning why he or she is retracting the object and then change the object's status to private again by clicking the Retract This Item button (see Figure 5.14).

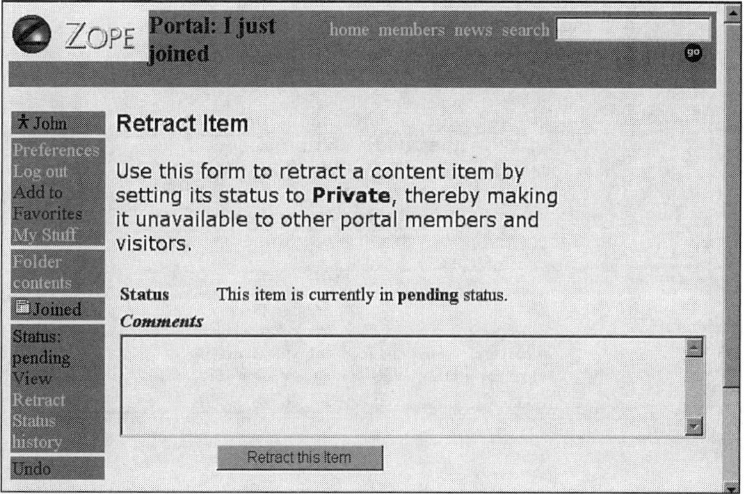

Figure 5.14
Retracting a published or submitted object.

Reject A reviewer that decides not to publish a pending object can do so by clicking the Reject link. The page that appears contains a form similar to the Submit, Publish, and Retract forms. Again, a comment can be entered and the status changed to private by clicking Reject This Item.

Folder Contents

This link directs the browser to the content view of the current folder. This folder may be the member's folder, a subfolder of the member's folder, or the CMF folder.

Undo

The Undo page (see Figure 5.15) lists transactions executed by the current member. Because a member only has permission to undo his or her own actions, the undo list does not contain any transactions executed by another member.

> **Warning**
> Because Undo itself cannot be undone, be careful when using this feature.

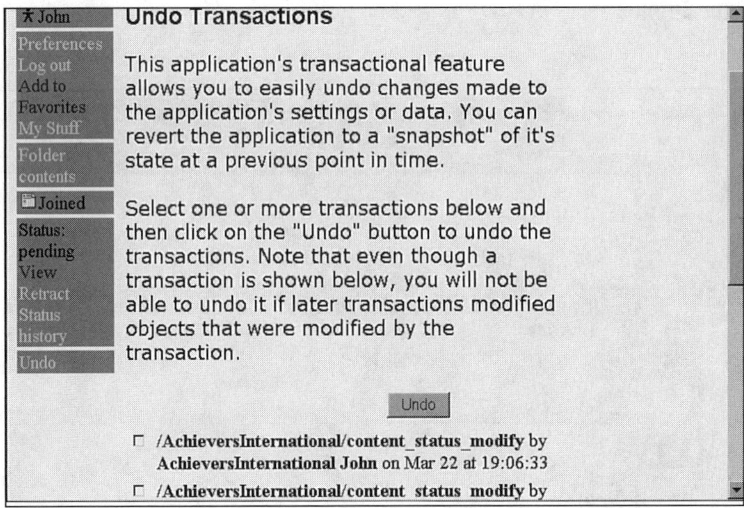

Figure 5.15
Undo transactions.

The transactions can be undone by activating the check box to the left of the transaction(s) and then clicking the Undo button.

Sometimes a transaction cannot be undone because later transactions have modified the object that the transaction concerns.

Pending Review (Number)

A reviewer has another link in the actions box. Whenever a member submits an object and its status is pending, the link Pending Review (Number) appears in the reviewer's actions box. The number shown in brackets is the number of pending objects. By clicking this link, the reviewer gets a list of the pending objects (see Figure 5.16). He or she then needs to view the different objects and decide for each one whether it should be published or rejected.

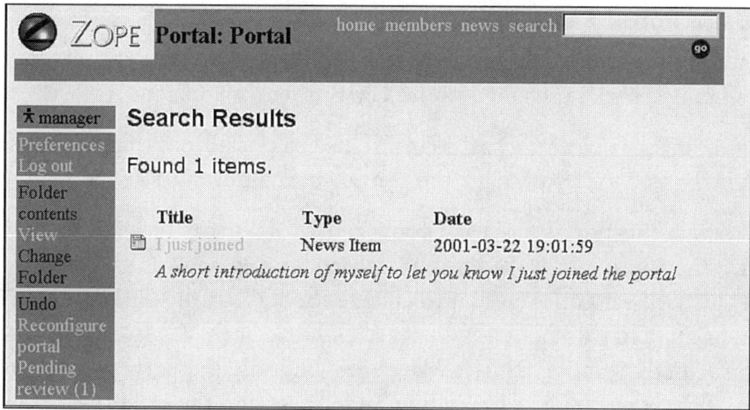

Figure 5.16
One object pending.

Customizing the Portal's Design and Layout

The default CMF instance has a certain design and layout. It has the Zope logo in the top-left corner and the blue and white background color. But this often is not what you want your portal to look like. You will want to put up a different logo and change the colors of the links, standard font, background, and so on to create your own portal.

Everything you see on the portal is defined in a skin. That means each color and every part of a page has a specific name and value that can be customized individually to create a different look. The new look then becomes a new skin. The default design and layout of the CMF is called the *Basic skin*.

Changing the Portal Skin

Every member can change the look of his or her view of the portal. The skin he or she chooses is saved as member data. Therefore, depending on which member is logged in and which skin that member chose, the look of the CMF differs.

However, a member can only choose from a list of existing skins. He cannot create his own skins because creating a skin is done via the management screen, and a normal portal member does not have access to Zope's Management screen.

To choose a different skin, log on to the portal and go to the Preferences page. At the bottom of the form, there is a select box labeled Skin. The select box contains the three predefined skins—and yours after you've created your own skins.

The Basics of Portal Skins

As already stated, a new skin is created via the Zope Management screen. Access the Management screen and change to the CMF instance you created.

There you find an object `portal_skins`. This is a portal tool that contains all the skins of this CMF instance. Now, click the `portal_skins` portal tool.

The folders in this portal tool each contain part of what makes up the portal. You may recognize the names of two of the folders: `no_css` and `nouvelle`. These two objects contain the necessary information to change the look of the CMF to the No CSS or Nouvelle skin. They do not contain every element of the CMF design and layout, the DTML methods that create the CMF pages, but only the parts that actually make the changes. That is namely the Cascading Style sheet and the style sheet properties.

Choose the `nouvelle` folder. You see two objects: `nouvelle_stylesheet` and `stylesheet_properties (New Skin)`.

The style sheet properties define certain parts of a CMF page (link, vlink, and so on) and give each one a value (#CC0033, for example). These properties are then used in the `nouvelle_stylesheet` as variables.

The style sheet for the `Basic` skin can be found in the `generic` folder in the `portal_skin` tool. Here, you also find some of the DTML methods that create the CMF pages. The rest of the DTML methods are in the `content` and `control` folders, depending on their purpose. DTML methods that are responsible for creating and presenting content, such as the form to create a news item or to edit metadata, are combined in `content`. The `control` folder contains DTML methods that help configure and maintain the CMF from a member's viewpoint.

Creating a New Portal Skin

The first thing you need to do is add a new folder to the `portal_skin` tool. Click the portal tool and add the folder `MySkin` there (see Figure 5.17).

Now you need to decide what you want your skin to look like. If you just want to change the colors of links, background, and so on, your new skin will be finished in just a few minutes. But if you want to change the layout, you will need to change actual HTML pages, and this may take a lot longer. For now, we will create a new skin that uses the same layout but different colors.

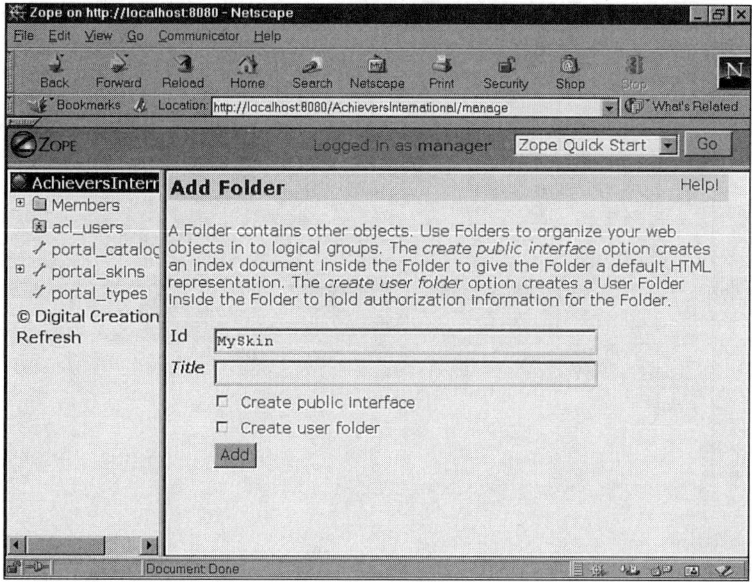

Figure 5.17

Adding the MySkin folder.

Changing Colors

You know that there are three existing skins and that the style sheet properties define the colors of a skin. This is what you need to customize now. The easiest way to do this is using the style sheet properties of one of the existing skins.

1. Go to the `nouvelle` folder in `portal_skins` tool. Here you find the `stylesheet_properties` object that belongs to the Nouvelle skin.

2. Click `stylesheet_properties` to see its contents. The object has only one tab—Customize—on which you see the various properties that are defined for the Nouvelle skin, each with a name and a value (see Figure 5.18).

3. At the top of the list of properties is a drop-down menu and a Customize button. You will find the new folder `MySkin` in this drop-down menu because you created it earlier. MySkin should already be selected in the menu; if not, choose it now.

4. Click the Customize button. A new folder labeled `stylesheet_properties` is added to the `MySkin` folder, and it receives all the properties that the original `stylesheet_properties` has (see Figure 5.20).

   You are now in the `stylesheet_properties` folder in your MySkin folder. The list of properties has become a form where the value fields can be edited (see Figure 5.19).

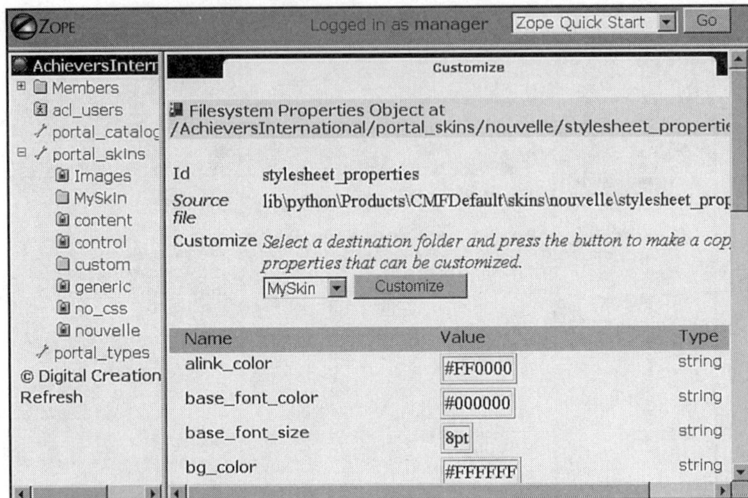

Figure 5.18

The `stylesheet_properties` *object of the* `nouvelle` *folder.*

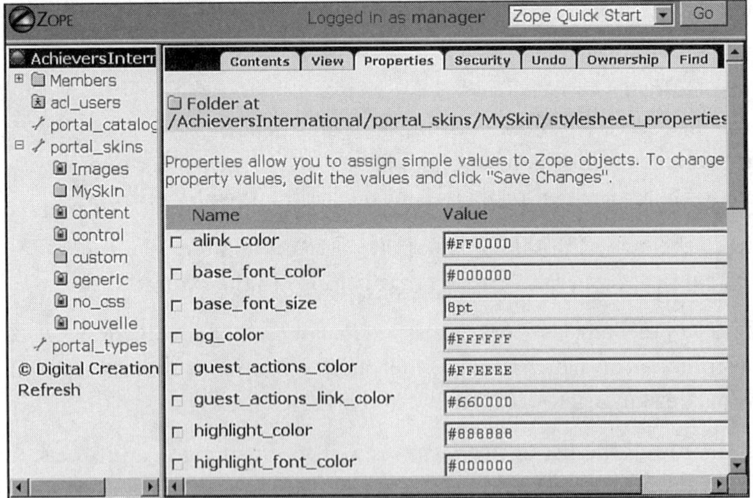

Figure 5.19

The customizable `stylesheet_properties` *object.*

5. Change the values of `primary_accent_color` and `secondary_accent_color` to `#00FFCC`. Then save the changes by clicking the Save Changes button at the bottom of the form.

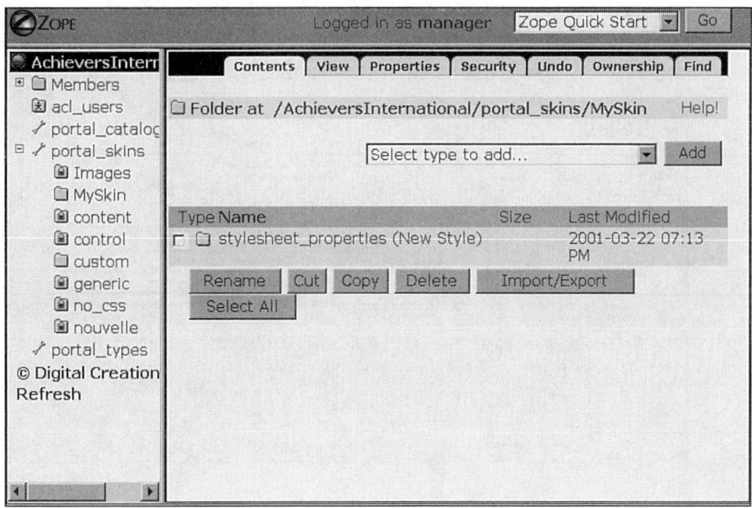

Figure 5.20
MySkin with the `stylesheet_properties` *folder.*

Whenever you want to change other colors of MySkin, go to the `stylesheet_properties` in the `MySkin` folder and click the Properties tab to get the properties form.

A color guide that will help you find the correct properties for the different parts of a CMF page can be found at `http://cmf.zope.org/Members/bowerymarc/stylesheet_colorguide`.

But changing the style sheet properties is not enough to finish the new skin. You need to tell the CMF that there is a new skin that should be available to the members. This is done in the Properties view of `portal_skins`. Go to `portal_skins` and click the Properties tab (see Figure 5.21).

You see the Properties form containing the following properties:

- Skin Selections
- Default Skin
- REQUEST Variable Name
- Skin Flexibility

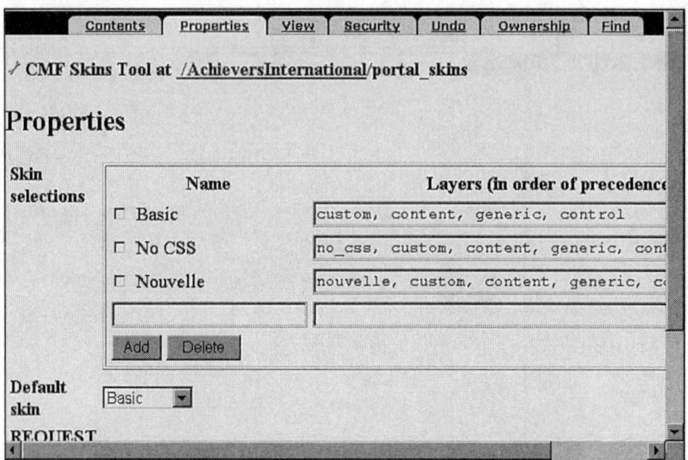

Figure 5.21
The Properties view of `portal_skins`.

To make the new skin available in the CMF, add it to Skin Selections. Fill out the fields below the existing skins as follows:

Name:	**`My Skin`**
Layers:	**`MySkin, custom, nouvelle, content, generic, control`**

The layers, the folders that are to be searched for any specific object, have to be ordered in a certain order. The name of the new skin folder has to be first because any object that needs to be found should first be looked up in the that folder. As you know, there is more than one object called `stylesheet_properties`—each skin has one. But if a member has chosen `MySkin` as his or her preference, Zope should find the `stylesheet_properties` object of `MySkin` and not the one in `nouvelle` or `generic`.

The `nouvelle` folder has to be in this list because one property (`select_stylesheet_id`) in `stylesheet_properties` refers to the `nouvelle_stylesheet` object. Zope will throw an error if you do not include `nouvelle` in the list of layers, because it won't be able to find the `nouvelle_stylesheet`.

You could also customize `nouvelle_stylesheet` so that a copy of it is transferred to the `MySkin` folder. Then you would not have to include `nouvelle` in the layers list. Either way works.

Now, click the Add button, and the skin will be added to the list of skins (see Figure 5.22).

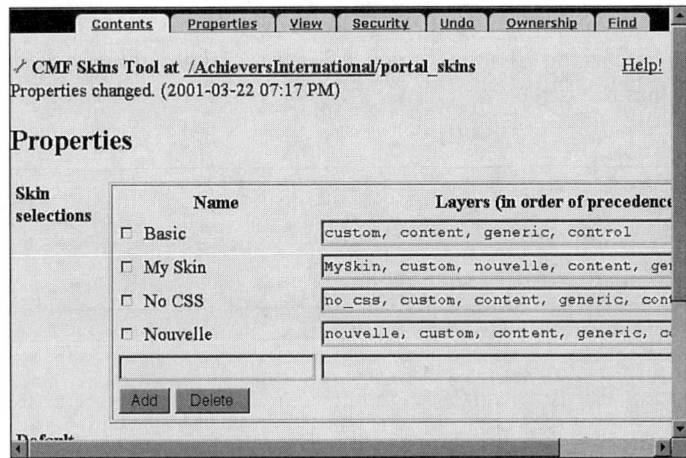

Figure 5.22

The new skin has been added.

Now when you enter the Preferences page of the CMF, you will see that `My Skin` is included in the drop-down Skin menu (see Figure 5.23).

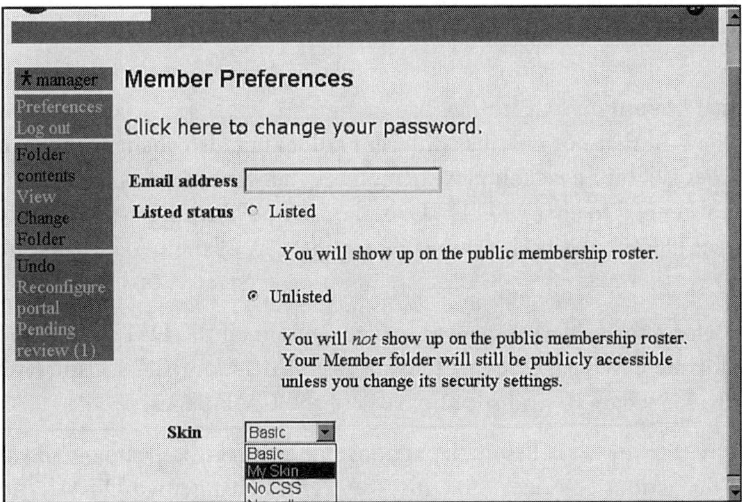

Figure 5.23

The Preferences page with the new skin in the Skin menu.

Change the skin to `My Skin` by choosing it from the drop-down menu and save the preferences by clicking Change. Figure 5.24 shows what a difference changing just two property values can make.

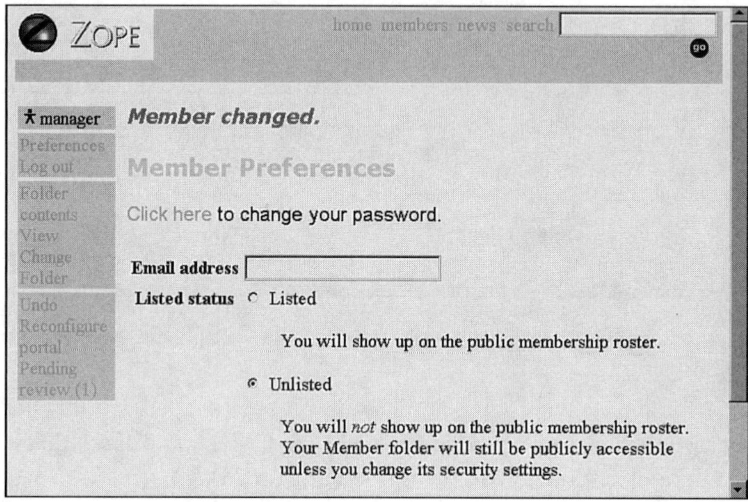

Figure 5.24
The portal's new look due to the `MySkin` skin.

Changing Layout

Creating a skin that not only has different colors but also changes the layout of the CMF pages is a bit more complex. It requires the same steps as previously shown, but you will also need to change DTML methods. The hardest part is probably finding the correct DTML method responsible for the part of the CMF that you want to change.

As said before, the folders in `portal_skins` contain all the DMTL methods that are needed for the CMF pages. See "The `portal_skins` Content" section later in this chapter to see where to find specific parts of the CMF pages.

Let's move the news box below the actions box so that it appears on all CMF pages, just like the actions box does. For this, we need to change two DTML methods:

- `standard_html_header`
- `index_html`

Both DTML methods are in the generic folder.

Because all elements of the CMF pages are split up into small parts, that is to say that they are in different DTML methods, it is very easy to put the news box on the left.

Go to the generic folder and click index_html. Customize the DTML method by choosing MySkin from the drop-down menu and clicking the Customize button.

Do the same with the standard_html_header method. Now look at line 13 in index_html, as shown in Listing 5.1.

Listing 5.1

index_html *in the* generic *Folder*

```
 1: <dtml-var standard_html_header>
 2: <dtml-with portal_properties>
 3: <table cellpadding="0" cellspacing="0" width="100%">
 4:  <tr>
 5:   <td valign="top" width="80%">
 6: <h1> Welcome to &dtml-title; </h1>
 7: <dl>
 8:  <dt> Overview </dt>
 9:  <dd> <dtml-var description> </dd>
10: </dl>
11:   </td>
12:   <td valign="top" width="20%">
13:    <dtml-var news_box>
14:   </td>
15:   </tr>
16:  </table>
17: </dtml-with>
18: <dtml-var standard_html_footer>
```

In line 13, you see the <dtml> command <dtml-var news_box>. As you know, this calls an object or property called news_box. This is the first part that needs to be changed.

Replace line 13 in index_html with   so that there is a space instead of the news box and the news box does not appear on both sides of the homepage.

Now look at line 26 in standard_html_header, shown in Listing 5.2.

Listing 5.2

`standard_html_header` *in the* `generic` *Folder*

```
<dtml-if "_.hasattr(this(),'isEffective') and not isEffective( ZopeTime()
 )">
<dtml-unless "portal_membership.checkPermission('Request review',this())
or portal_membership.checkPermission('Review portal content',this())">
<dtml-var "RESPONSE.unauthorized()">
</dtml-unless>
</dtml-if>
<html>
<head>
<title><dtml-with portal_properties>&dtml-title;</dtml-with
><dtml-if name="Title">: &dtml-Title;</dtml-if></title>
<dtml-var css_inline_or_link>
</head>
<body>
<dtml-var standard_top_bar>
<table width="100%" border="0" cellpadding="0" cellspacing="0">
<tr>
<!-- Vertical whitespace -->
<td colspan="4"><br /></td>
</tr>
<tr valign="top">
<td class="SideBar" width="15%" align="left" valign="top">
<dtml-comment> Menu is now in top bar.
<dtml-var menu> <br />
</dtml-comment>
<dtml-var actions_box>
</td>
<!-- Horizontal whitespace -->
<td width="1%"> </td>
<td class="Desktop" colspan="2" width="84%" valign="top">
<dtml-if "not portal_membership.isAnonymousUser() and
not _.hasattr(portal_membership.getAuthenticatedMember(),
'getMemberId')">
<div class="AuthWarning">
<table>
<tr class="Host">
<td> Warning! </td>
<tr>
<td> You are presently logged in as a user from outside
this portal. Many parts of the portal will not work!
You may have to shut down and relaunch your browser to
```

Listing 5.2

Continued

```
42:  log out, depending on how you originally logged in.
43:  </td>
44:  </tr>
45:  </table>
46:  </div>
47:  </dtml-if>
48:  <dtml-if portal_status_message>
49:  <p class="DesktopStatusBar">&dtml-portal_status_message;</p>
50:  </dtml-if>
51:  <dtml-if localHeader>
52:  <dtml-var localHeader>
53:  </dtml-if>
```

Line 26 contains the `<dtml>` command `<dtml-var actions_box>`. Enter the following line

```
<dtml-var news_box>
```

between lines 26 and 27. That's it! If a member now uses the MySkin skin, the news box will appear on the left side below the actions box in all CMF pages.

Using Scripts in Skins

There is another way to customize a skin. You can use a Python script to create Python commands that, for example, calculate the background color from the member's name. As you already know, the background color is defined as a property for the skin's style sheet. It is called `bg_color`. Because Zope first looks for this property in `stylesheet_property`, you have to delete it there before you can use a Python script with the same name.

So, go to the `stylesheet_property` object in `MySkin` and click the Properties tab. Now activate the check box in front of the `bg_color` property and click the Delete button.

Go back to the `MySkin` folder and select Script (Python) from the drop-down menu. Add the script with the ID `bg_color`.

To have the background color calculated from the name of the currently logged in member, we need to give the member's name to the Python script as a parameter. Click the `bg_color` Python script and enter **`name`** in the field for the parameters (see Figure 5.25).

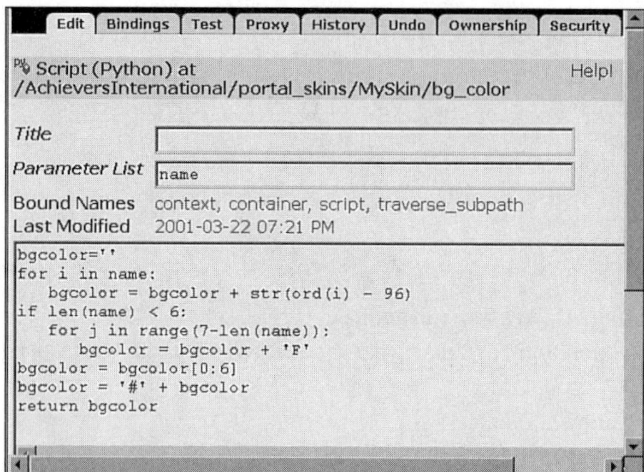

Figure 5.25

The `bg_color` *Python script.*

Enter the code in Listing 5.3 in the text area of the Python script.

Listing 5.3

`bg_color` *Python Script*

```
1: bgcolor=''
2: for i in name:
3:     bgcolor = bgcolor + str(ord(i) - 96)
4: return ('#' + bgcolor + 'FFFFFF')[:7]
```

Line 1 initializes the variable `bgcolor` so that it can be used in line 3. The loop in lines 2 and 3 goes through the member's name and takes each letter. With `ord(i)`, we get the ASCII number for the respective letter. We take away `96` because "a" has the ASCII number 97, and all the other letters in the alphabet come after that. By taking away 96, we make sure to not get three-digit numbers.

Because an HTML color has six digits, we need to catch the possibility that a member's name has less than six letters and so we might not have enough digits after the loop in lines 2 and 3. That is why we add six Fs in line 4. Consequently, no matter how long or short the user's name, we always have at least the six Fs. In line 4, we also put a `'#'` in front of the letters and then reduce the string we created to seven digits using `[:7]`. The complete HTML color is then returned.

Writing this script, however, is not enough. It needs to be called from somewhere, and the member's name needs to be handed over. This is done in the object that contains the Cascading Style sheet. So, we need to customize `nouvelle_stylesheet` because that is the object that is used in `stylesheet_properties`. Customize the style sheet and replace

```
&dtml-bg_color;
```

with

```
<dtml-var "bg_color(
➥_.str(portal_membership.getAuthenticatedMember().getUserName()))">
```

everywhere in the style sheet. Make sure you have replaced all `&dtml-bg_color;`, or you will get an error when you try to view any CMF page.

> **Tip**
> You can also use a parameterless `bg_color` script and insert the following line at the beginning:
>
> ```
> name = str(context.portal_membership.getAuthenticatedMember().getUserName())
> ```

The portal_skins Content

The following sections will give you an overview of the different folders in `portal_skins`. They will help you find the parts that need to be changed for a new skin.

The Images Folder

As the name says, this folder contains images. There are six default images:

- `UpFolder_icon.gif` This icon appears in front of the Up To <Foldername> link in the My Stuff page.
- `go.gif` This is the Go icon for the quick search at the top of the CMF portal.
- `logo.jpg` This is the Zope logo (upper-left rounded corner) that is used in the upper-left corner of each portal page.
- `logo.png` Same as `logo.jpg` without rounded corner.
- `spacer.gif` This image is used for design purposes to be put between images or other parts of a page.
- `tinyzope.jpg` A small Zope logo consisting only of the blue Zope logo.

When you use your own images, you can either store them in this folder or in the folder of the your skin. It may be better to put images in the Images folder because if you use an image in different skins and then delete one skin, you may accidentally delete an image that is needed in another skin.

The `content` Folder

The `content` folder contains DTML methods that produce CMF pages that deal with creating and maintaining content (edit pages or forms to add new objects, for example). It also contains the icons for the different objects, such as documents or folders.

- `content_publish_form`
- `content_reject_form`
- `content_retract_form`
- `content_status_history`
- `content_status_modify`
- `content_submit_form`
- `document_edit`
- `document_edit_form`
- `document_icon.gif`
- `document_view`
- `favorite_view`
- `file_edit`
- `file_edit_form`
- `file_icon.gif`
- `file_view`
- `folder_edit`
- `folder_edit_form`
- `folder_icon.gif`
- `full_metadata_edit_form`
- `image_edit`

- image_edit_form
- image_icon.gif
- image_view
- link_edit
- link_edit_form
- link_icon.gif
- link_view
- metadata_edit
- metadata_edit_form
- newsitem_edit
- newsitem_edit_form
- newsitem_icon.gif
- newsitem_view

There are four objects here for each of the standard types in a CMF: `typename_edit`, `typename_edit_form`, `typename_icon.gif`, and `typename_view`. The edit form is used to modify an object. The new data is then sent to the `typename_edit` object that saves the changes.

The `control` Folder

This folder contains the DTML methods that are responsible for "controlling" portal contents. For example, they allow you to cut, copy, paste, and delete content. They also let you register, personalize, and log out.

- `addtoFavorites` This method adds an object to the current member's Favorites when he or she clicks the Add to Favorites link in the actions box.
- `change_password` This method saves the new password when a user changes his or her password in the preferences.
- `finish_portal_construction` This is the Welcome page you see when creating a new CMF.
- `folder_copy` This method allows the copying of folders in the members' areas.
- `folder_cut` This method lets members cut out folders in their areas.

- `folder_delete` This method is responsible for deleting folders in member areas.
- `folder_paste` This method allows the pasting of folders into member areas.
- `folder_rename` This method is called when renaming folders in member areas.
- `logout` This method is called when a user clicks the Log Out link in the actions box.
- `mail_password` This method mails the password to a member if he or she forgot it.
- `personalize` This method is called from the Preferences page and saves the changes made to the preferences.
- `reconfig` This method saves the changes made to the portal's configurations.
- `register` This method registers new users after they have entered the Join form.
- `search_debug` This method is not linked within the CMF and is only used to debug the search.
- `undo` This method undoes the transactions chosen on the Undo page of the CMF portal.

The `custom` Folder

The `custom` folder is empty by default. It can be used to customize the `Basic` skin. You can also customize other skins, but then you need to change the order of the layers in the Properties view of `portal_skins`.

The `generic` Folder

The `generic` folder contains all the other DTML methods for the CMF pages, as well as the `stylesheet_properties` and the `default_stylesheet` used by the `Basic` skin.

- `actions_box` This method creates the actions box at the left side of the CMF pages.
- `clearCookie` This method deletes the filter cookies that were set in the member's area to only show certain objects.
- `content_byline` This method produces the lines Created By and Last Modified On that appear in the third view of objects.
- `css_inline_or_link` This method creates the HTMl code for the CSS either as inline or as link depending on the browser.

- `default_stylesheet` This is the stylesheet for the classic PTK style.
- `discussion_reply_form` This method creates a form that is shown when a member wants to reply to a published object.
- `discussion_reply_preview` This method shows a preview of the reply created using the `discussion_reply_form` method.
- `discussion_thread_view` This method shows a tree structure of all replies in a thread.
- `folder_add` This is the form with which folders can be added to a member area.
- `folder_contents` This method shows the contents of the current folder and is called via the Folder Contents link in the actions box.
- `folder_factories` This method is called when a member clicks the New button on a `Folder_contents` page and creates a form with the list of types that a member can add to his or her area.
- `folder_filter_form` This method either shows or hides the additional filter form in a member's folder.
- `folder_rename_form` This is the form with which a member can rename a folder.
- `index_html` This is the CMF's Welcome page, which shows the overview for the CMF.
- `join_form` This method creates the Join form that new members have to fill out.
- `logged_in` This method tells the member whether he or she was logged in successfully.
- `logged_out` This method is called when the member clicks the Log Out link, and tells him or her that he or she was logged out successfully.
- `login_form` This is the form that members have to fill out to log in to the CMF.
- `mail_password_form` This form is called when a member clicks the I Forgot My Password link on the login form. Here, the member can enter his or her username to receive his or her password by e-mail.
- `mail_password_response` This method tells the member that his or her password was sent to his or her e-mail address.

- `mail_password_template` This is a template for the mail the member gets when he or she receives his or her password.
- `metadata_help` This method lists and describes the Dublin Core Metadata.
- `news_box` This method creates the news box that is shown on the right side of the CMF's homepage.
- `password_form` With this form, a member can change his or her password.
- `personalize_form` This method creates the Member Preferences page.
- `recent_news` This method creates the News page where all news is listed in batches of ten.
- `reconfig_form` This method shows the Configure the Portal page that site administrators can access by clicking the Reconfigure link in the actions box.
- `registered` This method tells a new member that he or she was registered successfully.
- `registered_notify` This is the template for the e-mail a new member receives when he or she chooses to get their password in an e-mail.
- `roster` This method creates the Members page that lists all members that chose to be listed.
- `search` This method lists the search results.
- `search_form` This is the advanced search form that can be accessed by clicking the Search link at the top of a CMF page.
- `showThreads` This method shows all replies to an object in a tree structure.
- `standard_html_footer` This is the `standard_html_footer` of the CMF that only shows a `localFooter` if one exists and that closes the HTML page.
- `standard_html_header` This `standard_html_header` arranges the top bar and the actions box on each CMF page.
- `standard_top_bar` This method creates the top bar on each CMF page that contains the Home, Members, and Search links, for example.
- `stylesheet_properties` (Classic PTK Style) This is the stylesheet for the `Basic` skin.
- `undo_form` This form shows all transactions available to be undone by the current member.
- `viewThreadsAtBottom` This method shows the replies to an object using the `showThreads` method.

The no_css Folder

This folder contains the stylesheet_properties object for the skin that uses no Cascading Style sheet (CSS). It is the only object in this folder, because it is the only object necessary to overwrite the CSS of the Basic skin in the generic folder.

The nouvelle Folder

This folder contains the stylesheet_properties and nouvelle_stylesheet for the Nouvelle skin. The nouvelle_stylesheet is necessary, because the Nouvelle skin assigns the properties differently to the CSS.

Example: AchieversInternational Skin

In this section, we will create the AchieversInternational skin. Figure 5.26 shows what this skin will look like.

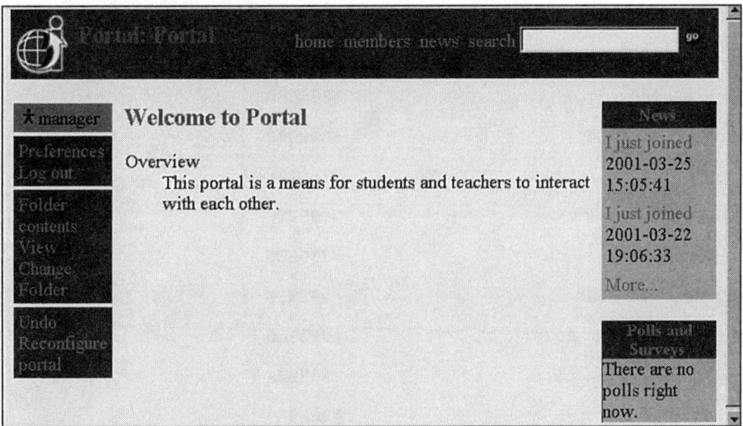

Figure 5.26
The CMF with the AchieversInternational skin.

To create this skin, we need a new image—the Achievers International logo. All the other changes can be made using the existing DTML methods.

The DTML methods that need to be customized are as follows:

- actions_box
- news_box
- nouvelle_stylesheet
- standard_top_bar

The skin is based on the `Nouvelle` skin, so `Nouvelle`'s `stylesheet_properties` needs to be modified as well.

Let's start with the new folder for our skin. Create a folder called `AchieversInternational` in `portal_skins`. Now, customize Nouvelle's `stylesheet_properties` according to Table 5.1.

Table 5.1

`AchieversInternational` *Skin's* `stylesheet_properties`

Property Name	Property Value
alink_color	**lightgrey**
base_font_color	**#000000**
base_font_size	**8pt**
bg_color	**#FFFFFF**
guest_actions_color	**#FFEEEE**
guest_actions_link_color	**#660000**
highlight_color	**#888888**
highlight_font_color	**#000000**
hover_color	**lightgrey**
link_color	**#009966**
primary_accent_alink_color	**#009966**
primary_accent_color	**#003366**
primary_accent_font_color	**#009966**
primary_accent_link_color	**#009966**
primary_accent_text_color	**#009966**
primary_accent_vlink_color	**#009966**
primary_font_family	**Arial, Verdana, Helvetica, sans-serif**
secondary_accent_alink_color	**#009966**
secondary_accent_color	**#666666**
secondary_accent_font_color	**#000000**
secondary_accent_link_color	**#FFFFFF**
secondary_accent_vlink_color	**#FFFFFF**
secondary_font_family	**Verdana, Arial, Helvetica, sans-serif**
select_stylesheet_id	**nouvelle_stylesheet**
title	**Achievers International Style**
vlink_color	**#009966**

Now, we can customize the `nouvelle_stylesheet` object. Only two parts of the style sheet need to be modified—the `table.ActionBox` and the `tr.NewsItemRow td`. Both the ActionBox table and a cell within the NewsItemRow will get a new background color. Change these two parts in `nouvelle_sheet` as shown in Listing 5.4.

Listing 5.4

Modified Parts of `nouvelle_stylesheet`

```
....
table.ActionBox {
     font-family: &dtml-primary_font_family;;
     background-color: lightgrey;
}
....
tr.NewsItemRow td {
     background-color: #cdcdcd;
     font-size: 70%;
}
```

At this point, we can upload the new image we need for the skin. This is a logo that will replace the Zope logo in the upper-left corner of the portal pages. Use your own logo, which should be about 60×65 pixels in size.

To upload the image, go to the `AchieversInternational` skin folder, add an `Image` object, and name it `portal_logo`.

The next step is to modify the necessary DTML methods. Use Listings 5.5, 5.6, and 5.7 to customize the `actions_box`, `news_box`, and `standard_top_bar` DTML methods.

Listing 5.5

Modified `actions_box` *DTML Method*

```
<dtml-let isAnon="portal_membership.isAnonymousUser()"
          AuthClass="isAnon and 'GuestActions' or 'MemberActions'"
          uname="isAnon and 'Guest'
                 or portal_membership.getAuthenticatedMember().
➥getUserName()"
          obj="this()"
          actions="portal_actions.listFilteredActionsFor(obj)"
          user_actions="actions['user']"
          folder_actions="actions['folder']"
          object_actions="actions['object']"
          global_actions="actions['global']">
<table class="ActionBox" width="100%" cellpadding="4">
```

Listing 5.5
Continued

```
 <tr class="&dtml-AuthClass;">
  <td bgcolor="#009966">
   <img src="user_icon" align="left" alt="User">
   <dtml-var uname>
  </td>
 </tr>
 <tr class="&dtml-AuthClass;">
  <td bgcolor="#003366">
   <dtml-in user_actions mapping>
    <a href="&dtml-url;"><dtml-var name></a><br>
   </dtml-in>
  </td>
 </tr>
<dtml-if folder_actions>
 <tr class="&dtml-AuthClass;">
  <td bgcolor="#003366"> <dtml-in folder_actions mapping>
        <a href="&dtml-url;"><dtml-var name></a><br>
       </dtml-in>
  </td>
 </tr>
</dtml-if>
<dtml-if object_actions>
 <tr class="&dtml-AuthClass;">
  <td bgcolor="#003366">
     <font color="lightgrey">
   <dtml-let icon="obj.icon"
             mt="obj.meta_type"
             objID="obj.id"
   >
     <img src="&dtml-portal_url;/&dtml-icon;" align="left"
          alt="&dtml-meta_type;">
     &dtml-objID;
    </dtml-let>
  </td>
 </tr>
 <tr class="&dtml-AuthClass;">
  <td bgcolor="#003366">
      <font color="lightgrey">
     <dtml-if expr="_.hasattr(obj, 'review_state')">
     Status: <dtml-var "obj.review_state"><br>
     </dtml-if>
```

Listing 5.5

Continued

```
    <dtml-in object_actions mapping>
     <a href="&dtml-url;"><dtml-var name></a><br>
    </dtml-in>
    </td>
  </tr>
</dtml-if>
<dtml-if global_actions>
  <tr class="&dtml-AuthClass;">
    <td bgcolor="#003366">
     <dtml-in global_actions mapping>
      <a href="<dtml-var url>"><dtml-var name></a><br>
     </dtml-in>
    </td>
  </tr>
</dtml-if>
</table>
</dtml-let>
```

The changes made to the `actions_box` DTML method are the background colors in the table cells and some text colors within the cells. Note that the table cells do not all have the same background color. Also, a cell padding of 4 has been added to the table.

Listing 5.6

Modified `news_box` *DTML Method*

```
<table class="NewsItems" cellspacing="0" cellpadding="4" border="0"
➥width="100%">
  <tr><td valign="top" class="NewsTitle" width="100%">
      <b>News</b>
   </td>
  </tr>
  <dtml-in "portal_catalog.searchResults( meta_type='News Item'
                                        , sort_on='Date'
                                        , sort_order='reverse'
                                        , review_state='published'
                                        )" size="10">
  <tr class="NewsItemRow">
   <td valign="top">
    <a href="<dtml-var "portal_catalog.getpath( data_record_id_ )"
    >"> &dtml-Title; </a><br>
    <dtml-var Date>
```

Listing 5.6

Continued

```
   </td>
  </tr>
  <dtml-else>
  <tr class="NewsItemRow">
   <td valign="top">
     No news is no news.
   </td>
  </tr>
  </dtml-in>
  <tr class="NewsItemRow">
   <td>
     <a href="&dtml.url-recent_news;">More...</a>
   </td>
  </tr>
 </table>
```

Again, a cellpadding of 4 was added to the table in the `news_box` DTML method. Also, the first table cell was deleted.

Listing 5.7

Modified `standard_top_bar` *DTML Method*

```
<!-- Top bar -->
<table width="100%" border="0" cellpadding="0" cellspacing="0">
<tr><td colspan="3" witdth="100%">
<!-- hack around Netscape 4.x to ensure top table is solid black -->
<table class="Masthead" cellspacing="0" cellpadding="4" border="0"
       width="100%">
 <tr class="Masthead">
  <td class="PortalLogo" align="left" valign="top" width="1%"><a
    href="&dtml-portal_url;"><img src="portal_logo" width="60" height="65"
    alt="Achievers International Logo" border="0"></a></td>
  <td class="PortalTitle" width="29%" align="left"
      valign="center">
   <h1><dtml-with portal_properties>&dtml-title;</dtml-with
   ><dtml-if name="Title">: &dtml-Title;</dtml-if></h1>
  </td>
  <td class="NavBar" align="right" valign="bottom" width="70%" wrap="no">
   <form action="&dtml-portal_url;/search">
    <a href="&dtml-portal_url;">home</a> 
    <a href="&dtml-portal_url;/roster">members</a> 
```

Listing 5.7
Continued

```
20:      <a href="&dtml-portal_url;/recent_news">news</a> 
21:      <a href="&dtml-portal_url;/search_form">search</a>
22:      <input name="SearchableText" size="16">
23:      <input border="0" type="image" name="go" src="Images/go.gif">  
24:     </form>
25:   </td>
26:  </tr>
27: </table>
28: </td></tr></table>
```

In the `standard_top_bar` DTML method, we have changed the image source for the logo (lines 9 and 10) and added the cell padding of 4.

The last step is to add the skin to the Properties view of `portal_skin`. Now, a member of your portal can choose to use the `AchieversInternational` skin.

The CMF Types

In this section, you will learn about the different ways CMF types can be created and how to create new ones that will enhance your portal.

What Is a Type?

A CMF type is an object that contains certain data and metadata. Each type has a set of properties and actions.

The properties define the title, description, metatype, icon, and some information that the CMF needs to add an object of this type. You can also define whether a member can reply to an object (whether the object can be discussed).

The type's actions define which DTML method or DTML document is to be called to be used as an Add or Edit page.

The standard CMF types are as follows:

- `News Item`
- `Document`
- `File`
- `Image`

- `Link`
- `Folder`
- `Favorite`

The Properties View of a Type

The types are defined in the `portal_types` portal tool. Clicking a type calls up the type's Properties view (see Figure 5.27).

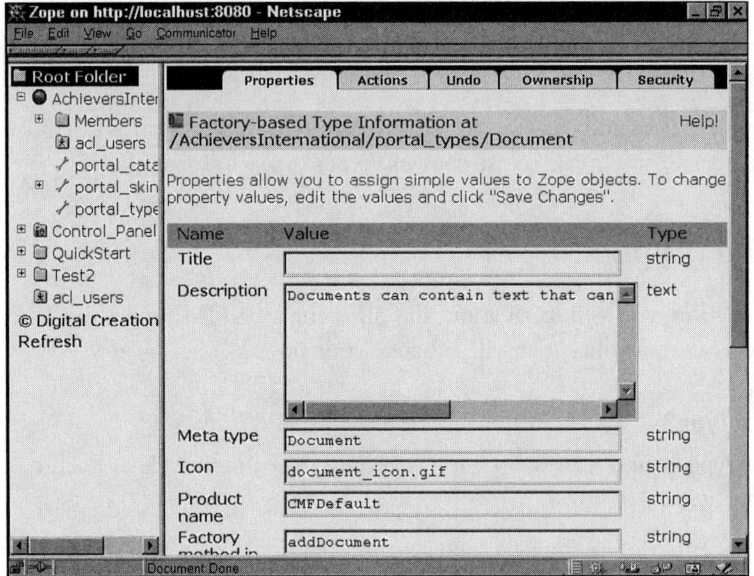

Figure 5.27

Properties view of the Document type.

Giving a title for the type is voluntary, but you should give a description. The description appears below the type's name on the page where a member can choose which type of object he or she wants to add to his or her folder.

The next property is the metatype. The metatype is important for filtering objects when a member only wants to have certain types listed in his or her folder.

In the Icon field on the Properties view, you see the name of the image that appears in front of an object of this type.

Product name and factory method define where Zope has to look for the method that actually creates the new object in the member's folder. The factory method is a Python method within a Zope product (the `addDocument()` method in the CMFDefault product, for example).

On the Properties view, you also find an Allow Discussion? check box. If this check box is activated, members can reply to an object of this type by clicking the action reply that appears in the actions box. The links to reply to an object are then shown at the bottom of the object.

The Actions View of a Type

In the Actions view of a type (see Figure 5.28), you define the different views that are necessary to add and edit an object of this type. You do not add the DTML methods here that create the views, but you state what the DTML methods are called and what permission a member must have to be able to see the respective view.

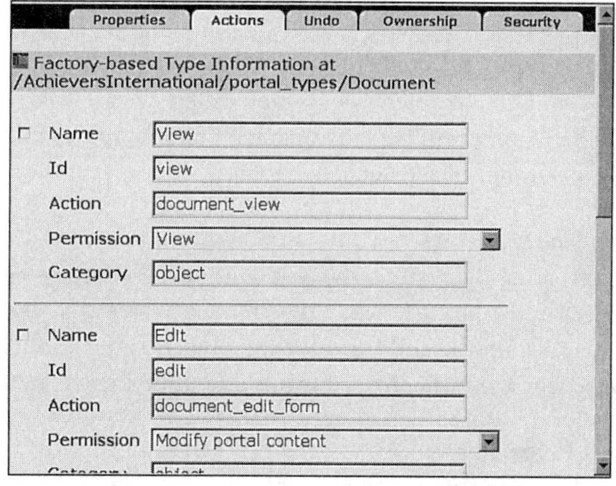

Figure 5.28
The Actions view with defined actions.

Each action contains a Name, ID, Action, Permission, and Category. There need to be at least three actions for a type:

- View
- Edit
- Metadata

The View action is needed so that a member can see the third view of an object, and the Edit action needs to be defined so that an object can be created and edited. The Metadata view is necessary for creating and editing an object, but it is for editing the object's metadata.

The name of an action appears as a link in the actions box in the CMF when an object of the respective type is viewed. In the Action field of an action, you find the name of the DTML method that is called when a member clicks the respective link for this action.

Creating a New Type

There are a couple of ways to create a new type, depending on what type you want to create. If you want to create a type that is only slightly different from one that already exists (if you want to change the name and representation of a type, for example), you base your new type on the existing one. This is what we will do first. Later, we will explain how to add default values for a type and how to create a new product as a type by using a ZClass.

Using an Existing Type to Create a New One

In this section, we will create a new portal type called `CV` that will be based on the `Document` type. The `CV` type will have its own icon and its representation will be slightly different from that of the `Document` type.

Adding the New Type

The first step in creating a new type this way is to add a `Factory-based Type Information` object in the `portal_types` type folder. Select this object from the drop-down-menu. This calls up the add form for the object. Enter the ID **`CV`** and choose `CMFDefault: Document` from the drop-down menu. (See Figure 5.29.)

Editing the Types Properties

Now we change the properties so that this new type does not have the same description, metatype, and icon as the `Document` type on which it is based.

Enter the following description, which will appear below the type's name in the list of types a member can choose from when creating a new object, for the CV type:

```
CVs contain text that can be formatted using Structured Text.
```

The type's metatype will be `CV`, so type **`CV`** into the Metatype field. In the Icon field, we need to give the name of the icon that will appear in front of an object of the `CV` type. You can either use an existing icon or create a new one with a program such as Adobe Photoshop. Because we want `CV` objects to have a different icon than the other types, we created the simple icon shown in Figure 5.30.

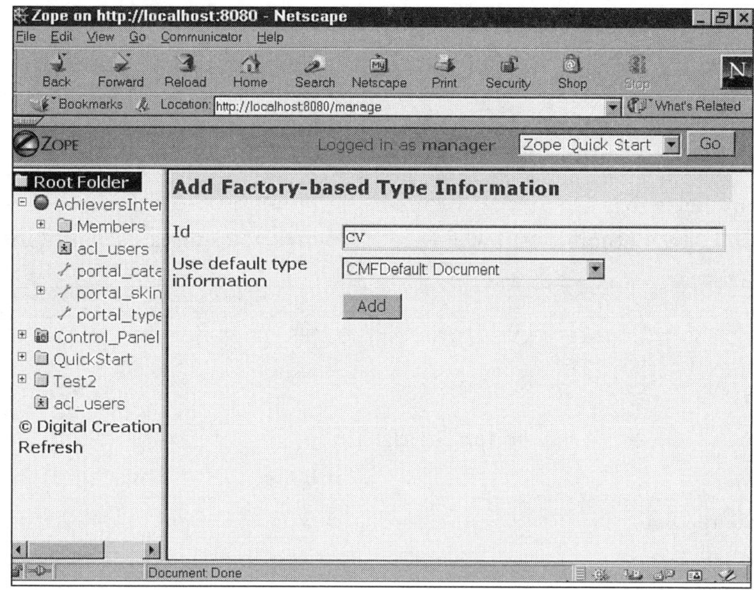

Figure 5.29

Adding the new CV type.

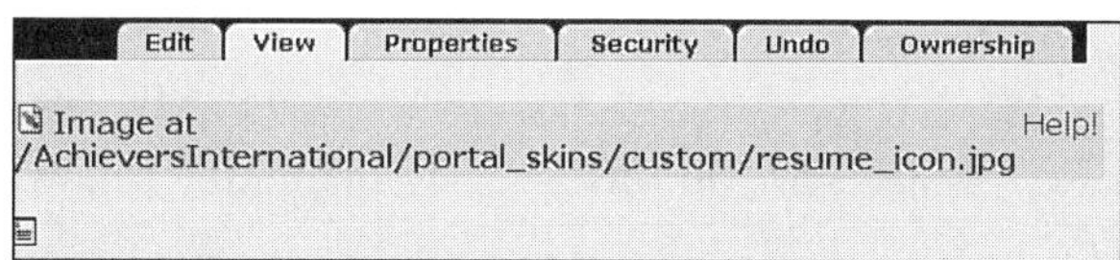

Figure 5.30

The CV icon.

Enter **`cv_icon.jpg`** in the Icon field because this is what we will call the icon when we add the respective image object to Zope. The Product Name and Factory Method fields need to stay the way they are, but the Initial field's view name has to be changed. Enter **`cv_metadata_edit_form`** in this field and save the changes. The `cv_metadata_edit_form` DTML method does not exist yet, but we will create it after editing the type's actions.

Modifying the CV Type's Actions

Changing the actions to fit our new type does not require much editing. Because we used the `Document` type as a basis, the `CV` type already has the usual three actions defined for it:

- View
- Edit
- Metadata

The only fields that need to be changed are the Action fields, because they define which DTML method to call when the respective action link is clicked in the object's action box.

To fit our type, change the action fields as shown in Table 5.2.

Table 5.2
Old and New Values of the Action Fields

Old Value	New Value
`document_view`	`cv_view`
`document_edit_form`	`cv_edit_form`
`metadata_edit_form`	`cv_metadata_edit_form`

Save the changes by clicking the Save button.

Customizing the DTML Methods

Before we can use the CV type, we need to create the DTML methods we just defined to add and edit a CV object. We do this by customizing the following existing DTML methods:

- `document_view`
- `document_edit`
- `document_edit_form`
- `full_metadata_edit_form`
- `metadata_edit`
- `metadata_edit_form`

and renaming them as shown in Table 5.3.

Table 5.3

Original and New Names of DTML Methods

Original Name	New Name
document_view	cv_view
document_edit	cv_edit
document_edit_form	cv_edit_form
full_metadata_edit_form	full_cv_metadata_edit_form
metadata_edit	cv_metadata_edit
metadata_edit_form	cv_metadata_edit_form

You find these DTML methods in the `content` folder in `portal_skins`. Go through the following steps for each of the DTML methods before continuing with the text:

1. Click the DTML method.
2. Select Custom from the drop-down-menu.
3. Click the Customize button.
4. Go to the `custom` folder.
5. Activate the check box in front of the DTML method.
6. Click the Rename button.
7. Rename the DTML method in accordance with Table 5.3.

The DTML methods themselves do not need much changing. It is mostly the relating links that need to be modified to fit the new DTML methods' names. But we will change the layout of the third view of a CV; in other words, we will change the `cv_view` DTML method. Let's start with that DTML method. Figure 5.31 shows what an object of the `CV` type will look like.

In the Management screen, edit the `cv_view` DTML method by clicking it. Replace the existing code with the code in Listing 5.8.

Listing 5.8

The `cv_view` DTML Method

```
<dtml-var standard_html_header>
<div class="Desktop">
 <div class="CV">
  <b>CV:</b> <dtml-var title_or_id>
```

Listing 5.8

Continued

```
 5:     <hr>
 6:     <dtml-var cooked_text><br>
 7:     <hr>
 8:     <br>
 9:     <dtml-var content_byline>
10:     <div class="Discussion">
11:       <dtml-var viewThreadsAtBottom>
12:     </div>
13:   </div>
14: </div>
15: <dtml-var standard_html_footer>
```

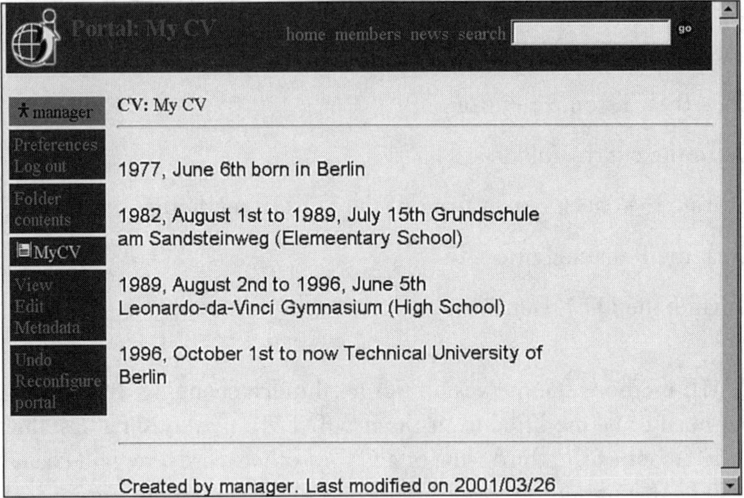

Figure 5.31

An object of the CV type.

The changes are not that complicated, but the difference they make in the layout are considerable. Listing 5.8 changes the order in which the object's content, creation date, and author are shown (lines 6 and 9). It also adds the title—or ID, depending on whether the object has a title or not—in line 4. The title, content, and date of creation are divided by two horizontal lines (lines 5 and 7).

Now we need to change the `cv_edit` DTML method. This is shown in Listing 5.9.

Listing 5.9

The `cv_edit` *DTML Method*

```
1: <dtml-call expr="edit(REQUEST['text_format'],
2:                      REQUEST['text'], REQUEST.get('file', ''))">
3: <dtml-let portal_status_message="'CV changed.'">
4: <dtml-return cv_edit_form>
5: </dtml-let>
```

The only change in this DTML method occurs in line 4. The name of the returned DTML method has to be changed to `cv_edit_form`, according to the modified `document_edit_form`. Save the change and go to the `cv_edit_form` DTML method.

Listing 5.10 shows the `cv_edit_form` DTML method that is called by `cv_edit`.

Listing 5.10

The `cv_edit_form` *DTML Method*

```
<dtml-var standard_html_header>
<div class="Desktop">
<dtml-if message>
 <p>&dtml-message;</p>
 <hr>
</dtml-if>
<div class="CV">
<h2>Edit &dtml-id;</h2>
<form action="cv_edit" method="post" enctype="multipart/form-data">
<table class="FormLayout">
 <tr>
  <th>
    Title
  </th>
  <td>
   <dtml-var Title>
  </td>
 </tr>
 <tr>
  <th>
    Introductory Self-Description
  </th>
  <td>
   <dtml-var description>
  </td>
 </tr>
```

Listing 5.10
Continued

```
<tr>
 <th>
  Format
 </th>
 <td>
  <input type="radio" name="text_format" value="structured-text"
         <dtml-if "text_format=='structured-text'">checked</dtml-if>
         id="cb_structuredtext" />
         <label for="cb_structuredtext">structured-text</label>
  <input type="radio" name="text_format" value="html"
         <dtml-if "text_format=='html'">checked</dtml-if>
     id="cb_html" />
     <label for="cb_html">html</label>
 </td>
</tr>
<tr>
 <th> Upload </th>
 <td>
  <input type="file" name="file" size="25">
 </td>
</tr>
<tr>
 <th class="TextField"> Edit CV</th>
 <td class="TextField">
  <textarea name="text:text"
            rows="20" cols="80"><dtml-var text html_quote></textarea>
 </td>
</tr>
<tr>
 <td> <br> </td>
 <td>
   <input type="submit" value=" Change ">
 </td>
</tr>
</table>
</form>
</div>
</div>
```

In the `cv_edit_form` DTML method, we need to change the action of the form (line 9) to `cv_edit` so that the correct DTML method is called to commit the changes to the CV object. We also change two of the forms' field titles: Description is changed to Introductory Self-Description (line 21) and Edit is changed to Edit CV (line 49).

Next is the `cv_metadata_edit` DTML method (see Listing 5.11), which needs two changes:

1. We need to modify the status message that tells the member that the metadata of the CV object was successfully changed (line 13).
2. The call that returns the next view has to be changed to `cv_view` (line 17).

Listing 5.11

The `cv_metadata_edit` DTML Method

```
 1: <dtml-call expr="editMetadata(
 2:       title=REQUEST.get('title', ''),
 3:       subject=REQUEST.get('subject', ()),
 4:       description=REQUEST.get('description', ''),
 5:       contributors=REQUEST.get('contributors', ()),
 6:       effective_date=REQUEST.get('effective_date', _.None),
 7:       expiration_date=REQUEST.get('expiration_date', _.None),
 8:       format=REQUEST.get('format', 'text/html'),
 9:       language=REQUEST.get('language', 'en-US'),
10:       rights=REQUEST.get('rights', ''))">
11: <dtml-if expr="REQUEST.get('change_and_edit', 0)">
12:    <dtml-let method="restrictedTraverse(getTypeInfo().
➥getActionById('edit'))"
13:              portal_status_message="'CV Metadata changed.'">
14:       <dtml-return method>
15:    </dtml-let>
16: <dtml-else>
17:    <dtml-return cv_view>
18: </dtml-if>
```

Listings 5.12 and 5.13 show the modified edit forms for the metadata. There are two listings because a member can either edit a short version of the metadata or the full version.

Listing 5.12

The `cv_metadata_edit_form` *DTML Method*

```
<dtml-var standard_html_header>
<div class="Desktop">
<dtml-if message>
 <p>&dtml-message;</p>
 <hr>
</dtml-if>
<div class="Metadata">
<h2>Resource Metadata </h2>
<form action="cv_metadata_edit" method="post">
<table class="FormLayout">
 <tr valign="top">
  <th align="right"> Identifier
  </th>
  <td>
   <dtml-var Identifier>
  </td>
  <td colspan="2" align="right">
   <a href="full_cv_metadata_edit_form"> Edit all CV metadata </a>
  </td>
 </tr>
 <tr valign="top">
  <th align="right"> Title
  </th>
  <td colspan="3">
   <input type="text"
          name="title"
          value="&dtml-Title;"
          size="65">
  </td>
 </tr>
 <tr valign="top">
  <th align="right"> Introductory Self-Description
  </th>
  <td colspan="3">
   <textarea name="description:text" rows="5"
              cols="65">&dtml-Description;</textarea>
  </td>
 </tr>
 <tr valign="top">
  <th align="right"> Subject
  </th>
```

Listing 5.12

Continued

```
42:    <td>
43:     <textarea name="subject:lines" rows="5"
44:               cols="30"><dtml-in Subject><dtml-var sequence-item>
45: </dtml-in></textarea>
46:    </td>
47:    <th align="right"> Format
48:    </th>
49:    <td> <input type="text" name="format" value="&dtml-Format;">
50:    <br> <input type="submit" name="change_and_edit" value=" Change & Edit
➥">
51:    <br> <input type="submit" name="change_and_view" value=" Change & View
➥">
52:    </td>
53:   </tr>
54: </table>
55: </form>
56: </div>
57: </div>
58: <dtml-var standard_html_footer>
```

There are three lines in the `cv_metadata_edit_form` DTML method that were changed to fit the CV type.

- In line 9, the form action was changed to `cv_metadata_edit` to call the correct DTML method.
- In line 18, the link to the full metadata edit form was modified for the new `full_cv_metadata_edit_form` DTML method.
- In line 32, the Description field is now called Introductory Self-Description.

Listing 5.13

The `full_cv_metadata_edit_form` DTML Method

```
<dtml-var standard_html_header>
<div class="Desktop">
<dtml-if message>
 <p>&dtml-message;</p>
 <hr>
</dtml-if>
<div class="Metadata">
<h2>Resource Metadata </h2>
```

Listing 5.13

Continued

```
<dtml-let effectiveString="effective_date and effective_date.ISO() or
➥'None'"
          expirationString="expiration_date and expiration_date.ISO() or
➥'None'"
>
<form action="cv_metadata_edit" method="post">
<table class="FormLayout">
 <tr valign="top">
  <th align="right"> Identifier
  </th>
  <td colspan="3"> <dtml-var Identifier>
  </td>
 </tr>
 <tr valign="top">
  <th align="right"> Title
  </th>
  <td colspan="3">
   <input type="text"
          name="title"
          value="&dtml-Title;"
          size="65">
  </td>
 </tr>
 <tr valign="top">
  <th align="right"> Introductory Self-Description
  </th>
  <td colspan="3">
   <textarea name="description:text" rows="5"
             cols="65">&dtml-Description;</textarea>
  </td>
 </tr>
 <tr valign="top">
  <th align="right"> Subject
  </th>
  <td>
   <textarea name="subject:lines" rows="5"
             cols="30"><dtml-in Subject><dtml-var sequence-item>
</dtml-in></textarea>
  </td>
  <th align="right"> Contributors
  </th>
```

Listing 5.13

Continued

```
  <td>
   <textarea name="contributors:lines" rows="5"
             cols="30"><dtml-in Contributors><dtml-var sequence-item>
</dtml-in></textarea>
  </td>
 </tr>
 <tr valign="top">
  <th align="right"> Creation Date
  </th>
  <td> <dtml-var CreationDate>
  </td>
  <th align="right"> Last Modified Date
  </th>
  <td> <dtml-var ModificationDate>
  </td>
 </tr>
 <tr valign="top">
  <th align="right"> Effective Date
  </th>
  <td> <input type="text" name="effective_date"
                           value="&dtml-effectiveString;">
  </td>
  <th align="right"> Expiration Date
  </th>
  <td> <input type="text" name="expiration_date"
                           value="&dtml-expirationString;">
  </td>
 </tr>
 <tr valign="top">
  <th align="right"> Format
  </th>
  <td> <input type="text" name="format" value="&dtml-Format;">
  </td>
 </tr>
 <tr valign="top">
  <th align="right"> Language
  </th>
  <td> <input type="text" name="language" value="&dtml-Language;">
  </td>
 </tr>
 <tr valign="top">
```

Listing 5.13
Continued

```
 89:    <th align="right"> Rights
 90:    </th>
 91:    <td> <input type="text" name="rights" value="&dtml-Rights;">
 92:    </td>
 93:   </tr>
 94:   <tr valign="top">
 95:    <td> <br> </td>
 96:    <td>
 97:      <input type="submit" value=" Change ">
 98:    </td>
 99:   </tr>
100: </table>
101: </form>
102: </dtml-let>
103: </div>
104: </div>
105: <dtml-var standard_html_footer>
```

The two changes in the `full_cv_metadata_edit_form` DTML method occur in line 12, where the action again was changed to fit the new DTML methods, and in line 31 where the description field name was modified.

Now, the new type is ready to be used by the portal's members. They can add and edit objects of this type just as with any of the default CMF types.

Creating a Type with ZClasses

Most of the time, it will not be enough to just derive types from the default types. We want the new type to be more and do more than the existing ones. That is where we use ZClasses to create our own version of a portal type.

The type we will create in this section is called `TermPaper`. It is a folder-like object that can contain documents and files and nothing else. It will also have its own icon.

The type will help students better organize their term papers online by keeping unwanted objects out of the term paper folder. This is achieved by not allowing any objects other than documents and files to be added to the `TermPaper` folder.

Figure 5.32 shows the `TermPaper` type in the list of types that portal members can add to their space:

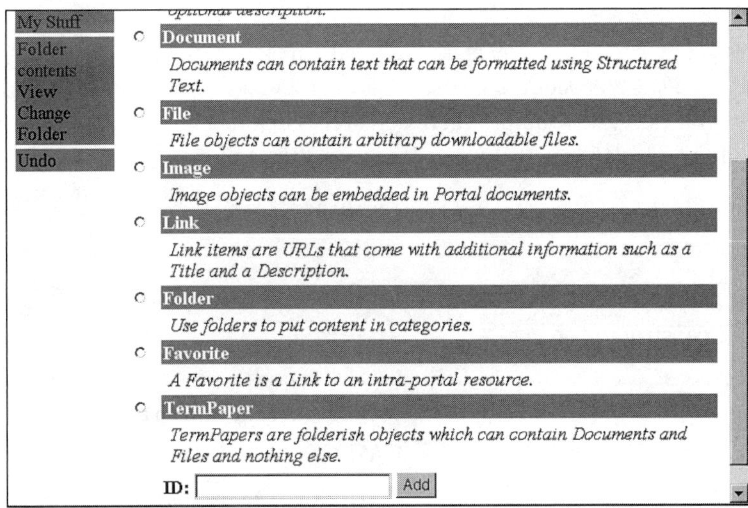

Figure 5.32
The list of types in the portal.

Figure 5.33 shows the folder of portal member `kris_k`. Kris has already added several `TermPaper` objects.

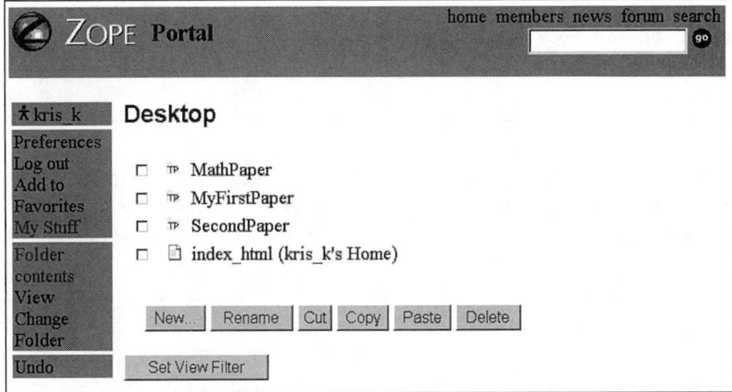

Figure 5.33
A member's folder with several `TermPaper` objects.

The first step is creating the ZClass.

Creating the ZClass

ZClasses are created in products, so we need a new product for our ZClass. Go to the `Control_Panel/Product_Management` folder and add a new product with the ID `SchoolProjects`. When the product is created, click its name in the list of products. Now add the new ZClass `TermPaperClass` with the following data:

ID:	**`TermPaperClass`**
Title:	**`<no title>`**
Meta Type:	**`TermPaper`**
Create constructor objects?	**Activated**
Base classes:	**CMF Default: `DefaultDublinCoreImpl`** **CMFCore: `PortalContent`** **CMFCore: `PortalFolder`** **CMF Default: `Document`**
Include standard Zope persistent object base classes?	Activated

> **Note**
> The order in which the base classes are selected is very important. If you change the order, the ZClass might not work or only partly work.

> **Warning**
> Base classes cannot be changed after the ZClass is created. You need to decide carefully which ZClasses you need when creating your own ZClasses. If you want your ZClass to become a portal type, you need to choose CMFCore: PortalContent as one of the base classes.

The new ZClass and its default constructor objects are created:

- `TermPaperClass`
- `TermPaperClass_add`
- `TermPaperClass_addForm`
- `TermPaperClass_addPermission`
- `TermPaperClass_Factory`

Figure 5.34 shows the Contents view of the `SchoolProjects` product with the listed objects.

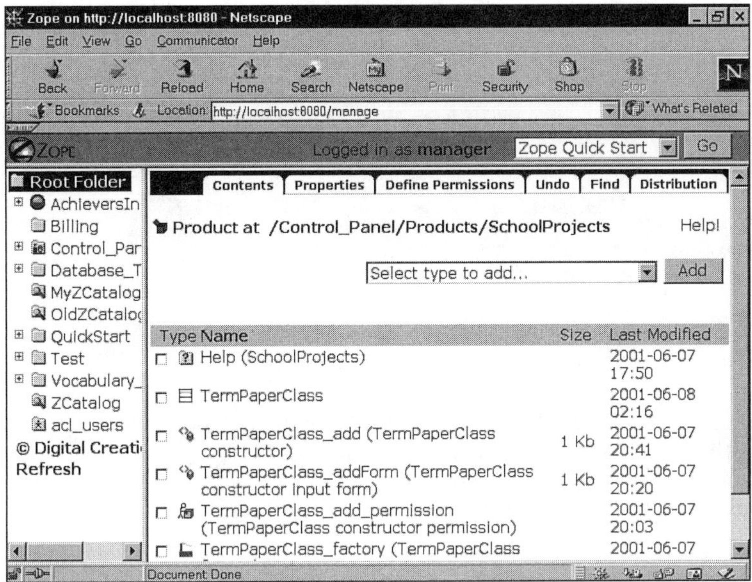

Figure 5.34

The Contents view of `SchoolProjects` *after adding the ZClass.*

The first thing we should do now is create a Python script that will be called whenever a member wants to add a `TermPaper` object. This script will create the instance of the ZClass.

Add a Python script called `addTermPaper.py` to the Contents view of the `SchoolProjects` product using the code from Listing 5.14.

Listing 5.14

`addTermPaper.py` *Python Script*

```
return context.manage_addProduct['SchoolProjects'].
➥TermPaperClass.createInObjectManager(id,context.REQUEST)
```

Figure 5.35 shows the Edit view of the `addTermPaper.py` Python script.

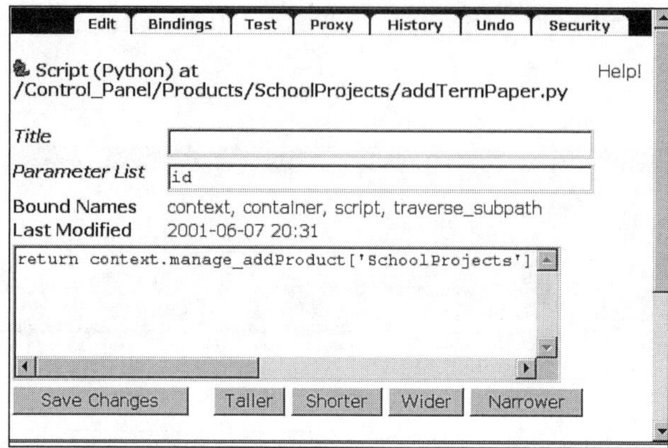

Figure 5.35
The `addTermPaper.py` *Python script.*

Now, click the `TermPaperClass` ZClass to enter the Methods view of the ZClass. We will need three DTML methods for our class:

- `editTermPaper`
- `editTermPaperForm`
- `showTermPaper`

But first, we should define the ZClass's properties. Click the Property Sheets tab and then click the Add Common Instance Property Sheet button. Enter the ID **`TermPaperClass_Properties`** and click Add.

Click the new Property Sheet to go to its Properties view (see Figure 5.36). Here you can add properties for the ZClass. In our case, we need the `Version` property. Add it as a string.

Next, we have to define one permission so that instances of the ZClass can be added as portal objects. This is done in the Define Permissions view (see Figure 5.37).

Select the permission Add Portal Content from the drop-down menu of Create Class Instances and save the changes.

Before we can create the views of the ZClass, we have to create the three DMTL methods mentioned earlier. Listings 5.15, 5.16, and 5.17 contain the three DTML methods.

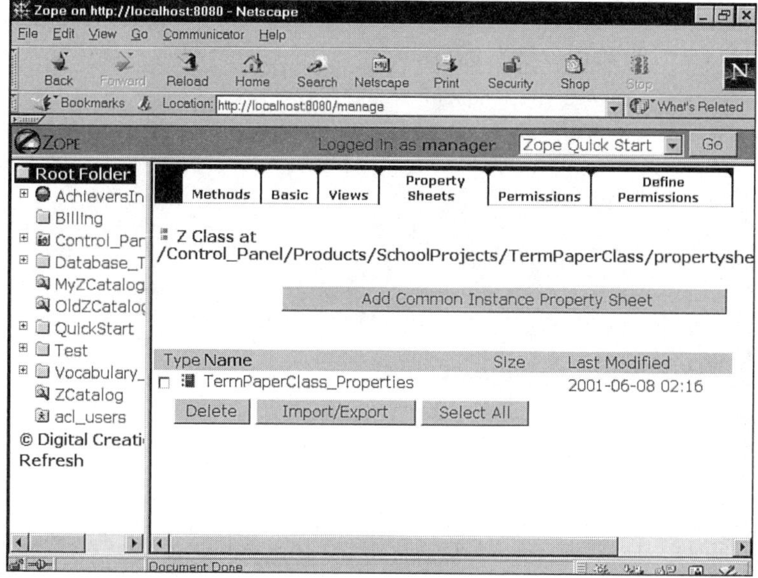

Figure 5.36

The Property Sheet for `TermPaperClass_Properties`.

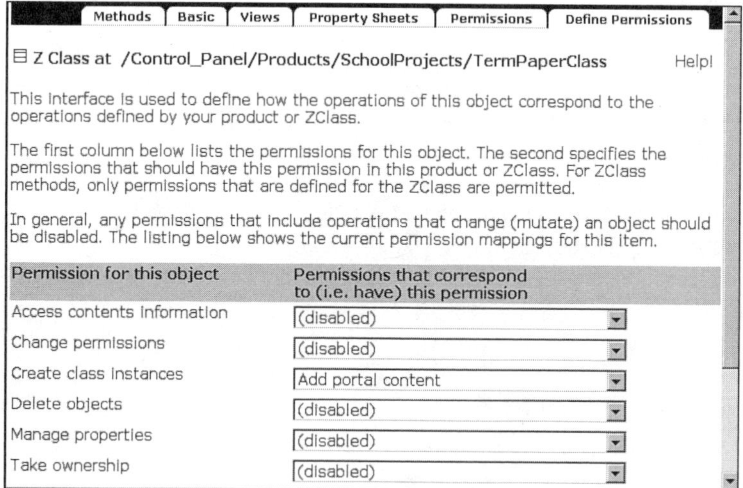

Figure 5.37

The Define Permissions view with the correct permissions.

Listing 5.15

The `editTermPaperForm` *DTML Method*

```
<dtml-var standard_html_header>
<h2><dtml-var document_title></h2>
<p>
<form action="./" method=post>
<table>
<tr>
<th>Title</th>
<td><input type=text name=title value="<dtml-var title>">
</tr>
<tr>
<th>Version:</th>
<td><input type=text name=Version value="<dtml-var Version>"></td>
</tr>
<tr>
<td><input type=submit name="editTermPaper:method" value="Save
➥Changes"></td>
</tr>
</table>
</form>
<dtml-var standard_html_footer>
```

Listing 5.16

The `editTermPaper` *DTML Method*

```
<dtml-call
➥"propertysheets.TermPaperClass_Properties.manage_changeProperties(REQUEST)">
<dtml-call "manage_changeProperties(REQUEST)">
<dtml-call indexObject>
<dtml-call "RESPONSE.redirect(URL2+'/folder_contents')">
```

Listing 5.17

The `showTermPaper` *DTML Method*

```
<dtml-var standard_html_header>
<h2><dtml-var title_or_id></h2>
<p>
This is the TermPaper <dtml-var title_or_id>. <br>
The version is <dtml-var Version>.
</p>
<dtml-var standard_html_footer>
```

The `editTermPaperForm` DTML method contains a simple form where the title and the `Version` of the instance can be edited. As you remember, `Version` is the property we defined earlier.

The form is sent to the `editTermPaper` DTML method, which changes the properties of the instance according to what was entered in the form and re-indexes the object. Then it directs the browser to the folder contents of the `TermPaper` instance.

`showTermPaper` shows the properties of the instance.

Now that we have the three DTML methods, we can create the views for the ZClass. Click the Views tab and create the views as follows:

Name:	**`View`**
Method:	**`showTermPaper`**
Help Topic:	

Name:	**`Edit`**
Method:	**`editTermPaperForm`**
Help Topic:	

Figure 5.38 shows the two views—`View` and `Edit`—as they appear in the Views view.

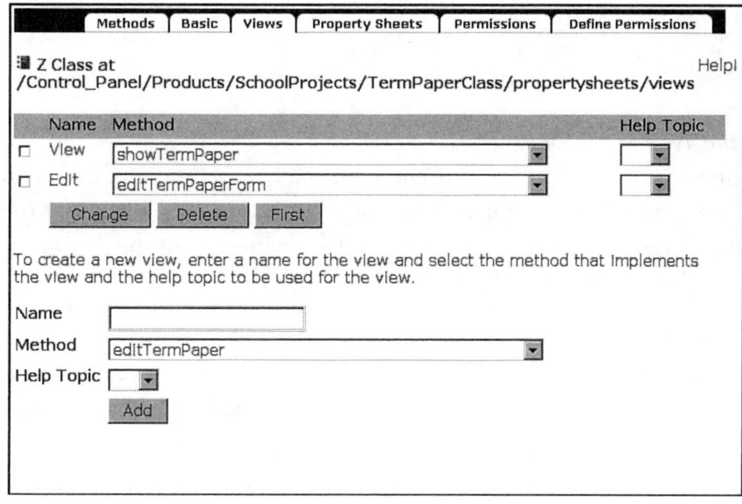

Figure 5.38

The Views view with the two defined views.

This next part is optional. To define an icon for a ZClass, you need a 16×16 GIF image. Go to the Basics view of the ZClass and click the Browse button. Select your icon image and open it. Then save the changes.

Figure 5.39 shows the Basic view with the icon that will be used for `TermPaper` objects. You can see the icon above the Icon Image text field.

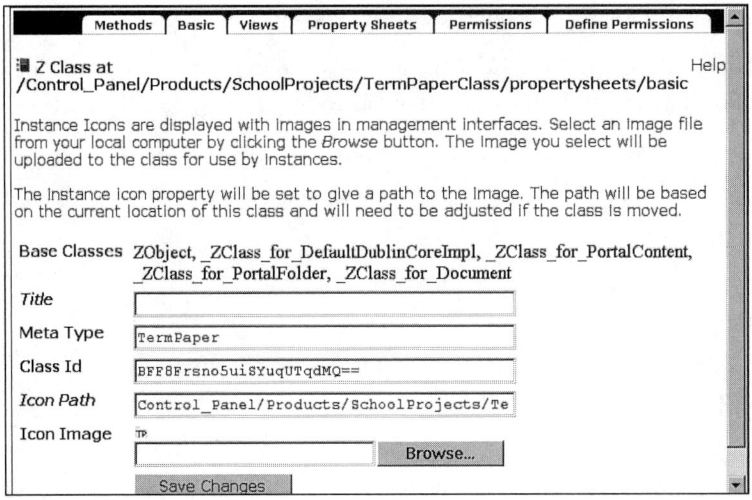

Figure 5.39
The Basic view with the ZClass's icon.

Our ZClass is finished and we can go on to linking it to a portal type.

Adding the Type

To complete the process of creating the type, we have to add a new type in the `portal_types` portal tool in the instance of the CMF in which we want to add the type. There we select Factory-Based Type Information form the drop-down menu and enter the following data:

Title:	**<no title>**
Description:	**`TermPapers are folderish objects which can contain Files and Documents.`**
Meta type:	**`TermPaper`**
Icon:	**`icon.gif`**
Product name:	**`SchoolProjects`**

Factory method in product: **addTermPaper.py**

Initial view name: **editTermPaperForm**

Filter content types? **Activated**

Allowed content types: **Documents**

Files

Allow discussion? **Deactivated**

The description will be shown under the type name in the list of types a portal member can add.

The `Meta` type used here must be the same as used in the ZClass or the instances of the ZClass will not appear in the member's folder.

Figure 5.40 shows the Properties view of the factory-based type information with the defined properties defined.

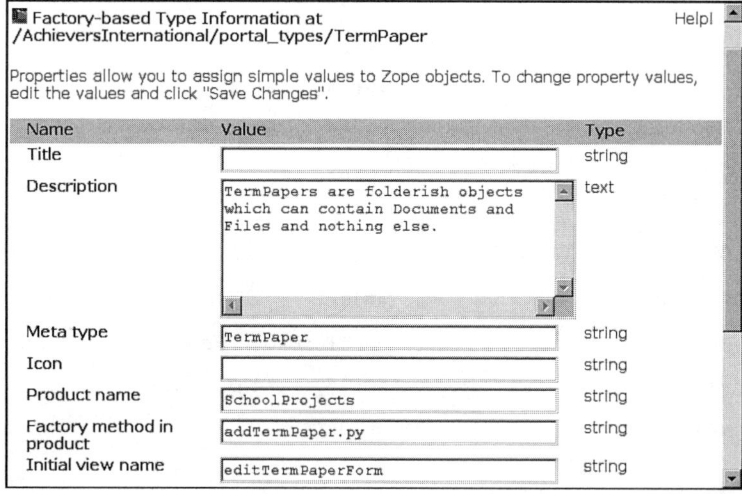

Figure 5.40

The Properties view of the factory-based type information.

The Product Name is the name of the product we defined at the very beginning and that contains our ZClass.

The Factory Method in Product is the `addTermPaper.py` Python script that adds the instance of the ZClass in the current folder.

In the Initial View Name field is the name of the DTML method in our ZClass that will be called right after the new instance of the type is created. In our case, this is `editTermPaperForm` because we have to add a value for the `Version` property.

Because `TermPaper` objects should only contain documents and files, we have to limit the allowed content types to those two types.

Next, we have to define actions for the type. The actions appear in the actions box for instances of the type. Go to the Actions view by clicking the corresponding tab and add the following actions:

Name:	**`View`**
ID:	**`view`**
Action:	**`showTermPaper`**
Permission:	**`View`**
Category:	**`object`**

Name:	**`Metadata`**
ID:	**`metadata`**
Action:	**`metadata_edit_form`**
Permission:	**`Modify portal content`**
Category:	**`object`**

Name:	**`Edit`**
ID:	**`edit`**
Action:	**`editTermPaperForm`**
Permission:	**`Modify portal content`**
Category:	**`object`**

Figure 5.41 shows the Actions view of the factory-based type information with the `View` and the `Edit` actions.

The necessary steps to create a type with ZClasses are completed and the portal members can now start adding `TermPaper` objects to their spaces.

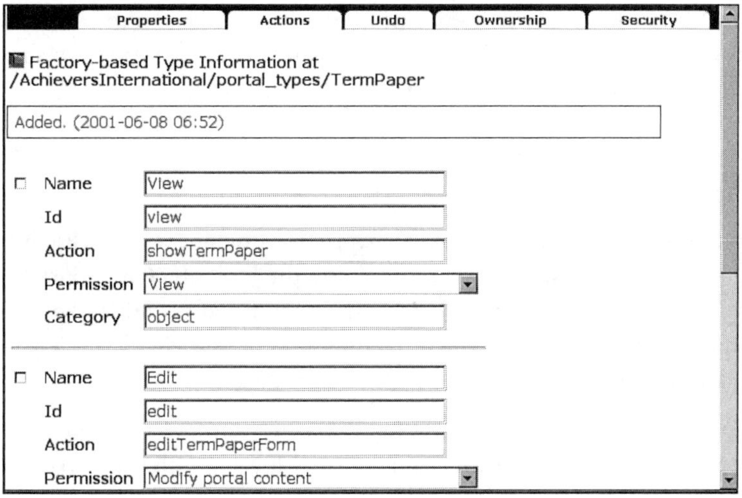

Figure 5.41

The Actions view of the factory-based type information.

Future of CMF

If you visit `http://cmf.zope.org/doc`, you will find a series of documents, such as the "Project Charter/Vision Statement," that describe the CMF and the design aspects behind its construction. Additionally, you will also find documents discussing or announcing several future features.

One of these documents, "Thoughts on different Portal designs and the CMF," describes potential features, such as ParserHandlers that would parse incoming files, such as Word or PDF documents, and extract the content and relevant metadata for indexing with Zope's built-in ZCatalog search index. Especially for long texts or visually appealing documents, such as product brochures, this is a vital feature because the ZCatalog would otherwise be blind to some of the most interesting resources available via the portal.

For some, non-technical working that stays within the Windows/Office world with which they are familiar may be ideal. For them, their user directories on the Zope server would show up simply as regular (Web) folders in their Windows Explorer.

This is possible because Zope works with Internet standards, such as FTP and WebDAV. WebDAV is gaining popularity and can already be used with recent versions of Internet Explorer, Mac OS X Finder, Eazel, and Adobe GoLive 5. Using WebDAV, portal members can simply drag-and-drop their files, with future versions of CMF taking care of the actual indexing. This will make it so much easier to share information with people on the Internet or their intranets.

Summary

This chapter explained the Content Management Framework (CMF) and showed its various features. It also showed how to modify the look of a CMF portal by changing the existing skin or creating new skins. It then explained how new types are added so that portal members can add types of content other than what is already available with the standard CMF.

The next chapter will introduce the MetaPublisher, another free Zope product. The version used in that chapter is especially created for use with the CMF.

CHAPTER 6

THE METAPUBLISHER

MetaPublisher is a complex and powerful tool that helps you integrate skillful Web applications into your Web site. The product is written by beehive's programmers Sebastian Lühnsdorf and Alexander Schad.

With a single MetaPublisher instance, you can easily create a guest book, picture books, or any other application dealing with input data. Data can be stored in relational databases as well as in the file system and the OFS.

Introduction

In the previous chapters, you learned how to use Zope together with relational databases, and we showed you how to set up a simple message board application using ZClasses.

This chapter will illustrate the use of beehive's MetaPublisher product with all the specifics.

You will learn the basics first—how to install MetaPublisher on your Zope server and how to add a MetaPublisher instance via the Management screen.

Then we will show you how to use MetaPublisher. You will get to know MetaPublisher's interfaces, and you will learn how to create an application step by step. Thus, you will create a simple feedback application.

The next section will illustrate the advanced use of MetaPublisher. We will show you how to optimize the results of your work. Thus, we will introduce you to some useful MetaPublisher methods.

MetaPublisher supports database storage and there is a section that will deal exclusively with that topic.

The final section of this chapter will describe how MetaPublisher can be used with the CMF. First, we will show you how to set up a MetaPublisher portal type. Then you will learn how to use MetaPublisher and CMF together.

Preparations

MetaPublisher is a Zope product and so it needs to be installed as such to work properly. The installation process works as easy as with any other Zope product. The following sections cover the installation process.

Downloading MetaPublisher

The latest downloadable version of MetaPublisher can be found at `www.beehive.de`. The MetaPublisher downloading area can be found at `http://www.beehive.de/zope/freeware/metapublisher.html`.

There are various MetaPublisher versions ready to download. The latest versions won't work with all Zope servers. The download section contains information about which MetaPublisher version works with which Zope server, so you can choose the installation file that meets your needs. We will work with MetaPublisher version 1.2.4 in this book.

Download the product file. It comes as a .zip file or a .tar file (e.g. `MetaPublisher_124.zip`) that needs to be unpacked.

Unpacking the Product File

Depending on your operating system, there are different ways to unpack the product file.

On Windows systems, use WinZip or WinRAR. Give the path of your Zope server as destination path and activate the Use Folder Names options. WinZip will then unpack the MetaPublisher files into the new MetaPublisher product folder.

On Linux systems, use `tar` to unpack the MetaPublisher product files.

Restarting Your Zope Server

The last step is to restart your Zope server. Simply execute the `start.bat` file on Windows systems, or run the `start` script on Linux systems.

Zope will then initiate the MetaPublisher product and two options are added to Zope's available options menu (see Figure 6.1):

- MetaEntry
- MetaPublisher

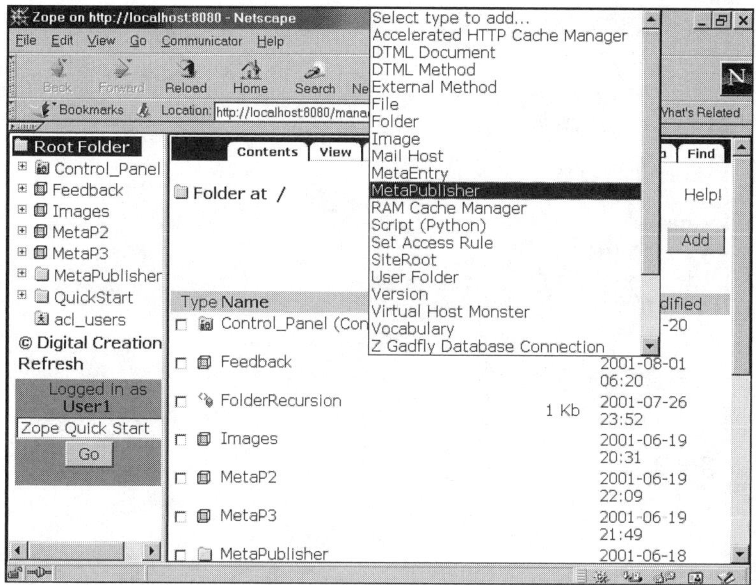

Figure 6.1

Two new Meta types come with MetaPublisher.

Using MetaPublisher

MetaPublisher is a powerful tool with a lot of features and advantages, but handling MetaPublisher is quite complex. We suggest you read this chapter in its original order—first learning the basics of MetaPublisher and later you will be introduced to its advanced features.

Goals and Preconditions

MetaPublisher can be used effectively to deal with user input. It is a powerful tool for administrating and maintaining data that has been received from visitors of a Web site. Consequently, you need to think about the kind of data you want to receive.

What Do We Want MetaPublisher to Do?

In our case, we want to add a feedback functionality to our Web site where our users can give us some information that we want to use for statistical purposes and Web site improvement. See Figure 6.2 for a first impression of the feedback Web page we want to create.

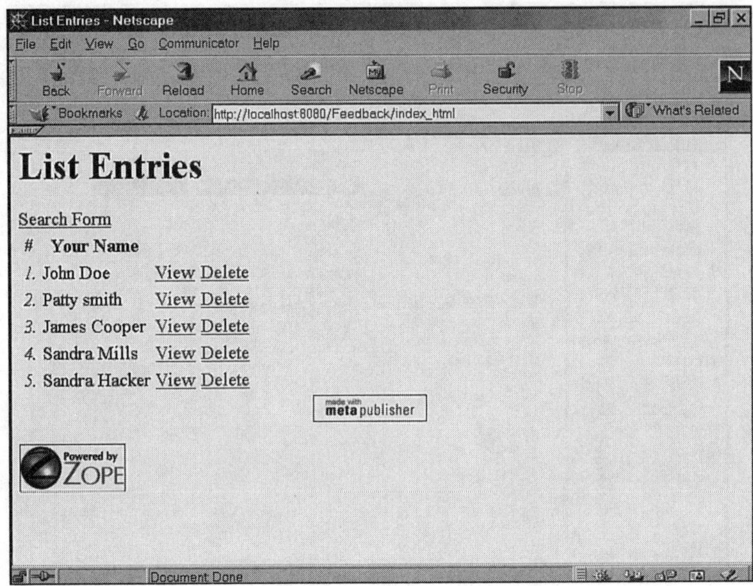

Figure 6.2

At the end of this section, you will have created a feedback function.

You may be familiar with these forms from certain Web sites where you can download programs but have to give some personal information first.

The information we want MetaPublisher to handle is as follows:

- Name
- Gender
- Age
- How did you get to know us?
- Comments

Forms and Input Fields

MetaPublisher uses forms to receive user input. These forms will contain several types of input fields, such as radio buttons or text area fields. You may certainly know these fields from HTML.

As all these fields are designed to obtain certain tasks, we also need to think about the kind of data that is concerned with each input field. We will discuss this topic in detail in the "Field Types" section, later in this chapter.

Functions and Interfaces

MetaPublisher doesn't only collect data, it offers functions to administrate information as well. You can add, edit, delete, and search data with MetaPublisher. These functions are organized using certain interfaces, and you have to think about which functions and interfaces will be useful for your purposes.

Our feedback Web page form will definitely need an interface where our users can type their information into certain input fields.

But we certainly won't need an interface where the data can be edited, because we don't want the users to alter any modification, and we do not want to modify any user input as well. See Figure 6.3 for a screenshot of the view interface where you can actually view the data an user has entered.

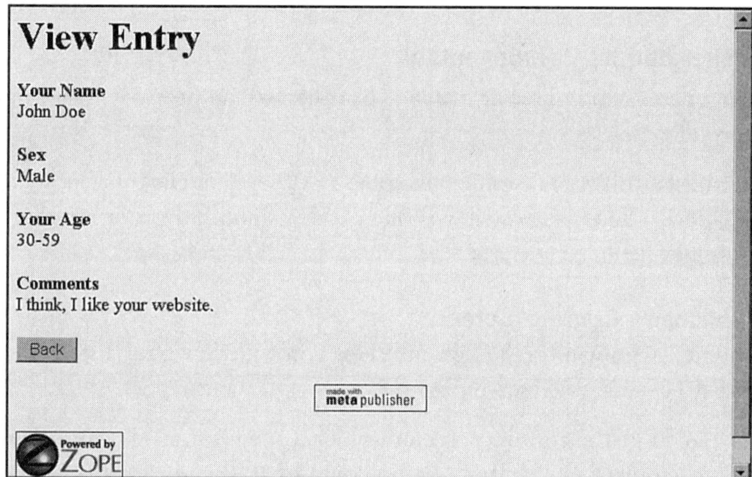

Figure 6.3

The view interface where you can see the data a user has entered.

General Steps

MetaPublisher can be used for numerous tasks and purposes. But there are five general steps you should follow when working with this product:

1. Create a new MetaPublisher instance.
2. Configure MetaPublisher.
3. Create the needed interfaces.
4. Adapt and optimize.
5. Link MetaPublisher to your Web site.

We will now introduce you to the basic usage of MetaPublisher and to all its interfaces.

Creating a New MetaPublisher Instance

Creating a MetaPublisher instance works just the same as with any other Zope product.

First, you need to choose MetaPublisher from the Available Objects menu and then you have to give an ID. During this chapter, we will use the ID `Feedback`.

There will be two more options for you to set—Presets and Storage. Please ignore those fields for now. We will discuss Presets and Data Storage later in this book.

If you need a more detailed description of how to set up a new MetaPublisher instance, see the "Creating a Feedback Web Page," section later in this book.

MetaPublisher and Its Components

Now that a new MetaPublisher instance has been set up properly, you can click its ID in the second view.

A MetaPublisher object is a folder-like object. When you click its ID, you enter its Contents view. The Contents view is one of MetaPublisher's user interfaces. The next sections will explain each interface.

MetaPublisher's Content Screen

The content screen will be the first interface you will view after a new MetaPublisher instance has been created (see Figure 6.4).

It works much like the content screen of older Zope versions. Because MetaPublisher is a folder-like object, the content screen contains all the objects that are stored inside that certain MetaPublisher. Moreover, you can see most of the usual features and some additional features as follows:

- *Available Objects*—This drop-down menu allows you to add any object that has been installed properly on your Zope server. Simply choose one option from the menu and click the Add button. The newly added object will then appear in the content screen as well.

- *Export Objects*—This drop-down menu enables you to import Zope objects. These objects must be contained in the import folder of the appropriate Zope installation. Those objects will then appear inside the export objects menu as options. All you need to do is choose one of the export files that are shown within the menu and click the Add button. The object will then be imported into the MetaPublisher folder.

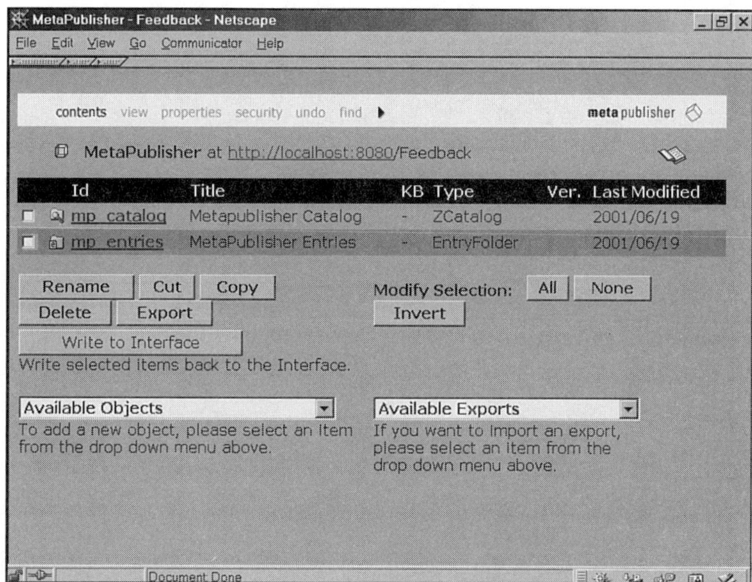

Figure 6.4

The content screen of our feedback MetaPublisher.

> **Note**
> Consider that you have to choose an object you want to import from the Export Objects menu.

- *Path information*—The path information shows a level trail from your Zope server's root folder to the object with which you are currently working. The path's single components are links so that you can easily navigate through the objects of your Zope server.
- *Contents Table*—Here you can see a list of the objects that are stored in the MetaPublisher. Each object is shown with information about its size, modification time, title, ID, and meta type. You can access an object by clicking its ID link in the table.
- *MetaPublisher Toolbar*—You can see the MetaPublisher Toolbar on the top of each MetaPublisher interface. It contains most of the tab options from the Zope Management screen and links to MetaPublisher's interfaces (see Figure 6.5).

Figure 6.5
The toolbar can be found on top of each MetaPublisher screen.

Note the small arrow on the right side of the toolbar. Clicking the arrow will take you to the Entries view. You will find more tab options in the toolbar there.

- *Delete, Rename, Cut, Copy, Export*—These are the buttons you already know from the usual Zope Management screen. Choose an object from the list by activating its check box, and than you can use these buttons to delete, rename, cut, copy, and export it.
- *Modify Selection*—These three buttons come in handy when you want to apply actions to several objects instead of only one.
    - *All*—The check box of each object in the content screen is activated.
    - *None*—Deactivates each of the check boxes that have been checked before. In the end, no check box will be activated.
    - *Invert*—Inverts the current selection of objects. That means that formerly activated check boxes become unchecked, whereas unchecked objects will become checked.
- *Write to interface*—This button is used to write the objects from the Contents view into the Interface view. Thus, the objects that have been edited and stored in the content screen can be stored in a preset. We will deal with this topic in the "Presets" section later in this chapter.

The first time you enter a MetaPublisher instance, the MetaPublisher folder will be empty except for the following two objects (refer to Figure 6.4):

- `mp_catalog` (ZCatalog)—The ZCatalog instance is used to provide searching capabilities.
- `mp_entries` (Entry Folder)—This folder will contain the so-called MetaPublisher entries.

The View Tab

The View tab can be found in the toolbar right beside the Contents tab. Click this tab, and Zope will try to show the `index_html` that is next on the acquisition path.

To view objects other than the `index_html`, click the object's link in the Contents view, the same as you've used in the Zope interface. Depending on the chosen object, several views will be shown.

Metapublisher's Properties View

There is no difference between MetaPublisher's Properties view and the Properties view in the usual Zope Management screen (see Figure 6.6).

In the Properties interface, you can set, edit, and delete properties for the current MetaPublisher.

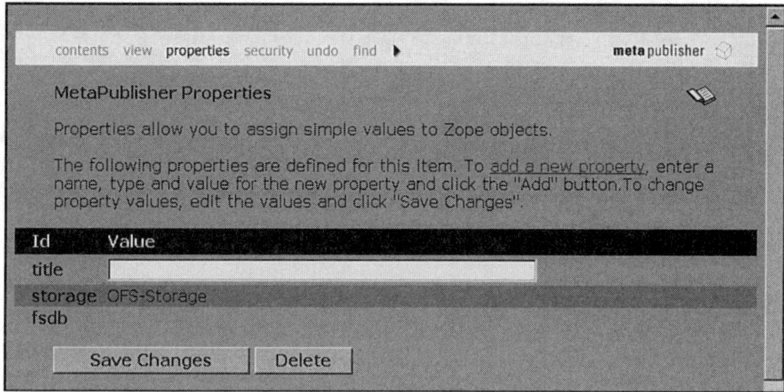

Figure 6.6

The Properties view works as usual.

The Security Interface

After you have clicked the Security tab (see Figure 6.7), you will see the familiar security interface where you can define security settings for the current MetaPublisher, as well as its ownership settings. You can also assign local roles to specified users as usual.

Undo

The undo interface enables you to undo transactions that have been done to the Zope database.

Undoable transactions are shown in a table, each transaction with a check box to its left. To undo a certain transaction, simply activate its check box and then click the Undo button.

MetaPublisher's undo interface (see Figure 6.8) works exactly as the undo function you already know from the management interface.

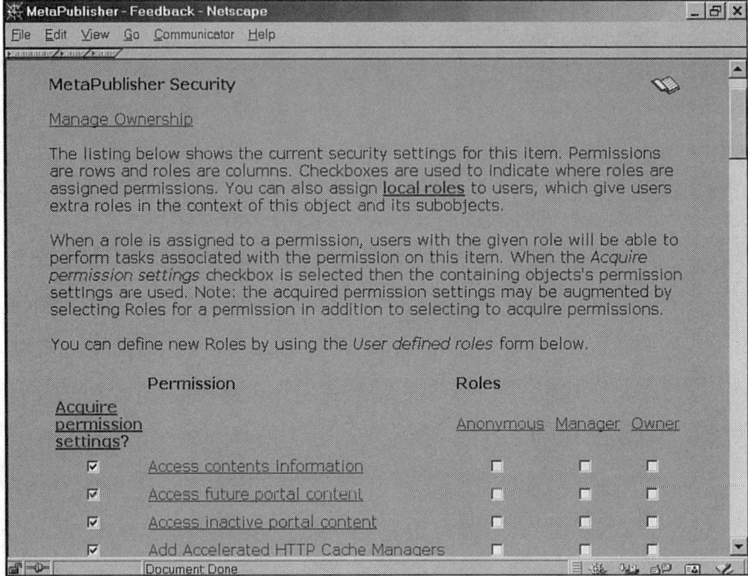

Figure 6.7

The security interface works exactly as in the usual Zope management interface.

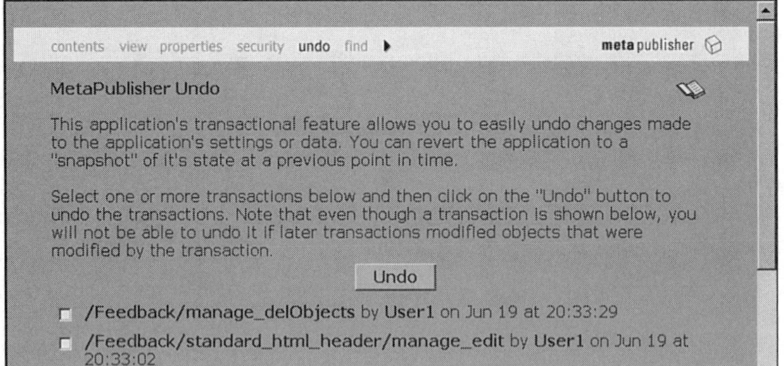

Figure 6.8

Transactions can be undone here.

> **Note**
>
> Your Undo view might look different than Figure 6.8—probably because you simply don't have any actions yet that can be undone. In that case, you are shown the following message: There are no transactions that can be undone.

MetaPublisher's Find Interface

This interface facilitates the search for Zope objects. This feature works like the Find tab of the usual management interface.

MetaPublisher's find interface combines a simple search for object IDs with an advanced search. Thus, the interface consists of two sections (see Figure 6.9).

The first section enables you to search for objects with the object's ID as the only search option.

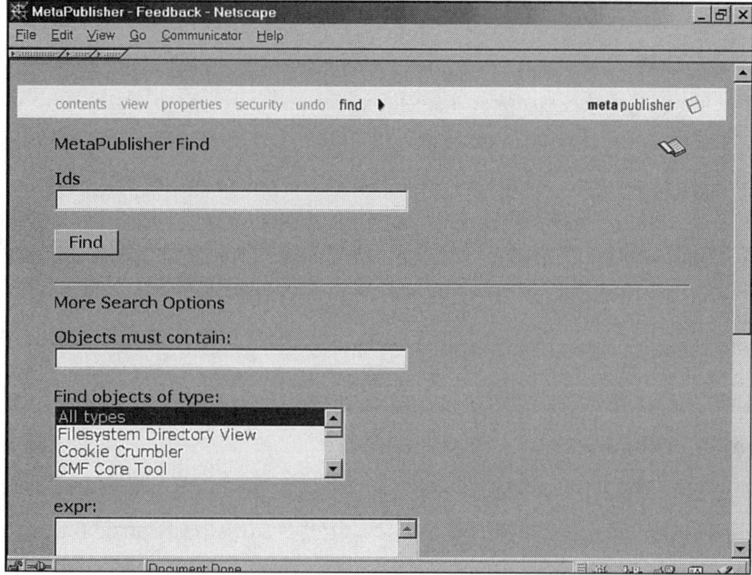

Figure 6.9

On top of the find interface, you will find a simple search function.

Simply enter the ID of the object you are looking for in the text field and then click the Find button.

MetaPublisher's find function will then search for any objects with the given ID, but in the current MetaPublisher folder exclusively.

> **Note**
> Please notice that you have to enter an exact ID because a partial ID search is not possible.

Objects that are found will be displayed directly under the Find button (see Figure 6.10).

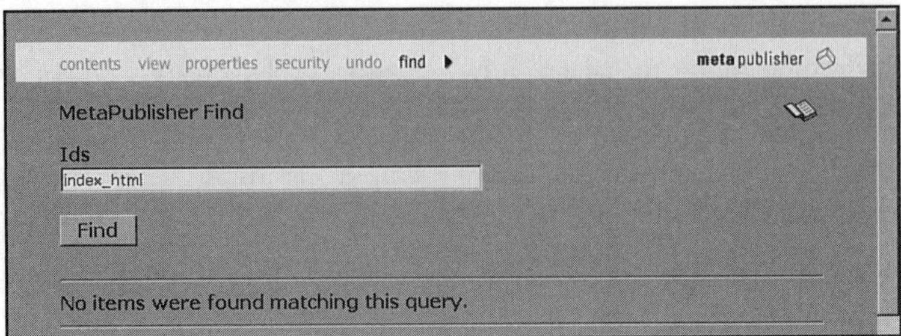

Figure 6.10
The current MetaPublisher doesn't contain an `index_html` *object.*

Below the simple search, you can see the advanced search options where you can search for objects by giving several parameters. This will help to optimize your search results.

- *Objects must contain*—Here you can state a phrase or a word that is contained in the requested object. Zope will search through text only; properties and the like are not overlooked.
- *Find objects of type*—A multiple selection box is given where you can choose from a list of meta types. Only objects of the chosen type are searched through. On Windows systems, you can choose various options by holding down the Ctrl key while clicking.
- *expr*—Type a valid DTML expression into the text area field. Only objects in whose context the evaluation of the stated expression returns true are searched. Others are rejected.
- *modified*—Here you can set a specific time period in which an object must have been modified to be found. At first you need to decide if objects have been modified before or after a certain time. Finally, simply enter a date into the text field beside the selection list. The entered date must be one of the following formats:

  YYYY/MM/DD hh:mm:ss

  YYYY-MM-DD, or hh:mm
- *where the roles*—A multiple selection list is given where you can choose the roles you want to be connected with the requested objects.
- *have permission*—Here you can choose from a list of roles you want to be associated with the object for which you are looking.

- *Search only in this folder*—Check this radio button if you want to restrict the search to the current folder.
- *Search all subfolders*—Check this radio button and the current folder, as well as all its subfolders, are searched.

After you have given all necessary parameters, you need to click the Find button to start the search (see Figure 6.11).

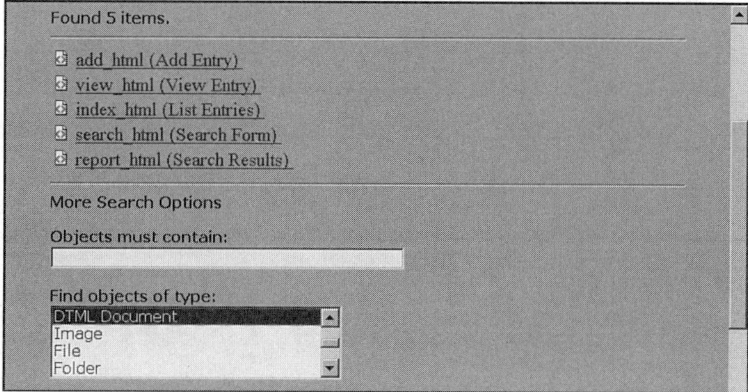

Figure 6.11
The result of the current advanced search is five items.

In the upper section, you can see the result of a search where the advanced search options have been used. In this example, we searched through all subfolders of the current folder to look for all objects with the `Meta` type DTML Document.

> **Note**
> MetaPublisher's find interface will search through the objects inside the current MetaPublisher exclusively.

The Configuration Interface

This interface is used to configure the current MetaPublisher. Here, you have to define the composition of the `mp_entries` in the configuration interface, the skeleton of the coming MetaPublisher application.

Remember our Feedback example? We want to give the users of our imaginary Web site the possibility to give us some feedback and information about themselves. For example, we wanted to know their names and their e-mail addresses. In the configuration form, we need to think about the input type of each piece of information we want to receive. Each of those "pieces," such as an e-mail address, is represented by one single entry field, so we need to choose the correct field types for each entry and these are created in the configuration interface (see Figure 6.12).

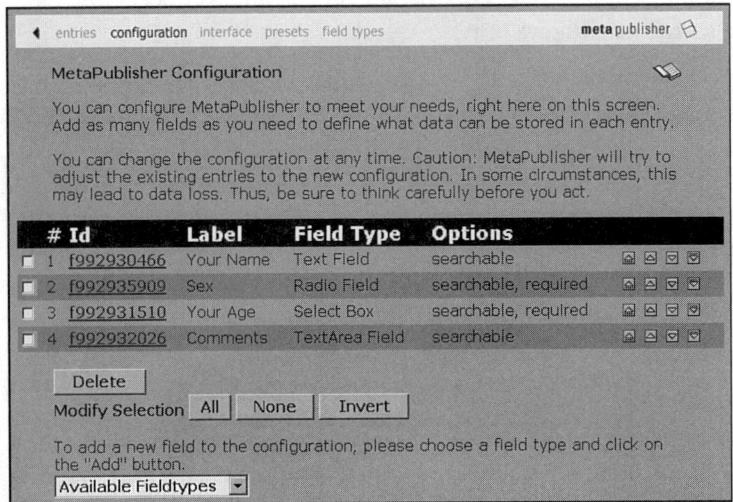

Figure 6.12
The configuration interface.

> **Note**
> Figure 6.12 might look slightly different than the view you can see on your computer because you might not have started to work with this view.

All the field types you can use are listed in the Available Fieldtypes menu. Simply choose a field type from the selection list and click the Add button. You then have to define the layout of the input field. The layout interface depends on the chosen field type, and we will give an overview of all available field types at the end of this section.

Entry fields that have already been configured are listed in a table on top of the configuration form. With the check boxes and the Delete button, you can remove entry fields. The entry field table gives some more information:

- *ID*—Each entry field needs a unique ID that is used to identify the entry field in the Zope database.

- *Label*—This is a short and significant description of the current field.
- *Fieldtype*—The field type of the current field.
- *Options*—The options that are associated with the entry field.

The buttons at the right of the entry field table help you arrange the entry fields (see Figure 6.13). The fields will appear in the user forms later in the same sequence as in the table.

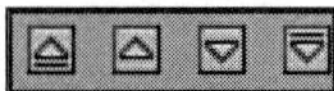

Figure 6.13
The button block.

- The leftmost button moves the current item to the top of the list.
- The second button moves the current item one position upward.
- The third button moves the current item one position downward.
- The rightmost button moves the current item to the bottom of the list.

The following are the field types that are currently supported by MetaPublisher:

- Date Field
- Email Field
- File Field
- Float Field
- Integer Field
- Image Field
- Select Box
- Radio Field
- Text Field
- Textarea Field

> **Note**
> Which of these field types are actually provided depends on the storage you have chosen. For example, images cannot be stored in a Gadfly database.
>
> Experienced users are able to create their own field types. See the "Defining New Field Types" section, later in this chapter, for details.

We will give detailed descriptions of each field type in the "Field Types" section later in this chapter.

The Entries Interface

This interface shows all the MetaPublisher entries administered by the current MetaPublisher. They are shown in a table (see Figure 6.14).

MetaPublisher entries contain the data of the MetaPublisher. One MP_`entry` corresponds to one data record in a database. The skeleton of the actual data is created in the Configuration view.

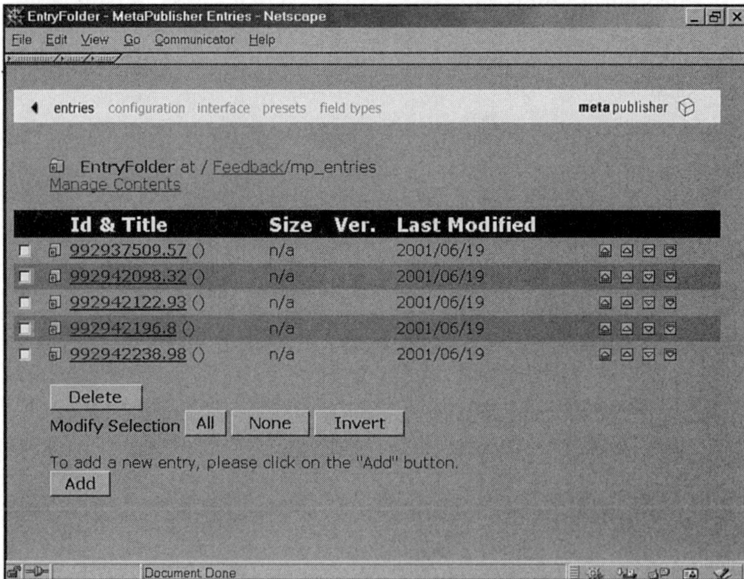

Figure 6.14
MetaPublisher entries are listed in a table.

Each MP_`entry` is listed with information about its size and time of modification. Similar to the contents interface, each table item has a check box at its side, but there is only one action you can apply to them—you can delete `MP_entries`.

Click the Delete button and each MP_entry that has been marked will be deleted and, thus, removed from the MP_entry table. The deletion of MP_entries can be undone. Simply use the Undo view for that purpose.

The four buttons on the right of each MP_entry can be used to alter the sequencing of the entries.

Click the Add button to add a new MP_entry. After clicking the button, you will see an interface that contains a form where you can enter all necessary data for an MP_entry. This Add form depends on the configuration of the current MetaPublisher.

You can get to the entries interview alternatively by clicking the MP_Entries folder within the Contents view.

> **Note**
> You cannot view the entries interface when the MP_Entries folder is empty. You are then directed to the configuration interface.

The MetaPublisher Interface Maker

The MetaPublisher application does not only need configured entry fields but various user interfaces, so that a user can actually work with the application.

Remember the mp_entries interface? You already know that there is an Add button that directs you to a form where you can type in all necessary data for a single mp_entry. After the MetaPublisher instance has been configured, you can access that interface. It simply shows all the entry fields that have been configured. Figures 6.15 and 6.16 show a form that consists of two parts. The first one contains basic information about the entry itself, where you are given the possibility to edit ID and Title of an entry. An entry's ID is auto-generated by default, using the system time to provide a unique value. Thus, we recommend you not change that value.

The second part of the add interface contains the previously configured entry fields. Here you can enter the actual data for your entry.

This form can be accessed by you and any other user who is given the permissions to modify a MetaPublisher instance. The user of a Web site (probably with the role of Anonymous User), who is actually supposed to give some information, certainly does not have those permissions.

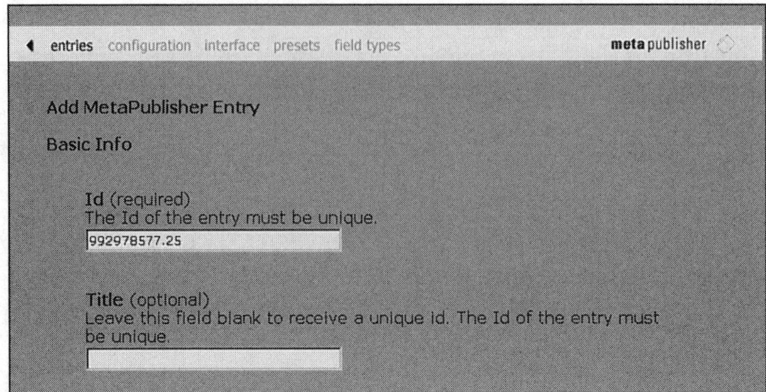

Figure 6.15
You may edit Title and ID of the new `mp_entry`.

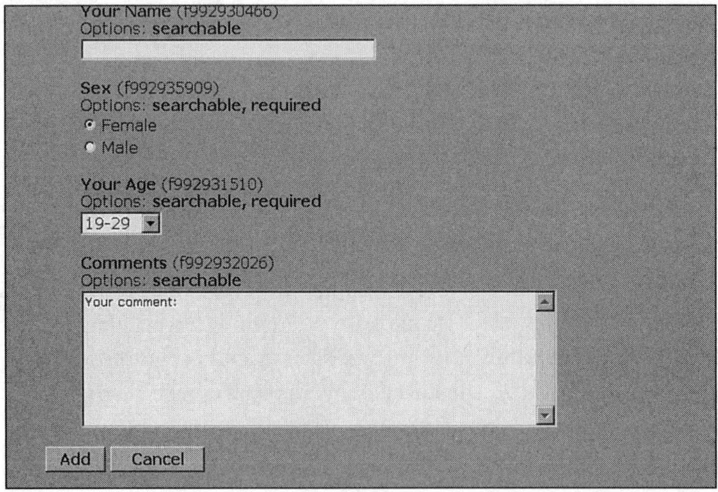

Figure 6.16
Fill in the data and click the Add button to add a new `mp_entry`.

So we need a form where users can type in their feedback data. Moreover, we will need an interface where the feedback entries are listed; we need a searching interface and so on. All that is organized within the Interface view (see Figure 6.17).

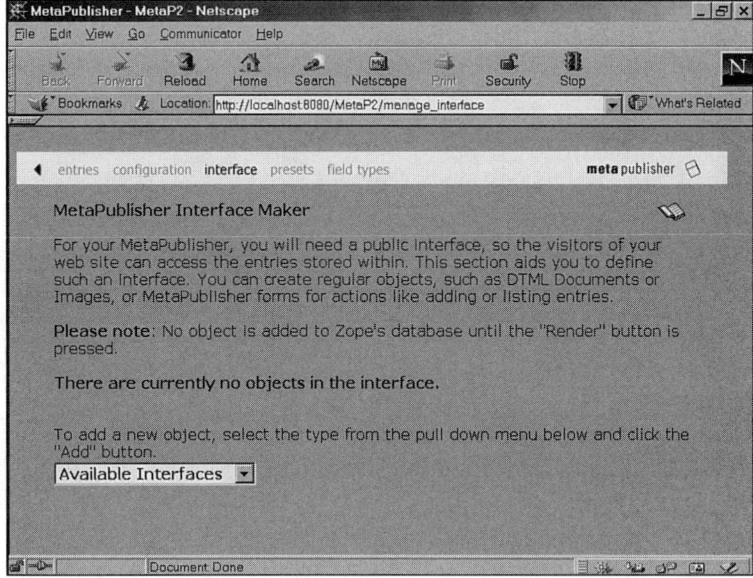

Figure 6.17
Here you can set up the necessary interfaces.

There are three steps to set up a MetaPublisher interface:

1. Select a certain interface from the list of supported interfaces.
2. Configure the interface so that it meets your needs.
3. Render the interface.

> **Note**
> If there are no fields in the configuration, you are automatically redirected to the configuration interface.

Supported MetaPublisher Interfaces

The following interfaces are currently supported by MetaPublisher:

- Add Entry Form
- Edit Entry Form
- List Entry Form
- View Entry Form

- Search Form
- Report Form
- Image
- File
- Document
- Method

Next, we will present each currently available interface and we explain their options in detail.

To illustrate the use of the aforementioned interfaces, we will use a simple MetaPublisher configuration as follows (see Table 6.1):

Table 6.1

Our Example Configuration

Label	Field Type	Options
Name	Text Field	searchable, required
Sex	Radio Field	searchable, required

Add Entry Form This form will be used with almost any MetaPublisher. It codes the form that is used to receive the requested information. Users will enter their data here.

You have to configure the form before it will be created:

- Basic Information:
  - *ID*—Define a unique ID for the interface; the default value is `add_html`.
  - *Title*—This field is optional. You can give a title to describe the interface.
- Options:
  - *Object*—Here you can decide whether you want the interface to be created as a DTML method or a DTML document.
  - *Security*—The multiple selection list contains the roles you can associate with the current interface. Hold down the Ctrl key on Windows systems to select more than one option. The default roles are `manager` and `owner`.

- Links:
    - *Add Method*—Choose the method where the user will be directed after the Add button has been clicked. Either choose a method from the Select list or check the other radio button and type in the ID of another method.
    - *Cancel*—Choose the method where the user will be directed after the Cancel button has been clicked. Simply type the ID into the text field. The default value is `index_html`.
- Layout:
    - *Header*—You can define a header for your interface using DTML and HTML code. The default header is as follows:

      ```
      <dtml-var standard_html_header>
      <h1><dtml-var title_or_id></h1>
      ```

    - *Footer*—You can define a footer for your interface using DTML and HTML code. The default footer is as follows:

      ```
      <dtml-var standard_html_footer>
      ```

- Fields—In this section, you will see each entry field you have configured before. Beneath each entry field's ID is a selection list where you can choose from various rendering options. These options depend on the relating field type.

  Look at the section called "Field Types" where you will find a general survey showing the rendering options for each field type.

Interfaces need to be rendered. With that, the actual DTML object is created that will then contain the appropriate DTML code. You can then look at that code when you go to the Contents view and click the object's ID inside the Contents table.

The result of the add interface, after it has been rendered, depends on the configuration that has taken place before. Look at the source code in Listing 6.1. We will explain how the configuration has affected the object's implementation beneath the code listing.

For the example interface, we used the default values and we activated the `Anonymous` role in the security section.

Listing 6.1

add_html

```
1: <dtml-var standard_html_header>
2: <h1><dtml-var title_or_id></h1>
3: <form action="./" method="post" enctype="multipart/form-data">
4: <input type="hidden" name="id" value="<dtml-var "get_time()">">
5: <b>Name</b><br>
6: <input type="text" name="f992827178:required" size="50" maxlength="250"
➥value="">
7: <p>
8: <b>Sex</b><br>
9: <select name="f992827209:required" size="1"><option selected>Female<option
➥>Male</select>
10: <p>
11: <input type="hidden" name="action" value="index_html">
12: <input type="submit" name="addEntry:method" value=" Add ">
13: <input type="submit" name="index_html:method" value=" Cancel ">
14: </form>
15: <div align="center"><img src="<dtml-var "REQUEST['SCRIPT_NAME']">
➥/misc_/MetaPublisher/made_with" alt="MetaPublisher" align="center"></div>
16: <dtml-var standard_html_footer>
```

- *Lines 1 and 2*—The code of the object's header as it has been defined in the layout section.
- *Line 4*—The `get_time` method is used to create a unique ID for the new `mp_entry` that is about to be added.
- *Lines 5 and 6*—The entry field for Name is created.
- *Lines 8 and 9*—The radio buttons for the Sex field are created.
- *Line 11*—This line of code causes the redirection to `index_html` after an entry has been added.
- *Line 12*—Creates the Add button and calls the `addEntry` method so that the `mp_entry` can eventually be created.
- *Line 13*—Creates the Cancel button that will redirect the user to the `index_html`.
- *Line 15*—Inserts the MetaPublisher logo.
- *Line 16*—Contains the code for the object's footer as it was defined in the layout section.

Figure 6.18 shows `add_html` as it can be seen via the third view.

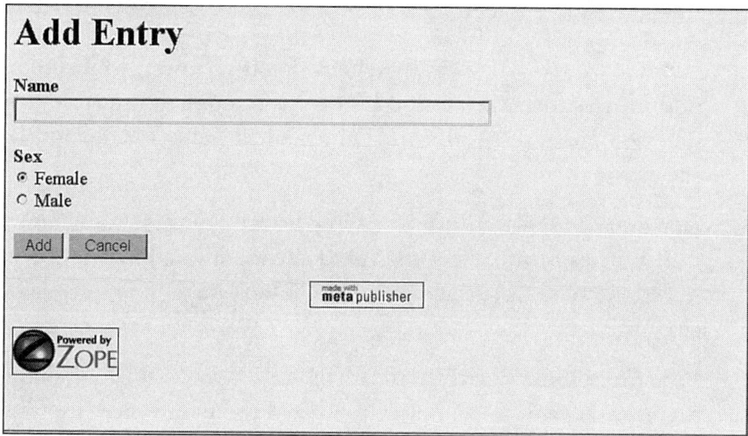

Figure 6.18
A simple form for user input.

List Entries Form This interface provides a survey of all entries that have been added to the current MetaPublisher instance. Configuring this interface is slightly more complex, because there are several links you might want to show or hide, and you have to decide what parts of the entries' information you want to be shown onscreen.

- Basic Information:
  - *ID*—Define a unique ID for the interface; the default value is `index_html`.
  - *Title*—This field is optional. You can give a title to describe the interface.
- Options:
  - *Security*—The multiple selection list contains the roles you can associate with the current interface. Hold down the Ctrl key on Windows systems to select more than one option. The default roles are `manager` and `owner`.
  - *Object*—Here you can decide whether you want the interface to be created as a DTML method or a DTML document.

    The selection list provides three options—Table, Ordered List, and Unordered List. That means you need to choose the way in which your data is to be represented. Choose Table to arrange the `mp_entries` in a simple HTML table, or choose Unordered or Ordered List to arrange the `mp_entries` in lists as created by the `<ul>` or `<ol>` HTML tags, respectively.
  - *Batches*—Activate the check box and the `mp_entries` are shown in batches of a specified size rather than in one very large list. You can specify the batch size in the text field.

- Links:
    - *Add Entry Link*—Activate the check box if you want to include a link to the Add Entries form. Select the ID of the mentioned interface from the selection menu or specify an ID in the text field. The default ID is `add_html`.
    - *Edit Entry Link*—Activate the check box if you want to include a link to the Edit Entries form. Select the ID of the mentioned interface from the selection menu or specify an ID in the text field. The default ID is `edit_html`.
    - *View Entry Link*—Activate the check box if you want to include a link to the View Entries form. Select the ID of the mentioned interface from the selection menu or specify an ID in the text field. The default ID is `view_html`.
    - *Search Form Link*—Activate the check box if you want to include a link to the Search form. Select the ID of the mentioned interface from the selection menu or specify an ID in the text field. The default ID is `search_html`.
    - *Delete Entry Link*—Activate this check box and a link will appear beside each `mp_entry` that, when clicked, deletes the entry.
- Layout:
    - *Header*—You can define a header for your interface using DTML and HTML code. The default header is as follows:

```
<dtml-var standard_html_header>
<h1><dtml-var title_or_id></h1>
```

    - *Footer*—You can define a footer for your interface using DTML and HTML code. The default footer is as follows:

```
<dtml-var standard_html_footer>
```

- Fields—In this section, you will see each entry field you have configured before. Beneath each entry field's ID will be a selection list where you can choose from various rendering options. These options depend on the relating field type.

  Look at the section called "Field Types" where you will find a general survey showing the rendering options for each field type.

Listing 6.2 shows the source code of the rendered `index_html`. Explanations can be found directly following the listing.

Listing 6.2

index_html

```
 1: <dtml-var standard_html_header>
 2: <h1><dtml-var title_or_id></h1>
 3: <a href="add_html">Add New Entry</a><br>
 4: <a href="search_html">Search Form</a><br>
 5: <table>
 6: <tr>
 7: <th><em>#</em></th>
 8: <th>Name</th>
 9: </tr>
10: <dtml-in entryIds>
11: <tr>
12: <td><em><dtml-var sequence-number>.</em></td>
13: <td><dtml-var "mp_entries.getEntryField(_['sequence-
➥item'],'f992827178')"></td>
14: <td><a href="view_html?key=<dtml-var sequence-item>">View</a></td>
15: <td><a href="edit_html?key=<dtml-var sequence-item>">Edit</a></td>
16: <td><a href="delEntry?key=<dtml-var sequence-item>">Delete</a></td>
17: </tr></dtml-in>
18: </table>
19: <div align="center"><img src="<dtml-var "REQUEST['SCRIPT_NAME']">
➥/misc_/MetaPublisher/made_with" alt="MetaPublisher" align="center"></div>
20: <dtml-var standard_html_footer>
```

- *Lines 1 and 2*—The code of the object's header as it has been defined in the layout section.
- *Line 3*—The hyperlink to `add_html` is inserted.
- *Line 4*—The hyperlink to the search interface is inserted.
- *Line 10*—A `<dtml-in>` tag is used to iterate over the `mp_entries`.
- *Line 13*—The `getEntryField` method is called to show the value of the Name field.
- *Line 14*—Creates the link to the View Entries form.
- *Line 15*—Creates the link to the Edit Entries form.
- *Line 16*—Creates the Delete hyperlink.

- *Line 19*—Inserts the MetaPublisher logo.
- *Line 20*—Contains the code for the object's footer as it was defined in the layout section.

Figure 6.19 shows the `index_html` document as it is shown via the third view.

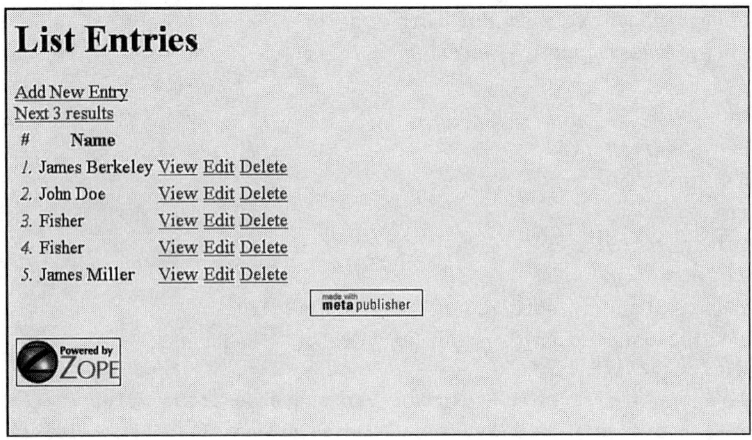

Figure 6.19
The List Entries form shows a batch of five entries.

View Entries Form This interface is used to show the actual data contained in one `mp_entry`. With the View Entries form, you can look at the contents of one `mp_entry`.

You have to configure the form before it is created:

- Basic Information:
  - *ID*—Define a unique ID for the interface; the default value is `view_html`.
  - *Title*—This field is optional. You can give a title to describe the interface.
- Options:
  - *Object*—Here you can decide whether you want the interface to be created as a DTML method or a DTML document.
  - *Security*—The multiple selection list contains the roles you can associate with the current interface. Hold down the Ctrl key on Windows systems to select more than one option. The default roles are `manager` and `owner`.

- Links:
    - *Edit Method*—The View Entry form contains a Back button. Here you can decide to where the user is redirected after the Back button has been pressed. Choose the ID of the according object from the selection list or enter an ID into the text field. The default ID is `index_html`.
- Layout:
    - *Header*—You can define a header for your interface using DTML and HTML code. The default header is as follows:

      ```
      <dtml-var standard_html_header>
      <h1><dtml-var title_or_id></h1>
      ```

    - *Footer*—You can define a footer for your interface using DTML and HTML code. The default footer is as follows:

      ```
      <dtml-var standard_html_footer>
      ```

- Fields—In this section, you will see each entry field you have configured before. Beneath each entry field's ID is a selection list where you can choose from various rendering options. These options depend on the relating field type.

  Look at the section called "Field Types" where you will find a general survey showing the rendering options for each field type.

Listing 6.3 shows the source code for our rendered `view_html`. Code explanations can be found following the listing.

Listing 6.3

view_html

```
<dtml-var standard_html_header>
<h1><dtml-var title_or_id></h1>
<form action="./" method="post" enctype="multipart/form-data">
<input type="hidden" name="id" value="<dtml-var "get_time()">">
<b>Name</b><br>
<dtml-var "mp_entries.getEntryField(_['key'],'f992827178')">
<p>
<b>Sex</b><br>
<dtml-var "mp_entries.getEntryField(_['key'],'f992827209')">
<p>
<input type="submit" name="index_html:method" value=" Back ">
```

Listing 6.3
Continued

```
12: </form>
13: <div align="center"><img src="<dtml-var "REQUEST['SCRIPT_NAME']">
➥/misc_/MetaPublisher/made_with" alt="MetaPublisher" align="center"></div>
14: <dtml-var standard_html_footer>
```

- *Lines 1 and 2*—The code of the object's header as it has been defined in the layout section.
- *Lines 5 and 6*—The value of the Name entry field is evaluated and displayed here.
- *Lines 8 and 9*—The value of the Sex radio field is evaluated and displayed.
- *Line 11*—The Back button is created. Users are redirected to `index_html`.
- *Line 13*—Inserts the MetaPublisher logo.
- *Line 14*—Contains the code for the object's footer as it was defined in the layout section.

Figure 6.20 shows `view_html` as it is shown via the third view.

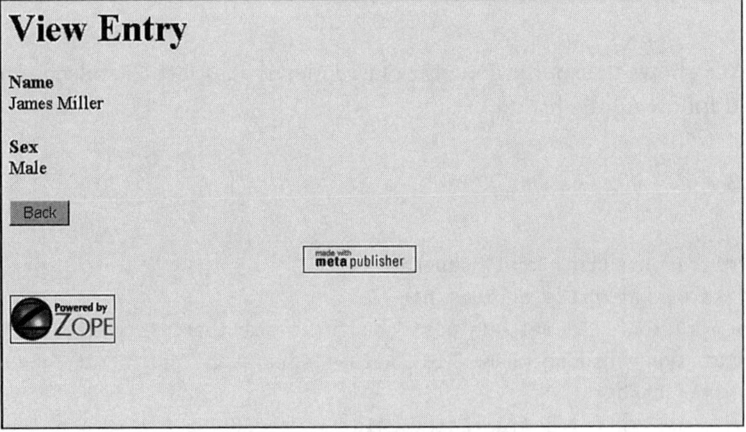

Figure 6.20
The contents of one single `mp_entry` *are shown here.*

Search Form This simple interface provides powerful searching capabilities. The search form contains one entry field for each MetaPublisher Entry field that has been made searchable via the configuration interface.

The interface needs some configuration:

- Basic Information:
    - *ID*—Define a unique ID for the interface; the default value is `search_html`.
    - *Title*—This field is optional. You can give a title to describe the interface.
- Options:
    - *Object*—Here you can decide whether you want the interface to be created as a DTML method or a DTML document.
    - *Security*—The multiple selection list contains the roles you can associate with the current interface. Hold down the Ctrl key on Windows systems to select more than one option. The default roles are `manager` and `owner`.
- Links:
    - *ID for report object*—An object is needed that calls methods to actually perform the search and that will display the search results. You can either choose the appropriate ID from the selection list or enter an ID into the text field. The default ID is `report_html`.
- Layout:
    - *Header*—You can define a header for your interface using DTML and HTML code. The default header is as follows:

      ```
      <dtml-var standard_html_header>
      <h1><dtml-var title_or_id></h1>
      ```

    - *Footer*—You can define a footer for your interface using DTML and HTML code. The default footer is as follows:

      ```
      <dtml-var standard_html_footer>
      ```

Listing 6.4 shows the rendered source code of our `search_html`. The explanation of the code follows the listing.

Listing 6.4

search_html

```
 1: <dtml-var standard_html_header>
 2: <h1><dtml-var title_or_id></h1>
 3: <form action="report_html">
 4: <table>
 5: <dtml-in "getSearchableEntries()">
 6: <dtml-try>
 7: <tr><th><dtml-var "_['sequence-item'][0]"></th>
 8: <td><input name="<dtml-var "_['sequence-item'][1]">"
➥width=30 value=""></td></tr>
 9: </dtml-try>
10: </dtml-in>
11: <tr><td colspan=2>
12: <input type="submit" value=" Find ">
13: </td></tr></table>
14: </form>
15: <div align="center"><img src="<dtml-var "REQUEST['SCRIPT_NAME']">
➥/misc_/MetaPublisher/made_with" alt="MetaPublisher" align="center"></div>
16: <dtml-var standard_html_footer>
```

- *Lines 1 and 2*—The code of the object's header as it has been defined in the layout section.
- *Line 5*—Iterates through all those fields that have been made searchable.
- *Lines 7 and 8*—Create input fields for the searchable fields.
- *Line 12*—The Find button is created. Users are redirected to `report_html`.
- *Line 15*—Inserts the MetaPublisher logo.
- *Line 16*—Contains the code for the object's footer as it was defined in the layout section.

Report Form The report form contains the results of a previously made search through the entries of a MetaPublisher.

- Basic Information:
    - *ID*—Define a unique ID for the interface; the default value is `report_html`.
    - *Title*—This field is optional. You can give a title to describe the interface.

- Options:
    - *Object*—Here you can decide whether you want the interface to be created as a DTML method or a DTML document.
    - *Security*—The multiple selection list contains the roles you can associate with the current interface. Hold down the Ctrl key on Windows systems to select more than one option. The default roles are `manager` and `owner`.
- Links:
    - *Return Method*—The View Entry form contains a Back button. Here you can decide to where the user is redirected after the Back button has been clicked. Choose the ID of the appropriate object from the selection list or enter an ID into the text field. The default ID is `index_html`.
    - *Edit Entry Link*—Decide whether you want to include a link that will redirect the user to a page where a single MP_entry can be edited.
    - *View Entry Link*—Decide whether you want to include a link that will redirect the user to a page where the MP_entry can be viewed.
    - *Delete Entry Link*—This will add a link to delete the current MP_entry.
- Layout:
    - *Header*—You can define a header for your interface using DTML and HTML code. The default header is as follows:

      ```
      <dtml-var standard_html_header>
      <h1><dtml-var title_or_id></h1>
      ```

    - *Footer*—You can define a footer for your interface using DTML and HTML code. The default footer is as follows:

      ```
      <dtml-var standard_html_footer>
      ```

- Fields—In this section, you will see each entry field you have configured before. Beneath each entry field's ID is a selection list where you can choose from various rendering options. These options depend on the relating field type.

  Look at the section called "Field Types" where you will find a general survey showing the rendering options in the different interfaces for each field type.

Listing 6.5 shows the rendered source code of our `report_html`. The explanation of the code follows the listing.

Listing 6.5

report_html

```
1: <dtml-var standard_html_header>
2: <h1><dtml-var title_or_id></h1>
3: <a href="index_html">Back</a><br>
4: <table>
5: <tr>
6: <th><em>#</em></th>
7: <th>Name</th>
8: <th>Sex</th>
9: </tr>
10: <dtml-in mp_catalog>
11: <tr>
12: <td><em><dtml-var sequence-number>.</em></td>
13: <dtml-in "[_['sequence-item'].id]">
14: <td><dtml-var "mp_entries.getEntryField(_['sequence-
➥item'],'f992827178')"></td>
15: <td><dtml-var "mp_entries.getEntryField(_['sequence-
➥item'],'f992827209')"></td>
16: <td><a href="view_html?key=<dtml-var sequence-item>">View</a></td>
17: <td><a href="edit_html?key=<dtml-var sequence-item>">Edit</a></td>
18: <td><a href="delEntry?key=<dtml-var sequence-item>">Delete</a></td>
19: </dtml-in>
20: </tr></dtml-in>
21: </table>
22: <div align="center"><img src="<dtml-var "REQUEST['SCRIPT_NAME']">
➥/misc_/MetaPublisher/made_with" alt="MetaPublisher" align="center"></div>
23: <dtml-var standard_html_footer>
```

- *Lines 1 and 2*—The code of the object's header as it has been defined in the layout section.
- *Lines 5 and 6*—The value of the Name entry field is evaluated and displayed here.
- *Lines 8 and 9*—The value of the Sex radio field is evaluated and displayed.
- *Line 11*—The Back button is created. Users are redirected to `index_html`.
- *Line 13*—Inserts the MetaPublisher logo.
- *Line 14*—Contains the code for the object's footer as it was defined in the layout section.

Rendering Interfaces

After the necessary interfaces have been configured, they need to be rendered. That means that the DTML code, which depends on the configuration of each interface itself, is generated and written to the Contents view.

Because many interfaces contain hyperlinks to other interfaces, and because they can be freely modified, there is a function that helps you find missing links and the like.

Mark all the interfaces you want to be checked and then click the Check Links button. The results will be shown in the MetaPublisher Interface Link Checker (see Figure 6.21). The links that are contained in the selected objects are verified and displayed. If everything goes right and each link is found, the single links are displayed in white. Otherwise, green, red, and yellow are used.

> **Note**
> Because the images in this book are only black and white, we cannot show you the different colors of the Link Checker.

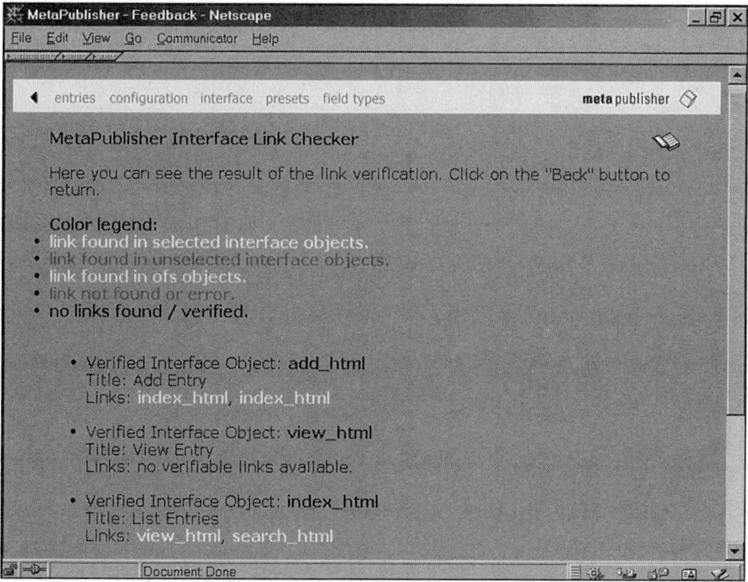

Figure 6.21
MetaPublisher Interface Link Checker helps you to remove missing links.

If the Link Checker has told you that everything seems to be all right with your interfaces, just mark the interfaces you want to be rendered.

Before actually clicking the Render button, look at the two radio buttons:

- *Never overwrite existing files*—Objects that already exist in the Contents view will not be overwritten.
- *Always overwrite existing files*—Objects that already exist in the Contents view are replaced.

Don't forget to activate the second radio button if you want to replace an old interface with a new one.

Now the Render button can be clicked. After the rendering has taken place, a line at the top of the interface informs you whether the action has been successful (see Figure 6.22).

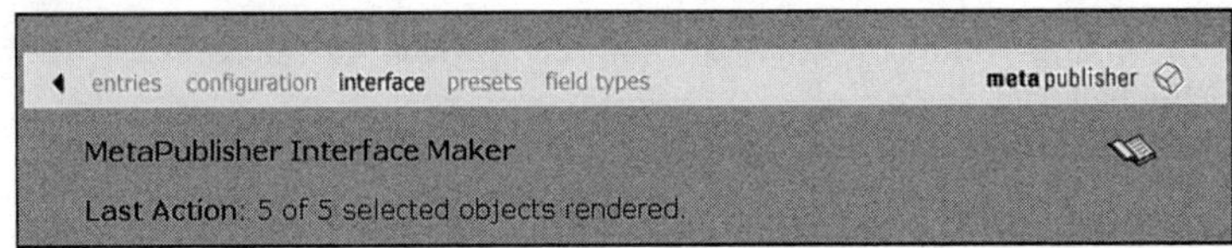

Figure 6.22
Five objects have been successfully rendered.

The Presets Interface

Presets are MetaPublisher configurations with the appropriate stored interfaces. The advantage of these is that the work you might once have invested in creating a sophisticated MetaPublisher application does not have to be done over and over again.

This interface is used to store, load, and delete presets.

- *Store*—When you enter a name for the preset you want to store and click the Store button, the current configuration, together with the interfaces, is saved in the file system.

  Stored presets can be found in the `/var/MetaPublisher/Presets` folder of the current Zope installation. A preset file consists of text, and its name matches the one of the preset.

- *Load*—Choose an available preset from the selection list. Click the Load button to load the requested preset.

> **Warning**
> Loading a preset means that the current configuration is entirely replaced by one of the loaded presets. But you can use the Undo view to undo the loading of a preset.

After the preset has been loaded, you will have to render the interfaces because the objects from the Contents view are not stored within a preset.

- *Delete*—Choose the preset you want to delete from the selection field and click the Delete button.

For more information about presets, see the "Presets" section later in this chapter.

The Field Types Interface

The field types interface lists all field types that are installed on the current MetaPublisher. Field types that may not be imported properly are shown with error messages.

The interface contains a Rescan button. Click the button if you want Zope to scan for new field types (see Figure 6.23). This is necessary whenever a new field type is implemented. Another way to search for installed field types is to restart the entire Zope server.

Implementing your own field types will be covered in the next section.

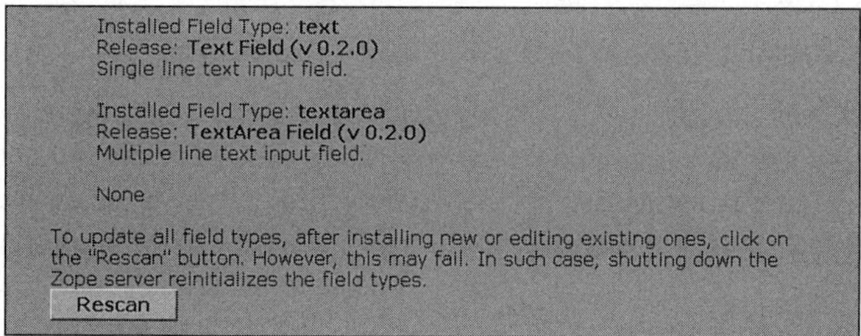

Figure 6.23

You can scan for new field types by clicking the Restart button.

Field Types

Field types are a fundamental element of MetaPublisher. Each entry field that is used to receive data or simply pass hidden data is based on a certain field type.

MetaPublisher provides several kinds of field types. Some of them work the same as well-known HTML entry types, such as the text area field or the select box field. Other field types are more sophisticated and specialized, such as the image field type or the e-mail field type.

The next section will give a general survey of the currently supported field types, and then we will explain the use of each field type in detail.

Another feature supported by MetaPublisher is the ability to import self-defined field types. We will illustrate how to set up the customized field type `date`.

Currently Supported Field Types The following lists the field types that are currently supported by MetaPublisher:

- Date Field
- Email Field
- File Field
- Float Field
- Integer Field
- Image Field
- Select Box
- Radio Field
- Text Field
- Textarea Field

As previously mentioned, each field type provides several so-called render options. The selected render option decides the way in which an entry field's value is handled in the user interfaces. For example, you can decide whether the value of an entry field is displayed in the `index_html` or whether you want the field's default value to be displayed.

Tables 6.2–6.5 show the common rendering options that are currently supported with explanations of their meanings.

Table 6.2

Render Options for `add_html`

Option	Explanation
input, default value by default	The default value you specified during the configuration is shown in the input field, and it can be edited by the visitor.
input, empty by default	Although you might have given a default value, the input field contains no data.
hide & pass default value	Default value is submitted always. It cannot be changed by the visitor, and the value is not shown in the input field.
view & pass default value	Default value is submitted always. It cannot be changed by the visitor, but it is displayed in the input field.

Table 6.3

Render Options for `edit_html`

Option	Explanation
input, current value by default	Passes the edited input data or the unmodified value. The current value is shown.
input, default value by default	Passes the edited input data or the default value. The default value is displayed.
input, empty by default	The entry field is empty and can be modified.
view & pass value	The value cannot be edited but is visible and passed anyway.
view & pass default value	The default value is displayed and passed; it cannot be modified.
hide & pass value	The input data is hidden but always passed.
hide & pass default value	The default value is hidden but passed anyway.
hidden_empty	The input field is hidden and empty.

Table 6.4 Render Options for `view_html`

Option	Explanation
view value	Shows the actual value of the entry field.
view default value	Shows the default value.
none	Doesn't show the entry field's value.

Table 6.5 Render Options for `index_html`

Option	Explanation
none	Shows none of the entry's value.
view value	Shows the actual value of the entry field.
view default value	Shows the entry field's default value.

The Date Field The date field is used to receive a date by a user. The required format is as follows:

```
Month/Day/Year
```

The next list shows all the options that can be set during the configuration of a date field.

- Basic Information:
  - *ID*—The entry field needs a unique ID to identify it in the Zope database. To guarantee a unique ID, the System time is used to automatically generate an ID. We recommend that you do not modify the ID field.
  - *Label*—Describes the information that is to be entered in a text row. The description should be simple and significant. Your goal is to ensure that the visitor knows exactly what data he or she is expected to enter.
- Options:
  - *Default*—Here you can define a standard value, which appears in the form and that can be edited by the visitor. A default value makes sense only when there is a high probability that the data sought will have, for the majority of visitors, the same (single standard) value.
  - *Searchable*—Makes the date field searchable via ZCatalog.
  - *Required*—Activate the check box and the user must type a value into this field before he or she can proceed.
- Available Render options for `add_html`:
  - input, default value by default
  - input, empty by default
  - view & pass default value
  - hide & pass default value

- Available Render options for `edit_html`:
    - input, current value by default
    - input, default value by default
    - input, empty by default
    - view & pass value
    - view & pass default value
    - hide & pass value
    - hide & pass default value
    - hidden_empty
- Available Render options for `view`:
- Available Render options for `edit_html`:
    - view value
    - view default value
    - none
- Available Render options for `index_html`:
    - none
    - view value
    - view default value

The E-mail Field This entry field requires a valid e-mail address—the value that is typed into an e-mail field must contain an "@".

- Basic Information:
    - *ID*—A unique ID.
    - Label—A significant description of the e-mail data you want to be entered.
- Options:
    - *Default*—Define a standard value.
    - *Searchable*—Makes the entry field searchable via ZCatalog.
    - *Required*—Activate the check box and the user must type a value into this field before he or she can proceed.

- Layout:
    - *Size*—Specify the length of the entry field itself.
    - *Maximum Length*—Specify the maximum length of the entered e-mail value.
- Available Render options for `add_html`:
    - input e-mail address
    - default value by default
    - input e-mail address, empty by default
    - view & pass default value
    - hide & pass default value
- Available Render options for `edit_html`:
    - input e-mail address
    - current value by default
    - input e-mail address
    - default value by default
    - input e-mail address
    - empty by default
    - view & pass value
    - link to & pass value
    - view & pass default value
    - hide & pass value
    - hide & pass default value
    - hidden_empty
- Available Render options for `view_html`:
    - view value
    - link to value
    - view default value
    - none

- Available Render options for `index_html`:
    - none
    - view value
    - link to value
    - view default value

The Float Field This entry field is used for floating-point numbers.

- Basic Information:
    - *ID*—A unique ID.
    - *Label*—A short description so the user knows what he or she is supposed to enter.
- Options:
    - *Default*—Define a standard value, such as 0.0.
    - *Required*—Activate the check box and the user must type a value into this field before he or she can proceed.
- Layout:
    - *Size*—Specify the length of the entry field itself.
    - *Maximum Length*—Specify the maximum length of the entered floating-point number.
- Available Render options for `add_html`:
    - input, default value by default
    - input, empty by default
    - view & pass default value
    - hide & pass default value
- Available Render options for `edit`:
    - input, current value by default
    - input, default value by default
    - input, empty by default
    - view & pass value
    - view & pass default value

  - hide & pass value
  - hide & pass default value
  - hidden_empty
- Available Render options for `view_html`:
  - view value
  - view default value
  - none
- Available Render options for `index_html`:
  - none
  - view value
  - view default value

The Integer Field The integer field is used for integer numbers.

- Basic Information:
  - *ID*—A unique ID.
  - *Label*—A short description so the user knows what he or she is supposed to enter.
- Options:
  - *Default*—Define a standard value, such as 0.
  - *Required*—Activate the check box and the user must type a value into this field before he or she can proceed.
- Layout:
  - *Size*—Specify the length of the entry field itself.
  - *Maximum Length*—Specify the maximum length of the entered integer.
- Available Render options for `add_html`:
  - input, default value by default
  - input, empty by default
  - view & pass default value
  - hide & pass default value

- Available Render options for `edit_html`:
    - input, current value by default
    - input, default value by default
    - input, empty by default
    - view & pass value
    - view & pass default value
    - hide & pass value
    - hide & pass default value
    - hidden_empty
- Available Render options for `view_html`:
    - view value
    - view default value
    - none
- Available Render options for `index_html`:
    - none
    - view value
    - view default value

The Select Box Field This entry field is shown as a simple selection list or as a multiple selection list where multiple options can be chosen.

- Basic Information:
    - *ID*—A unique ID.
    - *Label*—A significant description of the data from which to choose.
- Selections:
    - *Default*—Choose a standard value from the selection list.
    - *Add new option*—Adds a single option to the selection list.
    - *Delete option(s)*—Here you can delete option(s) you previously added to the selection list.

- Options:
    - *Searchable*—Makes the entry field searchable via ZCatalog.
    - *Required*—Activate the check box and the user must type a value into this field before he or she can proceed.
- Layout:
    - *Multiple*—Activate the check box if you want to create a selection box where multiple options can be chosen.
    - *Size*—Specify the number of rows of a multiple select box.
- Available Render options for `add_html`:
    - select box, default selection
    - select box, unselected
    - view & pass default selection
    - hide & pass default selection
- Available Render options for `edit_html`:
    - select box, current selection
    - select box, default selection
    - select box, unselected
    - view & pass current selection
    - view & pass default selection
    - hide & pass current selection
    - hide & pass default selection
    - hidden_empty
- Available Render options for `view_html`:
    - view selection
    - view default selection
    - none

- Available Render options for `index_html`:
    - none
    - view selection
    - view default selection

The Radio Field This field creates a list of options where only one option can be chosen.

- Basic Information:
    - *ID*—A unique ID.
    - *Label*—A significant description of the data from which you want to choose.
- Selections:
    - *Default*— Choose a value from the selection list that you want to be marked by default.
    - *Add new option*—Add a single option to the selection list.
    - *Delete option(s)*—Here you can delete option(s) you previously added to the list or radio buttons.
- Options:
    - *Searchable*—Makes the entry field searchable via ZCatalog.
    - *Required*—Activate the check box and the user must type a value into this field before he or she can proceed.
- Available Render options for `add_html`:
    - radio buttons, default selection
    - radio buttons, unselected
    - view & pass default selection
    - hide & pass default selection
- Available Render options for `edit_html`:
    - radio buttons, current selection
    - radio buttons, default selection

  - radio buttons, unselected
  - view & pass current selection
  - view & pass default selection
  - hide & pass current selection
  - hide & pass default selection
  - hidden_empty
- Available Render options for `view_html`:
  - view selection
  - view default selection
  - none
- Available Render options for `index_html`:
  - none
  - view selection
  - view default selection

The Image Field With this field, users are enabled to upload pictures. Along with the image, a thumbnail of the same image is stored. A thumbnail is a smaller representation of the original image.

PIL is imported and needed to create "real" thumbnails. If PIL is not available, a "fake" thumbnail is created, which means that the image is simply resized by the browser and no thumbnail is stored along with the original image.

For instructions on how to install and use PIL, see Chapter 11, "Creating Dynamic Graphs in Zope."

- Basic Information:
  - *ID*—A unique ID.
  - *Label*—A significant description of the images you want to be uploaded.
- Display Layout:
  - *Image Height*—Specify the height of an image. If no value is given, the image keeps its original height.

   - *Image Width*—Specify the width of an image. If no value is given, the image keeps its original width.
   - *Thumbnail Height*—Specify the thumbnail's height.
   - *Thumbnail Width*—Specify the thumbnail's width.
- Available Render option for `add`:
   - upload image, empty by default
- Available Render options for `edit`:
   - upload or delete image, view current image
   - upload image, view current image
   - upload or delete image
   - upload image, current image by default
   - upload image, empty by default
- Available Render options for `view`:
   - view thumbnail and image
   - view image only (no thumbnail)
   - view thumbnail link to image
   - view thumbnail only (no image)
   - none
- Available Render options for `list`:
   - view thumbnail link to image
   - view thumbnail only (no image)
   - view thumbnail and image
   - view image only (no thumbnail)
   - none

The Textarea Field In a textarea field, large amounts of text can be entered.

- Basic Information:
   - *ID*—A unique ID.
   - *Label*—A significant description of the data you want entered into the textarea field.

- Options:
    - *Default*—Define a standard value.
    - *Searchable*—Makes the entry field searchable via ZCatalog.
    - *Required*—Activate the check box and the user must type a value into this field before he or she can proceed.
    - *Wordwrap*—A new line is automatically started if the end of the current line is reached.
- Layout:
    - *Rows*—Specify the number of rows for the textarea field.
    - *Columns*—Specify the number of columns for the textarea field.
- Available Render options for `add_html`:
    - input, default value by default
    - input, empty by default
    - view & pass default value
    - hide & pass default value
- Available Render options for `edit_html`:
    - input, current value by default
    - input, default value by default
    - input, empty by default
    - view & pass value
    - view & pass default value
    - hide & pass value
    - hide & pass default value
    - hide & pass empty
- Available Render options for `view_html`:
    - view value
    - view default value
    - none

- Available Render options for `list`:
  - none
  - view value
  - view default value

The Text Field

A single line of text can be entered in the text field.

- Basic Information:
  - *ID*—A unique ID.
  - *Label*—A significant description of the text data you want entered.
- Options:
  - *Default*—Define a standard value.
  - *Searchable*—Makes the entry field searchable via ZCatalog.
  - *Required*—Activate the check box and the user must type a value into this field before he or she can proceed.
- Layout:
  - *Size*—Specify the length of the entry field itself.
  - *Maximum Length*—Specify the maximum length of the entered text value.
- Available Render options for `add_html`:
  - input, default value by default
  - input, empty by default
  - view & pass default value
  - hide & pass default value
- Available Render options for `edit_html`:
  - input, current value by default
  - input, default value by default
  - input, empty by default
  - view & pass value

    - view & pass default value
    - hide & pass value
    - hide & pass default value
    - hidden_empty
- Available Render options for `view_html`:
    - view value
    - view default value
    - none
- Available Render options for `index_html`:
    - none
    - view value
    - view default value

Defining New Field Types MetaPublisher supports the ability to import self-defined field types. That means that you can set up your own field type and make it work within a MetaPublisher instance.

MetaPublisher field types are all made of the same basic structure. Additionally, most of the field types are very similar to each other, so it is not necessary to rewrite a lot of code. In most cases, the easiest thing you can do will be to modify the source code of a similar field type implementation until it meets your needs.

Defining your own field types needs some modification within the file system. Knowledge of the Python programming language is necessary to do that.

We will first explain how MetaPublisher field types are stored within the file system. Next, we will illustrate one possibility how to define the simple field type `date`.

Each field type definition consists of one folder, named after the corresponding field type, and the following four files inside it:

- `__init__.py`
- `main.py`
- `add.dtml`
- `edit.dtml`

The main folder must be installed into another folder labeled `ftypes` that is part of your MetaPublisher installation.

The concrete path of the field type `date` is `Zope/lib/python/Products/MetaPublisher/ftypes`.

> **Note**
> There has to be one file, labeled `__init__.py`, inside a field type folder. Do not leave it out.

Now we will define the field type `date` step-by-step. But first, we need to think about the format of the `date` field type. We decided on a simple format, such as Month/Day/Year.

The `date` value itself can be entered, just like a simple text value. In fact, the most important difference between these two field types is a method called `verify()` that determines whether the format of the field type entry is correct.

1. Create the folder date inside the `ftypes` folder.
2. Copy the four files from the folder text into the new folder.
3. Modify the `__init__.py` file by changing the field type's name and the version number of your MetaPublisher.

The initialization file (see Listing 6.6) contains general data that differs only by the name of the concerning field type and the MetaPublisher's version number. In principle, the file's contents are not all that important; you might even leave it empty.

Listing 6.6

`init.py`

```
1: #
==========================================================================
2: #        MetaPublisher 1.1 - FTypes date Initialization
3: # --------------------------------------------------------------------------
4: #        read README.txt for more information or
5: #        visit http://www.zope.de/software/MetaPublisher/
6: #
==========================================================================
```

Line 1: The version of the current MetaPublisher and the field types ID have been changed to `date`.

4. Modify the `main.py` file:

a. Replace the title `text` by `date`.

b. Remove everything that is connected to the layout options `size` and `maxlength`.

c. Revise the `verify` method.

If an entry does not correspond to the field type's format, this method is supposed to raise an error message. In the case of the field type `date`, month, day, and year have to be entered and the entries for month and day are not allowed to go beyond 12 or 31, respectively. To get this working, the `string` module needs to be imported.

The `main.py` file, shown in Listing 6.7, is a Python module containing the field type's main implementation. It is structured into some sections that are explained in this section.

Listing 6.7

`main.py`

```
 1: # ======================================================================
 2: #        MetaPublisher 1.1 - FTypes Date
 3: # ----------------------------------------------------------------------
 4: #        read README.txt for more information or
 5: #        visit http://www.zope.de/software/MetaPublisher/
 6: # ======================================================================
 7: # ----------------------------------------------------------------------
 8: #        Initialization
 9: # ----------------------------------------------------------------------
10: from Products.MetaPublisher.ftypes.SimpleField import SimpleField
11: from Globals import HTMLFile
12: from Products.MetaPublisher.GUI import GUI
13: import time
14: import string
```

In lines 1–6, the head contains general data; you should modify the name of the field type and the version number of your MetaPublisher.

In lines 7–14, under `Initialization`, all necessary modules and classes are imported. `SimpleField`, `HTMLFile`, GUI, and time must be imported in each field type definition. Because we will need a method from the `string` module, that method needs to be imported as well.

```
15: # ---------------------------------------------------------------------
16: #       SimpleField Class
17: # ---------------------------------------------------------------------
18: class Field(SimpleField):
19:     """ Simple Date input field."""
20:     title = "Date Field"
21:     version = "v 0.2.0"
22:     type = "Property"
```

In lines 15–22, under `SimpleField Class`, the new `Field` class is derived from the basic `SimpleField` class.

In line 22, you set the way in which the configured field will be stored. Field types, based on the input of text, are stored as properties. To define binary field types, such as `ImageField`, set type on `"OFS"`.

The title and version settings will be shown in the field type screen of MetaPublisher.

```
23:     # -----------------------------------------------------------------
24:     #       config support
25:     # -----------------------------------------------------------------
26:     def __init__(self,REQUEST=None):
27:         SimpleField.__init__.im_func(self, REQUEST)
28:         if REQUEST is not None:
29:                 pass
30:         else:
31:             self.id='Date'
```

In lines 23–31, under `config support`, the methods of the `Field` class are implemented. The initialization method controls whether the layout options were set during the configuration.

If that is the case the values are passed, otherwise default values are used.

```
32:     def edit(self, REQUEST=None):
33:         """ change any attribute(s) """
34:         SimpleField.edit(self,REQUEST)
```

In this method, the editing of the field type's layout options is organized.

```
35:     def editForm(self,index,REQUEST):
36:         """ get edit form """
37:         _editForm = HTMLFile('edit',globals())
38:         return _editForm(
39:             self,
40:             id=self.id,
```

```
41:                 index=index,
42:                 label=self.label,
43:                 default=self.default,
44:                 searchable=self.searchable,
45:                 required=self.required,
46:                 manage_html_header=GUI.manage_html_header,
47:                 manage_html_footer=GUI.manage_html_footer,
48:                 manage_logo=GUI.manage_logo,manage_tabs3=GUI.manage_tabs3
49:                 )
```

In lines 35–49, the `editForm` method is used to generate the `edit.dtml` file. The data from the `add.dtml` file is added to the Namespace so that the existing settings can be shown in the form of the `edit.dtml` file.

Do *not* change the last three lines.

```
50:         # ----------------------------------------------------------------
51:         #       entry support
52:         # ----------------------------------------------------------------
53:         def verify(self,key,value,entry,data):
54:             """ add Property, return None if no error occurs"""
55:             entry._setProperty(key,value)
56:                     return None
57:             try:
58:                 value=str(value)
59:                 date_list=string.split(value, '/')
60:                 if len(date_list) != 3:
61:                     raise AttributeError, 'k'
62:                 month=int(date_list[0])
63:                 day=int(date_list[1])
64:                 year=int(date_list[2])
65:                 if month > 12:
66:                     raise AttributeError, 'k'
67:                 if day > 31:
68:                     raise AttributeError, 'k'
69:                 if year > 9999:
70:                     raise AttributeError, 'k'
71:                 entry._setProperty(key,value)
72:                 return None
73:             except:
74:                 return "Not a valid date input"
```

In lines 50–74, under entry support, the verify method is used to check whether the value that was given by the user corresponds to the field type. If that is the case, the value is set. The verify method checks whether the entry value matches the Month/Day/Year format. If not, an error message is shown (Not a valid date input).

```
75:     # ---------------------------------------------------------------------
76:     #       interface support
77:     # ---------------------------------------------------------------------
78:
79:     def render_editDynamic(self,value):
80:         """ support for edit in the zope administration interface """
81:         return '''<input type="text" name="%s" value="%s">''' %
➥(self.id,value)
82:         renderOptions= {
83:             'add':('input, default value by default',
➥'input, empty by default', 'view & pass default value',
➥'hide & pass default value'),
84:             'edit':('input, current value by default', 'input,
➥ default value by default', 'input, empty by default',
➥ 'view & pass value', 'view & pass default value',
➥'hide & pass value', 'hide & pass default value', 'hidden_empty'),
85:             'view':('view value', 'view default value', 'none'),
86:             'list':('none', 'view value', 'view default value'),
87:             'table':('input, current value by default', 'input,
➥ default value by default', 'input, empty by default',
➥ 'view & pass value', 'view & pass default value', 'view value',
➥ 'view default value', 'hide & pass value',
➥ 'hide & pass default value', 'none'),
88:             'requester':('none', 'view value', 'view default value',
➥ 'hide & pass value', 'hide & pass default value'),
89:             }
90:     def render(self,form='none',type='none',key='sequence-item'):
91:         """ render respective html code """
92:         # initialize
93:         name = self.id
94:         if self.required == 'yes':
95:             name = name + ':required'
96:         # verify form
97:         if type != 'input_default':
98:             if self.renderOptions.has_key(form):
99:                 if not type in self.renderOptions[form]:
100:                    type=''
101:            else:
102:                type=''
```

```
103:         # render type
104:         if type == 'view value':
105:             return """<dtml-var "mp_entries.getEntryField(_['%s'],'%s')
➥">"""
➥ % (key,self.id)
106:         elif type == 'view default value':
107:             return """%s""" % (self.default)
108:         elif type == 'hide & pass value':
109:             return """<input type="hidden" name="%s"
➥value="<dtml-var "mp_entries.getEntryField(_['%s'],'%s')">">"""
➥ % (name,key,self.id)
110:         elif type == 'hide & pass default value':
111:             return """<input type="hidden" name="%s"
➥value="%s">""" % (name,self.default)
112:         if type == 'view & pass value':
113:             return """<dtml-var "mp_entries.getEntryField(_['%s'],'%s')">
➥<input type="hidden" name="%s" value="
➥<dtml-var "mp_entries.getEntryField(_['%s'],'%s')">">"""
➥% (key,self.id,name,key,self.id)
114:         elif type == 'view & pass default value':
115:             return """<input type="hidden"
➥ name="%s" value="%s">%s""" % (name,self.default,self.default)
116:         elif type == 'input, current value by default':
117:             return '''<input type="text" name="%s"
➥value="<dtml-var "mp_entries.getEntryField(_['%s'],'%s')">">'''
➥ % (name, key,self.id)
118:         elif type == 'input, default value by default' or
➥type=='input_default':
119:             return """<input type="date" name="%s" value="%s">"""
➥% ( name, self.default )
120:         elif type == 'input, empty by default':
121:             return """<input type="text" name="%s">""" % (name)
122:         else:
123:             return ''
```

In lines 75–123, under `Interface Support`, the rendering options are defined and implemented. In addition to the chosen rendering options, the corresponding HTML code is generated.

```
124: # ------------------------------------------------------------------
125: #       Management Methods
126: # ------------------------------------------------------------------
127: def addForm(self,REQUEST):
128:     """ get add form - copy this in your file """
129:     _addForm = HTMLFile('add',globals())
130:     return _addForm(
131:         self,id='f'+string.split(str(time.time()),'.')[0],
132:         manage_html_header=GUI.manage_html_header,
133:         manage_html_footer=GUI.manage_html_footer,
134:         manage_logo=GUI.manage_logo,
135:         manage_tabs3=GUI.manage_tabs3
136:        )
```

In lines 124–136, under `Management Methods`, only the `addForm` method is used that, in turn, uses UNIX Standard Time to generate an ID for the new field. Moreover, the method is necessary so that all the objects, such as `manage_html_header`, can be called inside the `add.dml` file.

Do *not* modify this implementation.

Modify both DTML files. See Listing 6.8 for `add_dtml` and Listing 6.9 for `edit_dtml`. Again, you only need to remove the layout options and replace `text` by `date`:

Listing 6.8

add_dtml

```
<dtml-var manage_html_header>
<dtml-var manage_tabs3>
<b>Add Date Field</b><p>
<form action="./" method="post">
<input type="hidden" name="ftype" value="date">
<dl>
<dt><b>Basic Info</b><p>
<dd>
<b>Id</b> (required, must be unique)<br>
<input type="date" name="id:required" value="<dtml-var id>">
<p>
<b>Label</b><br>
<input type="date" name="label" value="Untitled"><p>
<dt><b>Options</b><p>
<dd>
<b>Default</b><br>
<input type="date" name="default" value=""><p>
```

Listing 6.8

Continued

```
<b>Searchable:</b><br>
<input type="checkbox" name="searchable" value="yes">
Click into the box, if you want to make field searchable.<p>
<b>Required:</b><br>
<input type="checkbox" name="required" value="yes">
Click into the box, if you want to make field required.<p>
<dt><b>Layout</b><p>
<dd>
</dl>
<b>
<input type="submit" name="manage_addConfigEntry:method" value=" Add ">
<input type="submit" name="manage_config:method" value=" Cancel ">
</b><p>
</form>
</body></html>
<dtml-var manage_html_footer>
```

Listing 6.9

edit_dtml

```
<dtml-var manage_html_header>
<dtml-var manage_tabs3>
<b>Edit Date Field</b><p>
<form action="./" method="post">
<input type="hidden" name="ftype" value="date">
<input type="hidden" name="old_id" value="<dtml-var id>">
<dl>
<dt><b>Basic Info</b><p>
<dd>
<b>Id</b> (required, must be unique)<br>
<input type="date" name="id:required" value="<dtml-var id>">
<p>
<b>Label</b><br>
<input type="date" name="label" value="<dtml-var label>"><p>
<dt><b>Options</b><p>
<dd>
<b>Default</b><br>
<input type="text" name="default" value="<dtml-var default html_quote>"><p>
```

Listing 6.9
Continued

```
<b>Searchable:</b><br>
<input type="checkbox" name="searchable" value="yes"
➥<dtml-if "searchable=='yes'">checked</dtml-if>>
Click into the box, if you want to make field searchable.<p>
<b>Required:</b><br>
<input type="checkbox" name="required" value="yes"
➥<dtml-if "required=='yes'">checked</dtml-if>>
Click into the box, if you want to make field required.<p>

<dt><b>Layout</b><p>
<dd>
</dl>
<b>
<input type="submit" name="manage_editConfigEntry:method" value=" Edit ">
<input type="submit" name="manage_config:method" value=" Cancel ">
</b><p>
</form>
</body></html>
<dtml-var manage_html_footer>
```

Finally, MetaPublisher needs to import the new field type. Choose the FieldTypes tab and click Rescan inside the field type screen.

If everything worked, the new field type will appear onscreen. Otherwise, an error message will be shown.

Creating a Feedback Web Page

We will now start building a user feedback utility following the process just discussed. We will do this step-by-step so you can follow our example.

Creating a New MetaPublisher Instance

As you've already seen, there are two new options inside the Available options menu—MetaPublisher and Meta Entry.

To create a new MetaPublisher instance, select MetaPublisher from the Available Objects menu, and click Add.

> **Warning**
> Although there is a MetaEntry option in the Available Objects menu, you cannot create a MetaPublisher Entry this way. You will receive an error message whenever you try.

Now you need to provide some initial information:

- *ID*—The new MetaPublisher instance needs an ID that must be unique inside the current folder. There are some rules to follow concerning IDs.

  Only use letters of any case, numbers, and symbols, such as _ or `.`. Also note that you should not use any reserved words, such as `id`, `title`, `type`, `str`, or `int` for any ID. Other storages may have reserved names or limitations, for example, the Gadfly database storage won't allow IDs that contain a period `.` or consist only of numbers.

  In our example, we will use the ID `Feedback`.

- *Title*—State an optional title that specifies the object.
- *Preset*—One of MetaPublisher's most appealing features is the ability to store already configured MetaPublishers as presets so they do not have to be reconfigured.

  MetaPublisher comes with the following presets:

  - PhotoAlbum
  - Guest Book
  - Address Book

> **Note**
> Depending on the MetaPublisher version you are currently using, there might be presets defined that are different from the previous list.

  Because we want to set up and configure a new utility, we will choose Custom.

- *Storage*—Finally, you have to decide the way in which you want your data to be stored. We will discuss this topic in detail in the "MetaPublisher and Relational Databases" section later in this chapter.

  Please choose OFS for the current example. Then the data is stored in Zope's object database. For details, see Chapter 3, "Connecting Zope to External Relational Databases."

- *Only for Database Storage*—Because we do not want to store our data in a relational database, we will ignore this check box for now.

To finally create the new MetaPublisher instance, click the Add button. A new `Feedback` object is created on your Zope server (see Figure 6.24).

Figure 6.24

The new MetaPublisher instance is a folder-like object.

Configuring MetaPublisher

At this point, we need to configure our MetaPublisher, so we'll move to the configuration interface where we will set up various input fields.

Remember the tasks we want to obtain with MetaPublisher. We intend to build a feedback application where we want visitors to our Web site to give the following information:

- Name
- Sex
- Age
- Comments

We now need to decide which field type would be the most useful for each piece of information.

Let's start with the Name entry field. A name usually consists of a first name and a family name, and both are usually written as simple text. Consequently, we decide to choose the input type Text Field from the menu of available field types.

If you want to follow our example, you might want to use the same configuration:

ID:	Do not modify the automatically generated ID
Label:	Your name
Default:	A default value does not make much sense, so this field stays empty

Searchable:	Yes
Required:	No, we do not want to force the visitor to reveal his or her name
Size:	`25`
Maximum Length:	`250`

Clicking the Add button adds the entry field.

For the Sex field, we will choose the Radio field, where only one option can be chosen at a time:

ID:	Do not modify the automatically generated ID
Label:	`Sex`
Options:	`Female, Male`
Default:	`Female`
Searchable:	Yes
Required:	Yes

The Age entry field will be best presented in a selection list:

ID:	Do not modify the automatically generated ID
Label:	`Your Age`
Options:	`19-29, 30-59, 60+`
Default:	`19-29`
Searchable:	Yes
Required:	Yes
Multiple:	No
Size:	Not required

A multiple selection box does not make sense because the user cannot be of more than one correct age.

The last entry field we need to configure is the Comments field. Here, we want our users to tell us whatever they want, so we need to give them enough space for that purpose. As a result, we choose the Textarea field type:

ID:	Do not modify the automatically generated ID
Label:	`Comments`
Default:	`Your comment:`
Searchable:	Yes
Required:	No
Wordwrap:	Yes
Rows:	`8`
Columns:	`40`

Now that all necessary entry fields have been configured, the configuration form should look like Figure 6.25.

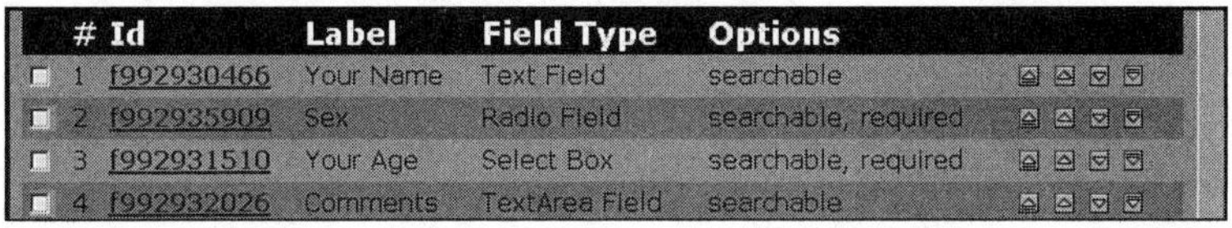

#	Id	Label	Field Type	Options
1	f992930466	Your Name	Text Field	searchable
2	f992935909	Sex	Radio Field	searchable, required
3	f992931510	Your Age	Select Box	searchable, required
4	f992932026	Comments	TextArea Field	searchable

Figure 6.25
Four entry fields have been configured.

The next step is to set up the necessary interfaces.

Creating the Needed Interfaces

Now we move to the MetaPublisher Interface Maker, where we will create the following user interfaces:

- Add Entry Form
- List Entry Form
- View Entry Form
- Search Form
- Report Form

The Add Entry Form

This is the only interface a user will see. We simply want to receive some data from our users. Users don't need to work with input. This form is configured as follows:

ID:	`dd_html`
Title:	`Add Entry`
Object:	`DTML Document`
Security:	`Anonymous, Manager, Owner`. Because we receive our data from users who have not necessarily joined our Web site we want to make the add form accessible for anonymous users.
Links	
Add Method:	`index_html`
Cancel Method:	`index_html`
Header:	Don't change the default value.
Footer:	Don't change the default value.
Your Name:	Input, default value by default.
Sex:	Radio buttons, default selection.
Your Age:	Select box, default selection.
Comments:	Input, default value by default.

The List Entry Form

The List Entry form is supposed to give an overview of all existing entries.

ID:	`index_html`
Title:	`List Entries`
Object:	DTML Document
Security:	Manager, Owner
Display:	Table
Add Entry Link:	No
Edit Entry Link:	No
View Entry Link:	Yes
Search Form Link:	Yes
Header:	Don't change the default value.
Footer:	Don't change the default value.
Your Name:	View value
Sex:	None

Your Age:	None
Comments:	None

The View Entry Form

We choose the View Entry form because we want to be able to look at the contents of a single `mp_entry`.

ID:	`view_html`
Title:	`View Entry`
Object:	DTML Document
Security:	`Manager, Owner`. Anonymous users are not given the permission to view other people's data.
Edit Field:	Leave this field empty. We do not need a form where data can be edited; we do not need a hyperlink to that page.
Header:	Don't change the default value.
Footer:	Don't change the default value.
Your Name:	View value
Sex:	View selection
Your Age:	View selection
Comments:	View value

The Search Form

This interface is very important to us, because, for example, we may want to search for certain age groups in the `mp_entries`.

ID:	`search_html`
Title:	`Search entries`
Object:	DTML Document
Security:	Manager, Owner
ID for report object:	`report_html`
Header:	Don't change the default value.
Footer:	Don't change the default value.

The Report Form

Because we have a Search form, we definitely need a Report form where the requested data is displayed.

ID:	`report_html`
Title:	`Search results`
Object:	DTML Document
Display:	Table
Security:	Manager, Owner
Return Link:	Yes, `search_html`
Edit Entry Link:	No
View Entry Link:	Yes
Delete Entry Link:	Yes
Header:	Don't change the default value.
Footer:	Don't change the default value.
Your Name:	View value
Sex:	None
Your Age:	None
Comments:	None

We have now set up all the necessary user interfaces (see Figure 6.26). But before we can use them, we need to render our objects.

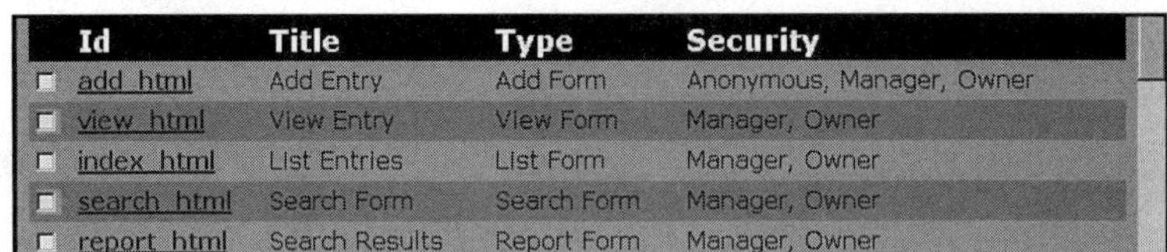

Id	Title	Type	Security
add_html	Add Entry	Add Form	Anonymous, Manager, Owner
view_html	View Entry	View Form	Manager, Owner
index_html	List Entries	List Form	Manager, Owner
search_html	Search Form	Search Form	Manager, Owner
report_html	Search Results	Report Form	Manager, Owner

Figure 6.26

If you followed our example, your Interface Maker table should look like this.

Before actually rendering your objects, you should check the contained links via the Check Links button. Consequently, check each check box in the Interface view's table and then click the Check Links button.

If everything is okay with the links, you can render the interfaces. In the Interface view, check all the check boxes in the table and click the Render button.

At this point you should test the feedback application. You can start by adding a few entries via the `add_html`. You can also go to the Contents view and use the View tab. That will show the `index_html` of the feedback Web page.

Figure 6.27 shows the `index_html` containing five entries.

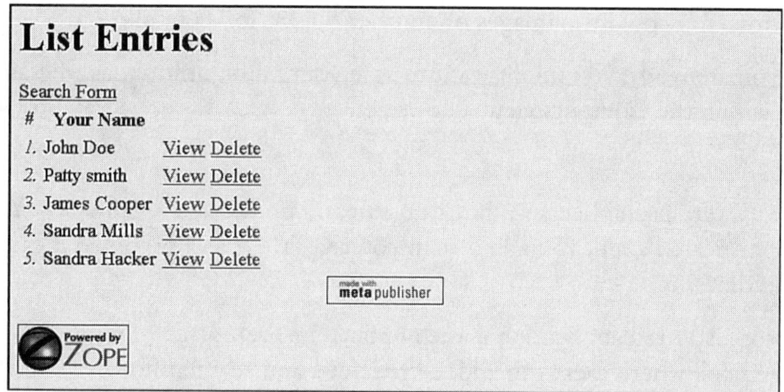

Figure 6.27
Five entries have been made so far.

In addition, we will test the searching function. The search results you can see in Figure 6.28 are correct. We were searching for all entries with the name Sandra.

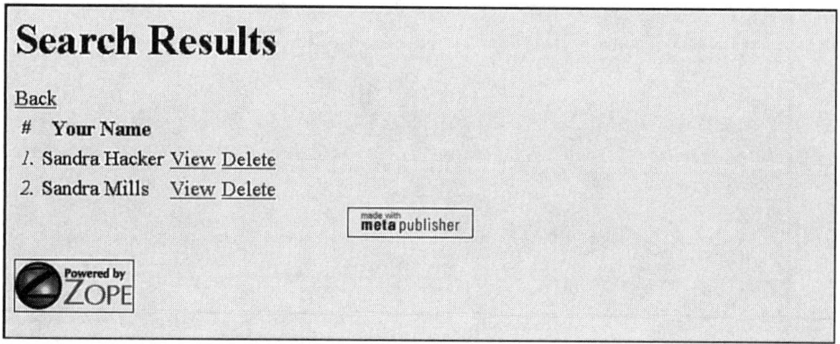

Figure 6.28
Two people with the name Sandra could be found.

Adapting and Optimizing

The previous checks might have shown that the feedback application works correctly. But there are still some things we'd like to change.

We didn't give anonymous users the permission to view the `index_html`. But we want each user to be directed to the `index_html` after he or she has added an entry.

The first thing we could do is modify the `add_html`. We can edit the `add_html` by inserting a simple user check.

In addition to editing DTML code, you can do whatever you need to modify your application. You could use images or another object, for example.

When you are ready, you might want to save your configuration, as well as the actual objects within the Contents view, as a preset.

Presets

Presets are very useful because they can save you time and a lot of work. You can set up a sophisticated application, and then you can save it as a preset so it can be used multiple times.

A very sophisticated application is the `PhotoAlbum` preset (see Figure 6.29). It provides a picture book where users can add, edit, delete, and search photos. With the `PhotoAlbum` preset, users can even add multiple entries.

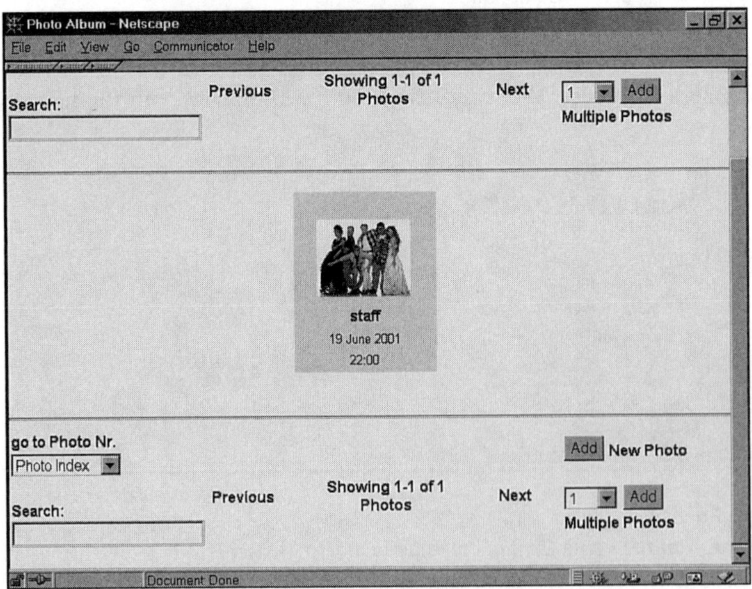

Figure 6.29
A complex picture book application.

If you have set up an application that you want to save as preset, you have certainly developed most of it in the Contents view. The problem is that objects inside the Contents view are not stored in a preset.

Consequently, you can use the Write to Interface button. When this button is selected, the objects from the Contents view are written to the Interface Maker and then can be stored in a preset.

This procedure is very easy. Imagine that you want to store the feedback Web page as a preset. Simply perform the following steps:

1. Go to the Contents view and check the objects you have modified. Then click the Write To Interface button. When you are asked if you want to replace the objects that already exist in the interface, click OK.

   Now the modified interfaces are copied to the Interface view and can be stored in a preset.

2. Go to the Preset view.
3. Enter a name for your new preset, such as **`feedback`**, into the entry field beside the Store Button.
4. Click the Store Button.

Now you have created a `feedback` preset. When you are inside the Presets view, you can check the menu beside the Load button to check whether it contains a `feedback` option.

Useful Methods from the `Entry.py` *Module*

The following are the public methods from the `Entry.py` module. You might want to use some of them to enhance your MetaPublisher application.

- `entryIds( self, order=None, sortdir=None )` Returns a list of current `mp_entry` IDs.
- `entryValues( self )` Returns a list of the current `mp_entry` objects.
- `entryItems( self )` Returns a list of tuples, consisting of (`entry id`, `entry object`).
- `delEntry( self, key, action='index_html', REQUEST=None, RESPONSE=None )` Deletes a certain `mp_entry`.
- `def addEntry( self, id='', title='', action='index_html', REQUEST=None, RESPONSE=None )` Adds a new `mp_entry`.

- `editEntry( self, id, title='', action='index_html', REQUEST=None, RESPONSE=None )` Edits an `mp_entry`.

Linking MetaPublisher to Your Web Site

The final task is rather simple. First, you need to think about the interface you want to use as an entrance to the MetaPublisher application.

That might be the List Entries form, that is `index_html`, so you can simply add a link to your Web site, such as

```
<a href="www.yourdomain.com/Feedback/index_html">Please Sign Our Feedback
➥Form!</a>
```

Now users can click that link and they will be directed to your feedback page.

MetaPublisher and Relational Databases

As we have mentioned already, there are several options for storing MetaPublisher data. That is, in fact, `mp_entries`.

The following storages are currently supported:

- OFS storage
- File system
- Sybase
- Oracle
- ODBC
- MySQL
- Gadfly

OFS storage means that `mp_entries` are stored in Zope's internal database.

File system storage means that the `mp_entries` are stored in the file system—that is, in the `var` folder of the current Zope installation. A folder is created for each MetaPublisher instance that uses file system storage. There is one folder for each `mp_entry` inside this folder with its ID. This is the folder in which the `mp_entries` are actually stored.

The following path states, for example, where the `mp_entries` of a MetaPublisher instance with the ID filetester are stored in the file system.

```
/Zope/var/MetaPublisher/MetaEntries/filetester
```

Sybase, Oracle, ODBC, and Gadfly are the relational databases that can be used to store `mp_entries`.

There are two ways in which you can use MetaPublisher together with relational databases.

- You can create a new MetaPublisher instance that will store its `mp_entries` in one of the aforementioned databases.
- You can also "hook" an existing database table to a MetaPublisher. The MetaPublisher will then take control of the database.

In the following sections, we'll discuss the first option, and then we'll explain how to hook a MetaPublisher to an existing database table.

Storing `mp_entries` in a Relational Database

There is no way to change the data storage after a MetaPublisher instance is created, so you have to decide about that before creating a MetaPublisher. The form that you can see when you enter the initial data for a new MetaPublisher contains an Available Storage line.

Here you can see which storages are available. MetaPublisher searches through the Zope server along the acquisition path for database connections. When a database connection is found, the accompanying storage will become available.

Because the ZGadfly database comes with Zope, you can easily create a ZGadfly database connection to your Zope server (see Figure 6.30).

In the following examples, we will use Gadfly storage for illustration purposes. The other database connections, such as Oracle and so on, can be found over the Internet.

We will now create a MetaPublisher instance with the ID MetaP that will store its entries in a Gadfly database. Simply select MetaPublisher from the Available Objects menu, enter **`MetaP`** in the ID field inside the following form, and then select an available Gadfly database connection.

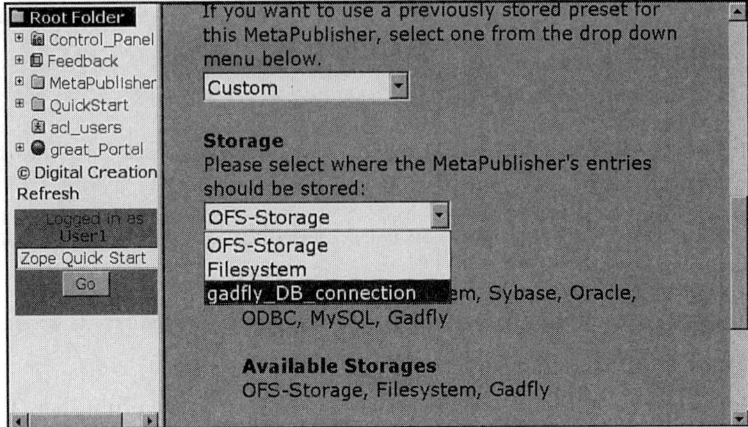

Figure 6.30

One Gadfly database connection is available.

We will add the following configurations:

Label	Type	Options
Name	Text	no options
Age	Integer	no options

Now we can use the Browse tab within the database connection to look at the database (see Figure 6.31).

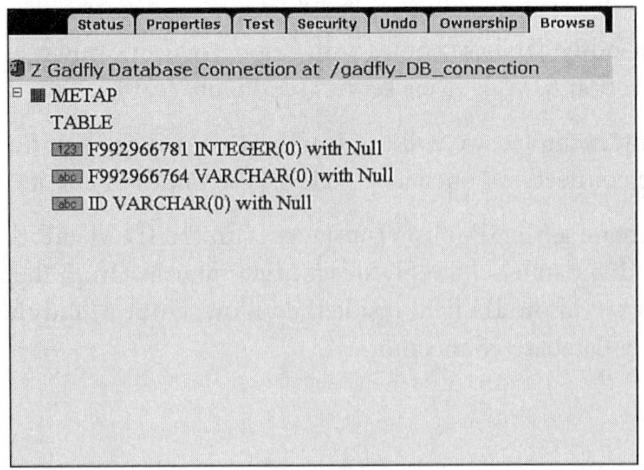

Figure 6.31

A new table with the ID of the MetaPublisher is created.

As you can see, the database has been modified. A table for the MetaPublisher instance has been created.

For each entry field that has been set up in the configuration interface, a column and one additional column has also been created.

The additional column with the label ID is auto-generated by MetaPublisher because a unique entry field (a column that contains unique entries exclusively) is required.

The `mp_entries` are stored in the Gadfly database. The items you can find in the `mp_entries` folder are simply a mapping so that you can access the single entries.

> **Note**
> If you should delete a MetaPublisher, the database table is not deleted. Also, the table entries are still within the database.

Hooking MetaPublisher to an Existing Database Table

If you have a database table and you need a powerful tool to administrate the database, you can easily use MetaPublisher. MetaPublisher will take control of the database and will provide you with interfaces for adding, editing, and deleting of data, as well as others.

But there are some things to consider to avoid the unintended loss of data.

Suppose that we have deleted the MetaPublisher from the previous section, but, because the data itself and the database table have not been removed, we still would like to use them. In this case, we will try to hook a new MetaPublisher instance to the table.

In the MetaPublisher Add form, we need to choose the right database connection, and we have to specify the name of the database table we want to use.

MetaPublisher will analyze the table data and ask you to set the right data type for each of the tables columns.

Moreover, you need to mark one single column that MetaPublisher needs as the unique entry field (see Figure 6.32). The column you choose here will be used by MetaPublisher internally and exclusively—the field will never show up, not in any interface nor in the configuration form.

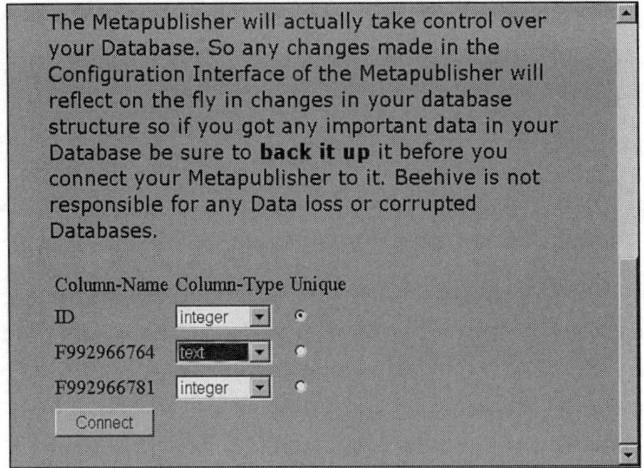

Figure 6.32

Choose a unique entry field and the appropriate data types for the other entry fields.

This means, in fact, that this field will be gone. In our example, it is not difficult to choose the appropriate field because one has been made for the purpose of providing a unique entry field.

> **Tip**
>
> You should always add a unique entry field to your database table before you connect the table to MetaPublisher.

You should also think about the data types of your entry fields before you choose them. For our Gadfly database, we can use the Browse tab to control the right settings; otherwise, the database could get corrupted. In any case, you should always make a backup of your data before you connect a table to MetaPublisher.

Now that we have created the new MetaPublisher instance, we can check whether the configuration is correct and whether we can access the `mp_entries`.

As you can see in Figure 6.33, the configuration is exactly as we have set it up.

We can also access the `mp_entries` we created (see Figure 6.34).

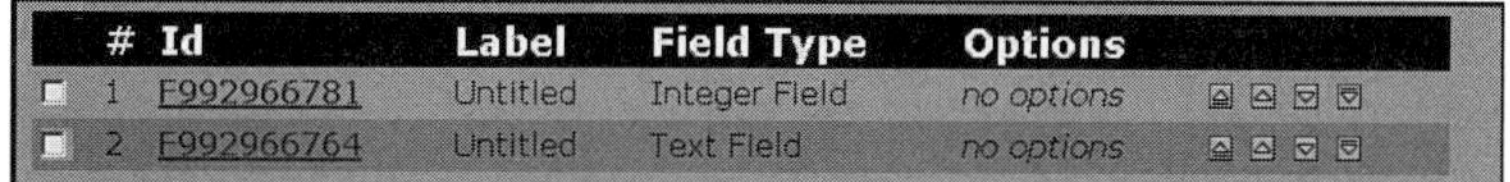

	#	Id	Label	Field Type	Options
	1	F992966781	Untitled	Integer Field	no options
	2	F992966764	Untitled	Text Field	no options

Figure 6.33

The new MetaPublisher contains the correct configuration.

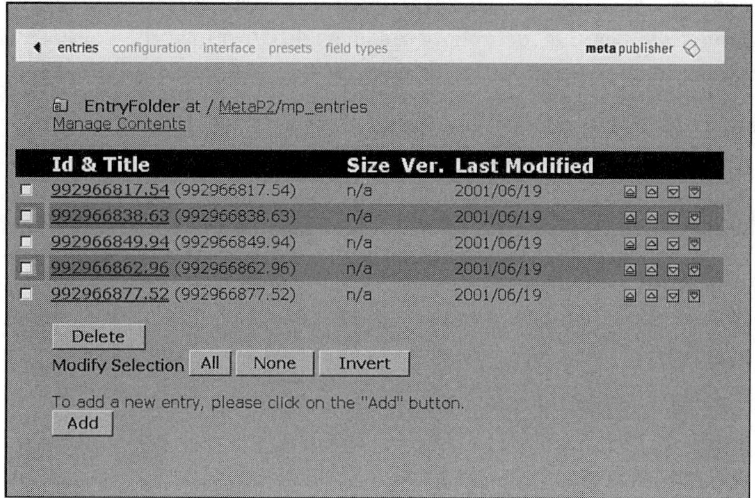

Figure 6.34

The entries from the database table have been received correctly.

MetaPublisher and CMF

As you have seen in previous chapters, the members and guests of a CMF portal can create portal-type instances, such as news items, file objects, or links.

With the MetaCMFPublisher, which is, in fact, an extension of MetaPublisher, you will be able to easily create new portal types that can then be used and published within a CMF portal. Members could, for example, add guest book entries and even news items that have been modified to meet their needs.

There are two steps to reach that goal:

1. A portal user with management permissions creates a new portal type with MetaCMFPublisher.
2. PortalUsers creates instances of the new portal type and starts using it.

Creating a New Portal Type with MetaCMFPublisher

Before you can actually start setting up a new portal type, you need to install MetaCMFPublisher, just as any other Zope product on your Zope server.

Installation

To install MetaCMFPublisher, do the following:

1. Go to `www.beehive.de`. Go to the main download area at `http://www.beehive.de/zope/freeware` and download the `MetaCMFPublisher` product file.
2. The product file needs to be unpacked. Use WinZip on Windows systems, or `tar` on Linux systems, to unpack it. For the destination path, use the path of your Zope installation. A new product with the name MetaCMFAddOn will then be installed in the products folder of your Zope installation.
3. Restart your Zope server. The new product will be initialized and will be ready for use.

Creating a MetaCMFPublisher Instance

MetaCMFPublisher instances need to be added to the root directory of the CMF portal (see Figure 6.35), where all the portal objects are, as `portal_actions` and `portal_skins`.

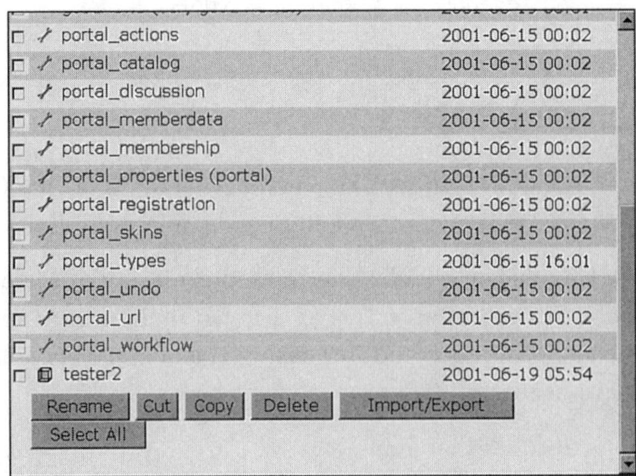

Figure 6.35
A new MetaCMFPublisher instance has been added to a CMF portal.

Choose the MetaPublisher (CMF based) option from the Available objects menu, and you will see the added interface of the new MetaPublisher.

In addition to the normal MetaPublisher, you need to specify an ID for the new portal type you are setting up (see Figure 6.36).

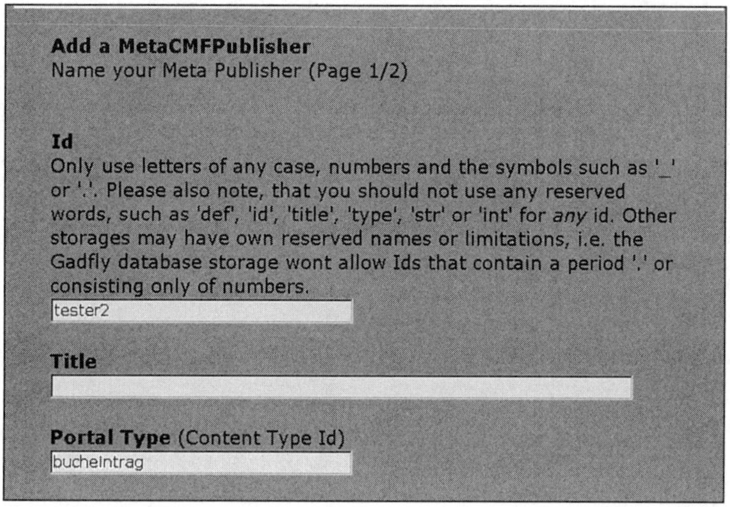

Add a MetaCMFPublisher
Name your Meta Publisher (Page 1/2)
Id
Only use letters of any case, numbers and the symbols such as '_' or '.'. Please also note, that you should not use any reserved words, such as 'def', 'id', 'title', 'type', 'str' or 'int' for any id. Other storages may have own reserved names or limitations, i.e. the Gadfly database storage wont allow Ids that contain a period '.' or consisting only of numbers.
tester2
Title
Portal Type (Content Type Id)
bucheIntrag

Figure 6.36

A MetaCMFPublisher with the ID tester2 created.

With that, a new FTI (factory-based type information) is added to the `portal_types` with the same ID as the MetaPublisher (see Figure 6.37).

The `/Control_Panel/Products/MetaPublisher` folder contains a new ZClass with the ID of the MetaPublisher as well.

Now, CMF portal members are able to add MetaPublisher entries (see Figure 6.38).

Configuring the MetaPublisher

Of course, you must not forget to configure the MetaPublisher you have created. The MetaPublisher configuration defines the entry fields of the new portal type.

You can work with MetaPublisher as usual, but it's not necessary for creating any user interfaces because they are not needed in the CMF portal. That means the CMF simply does not use them. When a member wants to add a MetaPublisher entry he or she will first state an ID for the new entry, such as goodNews (see Figure 6.38), and then the user is directed to the usual MetaData form (see Figure 6.39).

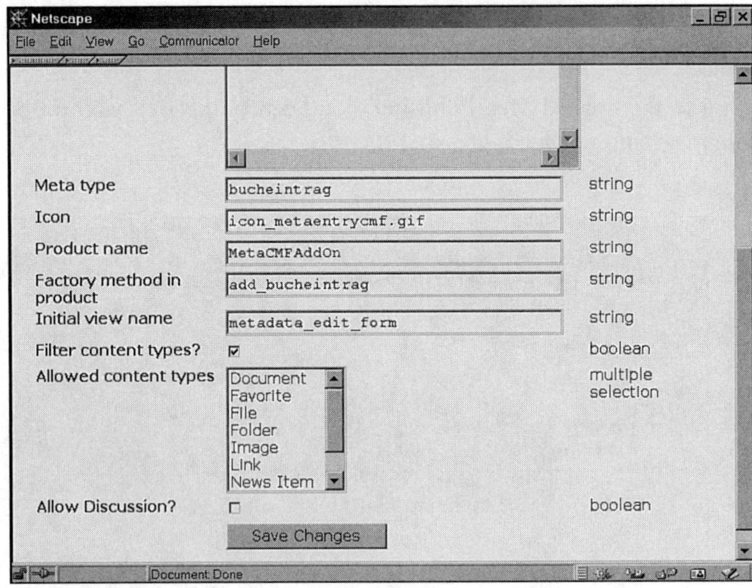

Figure 6.37

In the `portal_types` *folder, you can view the properties of the new FTI.*

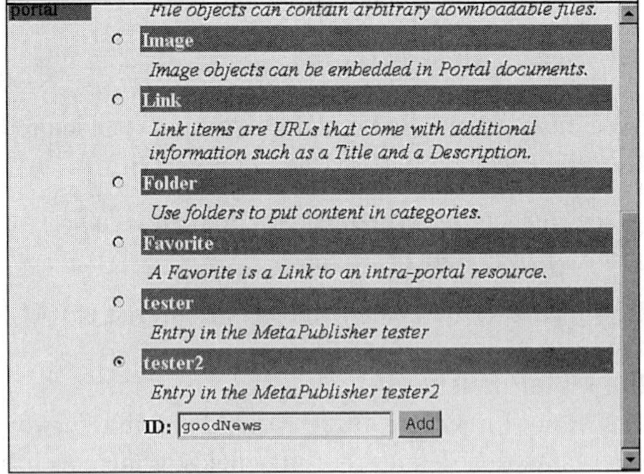

Figure 6.38

A new MetaPublisher entry with the ID goodNews is about to be created by a CMF portal member.

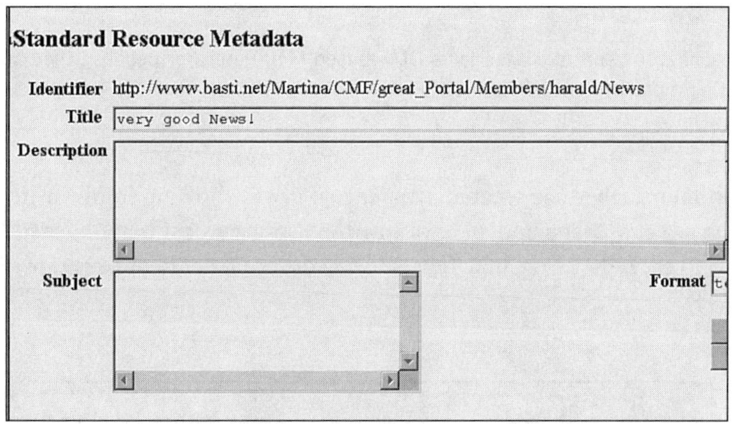

Figure 6.39

The portal member has stated a title for the new tester2 item he wants to add.

If the user then clicks the Add&Edit button, he or she will be directed to the form where he or she can specify all the necessary data for the `mp_entry` (see Figure 6.40). The entry fields that are provided by this form are taken from the MetaPublisher configuration. The actual entry is then stored in the MetaPublisher's `mp_entries` folder.

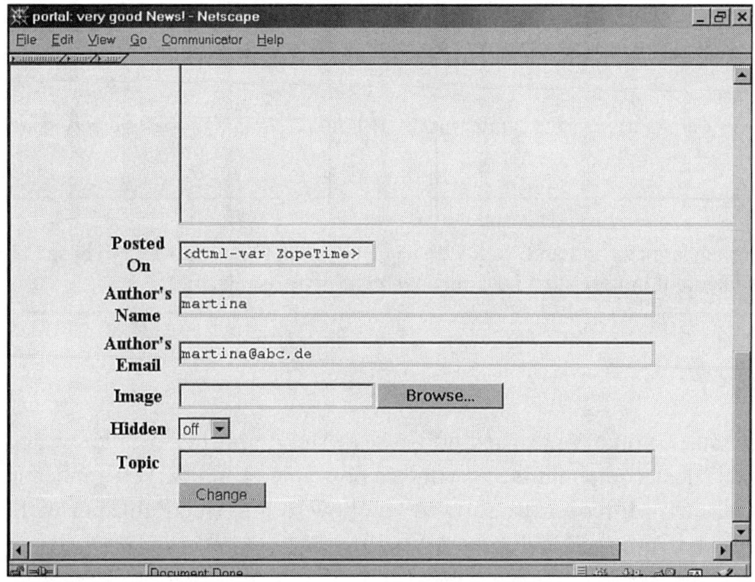

Figure 6.40

Portal members will use this form to add `mp_entries` *to tester2.*

> **Note**
> Do not configure user interfaces for a CMF-based MetaPublisher because they are not used by the CMF portal.

After a portal member has created a `mp_entry`, it will show up in his or her portal folder, just as `news_items` and so on. Now the user can let it be published by the reviewer and then the entry may be visible to other portal members as well (see Figure 6.41).

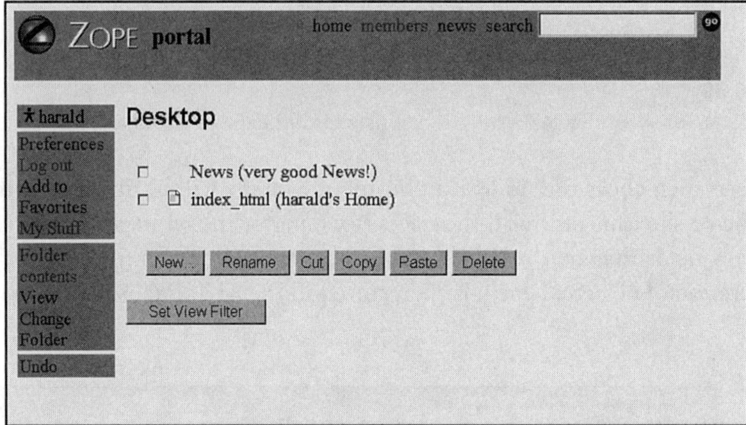

Figure 6.41
Portal user Harald has created an `mp_entry` *with the ID News and the title very good News!.*

> **Note**
> Portal members can add and work with `mp_entries`, but to set up a CMF-based MetaPublisher and configure it, a user must have management permissions.

Summary

In this chapter, you have learned how to use MetaPublisher. You know about MetaPublisher's components and you are now able to build Web applications with MetaPublisher. Moreover, we showed you how to use MetaPublisher with relational databases and with the CMF.

CHAPTER 7

CREATING A THREADED DISCUSSION GROUP

Providing your Web site visitors with a discussion forum will give them a means to interact with each other. Although they can publish news items to let others know about certain events, a forum will be more suitable to discuss topics.

In this chapter, we will create a discussion forum using ZDiscussions and ZUBB (Zope Ultimate Bulletin Board). The ZDiscussion product derives from the former Zope product Confera. This is why in the list of products that can be added to a folder, you will find the item Confera and not ZDiscussions.

> **Note**
> Within this chapter, we will use the terms Confera Topic and discussion forum—or just forum—synonymously.

Installation

Adding a discussion forum to your Zope server requires you to install two products instead of just one. Those two products are `ZDiscussion-0.2.0.tgz` and `ZDiscussionsZUBB-0.6.0.tar.gz`.

Download the products and unzip them to your Zope directory. Start with the first product. The second product will overwrite some of the first product's files. If you are asked whether to overwrite the files, answer Yes.

These two products will create the ZDiscussion and ZDBase directories in your Zope directory. ZDiscussion contains the standard DTML pages that are created when you add a discussion forum to your Zope server.

Remember to restart your Zope server. You will only be able to add new forums after a restart.

Creating a Portal Forum

Now we want to create a discussion forum for the members of our Achievers International portal. To do this, we need to

- Add a forum in the portal's folder
- Modify the portal to give the members access to the forum
- Modify the forum's look and
- Change the forum's security settings

You might like the original look of the forum. If not, the "Customizing the Discussion Forum" section later in this chapter will give you examples on how to add some extra information.

If you want to grant every portal visitor access to the forum, you do not need to change the security settings. However, you may want to restrict access to the registered portal members.

Adding a Confera Topic

If the installation was successful and the Zope server was restarted, you can start adding discussion forums. A folder's drop-down menu should contain a new item: Confera Topic.

Go to the Achievers International portal and select Confera Topic from the drop-down-menu. Fill out the Add form with the following data:

ID:	`Forum`
Title:	`Discussion Forum`
Options:	**Select This Topic Is Not Moderated, Messages in This Topic Do Not Expire, and Use Default Documents.**

Figure 7.1 shows the completed form with the different options.

A Confera Topic can be moderated or not. In our case, we don't want it to be moderated so that every message is shown at the Index page of the forum right after it is sent. If a Confera Topic is moderated, a reviewer has to approve the messages in the Management screen before they are shown at the Index page (see "The Options Tab" section later in this chapter).

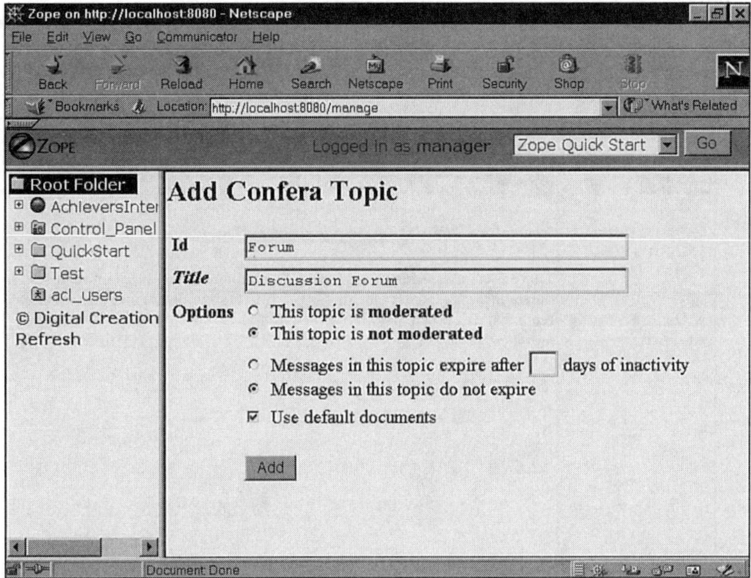

Figure 7.1
Adding a Confera Topic.

The Confera Tabs

In this section, we want to introduce the two tabs that are special for the Confera Topic. They are the Messages and Options tabs.

The Messages Tab

The Messages tab shows all the existing messages of a Confera Topic, similar to the `index_html` page. They are displayed with a tree structure, which means that you can expand and collapse the messages. You also have check boxes in front of each message. You can delete messages by activating the respective check boxes and pressing the Delete button at the bottom of the messages list.

> **Note**
> If you delete a message, you will automatically delete all the responses to this message.

As you know, a forum can be moderated or not moderated. Figure 7.2 shows the Messages tab of a non-moderated forum. As you can see, each message is also a link. If you click a message, you go to the Edit page for that message. The Edit page is similar to the page used to add a new message. Changes to a message are saved by clicking the Change button at the end of the Edit page.

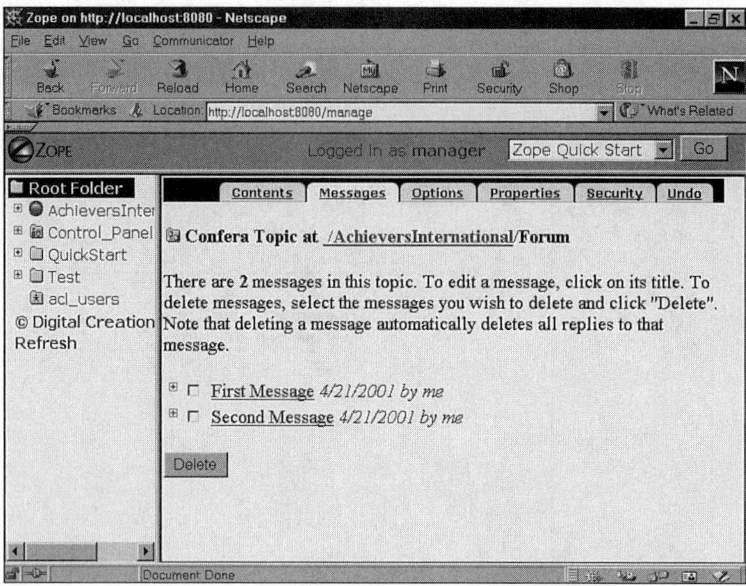

Figure 7.2

Messages view of a non-moderated forum.

If your forum is moderated, the Messages view looks slightly different. Some messages will have an asterisk in front of their title. The asterisk may be black or red. If it is black, that means a message within this thread (but not the message with the black asterisk) has not yet been reviewed and therefore is not visible in the `index_html` page. A red asterisk marks the message that needs to be reviewed. In Figure 7.3, First Message is a message that needs to be reviewed before it is shown on the `index_html` page, while Second Message only contains a message that has not been reviewed yet.

When using a moderated forum, you need to assign at least one moderator/reviewer who is allowed access to the Zope Management screen. This moderator could be the site administrator. To review a message and make it visible in the `index_html` page, click the respective message—the message with the red asterisk. In the message's Edit page (see Figure 7.4), you will see a This Item Has Been Reviewed check box. Activate the check box and save the message by clicking the Change button.

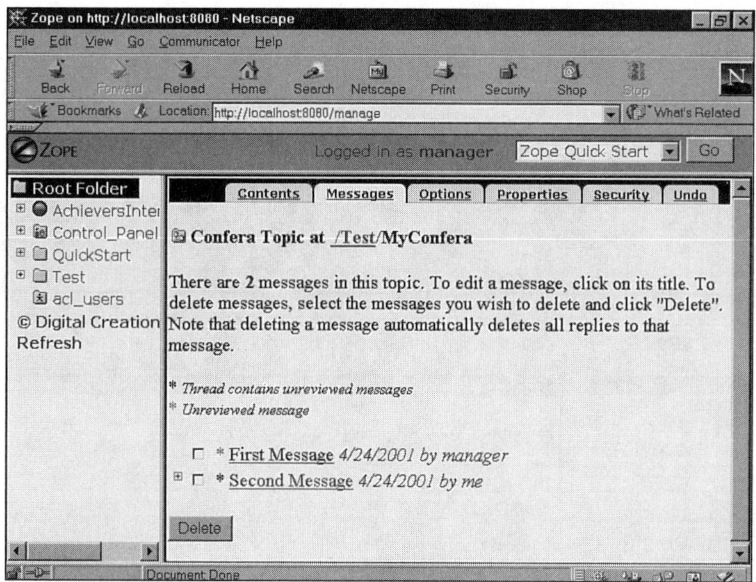

Figure 7.3

Messages view of a moderated forum.

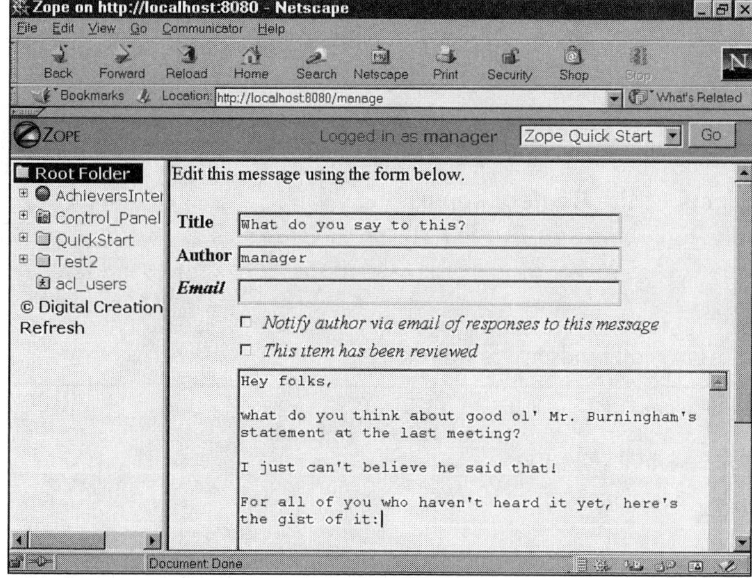

Figure 7.4

The Edit page of a message that has not been reviewed.

The Options Tab

The Options view of a Confera Topic enables you to change the forum's settings (see Figure 7.5). Here, the site administrator can decide whether a forum is moderated and whether the messages will expire after a stipulated amount of days.

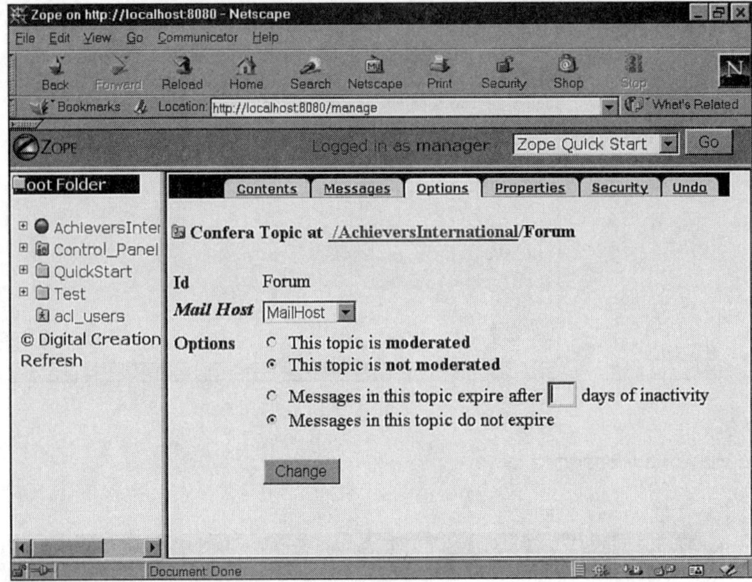

Figure 7.5

The Options view of a Confera Topic.

The Objects of the Confera Topic

A Confera Topic consists of six DTML methods as well as a vocabulary. The vocabulary is used to store the words used in the title, author, and body fields of a message.

The six DTML methods are as follows:

- `addMessageForm`
- `confera_searchResults`
- `index_html`
- `mail_html`
- `message_html`
- `searchForm`

The `addMessageForm` *DTML Method*

This DTML method provides the form used to add a new message to the discussion forum. The form consists of

- Three text fields—Title, Author, and E-mail
- A check box to indicate whether the author wants to be informed of responses to his or her message
- A text area for the body of the message
- A File field to attach a file to the message

> **Warning**
> A message is only accepted and sent if it contains a title and an author. If this information is not given, the message will be disregarded.

The check box will only appear in the form if the Zope server contains a `MailHost` object.

There are three variables that are stored after the first time a messages is added:

- `suggested_title`
- `suggested_author`
- `suggested_email`

The variables contain the information that was used the last time a user added a message. The next time the `addMessageForm` is called, this information is entered in the Title, Author, and E-mail fields.

The `confera_searchResults` *DTML Method*

This DTML method shows the results from a search. It is not called from another DTML method within the Confera Topic but from a Python method in the `ZDConfera.py` file.

The results are not shown using a tree structure but as a list. Top-level messages and replies can be recognized by their different icons.

The `index_html` *DTML Method*

This DTML method creates the homepage of a Confera Topic. It provides links to compose a new message and to search the existing messages. The messages are shown using the tree structure. Each message appears with its title, date created, and author.

As you know, a discussion forum can be moderated or not. Because only reviewed messages should appear on the homepage in a moderated forum, there are two tree structures that show the messages. One contains source code that will show only reviewed messages, and the other one shows all messages without first asking whether a message has been reviewed.

If there are no messages in the forum, the homepage will tell you so.

The `mail_html` DTML Method

The `mail_html` DTML method contains the contents of the mail that is sent when there has been a new reply to an author's message and the author wants to be informed of that.

The mail informs the author that a new response has been posted and to which message it belongs. It also gives the link where the response can be found and a link with which the author can deactivate the notification so that after he or she has been to the link, he or she will no longer be informed of new responses to the message.

The `message_html` DTML Method

This DTML method creates the page that shows a certain message. At the top, this DTML method shows the Return to Topic and Compose Reply links. The former takes you back to the forum's homepage, the latter to the form to add a new message.

The message's title is shown in bold letters, and below it is the date the message was created followed by the author of the message. The message body starts in the next line.

The `searchForm` DTML Method

The `searchForm` DTML method contains a simple form with two text fields: Search For and By Author.

The first text field is for searching the messages' body. The second, of course, is for searching for messages that were written by a certain author. By combining the two fields, you can minimize the number of results to your search.

Modifying the Portal

To grant the portal members access to the discussion forum, we need to change some DTML methods. Because there is no link yet that leads to the forum, we will have to add one. But let's change everything else that needs to be changed before giving the members access.

Besides adding the link to the forum, we will have to change the Confera Topic's security settings, because only registered members should be allowed to join in the discussions.

Another modification concerns the actions box. Because the Confera Topic is a separate product and not a portal type, it does not have actions applied to it. However, the actions box needs the object's actions to work correctly. Therefore, we need to change it so that it will work when the forum is called.

Changing the Forum's Security Settings

Because visitors that are not registered should not access the forum, we need to make sure that those anonymous users are not allowed to view the Confera Topic's pages. Go to the Confera Topic folder and click the Security tab.

The permission that needs to be changed is called `View`. Given to a group, it allows its members to see the respective objects in the third view. To ensure that the existing security settings from superfolders are not applied to the Confera Topic folder, deactivate the check box in front of the `View` permission. This interrupts the acquisition line and enables us to give this permission to only those groups we want to.

To grant the portal members access, activate the check boxes for the Member and Reviewer groups in the `View` permission row. Now, save the changes by clicking the Save Changes button (see Figure 7.6).

[x]	Set own password	[ ]	[x]	[ ]	[ ]	[ ]
[x]	Set own properties	[ ]	[x]	[ ]	[ ]	[ ]
[x]	Take ownership	[ ]	[x]	[ ]	[ ]	[ ]
[x]	Test Database Connections	[ ]	[x]	[ ]	[ ]	[ ]
[x]	Undo changes	[ ]	[x]	[ ]	[ ]	[ ]
[x]	Use Database Methods	[ ]	[x]	[ ]	[ ]	[ ]
[x]	Use Factories	[ ]	[x]	[ ]	[ ]	[ ]
[x]	Use mailhost services	[ ]	[x]	[ ]	[ ]	[ ]
[ ]	View	[ ]	[x]	[x]	[ ]	[x]
[x]	View History	[ ]	[x]	[ ]	[ ]	[ ]
[x]	View management screens	[ ]	[x]	[ ]	[ ]	[ ]
[x]	Vote	[ ]	[x]	[ ]	[ ]	[ ]

Save Changes

Figure 7.6

Security settings of the Confera Topic folder.

Modifying the Actions Box

As was already stated, the actions box needs an object's actions to work correctly. Therefore, we need to modify it to work with the discussion forum. Because it should work in all portal skins, there has to be a changed version of the `actions_box` DTML method in the `custom` folder of the `portal_skins` folder. Go to the `custom` folder and click the actions_box object. If there is no such object, read the “Creating a New Portal Skin” section in Chapter 5, “The Content Management Framework (CMF),” to see how to customize the portal.

Listing 7.1 shows the actions_box DTML method as it should be after the changes made in Chapter 5.

Listing 7.1

The actions_box *DTML Method*

```
<dtml-let isAnon="portal_membership.isAnonymousUser()"
          AuthClass="isAnon and 'GuestActions' or 'MemberActions'"
          uname="isAnon and 'Guest'
             or portal_membership.getAuthenticatedMember().getUserName()"
          obj="this()"
          actions="portal_actions.listFilteredActionsFor(obj)"
          user_actions="actions['user']"
          folder_actions="actions['folder']"
          object_actions="actions['object'] + actions['workflow']"
          global_actions="actions['global']"
>
<table class="ActionBox" width="100%">
 <tr class="&dtml-AuthClass;">
  <td class="ActionTitle">
   <img src="&dtml-portal_url;/p_/User_icon" align="left" alt="User">
   <dtml-var uname>
  </td>
 </tr>
 <tr class="&dtml-AuthClass;">
  <td>
   <dtml-in user_actions mapping>
    <a href="&dtml-url;"><dtml-var name></a><br>
   </dtml-in>
  </td>
 </tr>
<dtml-if folder_actions>
 <tr class="&dtml-AuthClass;">
  <td> <dtml-in folder_actions mapping>
         <a href="&dtml-url;"><dtml-var name></a><br>
       </dtml-in>
  </td>
 </tr>
</dtml-if>
```

Listing 7.1

Continued

```
<dtml-if object_actions>
 <tr class="&dtml-AuthClass;">
  <td class="ActionTitle">
   <dtml-let icon="_.getattr(obj, 'icon', '')"
             typ="_.getattr(obj, 'Type', '')"
             objID="obj.id"
   >
     <dtml-if icon>
     <img src="&dtml-BASEPATH1;/&dtml-icon;" align="left" alt="&dtml-typ;" />
     </dtml-if>
     <dtml-var objID size=15 html_quote>
    </dtml-let>
  </td>
 </tr>
 <tr class="&dtml-AuthClass;">
  <td>
    <dtml-let review_state="portal_workflow.getInfoFor(this(),
                             'review_state', '')">
    <dtml-if review_state>
    Status: &dtml-review_state;<br>
    </dtml-if>
    </dtml-let>
    <dtml-in object_actions mapping>
      <a href="&dtml-url;"><dtml-var name></a><br>
    </dtml-in>
  </td>
 </tr>
</dtml-if>
<dtml-if global_actions>
 <tr class="&dtml-AuthClass;">
  <td>
   <dtml-in global_actions mapping>
    <a href="<dtml-var url>"><dtml-var name></a><br>
   </dtml-in>
  </td>
 </tr>
</dtml-if>
</table>
</dtml-let>
```

The problem in the current source code is the line 5:

```
obj="this()"
```

Because of this line, the CMF takes the current object (`this()`) and tries to get its actions. Because the Confera Topic does not have any actions, we need to state a different object here whose actions can be shown in the actions box. Let's use the CMF itself, which has standard actions. However, if we just replaced the current line with the following line

```
5:              obj="AchieversInternational"
```

the actions box would always show the standard actions and not the different actions that belong to a document or link, for example. We can avoid this problem by using the `try...except` tags. We use the `try` part of this structure for the normal CMF pages and the `except` part for the forum. This way, the actions box will first try to find the actions of the current object (`this()`) and only if this fails (raises an error), will it use the code modified for the forum pages.

To use this structure, you need to duplicate the existing code in the `actions_box` DTML method and paste it at the end of the DTML method. Then change the `obj` line as shown in line 79 of Listing 7.2. Now you need to surround the two parts with the `try...except` tags. Listing 7.2 shows the modified code for the `actions_box` DTML method. Note the `try...except` tags in lines 1, 74, and 147.

Listing 7.2

Modified `actions_box` *DTML Method*

```
 1: <dtml-try>
 2: <dtml-let isAnon="portal_membership.isAnonymousUser()"
 3:              AuthClass="isAnon and 'GuestActions' or 'MemberActions'"
 4:              uname="isAnon and 'Guest'
 5:                        or portal_membership.getAuthenticatedMember().
➥getUserName()"
 6:              obj="this()"
 7:              actions="portal_actions.listFilteredActionsFor(obj)"
 8:              user_actions="actions['user']"
 9:              folder_actions="actions['folder']"
10:              object_actions="actions['object'] + actions['workflow']"
11:              global_actions="actions['global']"
12: >
13: <table class="ActionBox" width="100%">
14:  <tr class="&dtml-AuthClass;">
```

Listing 7.2

Continued

```
  <td class="ActionTitle">
   <img src="&dtml-portal_url;/p_/User_icon" align="left" alt="User">
   <dtml-var uname>
  </td>
 </tr>
 <tr class="&dtml-AuthClass;">
  <td>
   <dtml-in user_actions mapping>
    <a href="&dtml-url;"><dtml-var name></a><br>
   </dtml-in>
  </td>
 </tr>
<dtml-if folder_actions>
 <tr class="&dtml-AuthClass;">
  <td> <dtml-in folder_actions mapping>
        <a href="&dtml-url;"><dtml-var name></a><br>
       </dtml-in>
  </td>
 </tr>
</dtml-if>
<dtml-if object_actions>
 <tr class="&dtml-AuthClass;">
  <td class="ActionTitle">
   <dtml-let icon="_.getattr(obj, 'icon', '')"
             typ="_.getattr(obj, 'Type', '')"
             objID="obj.id"
   >
     <dtml-if icon>
     <img src="&dtml-BASEPATH1;/&dtml-icon;" align="left"
  alt="&dtml-typ;" />
     </dtml-if>
     <dtml-var objID size=15 html_quote>
    </dtml-let>
  </td>
 </tr>
 <tr class="&dtml-AuthClass;">
  <td>
    <dtml-let review_state="portal_workflow.getInfoFor(this(),
                            'review_state', '')">
    <dtml-if review_state>
    Status: &dtml-review_state;<br>
```

Listing 7.2

Continued

```
    </dtml-if>
    </dtml-let>
    <dtml-in object_actions mapping>
      <a href="&dtml-url;"><dtml-var name></a><br>
    </dtml-in>
  </td>
 </tr>
</dtml-if>
<dtml-if global_actions>
 <tr class="&dtml-AuthClass;">
  <td>
   <dtml-in global_actions mapping>
    <a href="<dtml-var url>"><dtml-var name></a><br>
   </dtml-in>
  </td>
 </tr>
</dtml-if>
</table>
</dtml-let>
<dtml-except>
<dtml-let isAnon="portal_membership.isAnonymousUser()"
           AuthClass="isAnon and 'GuestActions' or 'MemberActions'"
           uname="isAnon and 'Guest'
              or portal_membership.getAuthenticatedMember().getUserName()"
           obj="AchieversInternational"
           actions="portal_actions.listFilteredActionsFor(obj)"
           user_actions="actions['user']"
           folder_actions="actions['folder']"
           object_actions="actions['object'] + actions['workflow']"
           global_actions="actions['global']"
>
<table class="ActionBox" width="100%">
 <tr class="&dtml-AuthClass;">
  <td class="ActionTitle">
   <img src="&dtml-portal_url;/p_/User_icon" align="left" alt="User">
   <dtml-var uname>
  </td>
 </tr>
 <tr class="&dtml-AuthClass;">
  <td>
   <dtml-in user_actions mapping>
```

Listing 7.2

Continued

```
      <a href="&dtml-url;"><dtml-var name></a><br>
     </dtml-in>
    </td>
  </tr>
<dtml-if folder_actions>
  <tr class="&dtml-AuthClass;">
   <td> <dtml-in folder_actions mapping>
          <a href="&dtml-url;"><dtml-var name></a><br>
         </dtml-in>
   </td>
  </tr>
</dtml-if>
<dtml-if object_actions>
  <tr class="&dtml-AuthClass;">
   <td class="ActionTitle">
     <dtml-let icon="_.getattr(obj, 'icon', '')"
               typ="_.getattr(obj, 'Type', '')"
               objID="obj.id"
     >
       <dtml-if icon>
       <img src="&dtml-BASEPATH1;/&dtml-icon;" align="left"
    alt="&dtml-typ;" />
       </dtml-if>
       <dtml-var objID size=15 html_quote>
     </dtml-let>
   </td>
  </tr>
  <tr class="&dtml-AuthClass;">
   <td>
     <dtml-let review_state="portal_workflow.getInfoFor(this(),
                               'review_state', '')">
     <dtml-if review_state>
     Status: &dtml-review_state;<br>
     </dtml-if>
     </dtml-let>
     <dtml-in object_actions mapping>
       <a href="&dtml-url;"><dtml-var name></a><br>
     </dtml-in>
   </td>
  </tr>
</dtml-if>
```

Listing 7.2

Continued

```
<dtml-if global_actions>
  <tr class="&dtml-AuthClass;">
   <td>
    <dtml-in global_actions mapping>
     <a href="<dtml-var url>"><dtml-var name></a><br>
    </dtml-in>
   </td>
  </tr>
</dtml-if>
</table>
</dtml-let>
</dtml-try>
```

Save the changes to the DTML method, and the forum is ready for use by the portal members. That means we now need to give the members access to the forum.

Adding a Link to the Discussion Forum

The last thing we need to do is add a link to the discussion forum somewhere in the portal so that the members can access it. The best place to put the link might be the top bar together with the Home, Search, and so on links.

The top bar is defined in the `standard_top_bar` DTML method, which should already be in the `custom` folder in the `portal_skin` folder. If not, see the "Creating a New Portal Skin" section of Chapter 5. Add the link to the forum, as shown in Listing 7.3, line 21, and save the changes.

Listing 7.3

The `standard_top_bar` *DTML Method with the Link to the Forum*

```
 1: <!-- Top bar -->
 2: <table width="100%" border="0" cellpadding="0" cellspacing="0">
 3: <tr><td colspan="3" witdth="100%">
 4: <!-- hack around Netscape 4.x to ensure top table is solid black -->
 5: <table class="Masthead" cellspacing="0" cellpadding="0" border="0"
 6:        width="100%">
 7:  <tr class="Masthead">
 8:   <td class="PortalLogo" align="left" valign="top" width="1%"><a
 9:     href="&dtml-portal_url;"><img src="logo.png"
10:     alt="Zope Logo" border="0"></a></td>
11:   <td class="PortalTitle" width="29%" align="left"
```

Listing 7.3

Continued

```
      valign="center">
   <h1><dtml-with portal_properties>&dtml-title;</dtml-with
   ><dtml-if name="Title">: &dtml-Title;</dtml-if></h1>
  </td>
  <td class="NavBar" align="right" valign="bottom" width="70%" wrap="no">
   <form action="&dtml-portal_url;/search">
    <a href="&dtml-portal_url;">home</a> 
    <a href="&dtml-portal_url;/roster">members</a> 
    <a href="&dtml-portal_url;/recent_news">news</a> 
    <a href="&dtml-portal_url;/Forum">forum</a> 
    <a href="&dtml-portal_url;/search_form">search</a>
    <input name="SearchableText" size="16">
    <input border="0" type="image" name="go" src="go.gif">  
   </form>
  </td>
 </tr>
</table>
</td></tr></table>
```

The discussion forum is open to all members of the portal now. Non-members will be redirected to the login form if they click the forum link.

Customizing the Discussion Forum

You may want to change the look of the discussion forum or add some new features. This section will give some examples of how you can enhance a Confera Topic.

The “Useful Methods of the Discussion Product” section later in this chapter describes some methods that might give you some more ideas on how to modify a forum. You may also want to take a look for yourself at the two Python methods `ZDConfera.py` and `ZDiscussions.py`.

Example: Adding the Links Expand All and Collapse All

There are two very useful variables that can be used with the tree structure:

- `expand_all`
- `collapse_all`

If the expand_all variable is set to 1, the entire tree is expanded, all branches are opened down to the last leaf. Set this way, the variable is an easy way to see all the messages in a discussion forum.

If the collapse_all variable is set to 1, all expanded branches are closed, and only the top-level messages of a discussion forum are shown on the homepage. Figure 7.7 shows the index_html page with the two additional links.

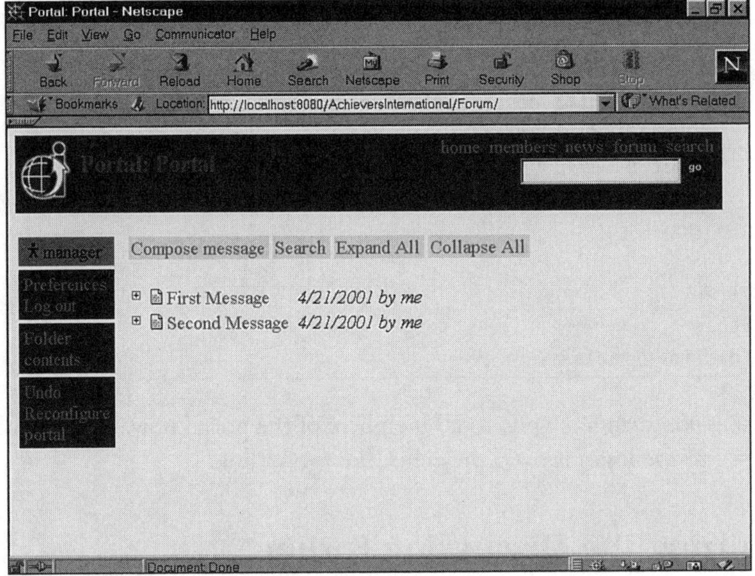

Figure 7.7
The forum's homepage with the additional links.

You can add these features to your discussion forum by adding two links to the Confera Topic's index_html DTML method. Listing 7.4 shows the modified DTML method. Lines 23–28 show the additional links. Essentially, what these two links do is call the DTML method again, but this time with the additional expand_all or collapse_all variable.

Listing 7.4
The index_html DTML Method with the Customized Link Table

```
1: <!--#var standard_html_header-->
2: <H2><!--#var title--></H2>
3: <P>
4: <TABLE>
```

Listing 7.4

Continued

```
<TR>
<!--#if parentObject-->
<!--#in parentObject-->
<!--#if sequence-var-index_html-->
<TD BGCOLOR="#EFEFEF" ALIGN="LEFT" VALIGN="TOP">
<A HREF="../index_html">Return
to <!--#if title--><!--#var title--><!--#else title--><!--#var id-->
➥ <!--#/if title-->
</A>
</TD>
<!--#/if index_html-->
<!--#/in parentObject-->
<!--#/if parentObject-->
<TD BGCOLOR="#EFEFEF" ALIGN="LEFT" VALIGN="TOP">
<A HREF="./addMessageForm">Compose message</A>
</TD>
<TD BGCOLOR="#EFEFEF" ALIGN="LEFT" VALIGN="TOP">
<A HREF="./searchForm">Search</A>
</TD>
<td bgcolor="#efefef" align="left" valign="top">
<a href="index_html?expand_all=1">Expand All</a>
</td>
<td bgcolor="#efefef" align="left" valign="top">
<a href="index_html?collapse_all=1">Collapse All</a>
</td>
</TR>
</TABLE>
<P>
<!--#if has_items-->
<table border=0>
<!--#if moderated-->
<tr>
<!--#tree branches="messageValues"-->
<!--#if reviewed-->
<td>
<A HREF="<!--#var tree-item-url-->/index_html">
➥ <IMG SRC="<!--#var SCRIPT_NAME-->/<!--#var icon-->" BORDER="0"></A>
<A HREF="<!--#var tree-item-url-->/index_html"><!--#var title--></A>
</td>
<td>
<EM><!--#var date_created--> by <!--#var author--></EM>
```

Listing 7.4

Continued

```
</td>
<!--#/if reviewed-->
<!--#/tree-->
</tr>
<!--#else moderated-->
<tr>
<!--#tree branches="messageValues"-->
<td>
<A HREF="<!--#var tree-item-url-->/index_html">
➥ <IMG SRC="<!--#var SCRIPT_NAME-->/<!--#var icon-->" BORDER="0"></A>
<A HREF="<!--#var tree-item-url-->/index_html"><!--#var title--></A>
</td>
<td>
<EM><!--#var date_created--> by <!--#var author--></EM>
</td>
<!--#/tree-->
</tr>
<!--#/if moderated-->
</table>
<!--#else has_items-->
<I>There are currently no messages in this topic.</I>
<!--#/if has_items-->
<!--#var standard_html_footer-->
```

Example: Displaying the Number of Messages in a Thread

Because the Confera Topic product was amended by the ZUBB product, there are some more useful methods you can use to enhance your discussion forum. For example, you can show the users how many replies have been made to a certain message. The Python `ZDiscussions.py` file provides the `childMessageCount()` method used here. Figure 7.8 shows what we will be doing in this section, namely, adding the number of messages in a thread behind the top message.

Showing the number of replies is obviously only necessary if the message is not expanded and its replies are not visible to the user. Therefore, we use the `if` tag to only show the number of replies if the item is not expanded and if there actually is a reply to the message:

```
<dtml-if "(_['tree-item-expanded']==0) and (childMessageCount() > 1)">
```

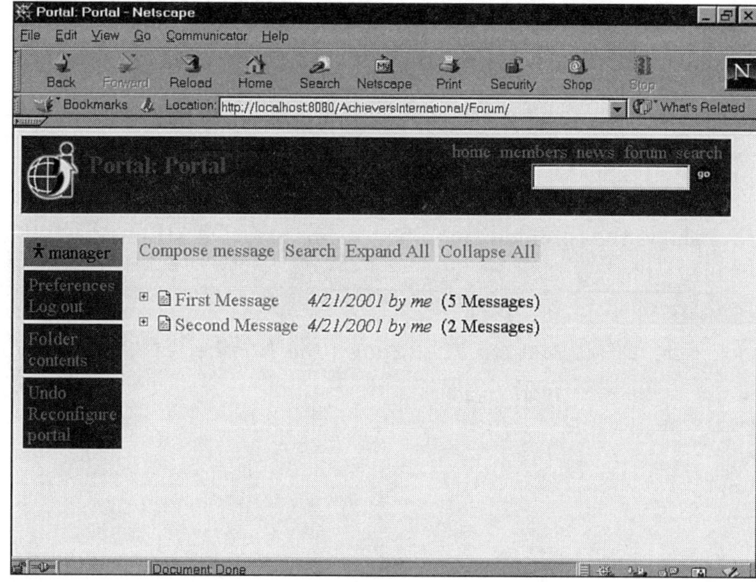

Figure 7.8

The discussion forum with the number of replies after a message.

The `tree-item-expanded` variable belongs to the tree structure. If it equals 0, the current tree item is not expanded. If it equals 1, the item is expanded.

If both conditions are true, we want to add the number of replies in brackets after the author. This is done as follows:

```
<td>
 (<dtml-var "childMessageCount()"> Messages)
</td>
```

Close the `if` tag after this table cell, or you will get an error message when you try to save the changes.

```
<dtml-if "(_['tree-item-expanded']==0) and (childMessageCount() > 1)">
<td>
 (<dtml-var "childMessageCount()"> Messages)
</td>
</dtml-if>
```

> **Note**
> You will have to add the previous code twice in the `index_html` DTML method—once for the moderated part (see Listing 7.5, lines 45–49) and once for the non-moderated part (see Listing 7.5, lines 63–67).

Listing 7.5 shows the complete, modified `index_html` DTML method.

Listing 7.5

The `index_html` DTML Method That Shows the Number of Messages in a Thread

```
1: <!--#var standard_html_header-->
2: <H2><!--#var title--></H2>
3: <P>
4: <TABLE>
5: <TR>
6: <!--#if parentObject-->
7: <!--#in parentObject-->
8: <!--#if sequence-var-index_html-->
9: <TD BGCOLOR="#EFEFEF" ALIGN="LEFT" VALIGN="TOP">
10: <A HREF="../index_html">Return
11: to <!--#if title--><!--#var title-->
➥ <!--#else title--><!--#var id--><!--#/if title-->
12: </A>
13: </TD>
14: <!--#/if index_html-->
15: <!--#/in parentObject-->
16: <!--#/if parentObject-->
17: <TD BGCOLOR="#EFEFEF" ALIGN="LEFT" VALIGN="TOP">
18: <A HREF="./addMessageForm">Compose message</A>
19: </TD>
20: <TD BGCOLOR="#EFEFEF" ALIGN="LEFT" VALIGN="TOP">
21: <A HREF="./searchForm">Search</A>
22: </TD>
23: <td bgcolor="#efefef" align="left" valign="top">
24: <a href="index_html?expand_all=1">Expand All</a>
25: </td>
26: <td bgcolor="#efefef" align="left" valign="top">
27: <a href="index_html?collapse_all=1">Collapse All</a>
28: </td>
29: </TR>
30: </TABLE>
```

Listing 7.5

Continued

```
<P>
<!--#if has_items-->
<table border=1>
#if moderated-->
<tr>
<!--#tree branches="messageValues"-->
<!--#if reviewed-->
<td>
<A HREF="<!--#var tree-item-url-->/index_html"> <IMG SRC="<!--#var SCRIPT_NAME-->/<!--#var icon-->" BORDER="0"></A>
<A HREF="<!--#var tree-item-url-->/index_html"><!--#var title--></A>
</td>
<td>
<EM><!--#var date_created--> by <!--#var author--></EM>
</td>
<dtml-if "(_['tree-item-expanded']==0) and (childMessageCount() > 1)">
<td>
(<dtml-var "childMessageCount()"> Messages)
</td>
</dtml-if>
<!--#/if reviewed-->
<!--#/tree-->
</tr>
<!--#else moderated-->
<tr>
<!--#tree branches="messageValues"-->
<td>
<A HREF="<!--#var tree-item-url-->/index_html"> <IMG SRC="<!--#var SCRIPT_NAME-->/<!--#var icon-->" BORDER="0"></A>
<A HREF="<!--#var tree-item-url-->/index_html"><!--#var title--></A>
</td>
<td>
<EM><!--#var date_created--> by <!--#var author--></EM>
</td>
<dtml-if "(_['tree-item-expanded']==0) and (childMessageCount() > 1)">
<td>
(<dtml-var "childMessageCount()"> Messages)
</td>
</dtml-if>
<!--#/tree-->
</tr>
```

Listing 7.5

Continued

```
<!--#/if moderated-->
<!--#else has_items-->
<I>There are currently no messages in this topic.</I>
<!--#/if has_items-->
<!--#var standard_html_footer-->
```

Example: Adding Links to the Replies of a Message

Another nice feature you might want to add to the discussion forum is adding links to the replies for a message at the bottom of the message. That way, it will be easier for readers to follow a thread.

Essentially, the code you need to do this is a copy of the tree code from the `index_html` DTML method. Put the code into a table and enter the resulting lines at the end of the `message_html` DTML method, but before the line

```
<!---#var standard_html_footer-->
```

Listing 7.6 shows the code you need to add.

Listing 7.6

Code for Adding Further Replies to the `message_html` *DTML Method*

```
<!--begin table with replies-->
<TABLE WIDTH="600" BORDER="0" CELLSPACING="0" CELLPADDING="0">
  <TR>
    <TD>
      <dtml-call "REQUEST.set('expand_all', '1')">
      <dtml-tree branches="messageValues">
      <A HREF="<dtml-var tree-item-url>/index_html">
      <IMG SRC="<dtml-var SCRIPT_NAME>/<dtml-var icon>" BORDER="0"></A>
      <A HREF="<dtml-var tree-item-url>/index_html"><dtml-var title></A>
      <EM> by <dtml-var author> (<dtml-var date_created>)</EM>
      </dtml-tree>
    </TD>
  </TR>
</TABLE>
<!--end table with replies-->
```

> **Note**
> The code in Listing 7.6 will automatically expand all replies. If you want the replies not to be expanded, delete line 5.

Figure 7.9 shows what a message will look like with the additional code.

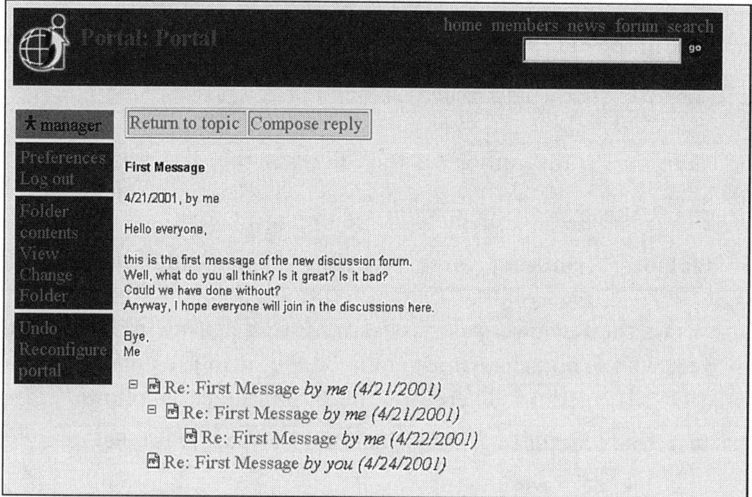

Figure 7.9
The Modified Message page.

Example: Marking Messages by Certain Authors

Sometimes, you might want to mark messages by certain authors, for example, messages sent by reviewers or by the moderator of a forum. You can do this simply by using the `if` tag to divide parts of the source code. You need the following methods to see if the author of a message has a certain role:

- `getUser()`
- `has_role()`

Let's build the `if` tag step by step:

getUser() is a method that belongs to the User folder object. Therefore, it has to be called on the object.

```
acl_users.getUser()
```

expects the name of a user. In this case, this will be the author of a message. The name of the author needs to be specifically transformed into a string:

```
acl_users.getUser(_.str(_['author']))
```

Now, we can call the has_role() method. This method expects a role as argument:

```
acl_users.getUser(_.str(_['author'])).has_role('Reviewer')
```

This line returns a 1 if the author has the Reviewer role and a 0 if he or she does not.

Now we can use this expression in an if tag:

```
<dtml-if "acl_users.getUser(_.str(_['author'])).has_role('Reviewer')">
```

If the author has the Reviewer role, we want his or her name to be bold and blue (color = #003366). If not, the name should be as it is in the default version of the index_html DTML method. Therefore, the if part looks as follows:

```
<dtml-if "acl_users.getUser(_.str(_['author'])).has_role('Reviewer')">
  <font color="#003366">
  <b><!--#var date_created--> by <!--#var author--></b>
```

and the following is how the else part looks:

```
<dtml-else>
  <!--#var date_created--> by <!--#var author-->
</dtml-if>
```

However, the if line may raise an error message if the name the author chose does not exist in the acl_users folder. That is why we need to put the if tag within a try...except construction. Listing 7.7 shows the lines that are necessary to mark messages of Reviewers.

Listing 7.7

Additional Lines to Mark Messages of Reviewers

```
<EM>
<dtml-try>
  <dtml-if "acl_users.getUser(_.str(_['author'])).has_role('Reviewer')">
    <font color="#003366">
```

Listing 7.7

Continued

```
      <b><!--#var date_created--> by <!--#var author--></b>
    <dtml-else>
      <!--#var date_created--> by <!--#var author-->
    </dtml-if>
  <dtml-except>
    <!--#var date_created--> by <!--#var author-->
  </dtml-try>
  </EM>
```

If you enter these lines in the `index_htm` DTML method, they will still cause error messages if the DTML method is called by users that are not Managers. This is because other users are not allowed to call the `getUser()` method. To avoid this problem, you need to give the `index_html` DTML method the proxy role Manager. That way, the DTML method can call methods that a user accessing the DTML method would normally not be allowed to call.

To change the DTML method's proxy role, go to its Proxy view by clicking the Proxy tab in its Edit view. Click Manager in the select list and save the changes (see Figure 7.10).

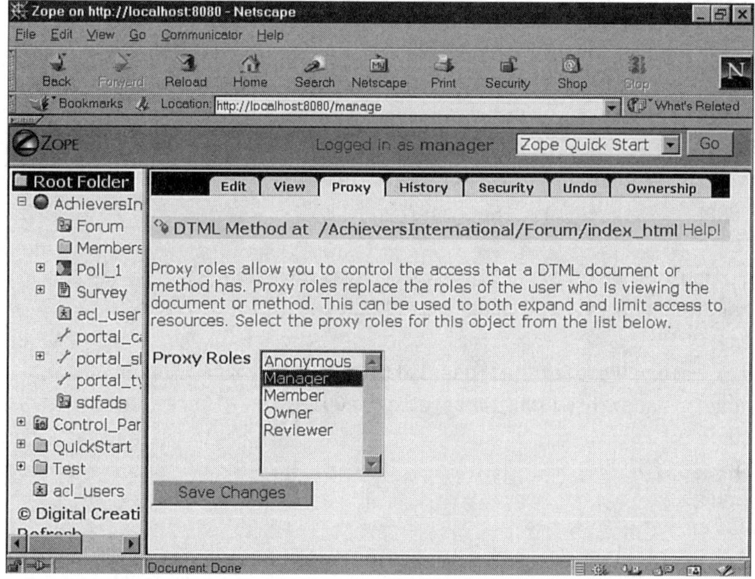

Figure 7.10

The Proxy view of the `index_html` *DTML method.*

Now the additional lines will not raise any error messages. Listing 7.8 shows the complete, new `index_html` DTML method. Note that you have to add the additional lines twice again: once for moderated (lines 43–54) and once for non-moderated (lines 72–83).

Listing 7.8

Complete, Modified `index_html` *DTML Method*

```
1: <!--#var standard_html_header-->
2: <H2><!--#var title--></H2>
3: <P>
4: <TABLE>
5: <TR>
6: <!--#if parentObject-->
7: <!--#in parentObject-->
8: <!--#if sequence-var-index_html-->
9: <TD BGCOLOR="#EFEFEF" ALIGN="LEFT" VALIGN="TOP">
10: <A HREF="../index_html">Return
11: to <!--#if title--><!--#var title-->
➥ <!--#else title--><!--#var id--><!--#/if title-->
12: </A>
13: </TD>
14: <!--#/if index_html-->
15: <!--#/in parentObject-->
16: <!--#/if parentObject-->
17: <TD BGCOLOR="#EFEFEF" ALIGN="LEFT" VALIGN="TOP">
18: <A HREF="./addMessageForm">Compose message</A>
19: </TD>
20: <TD BGCOLOR="#EFEFEF" ALIGN="LEFT" VALIGN="TOP">
21: <A HREF="./searchForm">Search</A>
22: </TD>
23: <td bgcolor="#efefef" align="left" valign="top">
24: <a href="index_html?expand_all=1">Expand All</a>
25: </td>
26: <td bgcolor="#efefef" align="left" valign="top">
27: <a href="index_html?collapse_all=1">Collapse All</a>
28: </td>
29: </TR>
30: </TABLE>
31: <P>
32: <!--#if has_items-->
33: <table border=0>
34: <!--#if moderated-->
35: <tr>
```

Listing 7.8

Continued

```
<!--#tree branches="messageValues"-->
<!--#if reviewed-->
<td>
<A HREF="<!--#var tree-item-url-->/index_html">
➥ <IMG SRC="<!--#var SCRIPT_NAME-->/<!--#var icon-->" BORDER="0"></A>
<A HREF="<!--#var tree-item-url-->/index_html"><!--#var title--></A>
</td>
<td>
 <EM>
 <dtml-try>
   <dtml-if "acl_users.getUser(_.str(_['author'])).has_role('Reviewer')">
     <font color="#003366">
     <b><!--#var date_created--> by <!--#var author--></b>
   <dtml-else>
     <!--#var date_created--> by <!--#var author-->
   </dtml-if>
 <dtml-except>
   <!--#var date_created--> by <!--#var author-->
 </dtml-try>
 </EM>
</td>
<dtml-if "(_['tree-item-expanded']==0) and (childMessageCount() > 1)">
<td>
(<dtml-var "childMessageCount()"> Messages)
➥  <dtml-var "threadNewestMessageDate()">
</td>
</dtml-if>
<!--#/if reviewed-->
<!--#/tree-->
</tr>
<!--#else moderated-->
<tr>
<!--#tree branches="messageValues"-->
<td>
<A HREF="<!--#var tree-item-url-->/index_html">
➥ <IMG SRC="<!--#var SCRIPT_NAME-->/<!--#var icon-->" BORDER="0"></A>
<A HREF="<!--#var tree-item-url-->/index_html"><!--#var title--></A>
</td>
<td>
 <EM>
 <dtml-try>
   <dtml-if "acl_users.getUser(_.str(_['author'])).has_role('Reviewer')">
```

Listing 7.8
Continued

```
     <font color="#003366">
     <b><!--#var date_created--> by <!--#var author--></b>
   <dtml-else>
     <!--#var date_created--> by <!--#var author-->
   </dtml-if>
 <dtml-except>
   <!--#var date_created--> by <!--#var author-->
 </dtml-try>
 </EM>
</td>
<dtml-if "(_['tree-item-expanded']==0) and (childMessageCount() > 1)">
<td>
(<dtml-var "childMessageCount()"> Messages)
</td>
</dtml-if>
<!--#/tree-->
</tr>
<!--#/if moderated-->
</table>
<!--#else has_items-->
<I>There are currently no messages in this topic.</I>
<!--#/if has_items-->
<!--#var standard_html_footer-->
```

Useful Methods of the Discussion Product

The Python `ZDiscussions.py` file can be found in the `/lib/python/Products/ZDBase` directory. It contains some useful methods that help show interesting information about the forum's messages on the `index_html` page of a forum. We have already used some of them in this chapter.

ZDiscussions.py

In this section we will introduce four methods of the `Zdiscussions.py` file:

- `childMessageCount()`
- `threadMessageCount()`
- `childNewestMessageDate()`
- `threadNewestMessageDate()`

Of course, there are more methods in this file, but these four are useful for forum administrators who want to add extra information in the forum for the users.

childMessageCount()

The `childMessageCount()` method returns the number of responses to a message plus one for the specified message. For example, if you have the following structure:

```
- UppermostMessage
  - Re: UppermostMessage
  - Re: UppermostMessage
    - Re: UppermostMessage
```

and you use the method on the `UppermostMessage` message, it will return the number 4, although there are only three children.

threadMessageCount()

This method works similar to `childMessageCount()`. However, it returns the number of messages within a thread. This means that even called on a reply to a message, it will return the number of all messages in the thread.

childNewestMessageDate()

The `childNewestMessageDate()` method looks through all messages in the replies to the current message and finds the most recent one. It then returns the date of the most recent message in the following form:

```
2001/04/22 11:08:42.96 GMT+2
```

threadNewestMessageDate()

This method is similar to `childNewestMeddageDate()`, but it looks for the most recent message within the entire thread. The format of the returned date is the same as `childNewestMessageDate()`'s.

Summary

In this chapter, you have learned how to create a discussion group using the Zope products ZDiscussions and ZUBB and how to fit the discussion group into the CMF portal. Then, you modified the group to enhance it and make it more useful for the portal members.

The next chapter will deal with adding polls and surveys to your portal to get feedback from the members.

CHAPTER 8

CREATING POLLS AND SURVEYS

This chapter will show you how to enhance your Web site—in our case, the CMF—with polls and surveys that may, for example, help you find out what visitors or members think about the design, layout, content, or searchability of your site.

For this, we do not need to start writing a long and complicated Python program or create difficult DTML methods with DTML and HTML. We simply use two existing Zope products that the Zope community provides—the Poll product and the Survey product. Both products can be found at `www.zope.org`:

```
http://www.zope.org/Members/sleeper/PMPSurvey
```

```
http://www.zope.org/Members/mega/poll
```

Installing the Products

Again, installing the products is very easy. Download the Poll and PMPSurvey products from `zope.org`. There are various survey products on that Web site, but we will be using the PMPSurvey product.

The files are compressed and need to be unpacked in the Zope directory because they already contain the correct pathnames. After decompressing the package, restart your Zope server, and you should be able to start working with the products. If either or both of the `Poll` and `pmp_survey` elements do not appear in the drop-down menu, make sure the `Poll` and `PMPSurvey` folders are in the Zope `/lib/python/Products` directory.

The Poll Product

A poll lets you pose questions to the members of the CMF. With the Poll product you can pose one or more questions, and you can decide whether the poll is to be anonymous. If you choose not to make the poll anonymous, each member can only vote once. Zope will remember the names of the members who have already voted.

The results of the poll can be seen either before or after voting, but after voting, the member is automatically directed to the Result page anyway.

Creating a Poll for the CMF

To give the members of the CMF a chance to state their opinions of the CMF, we will create a poll with the question: "How do you like this site?"

Creating a Poll Instance

Now let's start creating the poll. Go to the CMF directory and select the `Poll` element from the drop-down menu. Fill out the Add Poll form with the following data:

ID:	**`Poll_1`**
Title:	**`How do you like this site?`**

Add the `poll` object by clicking the Add button (see Figure 8.1).

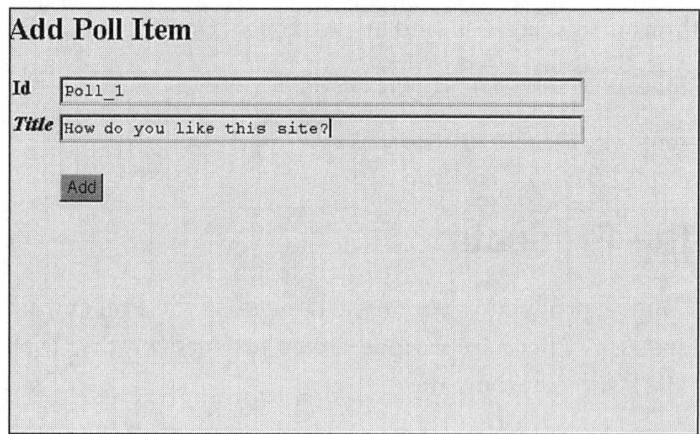

Figure 8.1
Add Poll form.

Adding a Question

Click the `Poll_1` object. You see the Properties view of this object. You can add new questions and edit existing ones here if needed (see Figure 8.2).

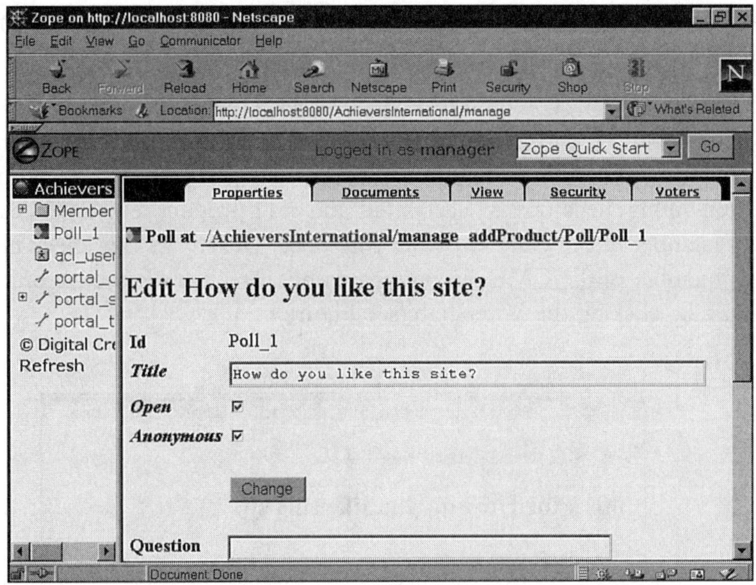

Figure 8.2
Properties view of `Poll_1`.

Enter the question **`How do you like this site?`** in the Question field, and the following answer choices in the Poll Answers text area—one answer per line:

a. **`It's fantastic.`**

b. **`It's alright.`**

c. **`I don't like it.`**

Click the Add button, and your first poll question is ready.

> **Note**
> If you have more than one question in a `poll` object, all questions must be answered by a voter for the vote to be counted. It is not possible to only answer part of the questions. If you want the voter to have a choice as to which question he or she wants to answer, create a `poll` object for each question. Do not forget to link the various `poll` objects on the CMF pages.

However, members of the CMF do not even know yet that there is a poll. They have no way to get to the poll from within the CMF, so we need to make some changes to the CMF to provide a link to the poll. But first, let's take a better look at the `poll` product.

On the Properties view, you have two check boxes: Open and Anonymous. Both are activated by default. If the Open check box is deactivated, the poll is closed and no more votes can be entered. As mentioned earlier, the poll can be anonymous or not. If the Anonymous check box is deactivated, the `poll` product remembers each voter so that each member of the CMF can only vote once. Deactivate this check box now, so that each member of the CMF can only vote once. You can see the list of voters on the Voters view by clicking the Voters tab (see Figure 8.3).

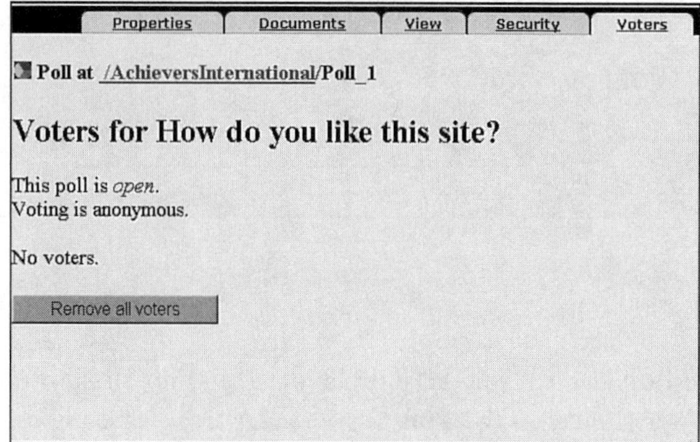

Figure 8.3
Voters view.

Changing the `legend.dtml` File

The questions and answers in the Properties view can be edited by clicking them. This way, even the number of votes for an answer can be edited. Figure 8.4 shows the Edit page for a question.

The way the questions and answers are shown here is the same as on the Results page that a voters sees. That means that, to the voter, the answers are links. That is not what we want, however, because clicking this link does not mean he or she votes—the browser would be directed to the Edit page for the respective answers.

Therefore, we need to change the file that returns the questions and answers information to the Results page. This file is on the file system in the `/lib/python/Products/Poll/` directory and is called `legend.dtml` (see Listing 8.1).

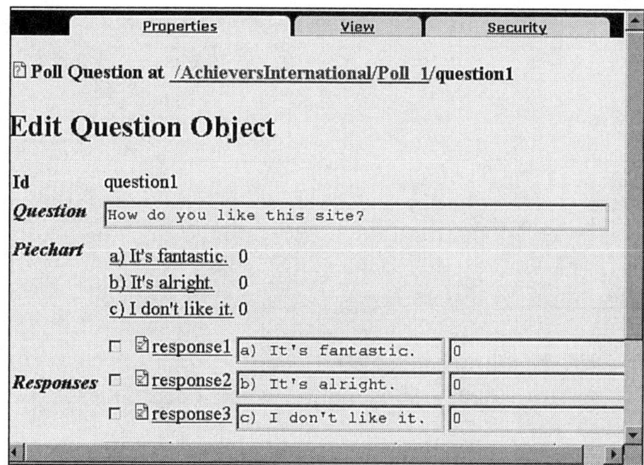

Figure 8.4

Edit page for a question.

Listing 8.1

The `legend.dtml` *File*

```
 1: <table border = "0">
 2:      <!--#if table-->
 3:      <!--#in table mapping-->
 4:      <tr>
 5:          <!--#if fancy_graphics-->
 6:             <td width="20" bgcolor="<!--#var colorCode-->"> </td>
 7:          <!--#/if-->
 8:          <td><a href='./<!--#if amPoll--><!--#var questionId-->/
➥<!--#/if--><!--#var responseId-->/manage_main'><!--#var response--></a></td>
 9:          <td><!--#var voteString--></td>
10:      </tr>
11:      <!--#/in-->
12:      <!--#else-->
13:      <tr><td>No Responses Yet!!!</td></tr>
14:      <!--#/if-->
15: </table>
```

Edit this file with a text editor and replace line 8 with the following line:

```
<td><!--#var response--></td>
```

This removes the hyperlink from the answer (see Listing 8.2). The questions will still be links, but only in the Properties view—not on the Results page.

Listing 8.2

Modified `legend.dtml` *File*

```
<table border = "0">
     <!--#if table-->
     <!--#in table mapping-->
     <tr>
        <!--#if fancy_graphics-->
          <td width="20" bgcolor="<!--#var colorCode-->"> </td>
        <!--#/if-->
        <td><!--#var response--></td>
        <td><!--#var voteString--></td>
     </tr>
     <!--#/in-->
     <!--#else-->
     <tr><td>No Responses Yet!!!</td></tr>
     <!--#/if-->
</table>
```

The Documents View

The Documents tab shows the DTML methods that are responsible for showing the poll questions and the results. (See Figure 8.5.) The two DMTL methods, `index_html` and `result`, can be edited by clicking them.

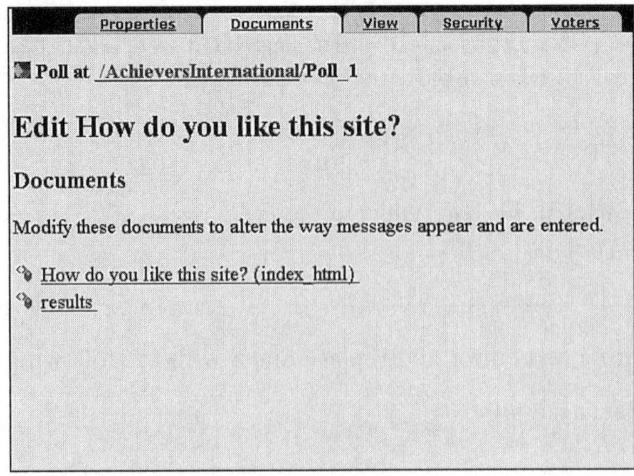

Figure 8.5

The Documents view of the poll.

Changing Security Settings

Another modification that needs to be done is to give the members of the CMF the permission to vote. This is done in the `Security` view of the poll. Deactivate the check box in front of the `Vote` permission at the bottom of the list and activate the check box behind the permission in the Members column (see Figure 8.6). Now click Save Changes, and members will be able to vote. If you also want to allow reviewers to vote, activate the respective check box in the column for Reviewers.

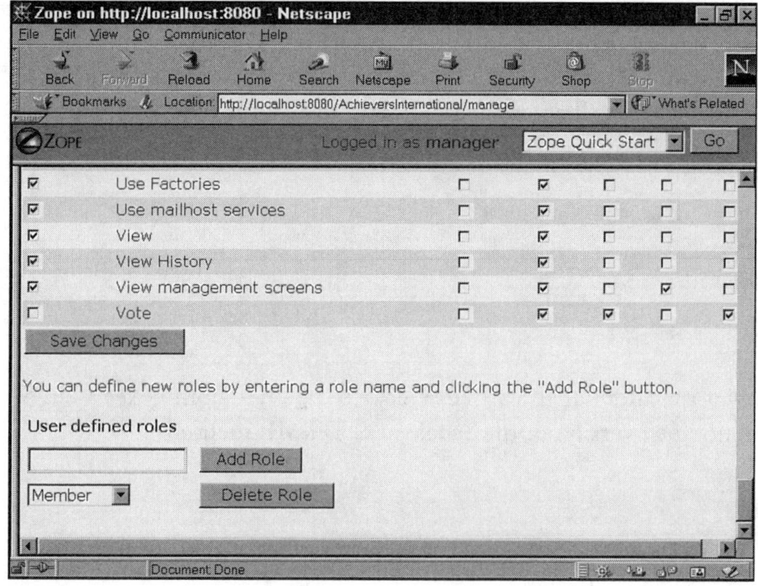

Figure 8.6
Security view.

You may also want to make the same changes with the View permission. This permission is given to the `Anonymous` role as well as the `Manager` role by default and, therefore, allows anyone to view pages of Zope—in the third view—that have not been explicitly blocked for visitors by taking the View permission from the `Anonymous` role.

You do not need to change any permissions for the two DTML methods within the poll—`index_html` and `result`—because Zope's acquisition causes the permission settings for the poll folder to automatically apply to any objects within it. The acquisition only applies to the permissions of an object for which the Acquire Permissions Settings? check box is activated. This is the check box in front of a permission in the Permissions view. We deactivated this box for the View and Vote permissions because we do not want the permission settings from the CMF to apply to the poll.

By taking away the permission from anonymous visitors to the CMF, you make sure that only logged-in members and reviewers can vote in the poll. This will keep your poll results accurate.

Opening the Poll to CMF Members

Now, let's make the poll accessible to members by creating a link to it on the CMF homepage. To do this, customize the `index_html` of the `Basic` skin—you will find it in the `generic` folder.

We want the links for the polls—and later the surveys—to be in a box similar to the news box. Consequently, we will use the `news_box` DTML method as a model. But first, we create a line in the `index_html` that calls the `polls_and_surveys` DTML method, which we will create in a moment, that creates the Polls and Surveys box.

Add the following line:

```
<dtml-var polls_and_surveys>
```

after the line

```
<dtml-var news_box>
```

Also add a <p> after `<dtml-var news_box>` to separate both boxes a bit. See Listing 8.3 for the modified version of the `index_html` DTML method.

Listing 8.3

Modified `index_html` *with* `polls_and_surveys` *Box*

```
<dtml-var standard_html_header>
<dtml-with portal_properties>
<table cellpadding="0" cellspacing="0" width="100%">
 <tr>
   <td valign="top" width="80%">
<h1> Welcome to &dtml-title; </h1>
<dl>
 <dt> Overview </dt>
 <dd> <dtml-var description> </dd>
</dl>
   </td>
   <td valign="top" width="20%">
    <dtml-var news_box><p>
    <dtml-var polls_and_surveys>
   </td>
   </tr>
```

Listing 8.3

Continued

```
  </table>
</dtml-with>
<dtml-var standard_html_footer>
```

Now we need to create the `polls_and_surveys` DTML method in the `custom` folder. We do this here because the `polls_and_surveys` box should be visible in all skins.

Because we want to use the `news_box` as a model for our new box, customize the `news_box` (you will find it in the `generic` folder) too. Listing 8.4 shows the unmodified version of the `news_box` DTML method.

Listing 8.4

The `news_box` DTML Method

```
<table class="NewsItems" cellspacing="0" cellpadding="0" border="0"
➥width="100%">
  <tr>
   <td class="NewsBorder" width="1" rowspan="13" bgcolor="#6699CC">
    <img src="Images/spacer.gif" alt=" "
         width="1" height="2" border="0">
   </td>
   <td valign="top" class="NewsTitle" width="100%">
     <b>News</b>
   </td>
  </tr>
  <dtml-in "portal_catalog.searchResults( meta_type='News Item'
                                        , sort_on='Date'
                                        , sort_order='reverse'
                                        , review_state='published'
                                        )" size="10">
  <tr class="NewsItemRow">
   <td valign="top">
    <a href="<dtml-var "getURL()"
    >"> &dtml-Title; </a><br>
    <dtml-var Date>
   </td>
  </tr>
  <dtml-else>
  <tr class="NewsItemRow">
   <td valign="top">
     No news is no news.
```

Listing 8.4

Continued

```
27:       </td>
28:     </tr>
29:     </dtml-in>
30:     <tr class="NewsItemRow">
31:       <td>
32:         <a href="&dtml.url-recent_news;">More...</a>
33:       </td>
34:     </tr>
35:   </table>
```

Replace lines 8 and 26 with the lines

<b>Polls and Surveys</b> (line 9 of Listing 8.5)

and

There are no polls right now. (line 24 of Listing 8.5)

Now delete lines 11–15 and replace them with the following line:

<dtml-in "AchieversInternational.objectIds(['Poll'])"> (line 12 of Listing 8.5)

This creates a loop through the object IDs within the AchieversInternational folder, but only does what is within the loop (everything until the </dtml-in> in line 27 of Listing 8.5) with objects that have the meta type poll. All other objects are disregarded.

The last thing to do is to replace lines 18–20 in Listing 8.4 with

```
<a href="<dtml-var sequence-item url_quote>/index_html"><dtml-var sequence-
➥item></a><br>
```

(line 15 in Listing 8.5)

The variable sequence-item contains the current item of the loop (the ID of an object with the meta type poll). If you want to get the title of the Poll object, for example if your poll has a descriptive title that sums up the questions within, you need to use the following line instead:

```
<a href="<dtml-var sequence-item url_quote>/">
➥ <dtml-var "_.getitem(_['sequence-item']).title"></a><br>
```

This way, Zope first looks up the object with the ID in the variable sequence-item and then gets the title of this object. You cannot get the title attribute from sequence-item directly because the value of sequence-item is a string and strings do not have attributes.

> **Warning**
> To use this second line, however, every poll and survey must have a title, or it will not appear in the `polls_and_surveys` box.

Listing 8.5

The `polls_and_surveys` *DTML Method*

```
<table class="NewsItems" cellspacing="0" cellpadding="0" border="0"
width="100%">
<tr>
<td class="NewsBorder" width="1" rowspan="13">
<img src="Images/spacer.gif" alt=" "
width="1" height="2" border="0">
</td>
<td valign="top" class="NewsTitle" width="100%">
<b>Polls and Surveys</b>
</td>
</tr>
<dtml-in "AchieversInternational.objectIds(['Poll'])">
<tr class="NewsItemRow">
<td valign="top">
<a href="<dtml-var sequence-item url_quote>/">
➥<dtml-var sequence-item></a><br>
</td>
</tr>
<tr class="NewsItemRow">
<td> </td>
</tr>
<dtml-else>
<tr class="NewsItemRow">
<td valign="top">
There are no polls right now.
</td>
</tr>
</dtml-in>
</table>
```

Poll Summary

Now the poll is really ready to be used by members of the CMF. Here, again, are the steps we used to create the poll and make it accessible to CMF members and reviewers:

1. Install the `Poll` product.
2. Create an instance of the `Poll` product in the CMF folder.
3. Add a question to the poll.
4. Change the `legend.dtml` file.
5. Change the security settings for the poll.
6. Customize the `index_html` of the CMF.
7. Create a `polls_and_surveys` DTML method.

The Survey Product

A survey is similar to a poll. However, results are not shown after a survey is filled out. In fact, the results will never be visible to the members of the CMF. Only a manager can see them in the Management screen of the `PMPSurvey` object.

Depending on how a survey question is configured, a question may be answered with one or more answers.

Creating a Survey for the CMF

In this survey, we want to find out a bit more about the members of the CMF. We would like to know the age of the member and what he or she likes about the CMF. Consequently, we need to create two questions with different types of answers within the survey. They will both appear on the same page.

Unfortunately, with this product, you cannot control that each member fills out the survey only once. A survey is always anonymous. It is also not possible to close the survey. You will have to delete the link to the survey from the homepage or change the security settings to keep members from taking the survey.

Creating the Survey Instance

Change to the CMF `AchieversInternational` object and select `pmp_survey` from the drop-down menu. Add the survey using the following data:

ID:	**`Survey`**
Title:	**`Short Survey`**

Do not fill out Description and Follow-up page. We will get back to that later. Click the Add button.

Adding a Question

When you click Survey in the CMF folder, you get to the Questions view of the survey instance. To add a question, type the question in the Question text area provided. Then decide whether a member should only be allowed to give one answer, or if he or she can give several answers. In the first case, you need to choose Radio Button for the question. In the latter, choose Checkbox.

For our survey, enter the question **`How old are you?`** in the text area, choose Radio Button, and click Add. Figure 8.7 shows the added question in the `Questions` view.

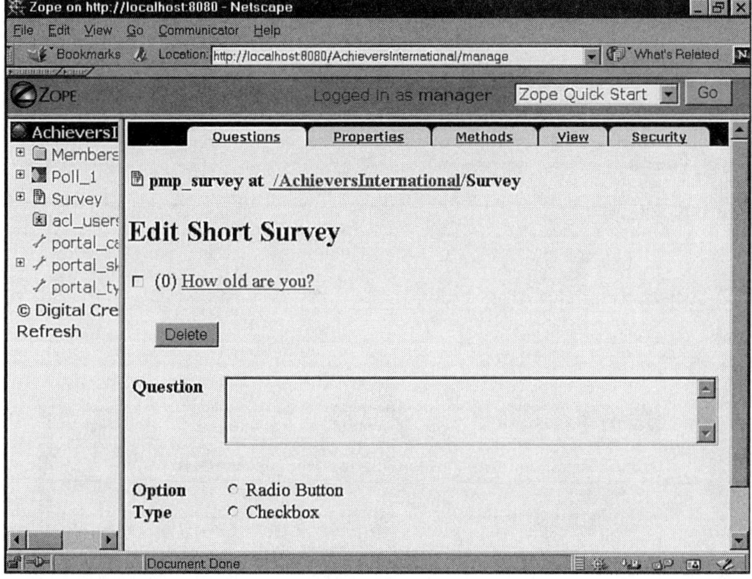

Figure 8.7

Questions view—one question added.

Now add the second question, "What do you like about this site?" This time, choose Checkbox as option type.

Because we have the questions, we can now go on to adding the answers. This is done in the Responses view that you get to by clicking the question in the Questions view of the survey.

The responses are added by typing them one by one in the Response text area and clicking the Add button.

> **Note**
> The responses for a question are added one at a time. This differs from how responses are added in the `Poll` object. If you enter more than one response in the text area and then click the Add button, the survey product will consider the input as one response and will treat it accordingly.

Add the response choices to the first question one by one:

- **`under 15 years`**
- **`16-18 years`**
- **`19-29 years`**
- **`30-39 years`**
- **`40-49 years`**
- **`over 50 years`**

Figure 8.8 shows the Responses view of the first survey question with all response choices added.

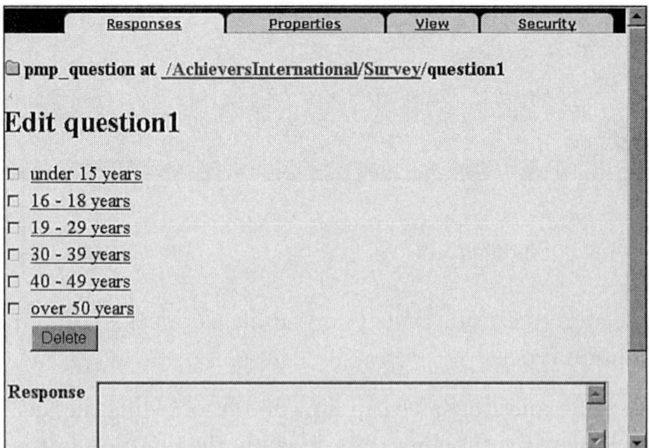

Figure 8.8
Responses view—all response choices added.

Now go back to the survey object and then to the Responses view of the second question. Add the response choices:

- `skins (basic, nouvelle)`
- `staging process`
- `search page`
- `news box`
- `actions box`

The questions are finished and we can now move on to changing the security settings so that only members and reviewers can participate in the survey.

Changing Security Settings

We need to change the security settings for the survey for the same reason that they needed to be changed for the poll:

- Only members and reviewers will be allowed to see the survey page. This will be achieved by setting the View permission accordingly.
- Members and reviewers do not yet have the permission to fill out the survey. The Respond to Survey permission needs to be set for both roles.

To set the permissions, go to the Security view of the survey object by clicking its Security tab. Deactivate the Acquire Permission Settings? check box in front of the View and Respond to Survey permissions.

This breaks the acquisition chain (the permission settings for those permissions from the parent object—`AchieversInternational`—do not apply in the survey object). Now we can decide which role we want to allow to view the survey page and to respond to the survey. Activate the check boxes for both roles in the Member and Reviewer columns. Save the new permission settings by clicking the Save Changes button.

Now the permissions are set so that members and reviewers can take part in the survey. The next step is to provide a description of the survey and a URL to which the browser is to be directed after a survey is filled out and sent.

The Properties View of the Survey

In the Properties view of a survey, you can edit the survey's title, description, and enter the URL to the follow-up page (see Figure 8.9).

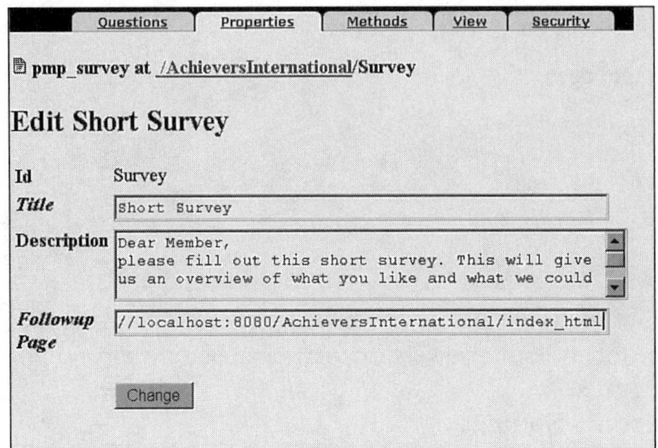

Figure 8.9
Properties view of the survey.

We already gave the survey a title when we created the instance. Now we need to enter a URL to a follow-up page. This is required because this URL will be needed whenever the survey is filled out by a member. After filling out and sending the survey, the member sees a page that notifies him or her that the responses were accepted and recorded and that contains an OK button. The URL given as the follow-up page is used in this page to define which URL should be called when the member clicks the OK button.

In our case, we want the member to go back to the CMF's homepage: `/AchieversInternational/`.

Enter this URL in the Followup Page field.

The Description text area can be used to give a short introduction to the survey. This introduction is shown at the top of the survey page. Enter the following description in the text area and click Change:

```
Dear Member,

Please fill out this short survey. This will give us an overview of what
you like and what we could improve.
```

Opening the Survey to CMF Members

Now we need to change the `polls_and_surveys` DTML method to include surveys. Go to `polls_and_surveys` in the `custom` folder of `portal_skins`.

There are two ways to include the surveys:

- You could change the code so the `<dtml-in>` loop combines polls and surveys.
- You could copy the code for the polls and change it so it works for surveys.

We will use the second choice because we want to put a line between polls and surveys in the box. This will be easier if there are two code parts for the polls and the surveys.

Listing 8.6 is the current code of `polls_and_surveys`.

Listing 8.6

polls_and_surveys *DTML Method*

```
<table class="NewsItems" cellspacing="0" cellpadding="0" border="0"
width="100%">
<tr>
<td class="NewsBorder" width="1" rowspan="13">
<img src="Images/spacer.gif" alt=" "
width="1" height="2" border="0">
</td>
<td valign="top" class="NewsTitle" width="100%">
<b>Polls and Surveys</b>
</td>
</tr>
<dtml-in "AchieversInternational.objectIds(['Poll'])">
<tr class="NewsItemRow">
<td valign="top">
<a href="<dtml-var sequence-item url_quote>/index_html">
➥ <dtml-var "_.getitem(_['sequence-item']).title"></a><br>
</td>
</tr>
<tr class="NewsItemRow">
<td> </td>
</tr>
<dtml-else>
<tr class="NewsItemRow">
<td valign="top">
There are no polls right now.
</td>
</tr>
</dtml-in>
</table>
```

Copy lines 12–27 and paste them after line 27. Now change the pasted line

```
<dtml-in "AchieversInternational.objectIds(['Poll'])">
```

to

```
<dtml-in "AchieversInternational.objectIds(['pmp_survey'])">
```

The resulting code looks like Listing 8.7.

Listing 8.7

First Modification of `polls_and_surveys`

```
 1: <table class="NewsItems" cellspacing="0" cellpadding="0" border="0"
 2: width="100%">
 3: <tr>
 4: <td class="NewsBorder" width="1" rowspan="13">
 5: <img src="Images/spacer.gif" alt=" "
 6: width="1" height="2" border="0">
 7: </td>
 8: <td valign="top" class="NewsTitle" width="100%">
 9: <b>Polls and Surveys</b>
10: </td>
11: </tr>
12: <dtml-in "AchieversInternational.objectIds(['Poll'])">
13: <tr class="NewsItemRow">
14: <td valign="top">
15: <a href="<dtml-var sequence-item url_quote>/">
➥<dtml-var "_.getitem(_['sequence-item']).title"></a><br>
16: </td>
17: </tr>
18: <tr class="NewsItemRow">
19: <td> </td>
20: </tr>
21: <dtml-else>
22: <tr class="NewsItemRow">
23: <td valign="top">
24: There are no polls right now.
25: </td>
26: </tr>
27: </dtml-in>
28: <dtml-in "AchieversInternational.objectIds(['pmp_survey'])">
29: <tr class="NewsItemRow">
30: <td valign="top">
```

Listing 8.7
Continued

```
31:  <a href="<dtml-var sequence-item url_quote>/ ">
➥<dtml-var "_.getitem(_['sequence-item']).title"></a><br>
32:  </td>
33:  </tr>
34:  <tr class="NewsItemRow">
35:  <td> </td>
36:  </tr>
37:  <dtml-else>
38:  <tr class="NewsItemRow">
39:  <td valign="top">
40:  There are no surveys right now.
41:  </td>
42:  </tr>
43:  </dtml-in>
44:  </table>
```

Now we want to put a line between polls and surveys. To create a simple line in HTML, you use the following command:

```
<hr>
```

Because the box is construed as a table, this `<hr>` needs to be inside a table cell. It also needs to be a new table row because it is supposed to be below the polls and not beside them.

To give the new table row the same color as the rest of the box (a color that depends on the skin the member chose), we need to define the class for this row. This is done by adding the class definition

```
class="NewsItemRow"
```

in the `<tr>` command. The code for the new table row is as follows:

```
<tr class="NewsItemRow">
<td><hr></td>
</tr>
```

Insert these lines between lines 27 and 28 of Listing 8.7. Click the Change button, and the survey will appear in the `polls_and_surveys` box on the CMF's homepage.

Survey Summary

The survey is ready to be filled out by members of the CMF now. We used the following steps to create the survey and make it accessible to CMF members and reviewers:

1. Install the `PMPSurvey` product.
2. Create an instance of the `Survey` product in the CMF folder.
3. Add questions to the survey.
4. Change the security settings for the survey.
5. Give a follow-up page for the survey and maybe a description.
6. Customize the `index_html` of the CMF.

Modifying the Poll Product

In this section, we will modify the Poll product so that a manager who looks at the list of voters in the Voters view not only sees the names of the people who have voted but also their roles. This will only be a slight modification, but it can be interesting to see how many members and how many reviewers have voted.

> **Note**
> Remember that voters will only be recorded and listed in the Voters view if the poll was not anonymous when the person voted.

Adding the User's First Role to the Voters View

This enhancement to the `Poll` product is done easily by changing one line in one of the `Poll`'s `dtml` files. The `dtml` files can be found on the file system in the `ZopeDir/lib/python/Products/Poll` directory.

The `pollVoters.dtml` file creates the Voters view in the Zope Management screen. We need to modify this file to have the voters' roles appear after their names.

Open the `pollVoters.dtml` file (see Listing 8.8) in a text editor (for example, Notepad or vi).

Listing 8.8

pollVoters.dtml *File*

```
 1: <html>
 2:   <head><title>Edit <!--#var title_or_id--></title></head>
 3:   <body bgcolor="#FFFFFF" link="#000099" vlink="#555555" alink="#77003B">
 4:     <!--#var manage_tabs-->
 5:     <h2>Voters for <!--#var title_or_id--></h2>
 6: <p>
 7: This poll is <em><!--#if open-->open
➥<!--#else-->closed<!--#/if--></em>.<br>
 8: Voting is <em><!--#if anonymous-->
➥<!--#else-->not<!--#/if--></em> anonymous.<br>
 9: </p>
10: <dtml-in "voted.keys()" sort>
11:   <dtml-if sequence-start>
12:     <table>
13:   </dtml-if>
14:   <tr><td>
15:   <dtml-var sequence-item html_quote>
16:   </td></tr>
17:   <dtml-if sequence-start>
18:     </table>
19:   </dtml-if>
20: <dtml-else>
21:   <p>No voters.</p>
22: </dtml-in>
23: <form action="./deleteVoters">
24: <input type="SUBMIT" name="SUBMIT" value=" Remove all voters "
25:   </body>
26: </html>
```

First, there is a small mistake in this file. It should say

```
<dtml-if sequence-end>
```

instead of

```
<dtml-if sequence-start>
```

in line 17.

The `<dtml-var sequence-item html_quote>` command in line 15 shows—when evaluated—the voter's name. Now we need to add some lines that will show the role(s). Because a Zope user can have more than one role (for example, Manager and Reviewer), we need to decide whether we want to know all the roles or just the first in the list of roles. CMF members will probably only have one role because they get the Member role when they join the CMF. Consequently, we will start with just the first role (see Listing 8.9). Later, we will see how to get all roles.

Listing 8.9

Additional Lines for `pollVoters.dtml` Showing One Role

```
1:            
2:        <dtml-try>
3:          ( <dtml-var "acl_users.getUser(_['sequence-item']).getRoles()[0]">
➥)
4:        <dtml-except>
5:          ( User not defined within the CMF )
6:        </dtml-try>
```

Python's `try...except` command is also implemented as a `dtml` command. It works as follows:

```
<dtml-try>
    do something that might cause an error
<dtml-except>
    do something else in case the something in the try-clause caused an error
</dtml-try>
```

Line 3 in Listing 8.9 tries to call the current user (`getUser(_['sequence-item'])`) to get the user's roles (`getRoles()`) and then to call the first of the roles (`[0]`). The `getUser()` method is used on the user folder of the CMF (`acl_users`). The role that hopefully results from this is then put between the two brackets at the beginning and the end of line 3.

It may be that this line causes an error, for example if the current user is not defined in the current `acl_users` folder but in a user folder above in the Zope hierarchy. We need to catch the error message that would result. Therefore, we state what should be done in such a case. We do this after the `<dtml-except>` clause.

Add the lines in Listing 8.9 in the text editor after line 15 in the `pollVoters.dtml` file (refer to Listing 8.8) and save the changes. If there are recorded voters for a poll, the Voters view will look something like Figure 8.10.

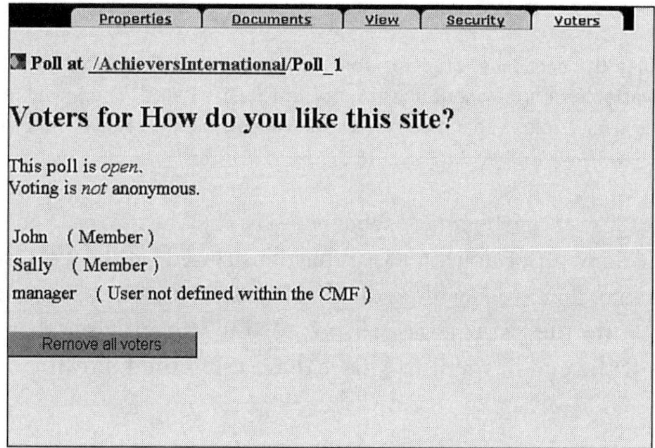

Figure 8.10

The improved Voters view.

Adding All the User's Roles to the Voters View

Now, we want to see all the roles a voter has. To do this, we use the code in Listing 8.10 instead of the code in Listing 8.9:

Listing 8.10

Additional Lines for `pollVoters.dtml` *Showing All Roles*

```
   
<dtml-try>
(
  <dtml-in "acl_users.getUser(_['sequence-item']).getRoles()">
   <dtml-var sequence-item> <dtml-unless sequence-end>,</dtml-unless>
  </dtml-in>
)
<dtml-except>
   ( User not defined within the CMF )
</dtml-try>
```

Because the roles of a user are contained in a list, we need to create a loop through this list this time. We do this using the `<dtml-in>` command.

> **Note**
> Do not confuse the `sequence-item` variable in line 4 with the variable with the same name in line 5. The variable in line 4 contains the current user's name. The variable in line 5 contains the list of the user's roles (specifically: `acl_users.getUser(_['sequence-item']).getRoles()`).

By calling `acl_users.getUser(_['sequence-item']).getRoles()` in the `<dtml-in>`, we get each role within the list and can have it printed on the Voters view (`<dtml-var sequence-item>`). The roles will be divided by commas. But because the loop would put a comma after the last role as well, we need to explicitly say that there should not be a comma at the end of the list. This is done using the following `<dtml-unless>` command:

```
<dtml-unless sequence-end>,</dtml-unless>
```

writes the comma unless we are at the end of the sequence. The `sequence-end` variable is a standard variable that comes with the `<dtml-in>` command, just like the `sequence-start` variable.

Using Listing 8.10 instead of Listing 8.9, the Voters view will look something like Figure 8.11.

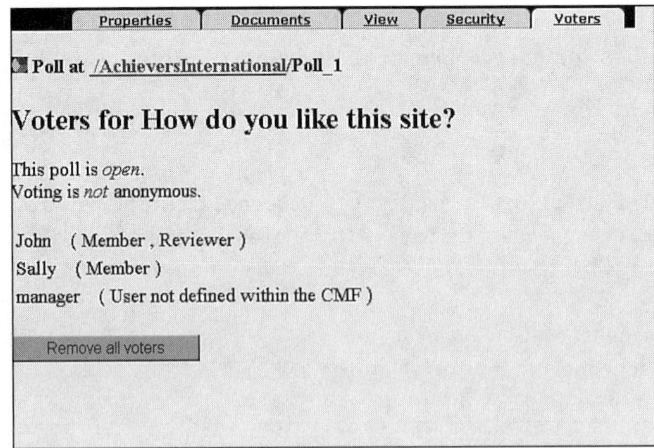

Figure 8.11

Voters view with all roles of the users.

Modifying the `Survey` Product

The `Survey` product as yet does not give you a list of users that have filled out a survey. In the `Poll` product, there is the Voters view and, with only a few changes, we can take this Voters view and put it into the `Survey` product.

For this, we need to change the main Python module of the `Survey` product. Python modules must be compiled before they can be used in Zope. When starting the Zope process, the last modification date of every product's Python modules is compared to the date of the respective compiled version. If the compiled version is older than the uncompiled version, the Python module is being compiled again. Changing a product's modules means that the Zope process needs to be restarted so that the new uncompiled version of the module gets compiled.

To change the `Survey` product in a way that it contains a Voters view, we need to do the following:

In the `Survey.py` file

- Add the new view to `manage_options` so that the View tab appears in the tab bar of a survey.
- Add the URL extension `manage_voters` to the View Management Screens permission so that the Voters view can be accessed by users having this permission.
- Initialize the `voted` variable as a dictionary in the method `__init__()`; the names of the users that have voted will be saved in this variable.
- Add the declaration of `manage_voters` so that Zope knows which file to call if the Voters tab is clicked.
- Add Python code to the `manage_updateFromPost` method so that the voters' names are stored in the `voted` variable.
- Add the `deleteVoters()` method from the `Poll.py` file at the end of the `Survey.py` file.

In the `Survey` product directory, copy and edit the `pollVoters.dtml` files from the `Poll` product directory to the `Survey` product directory.

> **Note**
> The `Poll.py` and `Survey.py` files are the main Python modules of the `Poll` and `Survey` product. They can be found on the file system in the `/lib/python/Products/Poll` and `/lib/python/Products/PMPSurvey` directories, respectively.

Changing the `Survey.py` File

Open the `Survey.py` file in a text editor. The changes that need to be made will be made by going through the file from top to bottom. Each change will be shown in listings that contain surrounding code. This way, you should be able to follow the step-by-step instructions.

> **Note**
> Remember that Python uses indentation to divide the different code parts. Be careful to use the right indentation, or changes will cause error messages.

The first part to change is the definition of the tabs that can be seen in an instance of the `Survey` product. At the moment, this definition contains the following tabs:

- Questions
- Properties
- Methods
- View
- Security

To add the Voters tab to this list, add the following line after the Security tab definition in `manage_options` (see Listing 8.11):

```
('label':'Voters', 'action':'manage_voters'),
```

The label defines the name of the tab—what is written on the tab in the Management screen. The action defines what URL should be called when a user clicks the tab. `manage_voters` has not been defined yet; we will do that later in this section.

Listing 8.11

Definition of the Tabs in the `Survey.py` File

```
manage_options = (
   {'label':'Questions', 'action':'manage_questions'},
```

Listing 8.11

Continued

```
        {'label':'Properties', 'action':'manage_main'},
        {'label':'Methods', 'action':'manage_documents'},
        {'label':'View', 'action':''},
        {'label':'Security', 'action':'manage_access'},
        ##### NEW ########
        {'label':'Voters', 'action':'manage_voters'},
        ##################
        )
```

Next, we have to add the manage_voters URL to the declaration of permissions. If we do not assign a specific permission to this URL, Zope will not grant anybody access to the URL. Assign manage_voters to the View Management Screens permission, as seen in line 3 of Listing 8.12.

Listing 8.12

Declaration of Permissions

```
1:    __ac_permissions__ = (
2:        ####### 'manage_voters' added #########
3:        ('View management screens', ('manage_tabs', 'manage_main',
➥'manage_voters')),
4:        ('Change permissions', ('manage_access',)),
5:        ('Change Surveys', ('manage_edit', 'manage_questions')),
6:        ('Respond to Survey', ('manage_updateFromPost',)),
7:        ('View', ('',)),
8:        )
```

We now have to initialize the variable voted in the __init__() method. This is done by simply adding the following line:

```
self.voted = {}
```

to the initializations done at the beginning of the method (see line 8 in Listing 8.13).

Listing 8.13

First Part of the __init__() Method

```
1:    def __init__(self, id, title = '', survey_text = '', follow =
➥'./index_html'):
2:        """Initialization function for Survey Class"""
3:        self.id = id
```

Listing 8.13

Continued

```
        self.title = title
        self.survey_text = survey_text
        self.followup = follow
        ##### NEW #####
        self.voted = {}
        ###############
```

The curly brackets indicate that `voted` is to be a dictionary. One element of a dictionary consists of a key and a value and is defined as follows:

```
{'aKey':'aValue', 'secondKey':'secondValue'}
```

Elements are divided by a comma.

The `manage_voters` URL that we used previously has not been defined yet. We do this in the part of the file where the other URLs are defined, such as `manage_documents` and `manage_questions`. Add the line

```
manage_voters = HTMLFile('surveyVoters', globals())
```

to the URL definitions (see Listing 8.14). `HTMLFile` is a standard Zope method that calls the `dtml` file whose name corresponds with the first parameter; in our case, it calls the `surveyVoters.dtml` `dtml` file. That means that whenever the `manage_voters` URL is called within an instance of the `Survey` product, Zope calls the `surveyVoters.dtml` file and returns it as pure HTML so that it can be understood by the browser.

Listing 8.14

Definition of the `manage_voters` *URL*

```
manage_documents=HTMLFile('surveyMethods', globals())
manage_questions = HTMLFile('surveyQuestionsEdit', globals())
manage_main = HTMLFile('surveyEdit', globals())
#########
manage_voters = HTMLFile('surveyVoters', globals())
#########
```

The next-to-last change is to add Python code to the `manage_updateFromPost()` method that will store the voters' names and also counts how often they have filled out the survey. Go to the end of this method and insert the code from Listing 8.15 (lines 3 to 13).

Listing 8.15

Part of the `manage_updateFromPost()` *Method with the Code That Stores Voters' Names*

```
 1:       for q in questionValues:
 2:         q.answered = 0
 3:       ########  NEW  ########
 4:       if REQUEST is not None and REQUEST.has_key('AUTHENTICATED_USER'):
 5:             if self.voted.has_key(REQUEST['AUTHENTICATED_USER'].
getUserName()):
 6:                 voted=self.voted
 7:                 voted[REQUEST['AUTHENTICATED_USER'].getUserName()] =
➥ voted[REQUEST['AUTHENTICATED_USER'].getUserName()] + 1
 8:                 self.voted=voted
 9:             else:
10:                 voted=self.voted
11:                 voted[REQUEST['AUTHENTICATED_USER'].getUserName()] = 1
12:                 self.voted=voted
13:       #########################
14:       return MessageDialog(
15:         title='Responses Accepted',
16:         message='Your responses were accepted and recorded.',
17:         action=self.followup)
```

The code consists of two `if` clauses. The first one, in line 4, is just to make sure there is a variable in the `REQUEST` that contains the name of the authenticated user. If there is not, the following lines would cause an error.

The second `if` clause, in line 5, checks if the authenticated user has already voted and is therefore stored in the `voted` variable. If that is the case, lines 6 to 8 are executed. Otherwise, the evaluation of the code continues in line 10.

If the user has already voted before, the number of times is increased by one and stored in the `voted` variable. For example, if the user Fred had voted twice before, the dictionary would contain the element

```
{'Fred':'3'}
```

at the end of the `if` clause.

If the user has not voted before, a new element is created in the `voted` dictionary with the name of the user as the key and the number 1 as the value.

The last change in the file is to take the method `deleteVoters()` method from the `Poll.py` (see Listing 8.16) and paste it at the end of `Survey.py`. This method does not need any modification; it can be used as it is. The method is necessary so that the list of voters can be removed from the Voters view and begins again.

Listing 8.16

`deleteVoters()` *Method Taken from the* `Poll.py` *File*

```
####### NEW ########
def deleteVoters(self, REQUEST=None):
        """Delete all voters"""
        self.voted = {}
        if REQUEST is not None:
            return MessageDialog(
                title='Voters deleted',
                message='<strong>%s</strong> has been edited.' % self.id,
                action ='./manage_voters',
                )
```

This completes the modifications necessary to the `Survey.py` file to add the Voters view to `Survey` instances. Now we need to create the `surveyVoters.dtml` file in the Survey directory.

Creating the `surveyVoters.dtml` File for the Voters View

Creating the `surveyVoter.dtml` file is simple. Take the `pollVoters.dtml` file from the `Poll` product directory, rename it to `surveyVoter.dtml`, and add the following `dtml` command to the file's code to include the number of times a user has filled out the survey:

```
  (<dtml-var "voted[_['sequence-item']]">)  
```

Add this line after the name of the user in line 11 in Listing 8.17. This listing shows the new file `surveyVoters.dtml`.

Listing 8.17

`surveyVoters.dtml` *File*

```
1: <html>
2:   <head><title>Edit <!--#var title_or_id--></title></head>
3:   <body bgcolor="#FFFFFF" link="#000099" vlink="#555555" alink="#77003B">
4:     <!--#var manage_tabs-->
5:     <h2>Voters for <!--#var title_or_id--></h2>
6: <dtml-in "voted.keys()" sort>
7:   <dtml-if sequence-start>
8:     <table>
9:   </dtml-if>
```

Listing 8.17
Continued

```
   <tr><td>
   <dtml-var sequence-item html_quote>  
➥(<dtml-var "voted[_['sequence-item']]">)  
  <dtml-try>
  (
    <dtml-in "acl_users.getUser(_['sequence-item']).getRoles()">
     <dtml-var sequence-item> <dtml-unless sequence-end>,</dtml-unless>
    </dtml-in>
  )
  <dtml-except>
      ( User not defined within the CMF )
  </dtml-try>
   </td></tr>
   <dtml-if sequence-end>
     </table>
   </dtml-if>
<dtml-else>
   <p>No voters.</p>
</dtml-in>
<form action="./deleteVoters">
<input type="SUBMIT" name="SUBMIT" value=" Remove all voters "
   </body>
</html>
```

Now, every survey has a Voters view. However, within surveys that have already been created, clicking the Voters tab will cause an error because they were created without the additional tab and therefore without the "knowledge" of what to do when the tab is clicked.

Summary

In this chapter, you have seen again how easy it is to put together different existing Zope products to add features to your Web site. Sometimes the products need to be modified slightly to fit your needs, but most of the time this is done much more easily than writing your own products.

Before beginning a project, take a look around the Zope community. Most of the time you will find that at least part of your problem has already been solved by someone else. Use the combined Zope and Python knowledge out there.

PART III

MORE COOL WEB APPLICATIONS

CHAPTER

CHAPTER 9

AUTOMATICALLY BUILDING SITEMAPS

In the last two chapters, you learned how to add several kinds of features to your Web portal. You know how to retrieve information from portal users via polls and surveys. Moreover you are able to set up a discussion board using ZDiscussions.

In this chapter, we will show you how to make navigating through your Web site easier. You will learn to create sitemaps. We will demonstrate different ways sitemaps can be built automatically so that you don't have to update your sitemap code by hand.

The first section will deal with the `<dtml-in>` tag for building sitemaps.

The next section will show you how to use the `<dtml-tree>` tag and how you can make it show hierarchically structured sitemaps.

In the last section of this chapter we will introduce the NFGnav products that make building complex sitemaps easy and comfortable.

Building Sitemaps with the `<dtml-in>` Tag

At first we will begin with a brief review of the use of the `<dtml-in>` tag in general. You will learn how different types of sequences are handled by the `<dtml-in>` tag, and we will describe each attribute of the tag in detail.

The main section will then deal with various kinds of sitemaps that can be built with the `<dtml-in>` tag.

The Use of the `<dtml-in>` Tag

The `<dtml-in>` tag is used to run through the items of sequences, such as tuples and lists. Thus, certain actions can be applied to each single item.

The `<dtml-in>` tag is a non-empty tag so it needs a starting and an ending tag. The code inside the tag body defines the actions that are applied to the sequence's items.

```
<dtml-in sequence>
     tag body
</dtml-in>
```

In the following code snippet, the `<dtml-in>` tag runs through the elements of a sequence with the ID `sequenceExample`.

```
<dtml-call REQUEST.set('sequenceExample', [(1,2,3,4,5,6,7,),'abc',{1:'take',
➥2:'go'}])">
<dtml-in sequenceExample>
<dtml-var sequence-index>:
<dtml-var sequence-item><br>
</dtml-in>
```

Each element of the sequence is displayed onscreen with its sequence index. The result that will be shown onscreen looks something like the following:

```
0:(1, 2, 3, 4, 5, 6, 7)
1:abc
2:{2: 'go', 1: 'take'}
```

Sequences with Different Data Types

The sequence used in the last example contains data stored in a tuple, in a string, and in a dictionary. In Table 9.1, you will see the way in which different types of sequences are handled by the `<dtml-in>` tag. The code that is used to render the table's examples is the same code we used to run through the sequence with the ID `sequenceExample`.

Table 9.1

The `<dtml-in>` Tag and Different Types of Sequences

	Sequence	Results
Tuples	(1,2,3)	0:1 1:2 2:3
Nested tuples	(1,(2,3))	0:1 1:3
List of strings	['george','ringo']	0:george 1:ringo
List of numeric values	[2,12.3,16L]	0:2 1:12.3 3:16L

Table 9.1
Continued

Mixed list	[,[(1,2),'abc',{1:'take',2:'go'}])">	0:(1,2) 1:abc 2:{1:'take', 2:'go'}
Dictionary	{1:'Autolycus',2:'Salmoneus',3:'Bart'}	Zope Error

Dictionaries

As you can see, it is not possible to run through the elements of a dictionary with the `<dtml-in>` tag directly. Any try will raise a Zope error (see Figure 9.1).

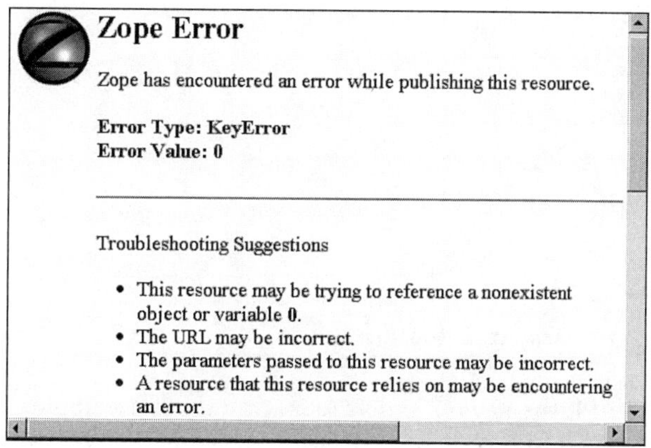

Figure 9.1
A Zope error is raised every time you try to run directly through the items of a dictionary.

The reason is that dictionaries are mappings rather than sequences. So sequence operations do not work here. Nevertheless, it is possible to run through a dictionary's elements. There are three Python methods that can be used for that purpose:

- `items()` This method returns a list of tuples containing the dictionary's items.
- `keys()` This method delivers a list of the dictionary's keys.
- `values()` This method returns a list of the dictionary's values.

> **Note**
> Dictionaries are mapping objects, so you cannot directly run through their elements. Use the Python methods `items()`, `values()`, and `keys()` instead.

Using the code in Listing 9.1, the keys and the values of a dictionary are displayed in a table.

Listing 9.1

Running Through a Dictionary's Elements

```
1: <dtml-var standard_html_header>
2: <p>
3: <dtml-call "REQUEST.set('dict',{'a':'John','b':'Paul',
4: 'c':'George','d':'Ringo'})">
5: <table border=1>
6: <tr><th>Key:</th>
7: <dtml-in "dict.keys()"><td>
8: <dtml-var sequence-item></td>
9: </dtml-in>
10: </tr>
11: <tr>
12: <th>Value:</th>
13: <dtml-in "dict.values()">
14: <td><dtml-var sequence-item></td>
15: </dtml-in>
16: </tr>
17: </table>
18: <dtml-var standard_html_footer>
```

In line 7 and line 14, the `keys()` and `values()` methods are applied to the example dictionary and passed to the `<dtml-in>` tag. The single items are displayed in a table, as you can see in Figure 9.2.

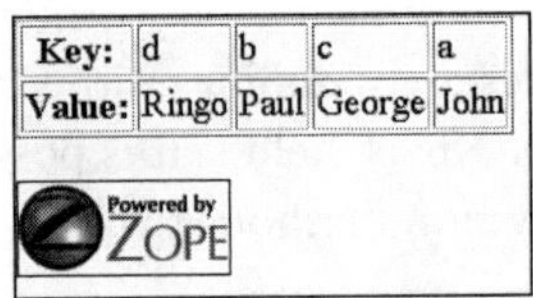

Key:	d	b	c	a
Value:	Ringo	Paul	George	John

Figure 9.2

Here, the `<dtml-in>` tag was used to display the elements of a dictionary in a table (refer to Listing 9.1).

Maybe you have noticed that the dictionary's elements are not listed in their original order. Because dictionaries are unordered collections of arbitrary objects that are looked up by `key`, there is no particular order to the elements. To keep the dictionary's items in a certain order, you should make use of the `sort` attribute. See the section "The Attributes of the `<dtml-in>` Tag" later in this chapter for details.

A Simple Sitemap

The `<dtml-in>` tag is rather powerful and the variety of the attributes and the variables that come with this tag enable the user to accomplish a considerable number of different tasks.

Because the `<dtml-in>` tag is not exclusively destined to make up sitemaps, some efforts have to be made by the user. But you have a lot of control over the look and feel of your implemented sitemaps.

There are various ways in which to set up a sitemap. For example, you could simply use some HTML code where you could manually insert the elements you want to be shown with the sitemap in a list or a table. But it is much more useful to implement code that can automatically traverse those objects that you want to be part of a sitemap. That's why we will use the `<dtml-in>` tag.

Listing 9.2 implements a basic sitemap.

Listing 9.2

A Basic Sitemap

```
1:   <dtml-in name="objectItems">
2: <a href="<&dtml-absolute_url>">
3: <dtml-var id></a><br>
4: </dtml-in>
```

In line 1, you can see that the value of the `name` attribute is the `objectItems` method. This method returns a list of sub-objects of the current object. See the "Useful Methods of the `ObjectManager.py` Module," later in this chapter, for details and for more methods you might want to use with the `<dtml-in>` tag.

Inside the tag body, the single objects are run through and displayed onscreen as hyperlinks. Figure 9.3 shows the result of the implementation from Listing 9.1.

With this very simple sitemap, the user can access an object by clicking it.

During the next sections, we will show you how to generate some advanced sitemaps.

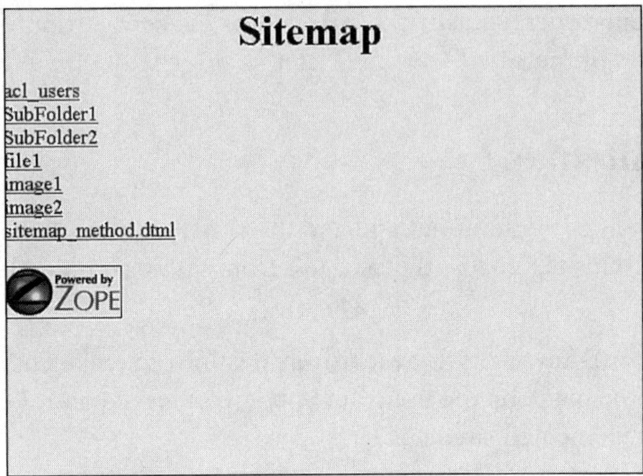

Figure 9.3
A basic sitemap.

Improving the Look and Feel

The basic sitemap that can be seen in the figure does not help the user navigate through the displayed objects. The user would probably be confused because the sitemap does not give any information about the hierarchical order and the type of the objects he or she might want to access.

A good way to present information about an object is to display it together with its Zope icon. To characterize the hierarchical structure of the displayed objects, you could state the superordinate folder and show the single objects in a list. In Listing 9.3 you can see how we made use of the HTML tags `<li>` and `<ul>` to structure a sitemap's elements hierarchically. An example sitemap that has been generated by this code can be seen in Figure 9.4.

Listing 9.3
An Advanced Version of the Basic Sitemap

```
<dtml-var id>
<ul>
<dtml-in objectItems>
<li><IMG SRC="<&dtml-icon>">
<a href="<&dtml-absolute_url>">
<dtml-var id></a></li><br>
</dtml-in>
</ul>
```

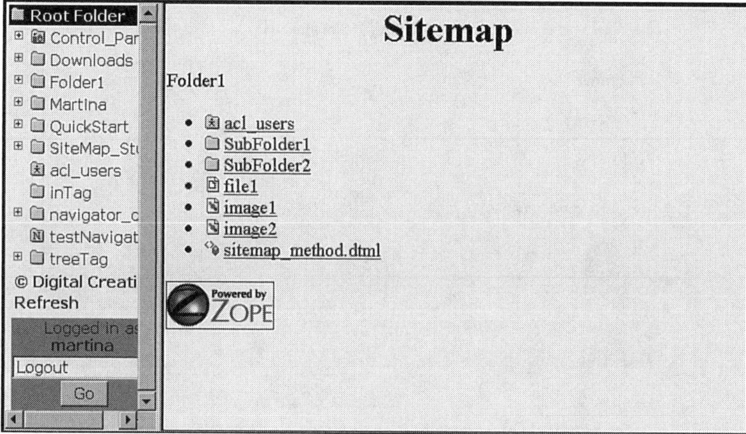

Figure 9.4

The sitemap is much better structured now.

Hiding Certain Objects from the User's View

Another important thing about sitemaps is that there will always be objects you do not want any user to see. Suppose that you want to generate a sitemap that displays the sub-objects of a folder, but you don't want the user to see the User folder and any DTML methods.

We will make use of the `<dtml-unless>` tag to solve this problem in Listing 9.4.

Listing 9.4

Hiding Objects from the User

```
 1: <dtml-var id>
 2: <ul>
 3: <dtml-in objectItems>
 4: <dtml-unless "meta_type in ('User Folder','DTML Method')">
 5: <li><IMG SRC="<dtml-var icon>">
 6: <a href="<dtml-var absolute_url>">
 7: <dtml-var id></a></li><br>
 8: </dtml-unless>
 9: </dtml-in>
10: </ul>
```

The `<dtml-unless>` tag encloses the body of the `<dtml-in>` tag (lines 4–8), so only those objects whose meta type is not specified in line 4 are displayed. You can see in Figure 9.5 that neither a User folder nor DTML methods are shown.

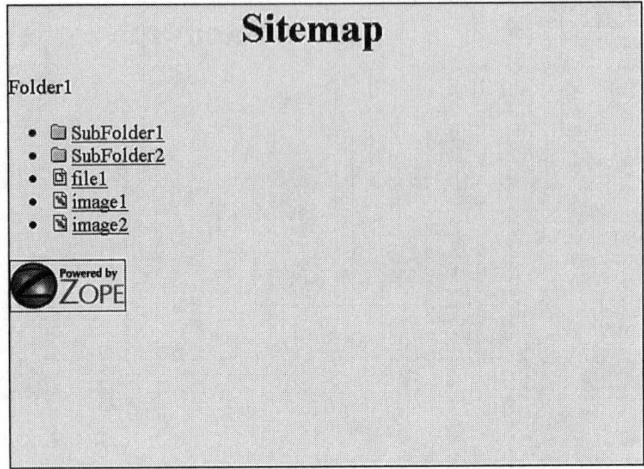

Figure 9.5

The user does not see any DTML methods or User folders.

Displaying Certain Objects

Another way to hide certain objects is to show the other objects exclusively. This can be done in passing the meta types of the appropriate objects to the method that returns the sequence of sub-objects for the `<dtml-in>` tag.

In Listing 9.5, we want to show only the file objects that are contained in the `SubFolder1` folder. Moreover, we want to show the objects' size and the last modification date. Figure 9.6 shows a table of those files that are contained in SubFolder1, and it also gives you information about each single file's size and modification time.

Listing 9.5

Only Certain Objects Are Displayed

```
<dtml-with SubFolder1><p>
<dtml-var id>
<table width="100%">
<dtml-in "objectItems('File')">
<tr>
<td><IMG SRC="<dtml-var icon>">
<a href="<dtml-var absolute_url>">
<dtml-var id></a></td>
<td><dtml-var "(_['sequence-item'].size)/1024">&#32Kb</td>
<td><dtml-var bobobase_modification_time></td>
</tr>
</dtml-in>
</dtml-with>
</table>
```

Because we wanted to retrieve the file objects inside `SubFolder1`, the `<dtml-in>` tag is used inside a `<dtml-with>` tag (lines 1 and 13).

In line 4, the meta type `File` is specified, so that the `objectItems` method returns a list of file objects.

Lines 9 and 10 implement the table columns that indicate the single file objects' size and last modification date.

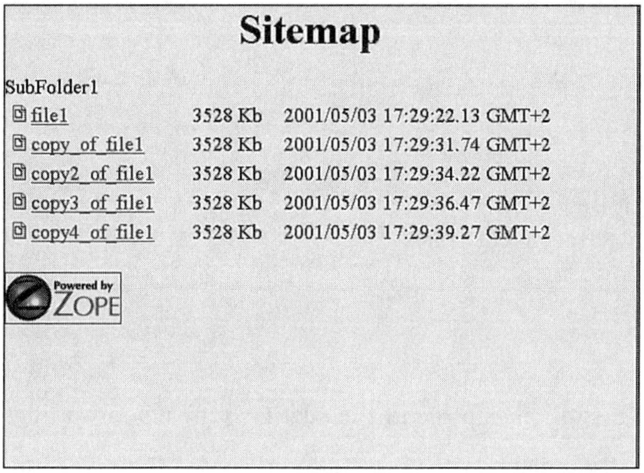

Sitemap

SubFolder1

file1	3528 Kb	2001/05/03 17:29:22.13 GMT+2
copy_of_file1	3528 Kb	2001/05/03 17:29:31.74 GMT+2
copy2_of_file1	3528 Kb	2001/05/03 17:29:34.22 GMT+2
copy3_of_file1	3528 Kb	2001/05/03 17:29:36.47 GMT+2
copy4_of_file1	3528 Kb	2001/05/03 17:29:39.27 GMT+2

Powered by ZOPE

Figure 9.6

The table shows the file objects inside `SubFolder1`.

Displaying Sub-Objects of Sub-Objects via Recursion

You have certainly noticed that all the examples so far simply show the sub-objects of an object. Complex sitemaps will often need to show sub-objects of sub-objects so that the user can traverse the whole object hierarchy of a folder.

Sub-objects of sub-objects can be traversed by using recursion. That means that we have to implement a message that will be called by itself.

In Listing 9.6, the DTML method with the ID `FolderRecursion` is called by itself and traverses the whole object hierarchy of the current folder.

Listing 9.6

`FolderRecursion`

```
<ul>
<dtml-in "objectItems(['Folder'])">
<img src="<&dtml-icon>">
```

Listing 9.6

Continued

```
 4: <dtml-var id>
 5: <dtml-in objectItems sort=size reverse>
 6: <dtml-unless "meta_type=='Folder' or meta_type=='User Folder'">
 7: <ul>
 8: <li>
 9: <img src="<&dtml-icon>">
10: <a href="<&dtml-absolute_url>">
11: <dtml-var id></a>
12: </li>
13: </ul>
14: </dtml-unless>
15: </dtml-in>
16: <dtml-with sequence-item>
17: <dtml-var FolderRecursion>
18: </dtml-with>
19: </dtml-in>
20: </ul>
```

The actual recursion takes place in the <dtml-with> tag, as in lines 16–18.

At first, the method displays Folder objects (line 4). Then a second <dtml-in> tag is used inside the first one to run through the sub-objects of each folder. Because of line 6, Folder objects are not run through again; otherwise, they would be displayed onscreen several times.

Listing 9.7 calls the FolderRecursion method for the first time.

Listing 9.7

index_html *Calls* FolderRecursion *Once*

```
<dtml-var standard_html_header>
<dtml-with aq_parent>
<dtml-var FolderRecursion>
</dtml-with>
<dtml-var standard_html_footer>
```

Figure 9.7 shows the rendered results of the code inside Listing 9.7 and Listing 9.6.

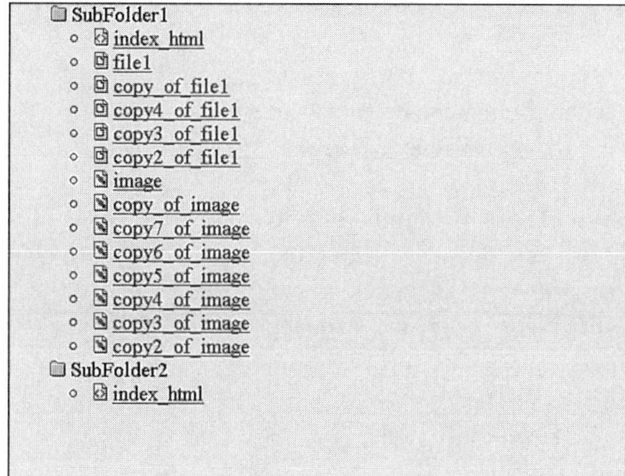

Figure 9.7

This sitemap shows objects and all their sub-objects.

Sitemaps and Batch Processing

The `<dtml-in>` tag provides several variables that make batch processing possible. Consequently, extensive sequences needn't be displayed in all their length but, rather, can be split into smaller batches.

With the code in Listing 9.8, a sitemap of the folder `SubFolder1` is created, where the single objects are displayed in several batches.

Listing 9.8

Batch Processing Is Used to Avoid Oversized Item Batches

```
<dtml-var standard_html_header>
<center><h1>Sitemap</h1></center>
<p>
<IMG SRC="<dtml-var icon>"><dtml-var id><p>
<dtml-with SubFolder1>
<dtml-if objectItems>
<table>
<dtml-in objectItems size=7 start=qs>
<tr><td><li><IMG SRC="<dtml-var icon>"><a href="<dtml-var absolute_url>">
➥<dtml-var id></a></li></td></tr>
</dtml-in>
</table>
<dtml-in objectItems next size=7 start=qs><p>
<a href="<dtml-var document_id><dtml-var sequence-query>
```

Listing 9.8

Continued

```
14: qs=<dtml-var next-sequence-start-number>">
15: (Next <dtml-var next-sequence-size> objects)</a>
16: </dtml-in>
17: <dtml-in objectItems previous size=7 start=qs><p<
18: <a href="<dtml-var document_id><dtml-var sequence-query>
19: qs=<dtml-var previous-sequence-start-number>">
20: (Previous <dtml-var previous-sequence-size> objects)</a>
21: </dtml-in>
22: <dtml-else>
23: No objects in Folder!.
24: </dtml-if>
25: </dtml-with>
26: <dtml-var standard_html_footer>
```

A `<dtml-if>` tag is used in line 6 to check whether `SubFolder1` is empty. If the folder is empty, the message No Objects in Folder1 is displayed, as defined in lines 22 and 23.

Three `<dtml-in>` tags are used to generate first the batches that contain the object items (line 8–10), and then a hyperlink to the next batch (lines 10–16), and then a hyperlink to the previous batch (lines 17–21). (See Figure 9.8.)

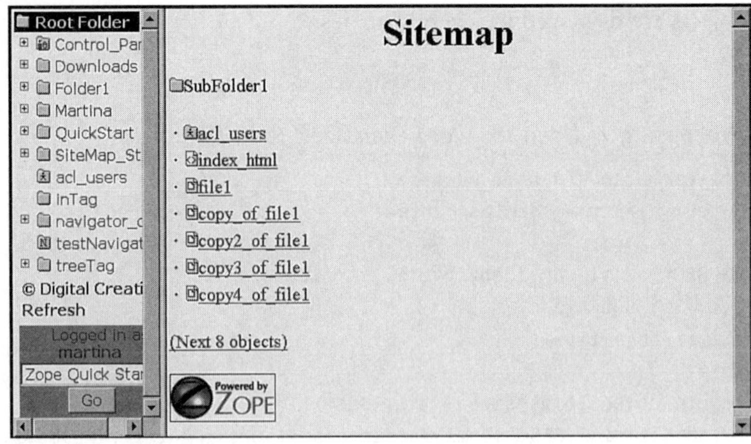

Figure 9.8

The sub-objects of `SubFolder1` are shown in batches of seven rows.

The Attributes of the `<dtml-in>` Tag

The use of the `<dtml-in>` tag is rather complex. A variety of attributes and variables are at your disposal that give you good control over the look of the sitemaps you intend to build. The next sections will discuss each attribute of the `<dtml-in>` tag in detail. Because we are dealing with sitemaps in this chapter, we will give examples that are sitemap-related.

To illustrate the functioning of the single attributes, we will use the folder structure shown in Figure 9.9.

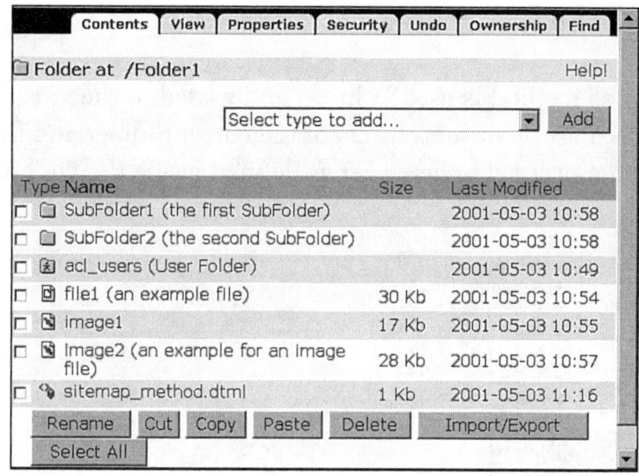

Figure 9.9

We will use this folder hierarchy as an example in this section.

The example code we will use is contained in the `sitemap_method.dtml` DTML method.

> **Warning**
> The `objectItems()` method does not work properly when used inside DTML documents. Use DTML methods instead.

The `name` Attribute

Function:

The name attribute's value is the variable that returns the sequence that is to be run through. When building sitemaps, you will certainly want to insert variables that return lists of objects and sub-objects, so that they can than build the structure of a sitemap.

There are certain methods that return lists of Zope objects or object IDs. See the "Useful Methods of the `ObjectManager.py` Module," later in this chapter, for further reference.

Example:

```
1: <dtml-var standard_html_header>
2: <ul>
3: <dtml-in objectItems>
4: <li><dtml-var id></li>
5: </dtml-in>
6: </ul>
7: <dtml-var standard_html_footer>
```

The `objectItems` method is used in line 3 and passed to the `<dtml-in>` tag. The method returns a list of all sub-objects of the current folder and the objects' IDs are displayed in an unordered bulleted list as defined inside the tag body (see Figure 9.10).

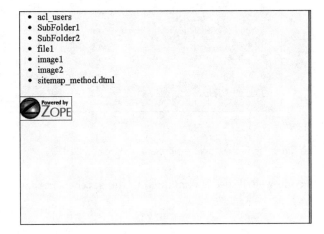

Figure 9.10
The sub-objects of `Folder1` are displayed in a bulleted list.

The `expr` Attribute

Function:

The `expr` attribute inserts a Python expression that returns a list of objects. The resulting list is passed to the `<dtml-in>` tag and the single objects can be run through.

Example:

```
<dtml-var standard_html_header>
<ul>
<dtml-in "objectItems(['Folder', 'DTML Method'])">
<li><dtml-var id></li>
</dtml-in>
</ul>
<dtml-var standard_html_footer>
```

In this example, the same `objectItems` method is used. But, because there are parameters passed to the `objectItems` method, a Python expression is used here. Consequently, only sub-objects of the specified meta type are considered (see Figure 9.11).

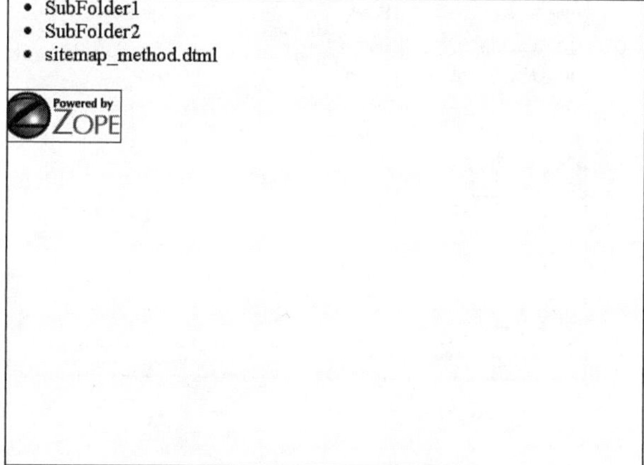

Figure 9.11
Only folders and DTML methods contained in `Folder1` *are displayed here.*

The `sort` Attribute

Function:

The `sort` attribute is used to run through a given sequence's elements in a specified order. The elements are sorted upwards.

Example:

```
<dtml-var standard_html_header>
<table>
<ul>
```

```
<dtml-in objectItems sort=meta_type>
<tr><td><li><dtml-var id>:</td>
<td><dtml-var meta_type></li></td></tr>
</dtml-in>
</ul>
</table>
<dtml-var standard_html_footer>
```

With this code, a table is implemented in which the sub-objects of `Folder1` are sorted by their meta type. The first table column contains the ID of the subject and the second column shows the corresponding meta type (see Figure 9.12).

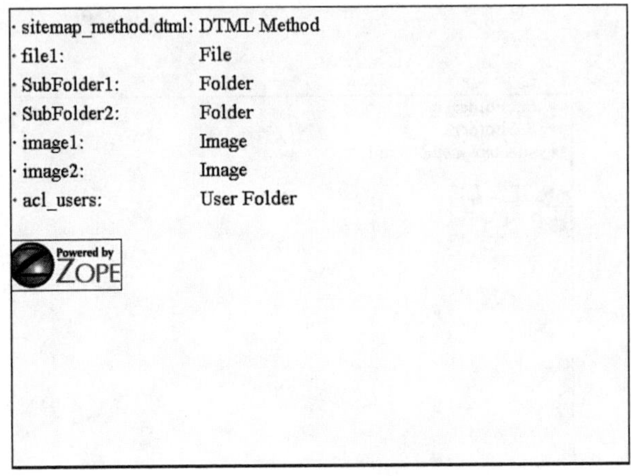

Figure 9.12

The sub-objects of `Folder1` are sorted by their meta type.

The `reverse` Attribute

Function:

The `reverse` attribute reverses the order in which the sequence's items are run through. That means that the original order, defined by the sort attribute, is reversed.

Example:

```
<dtml-var standard_html_header>
<ul>
<dtml-in objectItems sort=id reverse>
<li><dtml-var id></li>
</dtml-in>
</ul>
<dtml-var standard_html_footer>
```

As you can see in line 3, the elements are sorted by their IDs. But, because the `reverse` attribute has been set, the elements are sorted downwards rather than upwards (see Figure 9.13).

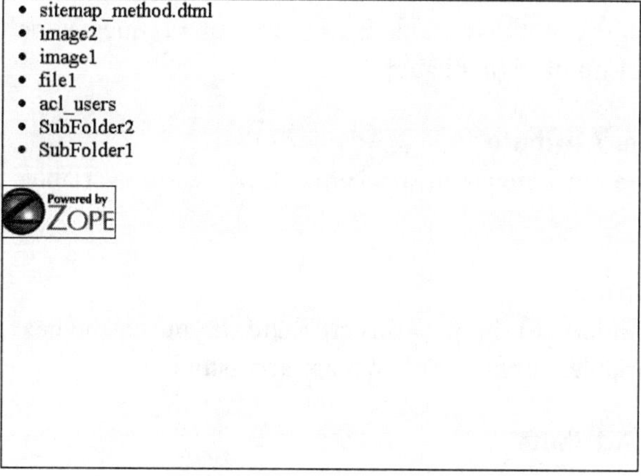

Figure 9.13
The sub-objects of `Folder1` are sorted downwards by their IDs.

The `skip_unauthorized` Attribute

Function:

The `skip_unauthorized` attribute is used to avoid Zope authentication errors. If this attribute is used, items that the current user is not allowed to access are skipped.

Example:

Setting the `skip_unauthorized` variable is rather simple. Because no value is required, simply insert the attribute into the `start` tag:

```
<dtml-in objectItems skip_unauthorized>
```

Batch Processing Variables of the `in` Tag

The following attributes are useful to control the results of the batch processing via the `<dtml-in>` tag. You should make use of the batch processing features when you have a long list of elements and it doesn't make sense to display all of them at once. Most of the time, it is better to split the sequence into several batches.

See "Sitemaps and Batch Processing," earlier in this chapter, for a detailed example.

The `size` Attribute

This attribute enables you to assign a value for the batch size, which means the number of items contained in one batch.

The `start` Attribute

The value assigned to this variable is the name of a request variable that is needed to define the start number of a batch.

The `previous` Attribute

If the `previous` attribute is set, special batch processing variables of the previous batch are accessible.

The `next` Attribute

This works similarly to the previous attribute. If you set the `next` attribute, batch processing variables of the next batch are accessible.

The `orphan` Attribute

The `orphan` attribute defines the minimum batch size. The default value is three.

Imagine a sequence containing 26 items. You want to display the sequence items in batches of 5 each. Theoretically, 6 batches should be generated and the last batch should contain one single item. But, because Zope is trying to combine batches smaller than the size of 2 with adjacent batches, Zope will generate 5 batches and the next one will contain 6 items. The `orphan` attribute is used to avoid that.

The `overlap` Attribute

The `overlap` attribute's value defines the number of overlapping batch items. That means that you can define how many rows you want to appear in one batch and in the neighboring batch.

Useful Methods of the `ObjectManager.py` Module

The following methods are defined in the `ObjectManager.py` module. These are the methods that can be applied for use with either the `<dtml-in>` or the `<dtml-tree>` tags.

To illustrate the function of the methods, we will give an example for each method. We will again use the folder structure that was shown in Figure 9.4.

`tpValues(self)`

The `self` parameter points to the object to which the method is applied. When the method is called from a DTML object, such as in the following example, the method is applied to the current DTML object or its superordinate folder.

This method returns a list of folder sub-objects of the current object. The method is used by default by the `<dtml-tree>` tag.

No parameters can be specified.

Example:

```
<dtml-in "tpValues()">
<dtml-var id>
</dtml-in>
```

Result:

```
SubFolder1 SubFolder2 acl_users
```

`objectIds(self, spec=None)`

This method returns a list of sub-object IDs of the current object.

You can specify a list of meta types if you want to receive a list that contains only those items that match the specified meta type.

Example:

```
<dtml-in "objectIds(['Image','Folder'])">
<dtml-var sequence-item>
</dtml-in>
```

Result:

```
SubFolder1 SubFolder2 image1 image2
```

`objectValues(self, spec=None)`

This method returns a list of sub-objects of the current object.

A list of meta types can be passed as an argument to the method. In that case, only those objects whose meta types match the given ones are returned.

Example:

```
<dtml-in "objectValues(['Image'])">
<dtml-var id>:&#32
<dtml-var "(_['sequence-item'].size)/1024">&#32Kb<br>
</dtml-in>
```

Result:

```
image1: 17 Kb
image2: 28 Kb
```

Because the method returns actual objects, the objects' properties can be accessed, as shown in line 3.

`objectItems(self, spec=None)`
This method returns a list of tuples of the scheme (IDs, sub-objects).

If a list of meta types is specified, the method returns only objects whose meta types match the given parameters.

Example:

```
<dtml-in objectItems>
<dtml-var sequence-key><br>
</dtml-in>
```

Result:

```
acl_users
SubFolder1
SubFolder2
file1
image1
image2
sitemap_method.dtml
```

`objectMap(self)`
This method returns a list of dictionaries that contain the ID and the meta type of an object. This method works faster and uses less memory than the `objectValues()` method.

Example:

```
<dtml-in objectMap>
<dtml-var sequence-item><br>
</dtml-in>
```

Result:

```
{'meta_type': 'User Folder', 'id': 'acl_users'}
{'meta_type': 'Folder', 'id': 'SubFolder1'}
{'meta_type': 'Folder', 'id': 'SubFolder2'}
{'meta_type': 'File', 'id': 'file1'}
{'meta_type': 'Image', 'id': 'image1'}
{'meta_type': 'Image', 'id': 'image2'}
{'meta_type': 'DTML Method', 'id': 'sitemap_method.dtml'}
```

Item Variables of the `<dtml-in>` Tag

There are certain variables that are valid as long as the contents of the `<dtml-in>` tag body are processed. These variables are referring to the elements of the appropriate sequence. Thus, certain actions can be applied to the sequence items.

`sequence-item`
Corresponds to the current item.

In passing this attribute's value to a `<dtml-var>` tag, the sequence item can be accessed and displayed.

`sequence-index`
This attribute returns the index of the current item from within the sequence. The sequence index starts with 0.

`sequence-key`
This variable works with lists of mapping objects. It returns the key of the current object.

`sequence-start`
This returns true or false. If the current element is the first element of the sequence, the result is true; otherwise, the variable returns false.

`sequence-end`
This returns true or false. If the current element is the last element of the sequence, the result is true; otherwise, the variable returns false.

Building Sitemaps with the `<dtml-tree>` Tag

The `<dtml-tree>` tag works much the same as the `<dtml-in>` tag because it runs through sequences of objects. But the `<dtml-tree>` tag automatically traverses sub-objects of sub-objects, and the result is displayed as a tree.

The following code snippet produces a rather simple tree and displays it onscreen (see Figure 9.14):

```
<dtml-var standard_html_header>
<dtml-tree>
<dtml-var id>
</dtml-tree>
<dtml-var standard_html_footer>
```

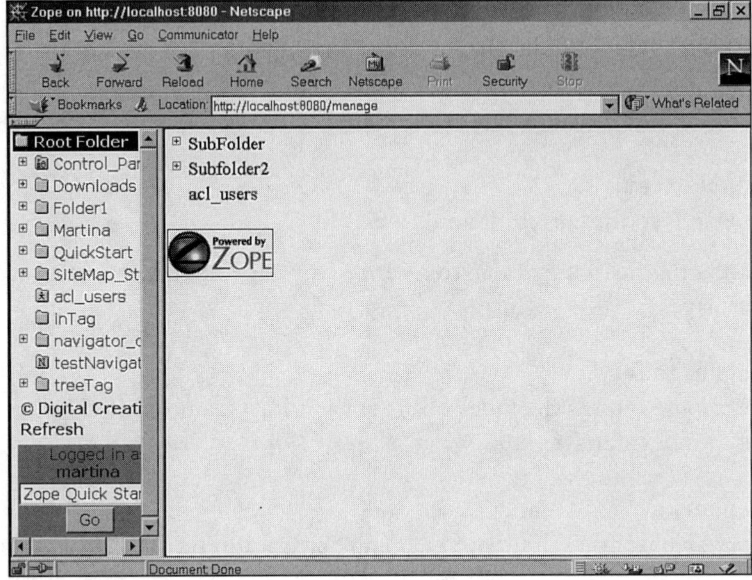

Figure 9.14

A very simple tree of Zope objects.

A tree consists of branches, sub-branches, and leaves. Branches and sub-branches illustrate the object hierarchy, and leaves are used to build groups of items of the same hierarchy.

Trees that have been generated with the `<dtml-tree>` tag will show small plus and minus symbols beside the tree items. These symbols are used to expand or collapse tree branches to make sub-objects visible or to hide them.

A Simple Sitemap

Because the `<dtml-tree>` tag already shows the full object hierarchy and, in addition, provides the capability to expand or collapse the tree's branches with a simple mouse click, this tag is easier to use to generate sitemaps than the `<dtml-in>` tag.

The following code extends the code from the previous section:

```
<dtml-tree branches=objectValues>
<IMG SRC="<dtml-var icon>">
<a href="<dtml-var absolute_url>"><dtml-var id></a>
</dtml-tree>
<dtml-var standard_html_footer>
```

As you can see, the `branches` attribute is set (line 1), and the assigned value is the `objectValues` method. Consequently, the `<dtml-tree>` tag traverses all sub-objects rather than only the folder-like ones (see Figure 9.15).

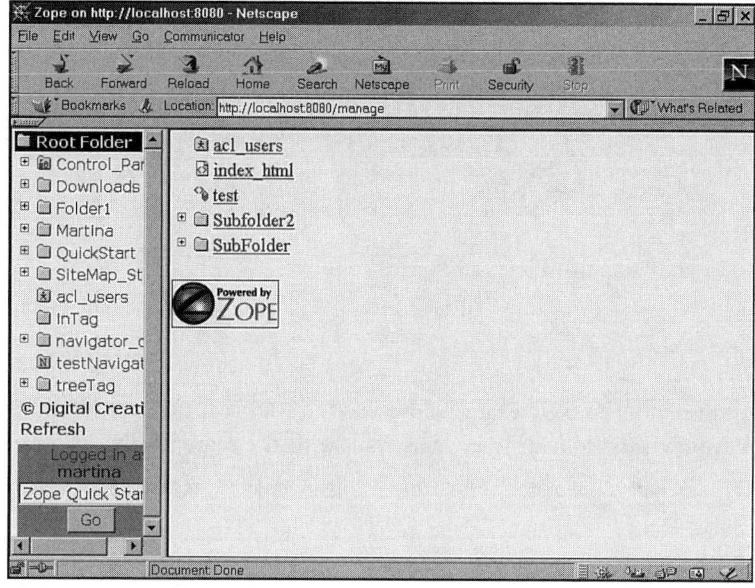

Figure 9.15

A sitemap made with the `<dtml-tree>` tag.

Attributes of the `<dtml-tree>` Tag

The `<dtml-tree>` tag provides a variety of attributes and variables that are very useful to control the design of the sitemaps you want to generate.

`name`

Insert the name of the variable that is supposed to be applied to the `<dtml-tree>` tag. This will usually be the name of the folder or folder-like object you want displayed as a tree.

The `<dtml-tree>` tag is applied to the current object by default.

Example:

```
<dtml-tree SubFolder>
<dtml-var id>
</dtml-tree>
```

This will display a tree of the sub-objects of `Subfolder`.

`expr`
Give an expression that is evaluated and whose result is then passed to the `<dtml-tree>` tag.

Example:

```
<dtml-tree "SubFolder.SubfolderA" branches=objectValues>
<dtml-var id>
</dtml-tree>
```

Result:

Shows a tree of all sub-objects of `SubfolderA`:

```
acl_users
   index_html
```

As you can see in the code example, we used the short form of the `expr` attribute. We could have used the following code as well, with the same results:

```
<dtml-tree expr="SubFolder.SubfolderA" branches=objectValues>
<dtml-var id>
</dtml-tree>
```

`branches`
Define the method that you want to be used to find sub-objects. The method used by default is `tpValues`. This method returns only folder-like objects. If you want to retrieve all objects, use `objectValues`. Check the "Useful Methods of the `ObjectManager.py` Module" section, earlier in this chapter, for more methods you might want to use.

Example:

```
<dtml-tree branches=objectValues>
<IMG SRC="<dtml-var icon>">
<a href="<dtml-var absolute_url>"><dtml-var id></a>
</dtml-tree>
```

Result:

Shows a tree that contains all objects inside the current folder.

`branches_expr`

This attribute is given an expression that is evaluated to find sub-objects. This attribute performs the same function as the `branches` attribute but uses an expression rather than the name of a method.

Example:

```
<dtml-tree branches_expr="objectValues(['Folder','DTML Method'])">
<dtml-var id>
</dtml-tree>
```

Result:

See Figure 9.16.

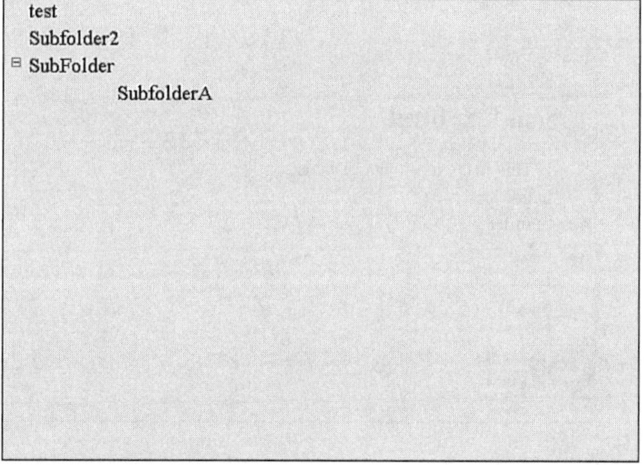

Figure 9.16

Only folders and DTML methods are displayed in the tree.

ID

The name of an attribute or a method that is used to set the ID of an object. The default method is `tpId`.

The attribute should be applied by advanced users only.

URL

Defines the name of an attribute or a variable that is used to retrieve the URL of the current object. The default method is `tpURL`.

The attribute should be applied by advanced users only.

`leaves`

Give the name of a document you want to be shown whenever a branch does not have any sub-branches.

Example:

```
<dtml-tree branches=objectValues leaves=index_html>
<dtml-var id>
</dtml-tree>
```

Result:

See Figure 9.17.

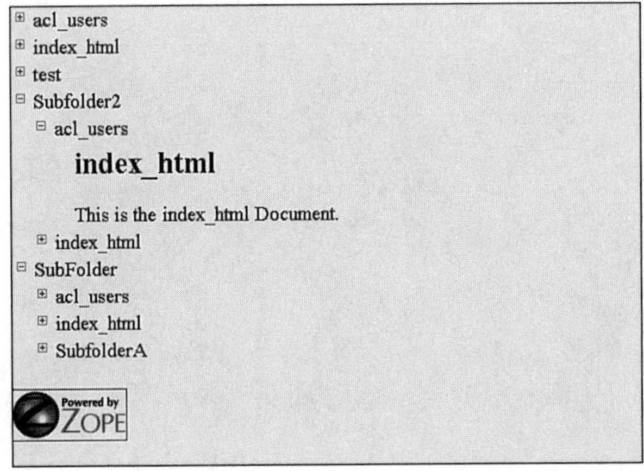

Figure 9.17

The contents of `index_html` *is displayed when a branch does not have sub-branches.*

`header`

Insert the name of the document you want to be displayed on top of each branch expansion.

`footer`

Insert the name of the document you want to be displayed on the bottom of each branch expansion.

`nowrap`

This attribute is used to truncate branches text. When set to 0, any text that does not fit is truncated rather than wrapped.

`sort`
Give the name of an attribute on which the tree's items can be sorted. They are sorted upwards.

`assume_children`
When set to 1, sub-objects are supposed to have subjects, but they are not searched. Thus, each item will have the plus symbol beside it. Only if the symbol is clicked is the search for sub-objects started.

`single`
If this attribute is set to 1, only one tree item can be expanded at a time. Every time one item opens, another one will collapse.

`skip_unauthorized`
The default value is 0. When set to 1, items that the user doesn't have the right permissions for are skipped, and no Authentication Error is raised.

Variables of the `<dtml-tree>` Tag

The following attributes are set by the `<dtml-tree>` tag, and they are associated with sub-objects.

`tree-item-expanded`
This attribute checks whether the current item is expanded. Returns true if it is expanded; otherwise, it returns false.

`tree-item-url`
This attribute gives the URL of the current item relative to the URL of the DTML document in which the tree tag is applied.

`tree-root-url`
Gives the URL of the document from where the `<dtml-tree>` tag is applied.

`tree-level`
This attribute gives the current item's depth. A level of 0 is associated with items on top.

`tree-colspan`
This attribute returns the number of nestings of the called tree.

`expand_all`
This attribute sets the variable to a true value, and all the branches will be expanded.

The following code implements a button that can be used to expand the whole tree:

```
<form action="<dtml-var URL0>">
<input type=hidden name=expand_all value=1>
<input type=submit value="expand all">
</form>
```

`collapse_all`
This attribute sets the variable to a true value, and all the branches will be collapsed.

The following code implements a button that can be used to collapse the whole tree:

```
<form action="<dtml-var URL0>">
<input type=hidden name=collapse_all value=1>
<input type=submit value="collapse all">
</form>
```

Building Sitemaps with NFGnav

A very useful and easy-to-manage product that helps you to build sitemaps automatically is NFGnav.

NFGnav was written by Guido A.J. Stevens and is a product of Net Facilities Group. Visit their Web site at `http://www.nfg.nl`.

First, we will show you how to install NFGnav, and then we will explain how you can efficiently build sitemaps with this product, as well as TreeMenus and LevelTrails.

Installing NFGnav

To install NFGnav, you will need to download the product first. Do as follows:

1. Visit the `www.zope.org` Web site. Type **NFGnav** into the search form and you will be lead to the product's downloading page.
2. After downloading, unpack the downloaded file into your Zope products directory.
3. Start or restart your Zope server.

Now you should be able to add a new NFGnav instance to your Zope server.

Getting Started

NFGnav comes with a DTML help environment. That means that you should move the `Navigation-0.7.zexp` file from the Zope product folder to your Zope server's Import directory. Next, import `Navigation-0.7.zexp`.

Now there's a folder with the Navigation ID on your Zope server that contains several objects:

- `INSTALL.txt`
- `NFGnav_ActiveMapItem`
- `NFGnav_ActiveTrailItem`
- `NFGnav_ActiveTreeItem`
- `NFGnav_CloseMapLevel`
- `NFGnav_CloseTreeLevel`
- `NFGnav_LinkMapItem`
- `NFGnav_LinkTreeItem`
- `NFGnav_OpenMapLevel`
- `NFGnav_OpenTreeLevel`
- `README.txt`
- `example_LevelTrail`
- `example_SiteMap`
- `example_TreeMenu`
- `index_html`

These objects will be of use later; now you have to add a new NFGnav instance first. Simply add the new instance to your root folder. The ID that is needed for the new instance to work with the help environment is NFGnavCore (see Figure 9.18).

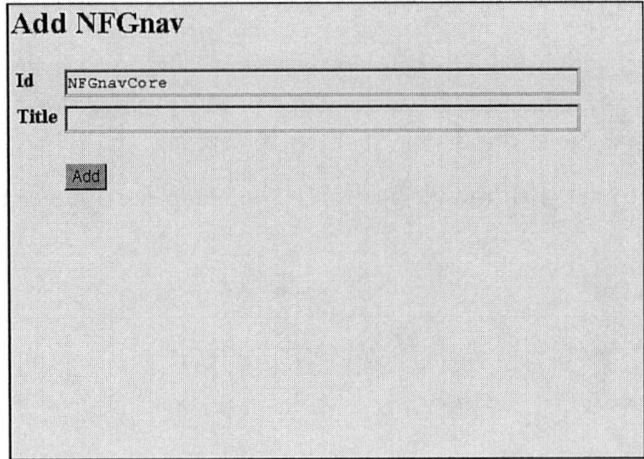

Figure 9.18
Add a new instance of NFGnav with the ID NFGnavCore.

Now you can view the three example methods—`example_SiteMap`, `exampleLevelTrail`, and `example_TreeMenu`. These methods will give you a good insight in how to work with this product.

Building a Sitemap

To build a Sitemap, simply apply the following method to your NFGnav instance:

```
SiteMap(self,
                    PARENTS,
                    REQUEST,
                    callerid=None,
                    context=None,
                    initlevel=1,
                    BaseURL="",
                    Meta_Types=['Folder'],
                    sort='id',
                    maxlevel=None)
```

Look at the following call:

```
<dtml-var "NFGnavCore.SiteMap(PARENTS,REQUEST,id(),initlevel=1,
    Meta_Types=['Folder','DTML Document','DTML Method'])">
```

The result will then look like Figure 9.19.

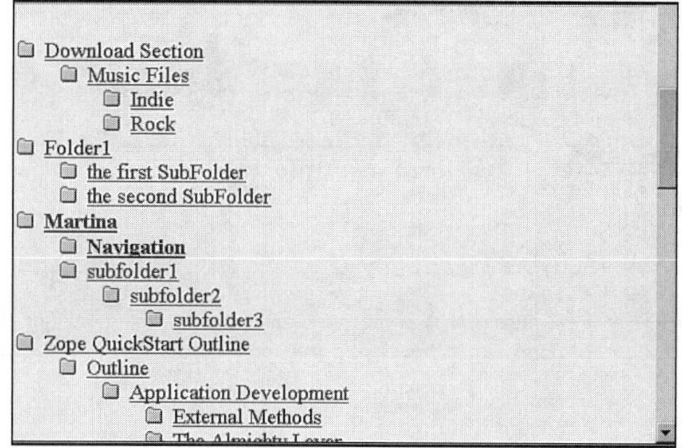

Figure 9.19

An excerpt of a sophisticated sitemap.

Building a `TreeMenu`

To build a `TreeMenu`, simply apply the following method to your NFGnav instance:

```
TreeMenu(self,
                    PARENTS,
                    REQUEST,
                    callerid=None,
                    context=None,
                    initlevel=1,
                    BaseURL="",
                    Meta_Types=['Folder'],
                    sort='id',
                    maxlevel=None)
```

We will call the method the following way:

```
&lt;dtml-var "NFGnavCore.TreeMenu(PARENTS,REQUEST,id(),initlevel=1,
Meta_Types=['Folder','DTML Document','DTML Method','Image'])"&gt;
```

The result will be as shown in Figure 9.20.

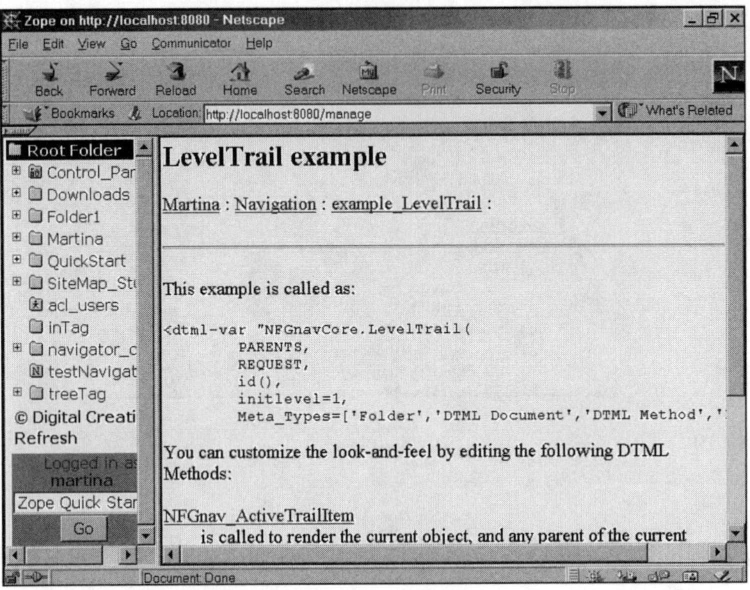

Figure 9.20
A tree menu.

Building a `LevelTrail`

To create a `LevelTrail`, simply apply the following method to your NFGnav instance:

```
def LevelTrail(self,
                    PARENTS,
                    REQUEST,
                    callerid=None,
                    context=None,
                    initlevel=1,
                    BaseURL="",
                    Meta_Types=['Folder'],
                    sort='id',
                    maxlevel=None)
```

If we would call the method as follows:

```
<dtml-var "NFGnavCore.LevelTrail(PARENTS,REQUEST,id(),initlevel=1,
    Meta_Types=['Folder','DTML Document','DTML Method','Image'])">
```

the result will be as shown in Figure 9.21.

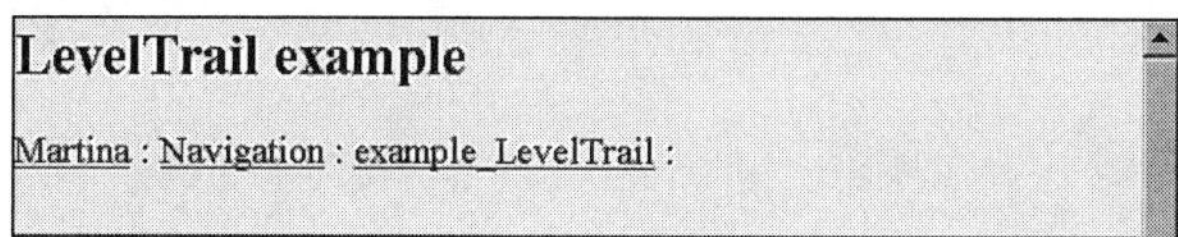

Figure 9.21
A LevelTrail as shown by NFGnav.

Summary

This chapter explained the commands `<dtml-in>` and `<dtml-tree>` and how they can be used to create a sitemap for your Web site. Then, you learned about an existing sitemap product, NFGnav, and how it is used.

The next chapter will introduce the ZCatalog, Zope's integrated catalog. It will show how to use the ZCatalog to add search capabilities to your Web site.

CHAPTER 10

ADDING SEARCH CAPABILITIES

One of the most important features of a Web site is its search capability. It is the easiest way for a visitor to find what he or she is looking for at your site. A sitemap, which you have learned about in the last chapter, helps with finding certain things but, sometimes, that is not enough—especially if your Web site has a lot of content that is added on a daily or weekly basis.

In this chapter, we will show you how to use the ZCatalog, a product integrated in Zope. After explaining the different views of the ZCatalog and how to index objects, we will show you how the cataloged objects can be searched using the Z Search Interface.

The ZCatalog

The ZCatalog has been a standard product in Zope since Zope version 2. With the ZCatalog, you can catalog either all existing objects or only those matching certain criteria. Those criteria can be:

- The object's meta type
- The object's ID
- Words that the object contains
- An expression the object matches
- The object's modification time and date
- The permission a certain group has concerning the object

How to define the criteria will be explained later in "The Find Objects View" section.

But first, we will create a ZCatalog.

> **Note**
> A ZCatalog only stores certain, defined information about objects. It does not store the objects themselves.

Adding a ZCatalog

A ZCatalog is created like any other instance of a product. There is a ZCatalog item in the drop-down menu of a folder. Go to the root folder and select ZCatalog from its drop-down menu. This will call up the Add page. In addition to the ID and title, which are common with every object in Zope, there is a select box labeled Vocabulary. The Vocabulary and its features are explained in "The Vocabulary View" section later in this chapter. For now, just choose Create One for Me (see Figure 10.1).

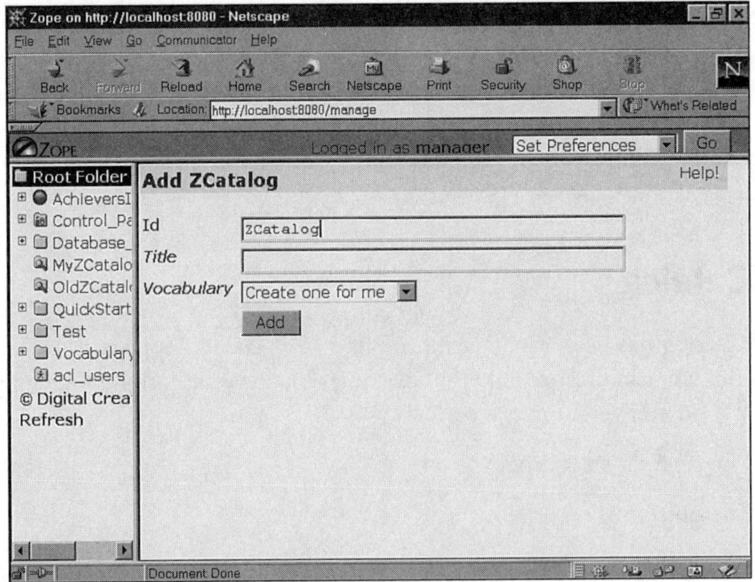

Figure 10.1
Adding a new ZCatalog.

After giving the object the ID `ZCatalog`, click the Add button. To search the objects in a ZCatalog, you will need a search and a result page, which we will talk about later in this chapter. First, we will introduce the different views of a ZCatalog.

The Views of the ZCatalog

In addition to the Content, Properties, Undo, and Security views, which you already know from other Zope objects, a ZCatalog has five catalog-specific views. Those views are as follows:

- Catalog
- Indexes
- Metadata
- Find Objects
- Advanced

This is the order the views appear in on the tab bar of a ZCatalog object. We will now go through these views and explain them, but in a slightly different order. We do this because you will need the Catalog view only after defining the indexes and metadata and finding objects that are to be cataloged.

The Indexes View

Before cataloging objects, you should define what attributes or properties are to be indexed. This is done in the Indexes view. The ZCatalog examines whether an object has any of the defined indexes and then indexes the value of every matching attribute (see Figure 10.2).

There are three types of indexes:

- Text Index
- Field Index
- Keyword Index

To add a new index, enter the name in the Add Index text field. Decide on the type of index and select it from the drop-down menu Of Type, and then click the Add button. You can delete an index by activating the check box in front of the index and clicking the Delete button.

Text Indexes

Text indexes divide the value of a property into words (the single words are indexed separately). Therefore, a user does not need to type in the exact value of a property—if it consists of several words—to get the respective object as a result. The results are sorted by score; that means the best hit comes first followed by the second best and so on.

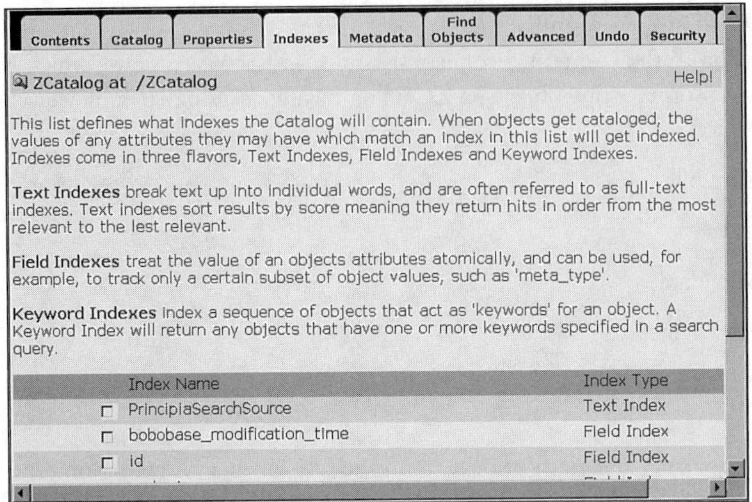

Figure 10.2
The Indexes view.

When searching text indexes, you can use Boolean expressions, such as AND, OR, AND NOT, and OR NOT, to specify your search. For example, if you are looking for objects that contain the word "standard," the word "HTML," but not the word "footer" in their titles, you would use the following query:

```
standard AND html AND NOT footer
```

> **Note**
> Querying the ZCatalog is done by using a search page. See "The Z Search Interface" section later in the chapter to see how to create such a page.

If your ZCatalog uses a Vocabulary (see "The Vocabulary" section later in this chapter), you can even use wildcards in your search. The previous query could look like the following, for example:

```
s* AND html AND NOT footer
```

This will give you all objects that have a title containing words that start with an "s" and contain the word HTML but not the word "footer." However, this will only work if the Vocabulary uses globbing. See the "Globbing or Not?" section later in this chapter for an explanation of globbing.

With text indexes, you can also use parentheses in your queries to define a hierarchy for the search. For example:

```
(s* AND html) AND NOT footer
```

will turn up different objects than:

```
s* AND (html AND NOT footer)
```

You see that the text index is very powerful and versatile.

Field Indexes

Field indexes preserve the property value as an entity. Therefore, a user needs to enter the exact value to get the respective object as a result. This might be a problem sometimes because, with certain properties, like a date, the user either does not remember the exact value or format or he or she does not know it.

In that case, a field index might be of better use for a range search. Doing a range search means, for example, that you are looking for objects that have been modified since yesterday or last week. How to do such a search is explained in the "Modifying the Search Page" section later in this chapter.

Keyword Indexes

Keyword indexes are used to search properties, such as tokens or lines. With these property types, you can put objects into different categories with each object belonging to either one or more of the categories.

For example, one book might be categorized as a novel, an adventure, and a historical text at the same time. Another book might be categorized as a poem and an adventure. If a user searches for an adventure, he and she will get both books as a result.

See the "Example: Searching Keyword Indexes" section later in this chapter for an example of keyword indexes.

The Metadata View

In addition to the indexes, a ZCatalog can store other information about the objects—metadata. Metadata is stored in a database, in the metadata table. While the indexes are used to search the cataloged objects, the metadata is used to show the search results. That means the defined indexes appear in the search form and the metadata appears on the Results page.

Indexes and metadata do not need to be the same. You can have the index `bobobase_modification_time`, which contains the latest date and time an object was modified, but you do not want to show this information on the Results page.

However, the metadata does not have to be shown explicitly on the Results page. It can be used to create the Results page. For example, if you store the information `absolute_url` as metadata, you can use it to create links to the objects on the Results page. Figure 10.3 shows the Metadata view where you define what metadata is to be stored.

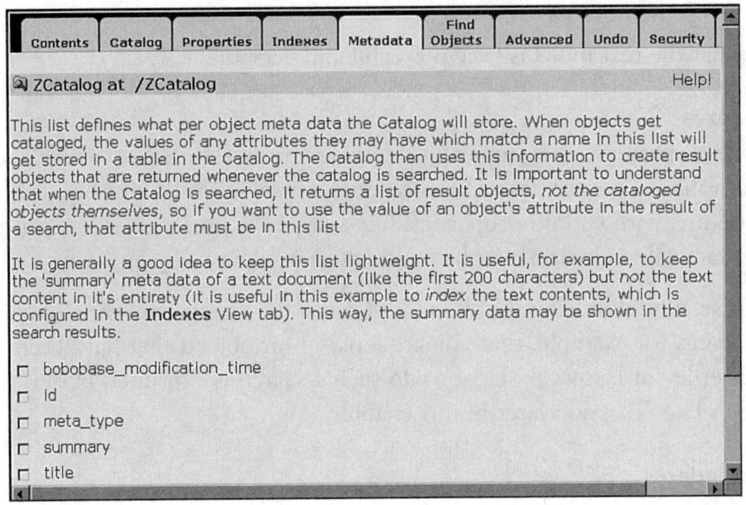

Figure 10.3
The Metadata view.

To add a Metadata item, enter its name in the Add Metadata text field and click the Add button. To delete a Metadata item, activate the check box in front of it and click the Delete button.

The Find Objects View

This is where you enter the criteria that will determine which objects are indexed in the ZCatalog (see Figure 10.4). Enter the criteria in the form and click the Find and Catalog button.

There are seven selection boxes on the Find Object view:

- *Find objects of type*—This list contains all the items that the drop-down menu of a folder-like object contains. You need to choose from this list which kinds of objects you want to index. The list contains the item All types, so you do not need to select all types by hand. You can either let the ZCatalog look for all types of objects, only one type, or a number of types by selecting multiple types.

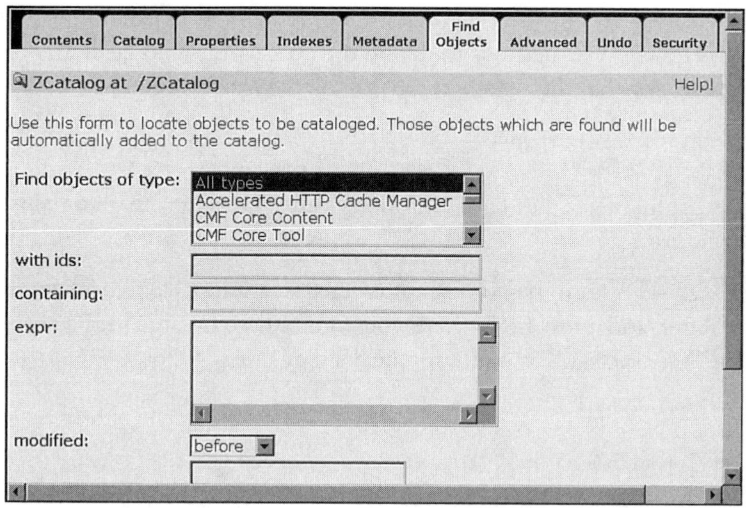

Figure 10.4
The Find Objects view.

> **Tip**
> The list is not in alphabetical order. If you want to change that, edit the `catalogFind.dtml` file in the `/lib/python/Products/ZCatalog/dtml` directory and change the line
>
> ```
> <dtml-in all_meta_types mapping>
> ```
>
> to
>
> ```
> <dtml-in all_meta_types mapping sort=name>
> ```

- *with ids*—This field is for the ID the objects should have. You can enter more than one ID in the field, separating them with spaces.
- *containing*—This field is for words, characters, parts of sentences, and so on that have to be contained in the objects. You can also enter DTML commands, such as the following:

  ```
  <dtml-var sequence-index>
  ```

- *expr*—Here, you can enter expressions that have to be true for an object if it is to be indexed in the ZCatalog. The following expression

  ```
  get_size()>5000
  ```

will ensure that only objects that are bigger than 5KB are indexed. This example shows how to use methods to define the criteria for an object. You can also use a property for that. For example, the following expression

```
'Adventure' in category
```

indexes all objects that have a property called `category` that contains the word Adventure.

- *modified*—This criteria consists of two parts: a select list with the items Before and After, and a text field where you enter a date or time in the correct DateTime format. Examples for such a date are as follows:

  2001/05/01

  2001/05/01 5:00

  2001/05/01 5:00:30.00 GMT-5

- *where the roles*—This selection box and the drop-down menu below it go together to define another criteria.

  Choose one or more roles from the selection box if you want to have all objects indexed where those roles have a specific permission.

- *have the permission*—Choose the permission that the roles defined in the Where The Roles selection box must have concerning an object.

Example

Figure 10.5 shows an example of how you can fill out the Find Objects form. Using the data in the figure, the ZCatalog will index all objects with the IDs `index_html` or `standard_html_header` that contain the words `<dtml-var title_or_id>`. The objects must have been modified after 5 p.m. on February 01, 2001 (2001/02/01 17:00:00.00). In addition, Anonymous must have the View permission for those objects.

The Catalog View

After you have filled out the form in the Find Objects view, you will be directed to the Catalog view.

In the Catalog view (see Figure 10.6), you can see a list of the objects that are currently indexed in the ZCatalog. The list is shown in batches of 20 entries per page. You can look through the list using the Previous 20 Entries and Next 20 Entries links at the top of the list.

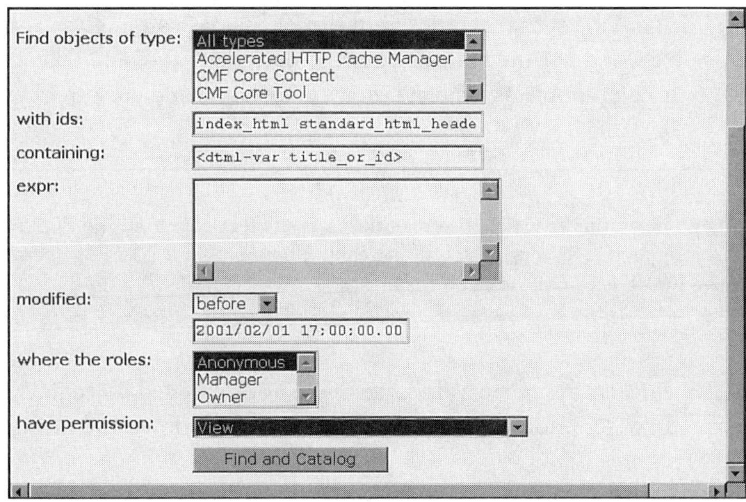

Figure 10.5

Example for the Find Objects view.

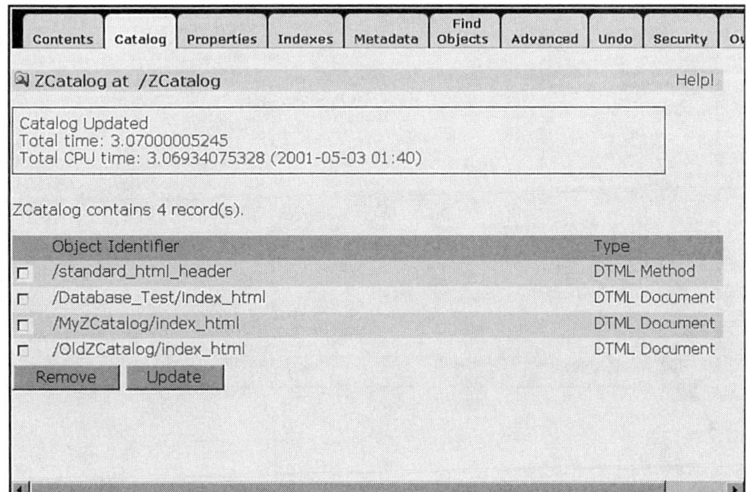

Figure 10.6

The Catalog view.

At the bottom of the list, you find two buttons—Remove and Update.

To remove an object from the ZCatalog, activate its check box and click the Remove button.

If you modified an object that is indexed in the ZCatalog, you might want to only update this object and not the entire ZCatalog, because that would take much longer. To update only certain objects, activate their check boxes and click the Update button.

> **Note**
> Removing an object in the Catalog view removes the object only from the ZCatalog. The object's information is no longer stored and cannot be found in a ZCatalog search. It will *not* remove the object from the Zope database.

The object identifiers are given as links in the list of cataloged objects. When you click a link, you see a description page of that object with its indexes and metadata (see Figure 10.7).

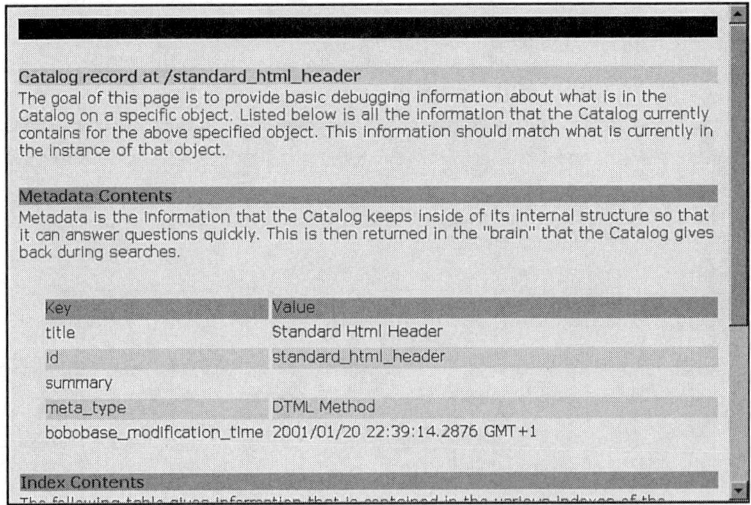

Figure 10.7
A cataloged object's Description page.

The Advanced View

This view is divided into two sections—Catalog Maintenance and Subtransactions (see Figure 10.8).

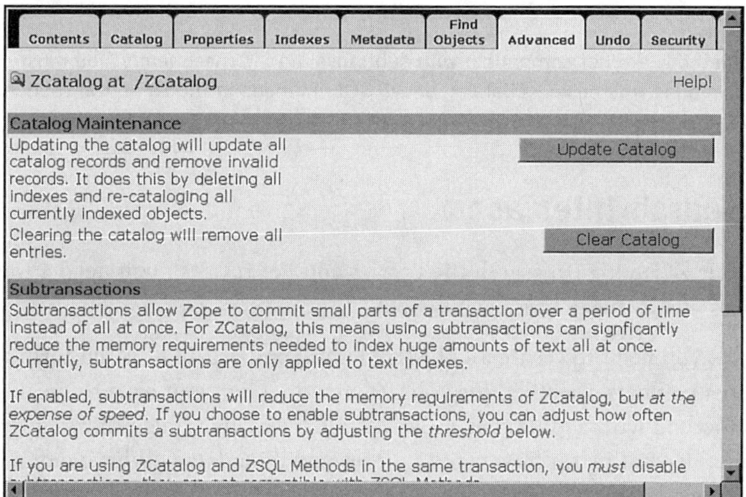

Figure 10.8
The Advanced view.

At the top, you find the Catalog Maintenance section. It consists of two buttons—the Update Catalog button and the Clear Catalog button. You know that you can update modified objects (for example, re-index them) by selecting them in the Catalog view and pressing the Update button. This, however, may be a time-consuming job if you have modified or deleted a lot of objects, and it may be even impossible if you cannot remember which objects you changed or modified. In that case, you can use the Update Catalog button in the Advanced view to update the entire ZCatalog. This will re-index all cataloged objects and will remove all invalid records. The Clear Catalog button removes all entries in the ZCatalog.

> **Note**
> Indexing is not an automatic process—cataloged objects are not re-indexed automatically whenever you modify them. You have to use the Update Catalog button to manually start the re-indexing process. However, re-indexing does not include newly created objects. You will have to catalog these objects by using the Find Objects view.

If subtransactions are enabled, the ZCatalog indexes objects in batches. Those batches are defined as threshold. A *threshold* is the number of objects that the ZCatalog indexes at one time. If you set a high threshold, indexing will go much faster, but it will also take more memory. If you set a low threshold, less memory is used but the indexing process will take longer.

> **Note**
> Z SQL methods are not compatible with subtransaction. Consequently, you must disable subtransactions when using ZCatalog and Z SQL methods in the same transaction.

The Z Search Interface

To use your ZCatalog (to search the entries and get results), you need a way to enter your query and to make the result visible.

Therefore, you need to create a DTML method and create a search form using all the indexes you have specified for your ZCatalog. Then you have to create another DTML method with a table that shows all the metadata. This process might take some time, depending on how many indexes and metadata you have defined, and is also very boring. You can save a lot of time by using the Z Search Interface, a standard Zope feature.

The Z Search Interface actually belongs to the Z SQL methods product. It is used to query a Z SQL method and to show the results. Consequently, the Z Search Interface can be used for both ZCatalogs and Z SQL methods.

The Z Search Interface creates two DTML methods—a Search page and a Results page. The Search page is created using the indexes defined at the time it is created. The Results page is created using the defined metadata.

> **Note**
> It is important that the indexes and metadata have been defined before the Search and Results pages are created using the Z Search Interface. This is necessary because the Z Search Interface uses the indexes and metadata currently defined.

Adding a Z Search Interface

To add a new Z Search Interface, select the item from the drop-down menu either in the ZCatalog or somewhere farther up in the hierarchy (perhaps in a superior folder). You will see the Add form (shown in Figure 10.9).

First select which ZCatalog and/or Z SQL method you want to be able to search with this Z Search Interface. Remember, you can have search forms for more than one ZCatalog/Z SQL method.

Now, enter IDs for both the Results page—the Report ID—and the Search page—the Search Input ID.

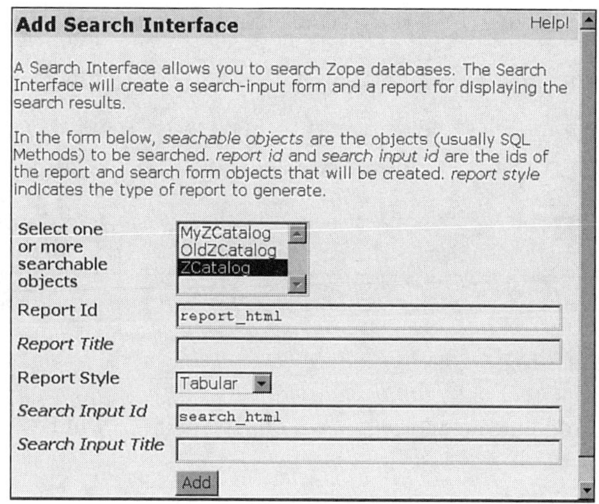

Figure 10.9
Adding a Search and Report page.

There are two different styles for the Results page—tabular and records. If you choose the tabular style, the results are shown as a table with a border (see Figure 10.10).

Title	Meta type	Id	Summary	Bobobase modification time	Data record id
Standard Html Header	DTML Method	standard_html_header		2001/01/20 22:39:14.2876 GMT+1	656686403
	DTML Document	index_html		2001/04/28 10:14:57.4 GMT+2	656686404
	DTML Document	index_html		2001/04/29 14:12:16.84 GMT+2	656686405
	DTML Document	index_html		2001/05/02 23:03:03.08 GMT+2	656686406

Powered by ZOPE

Figure 10.10
Tabular style Results page.

Figure 10.11 shows the Results page using the records style. Here, the information of an object is given in a line separated by commas.

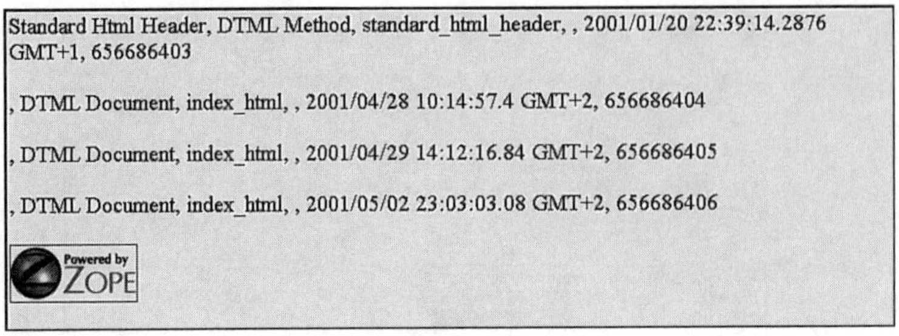

Standard Html Header, DTML Method, standard_html_header, , 2001/01/20 22:39:14.2876 GMT+1, 656686403

, DTML Document, index_html, , 2001/04/28 10:14:57.4 GMT+2, 656686404

, DTML Document, index_html, , 2001/04/29 14:12:16.84 GMT+2, 656686405

, DTML Document, index_html, , 2001/05/02 23:03:03.08 GMT+2, 656686406

Powered by ZOPE

Figure 10.11

Records style Results page.

Now click the Add button, and two new DTML methods will be created.

The Search

The search form contains a simple HTML form. If intended for a ZCatalog, the form's fields are created using the catalog's indexes (lines 5–19, Listing 10.1), as was previously mentioned.

Listing 10.1

Standard Search Form

```
 1: <dtml-var standard_html_header>
 2: <form action="report_html" method="get">
 3: <h2><dtml-var document_title></h2>
 4: Enter query parameters:<br><table>
 5: <tr><th>Title</th>
 6:     <td><input name="title"
 7:                width=30 value=""></td></tr>
 8: <tr><th>Id</th>
 9:     <td><input name="id"
10:                width=30 value=""></td></tr>
11: <tr><th>Meta type</th>
12:     <td><input name="meta_type"
13:                width=30 value=""></td></tr>
14: <tr><th>PrincipiaSearchSource</th>
15:     <td><input name="PrincipiaSearchSource"
16:                width=30 value=""></td></tr>
17: <tr><th>Bobobase modification time</th>
18:     <td><input name="bobobase_modification_time"
19:                width=30 value=""></td></tr>
20: <tr><td colspan=2 align=center>
```

Listing 10.1

Continued

```
21: <input type="SUBMIT" name="SUBMIT" value="Submit Query">
22: </td></tr>
23: </table>
24: </form>
25: <dtml-var standard_html_footer>
```

In line 2, you see the form's action. This is set to the ID of the Results page (Report ID). The code in Listing 10.1 creates the form seen in Figure 10.12.

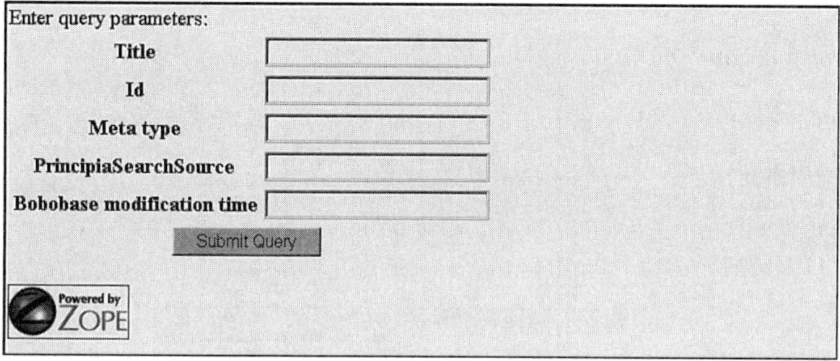

Figure 10.12

The standard search form.

Modifying the Search Page

Depending on which index types you are using, you might want to change the standard Search page. In "The Indexes View" section, we talked about the different types of indexes:

- Text Index
- Field Index
- Keyword Index

To search text indexes, you can use the normal text fields of an HTML form. But for field and keyword indexes, you might want to change that to make better use of those types of indexes.

Example: Searching Field Indexes 1

One index that is a default with the ZCatalog is the attribute `bobobase_modification_time`. This attribute keeps track of when an object was last modified. The modification time is stored in the DateTime format that a Web site's visitor may not know or may have a hard time remembering. Therefore, if a visitor wants to find objects that were last modified a day ago, he or she may not know exactly what to enter in the search form's text field.

We can make it easier for the visitor to search for the modification time by giving him or her a drop-down menu from which he or she can choose, for example, the following 'dates' (see Figure 10.13):

- Ever
- Last 6 hours
- Last 12 hours
- Yesterday
- Last week

Enter query parameters:
Title
Id
Meta type
PrincipiaSearchSource
Modified since: ever
ever
last 6 hours
last 12 hours
yesterday
last Week

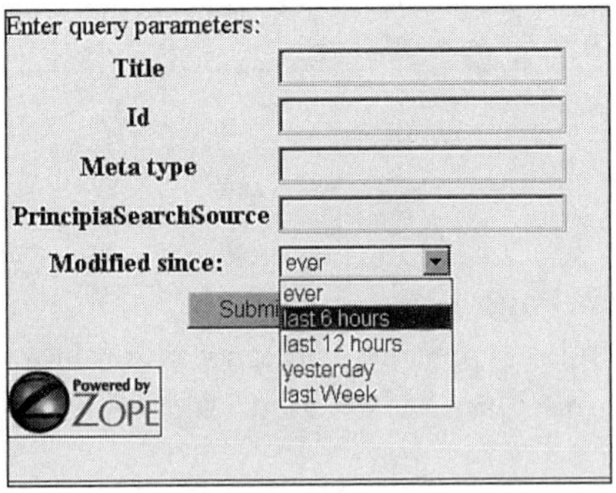

Figure 10.13
The modified Search page (`bobobase_modification_time`*).*

To do this, we need to change lines 17–19 of the standard Search page (Listing 10.1). First, change the field name from `bobobase_modification_time` to `modified since`. This will make the purpose clearer for the visitor.

Now, we need to create a drop-down menu (see Listing 10.2).

Listing 10.2

The Drop-Down Menu for `bobobase_modification_time`

```
1:      <select name="bobobase_modification_time:date">
2:        <option value="<dtml-var expr="_.DateTime(0)" >">ever</option>
3:        <option value="<dtml-var expr="_.DateTime() - 0.25">">last 6
➥hours</option>
4:        <option valur="<dtml-var expr="_.DateTime() - 0.5">">last 12
➥hours</option>
5:        <option value="<dtml-var expr="_.DateTime() - 1" >">yesterday</option>
6:        <option value="<dtml-var expr="_.DateTime() - 7" >">last Week</option>
7:      </select>
```

The name of this selection list must be `bobobase_modification_time`, of course, but we need to define that this entry will be a DateTime format. This is done by adding

```
:date
```

to the selection list name (see line 1, Listing 10.2).

The option values have to be dynamically created because they change, depending on the date and time that a visitor is entering the query. To calculate the respective option value, we use the `_.DateTime()` method. This method returns the current time and date in the correct DateTime format.

You can calculate with a DateTime format as if it was a number. You can add and subtract to get different times or dates. If you subtract a one from the result of `_.DateTime()`, you get the current time one day ago. If you subtract two, you get the time two days ago, and so on. To get the time six hours ago, you need to subtract 0.25 from the current time because six hours is one quarter of 24 hours.

Lines 3–6 in Listing 10.2 show the expressions used to calculate the option values for four of the options.

Line 1 shows that you can use a parameter with the `_.DateTime()` method. If you pass a number to the method, it returns the start date in computer language, which is

```
1970/01/01 01:00:00 GMT+1
```

plus the number as seconds. Therefore, line 2 in Listing 10.2 returns the start date, while the method call

```
ZopeTime(5)
```

returns the date

```
1970/01/01 01:00:05 GMT+1
```

and so on.

Having the drop-down menu, however, is not enough. We want to find all objects modified from the time given as the option value to the current time (a range search). For this, we need to define the use for the form entry `bobobase_modification_time`.

This is done with the following line:

```
<input type="hidden" name="bobase_modification_time_usage" value="range:min">
```

Here, you can see we used the form input of the type `hidden` and took the name of the index name (`bobobase_modification_time`) plus the word `_usage`. The value is the word `range` and the specific definition `:min`. That means the value of `bobobase_modification_time` is to be the minimum value, and the objects have to have a value greater than that. If you want to create a range search with a maximum value, you would have to use the `range:max` value.

Listing 10.3 shows the code block that needs to be used in the search form. It contains the complete table row with the heading (lines 2–4), the table cell (lines 5–14), the hidden usage field (line 6), and the drop-down menu (lines 7–13).

Listing 10.3

Code Block for the `modified bobobase_modification_time` *Search*

```
 1: <tr>
 2:    <th>
 3:      Modified since:
 4:    </th>
 5:    <td>
 6:      <input type="hidden" name="bobase_modification_time_usage"
➥value="range:min">
 7:      <select name="bobobase_modification_time:date">
 8:        <option value="<dtml-var expr="ZopeTime(0)" >">ever</option>
 9:        <option value="<dtml-var expr="ZopeTime() - 0.25">">
➥last 6 hours</option>
10:        <option valur="<dtml-var expr="ZopeTime() - 0.5">">
➥last 12 hours</option>
11:        <option value="<dtml-var expr="ZopeTime() - 1" >">yesterday</option>
12:        <option value="<dtml-var expr="ZopeTime() - 7" >">last Week</option>
13:      </select>
14:    </td>
15: </tr>
```

Example: Searching Field Indexes 2

In the last section, you learned about the range search using minimum and maximum values. Now we want to do a search using both. The goal is to create a search for IDs between two given letters (see Figure 10.14).

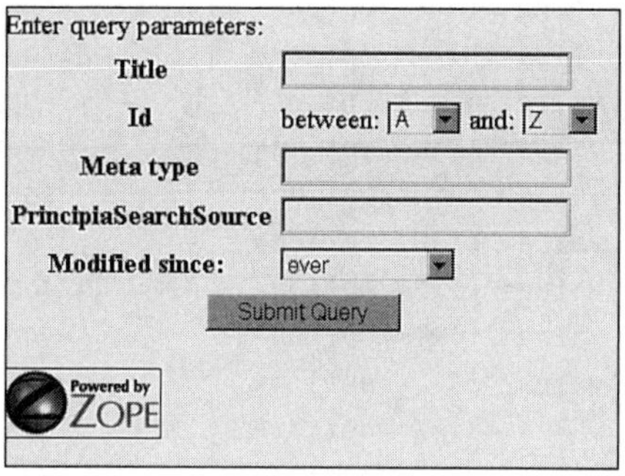

Figure 10.14

The modified Search page (ID).

For this, we need two selection lists with the letters of the alphabet. Both selection lists must have the name ID. We then have to define the usage for the index ID as follows:

```
<input type="hidden" name="id_usage" value="range:min:max">
```

Here, you see that the range has a minimum and a maximum value. Therefore, the entry for the index `id` has to consist of two values. Those values are each a letter of the two select lists. The letters have to be given to the ZCatalog as a list of two values or the search will not work correctly. This is done by adding the following expression:

```
:list
```

to each of the selection list names:

```
<select name="id:list">
```

Listing 10.4 shows the complete code block for the ID search.

Listing 10.4

Code Block for the Modified ID Search

```
<tr><th>Id</th>
<td><input type="hidden" name="id_usage" value="range:min:max">
    between:
```

Listing 10.4

Continued

```
 4:       <select name="id:list">
 5:          <option selected value="a">A</option> <option value="b">B</option>
 6:          <option value="c">C</option>          <option value="e">E</option>
 7:          <option value="f">F</option>          <option value="g">G</option>
 8:          <option value="h">H</option>          <option value="i">I</option>
 9:          <option value="j">J</option>          <option value="k">K</option>
10:          <option value="l">L</option>          <option value="m">M</option>
11:          <option value="n">N</option>          <option value="o">O</option>
12:          <option value="p">P</option>          <option value="q">Q</option>
13:          <option value="r">R</option>          <option value="s">S</option>
14:          <option value="t">T</option>          <option value="u">U</option>
15:          <option value="v">V</option>          <option value="w">W</option>
16:          <option value="x">X</option>          <option value="y">Y</option>
17:          <option value="z">Z</option>
18:       </select>
19:        and:
20:       <select name="id:list">
21:          <option value="a">A</option>          <option value="b">B</option>
22:          <option value="c">C</option>          <option value="e">E</option>
23:          <option value="f">F</option>          <option value="g">G</option>
24:          <option value="h">H</option>          <option value="i">I</option>
25:          <option value="j">J</option>          <option value="k">K</option>
26:          <option value="l">L</option>          <option value="m">M</option>
27:          <option value="n">N</option>          <option value="o">O</option>
28:          <option value="p">P</option>          <option value="q">Q</option>
29:          <option value="r">R</option>          <option value="s">S</option>
30:          <option value="t">T</option>          <option value="u">U</option>
31:          <option value="v">V</option>          <option value="w">W</option>
32:          <option value="x">X</option>          <option value="y">Y</option>
33:          <option selected value="z">Z</option>
34:       </select>
35:   </td>
36: </tr>
```

> **Note**
>
> Because the search returns nothing if the range for ID is A to A, the element A in the first and the element Z in the second selection list have been marked as the defaults (lines 5 and 33). This was done using the `selected` attribute of the `option` tag.

Example: Searching Keyword Indexes

A keyword index is intended to categorize objects. That means that there are a limited number of categories or keywords. Therefore, it would be a good idea to put all the categories in a list for the user to choose from when searching the ZCatalog. However, the user might look for objects that belong to two or more different categories. So we cannot use a drop-down menu for this search field. We need to provide a multiple selection list.

For this example, we added a Category index of the type Keyword Index to the ZCatalog (see Figure 10.15).

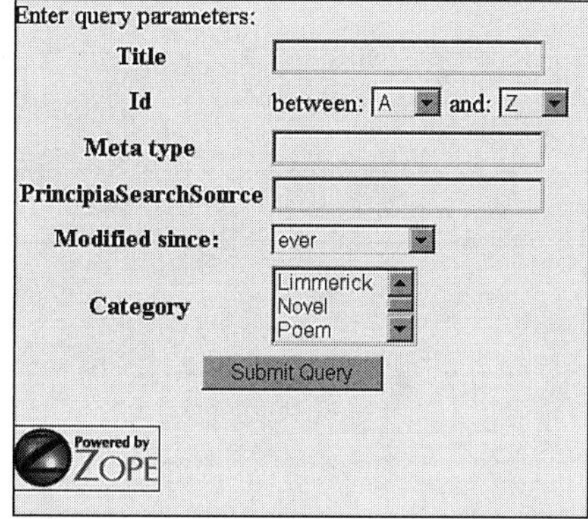

Figure 10.15

The modified Search page (Category).

The selection list needs to be created dynamically because the categories might change or more categories might be added. Listing 10.5 shows the necessary code snippet.

Listing 10.5

Code Block for the Category Search

```
<tr><th>Category</th>
    <td>
      <select name="Category" multiple size=3>
        <dtml-in expr="ZCatalog.uniqueValuesFor('Category')">
          <option value="&dtml-sequence-item;"><dtml-var sequence-item></option>
        </dtml-in>
      </select>
    </td>
</tr>
```

The selection list is started in line 3. The options for the list are created with the `in` tag. The `in` tag iterates over the values of the Category index (line 4). We get these values using the `uniqueValuesFor()` method. This method returns a list of all values for a specific index that exist in cataloged objects. The specific index is given as parameter (here: `Category`). For each item in this list, we create a selection option (line 5). The `sequence-item` variable contains the name of the category in each iteration.

> **Note**
>
> The `sequence-item` variable is called in two different ways in Listing 10.5.
>
> `&dtml-sequence-item;`
>
> is a special writing for DTML, called entity-syntax, for
>
> `<dtml-var sequence-item>`

The Results

The Results or Report page shows the result of a query to the ZCatalog. There are two layouts for this page: in a table (tabular) or in lines with the object's metadata separated by spaces (records).

The Tabular Layout

Listing 10.6 shows the standard source code for the tabular layout. The word standard in this case means that the indexes of the respective ZCatalog have not been edited in any way.

Listing 10.6

Standard Results Page (Tabular)

```
<dtml-var standard_html_header>
<dtml-in MyZCatalog size=50 start=query_start>
   <dtml-if sequence-start>
      <dtml-if previous-sequence>
        <a href="<dtml-var URL><dtml-var sequence-query
                 >query_start=<dtml-var
                 previous-sequence-start-number>">
        (Previous <dtml-var previous-sequence-size> results)
        </a>
      </dtml-if previous-sequence>
      <table border>
        <tr>
```

Listing 10.6
Continued

```
           <th>Title</th>
           <th>Meta type</th>
           <th>Id</th>
           <th>Summary</th>
           <th>Bobobase modification time</th>
           <th>Data record id </th>
         </tr>
    </dtml-if sequence-start>
         <tr>
           <td><dtml-var title></td>
           <td><dtml-var meta_type></td>
           <td><dtml-var id></td>
           <td><dtml-var summary></td>
           <td><dtml-var bobobase_modification_time></td>
           <td><dtml-var data_record_id_></td>
         </tr>
    <dtml-if sequence-end>
       </table>
       <dtml-if next-sequence>
          <a href="<dtml-var URL><dtml-var sequence-query
             >query_start=<dtml-var
             next-sequence-start-number>">
          (Next <dtml-var next-sequence-size> results)
          </a>
       </dtml-if next-sequence>
    </dtml-if sequence-end>
<dtml-else>
  There was no data matching this <dtml-var title_or_id> query.
</dtml-in>
<dtml-var standard_html_footer>
```

Figure 10.16 shows an example of the tabular layout of a Results page.

The tabular layout is very clearly arranged and easy to read because of the table. So this might be the preferred layout for a Web site search.

The Records Layout

Listing 10.7 shows the standard source code for the records layout. Here, standard means that the metadata of the ZCatalog has not been edited.

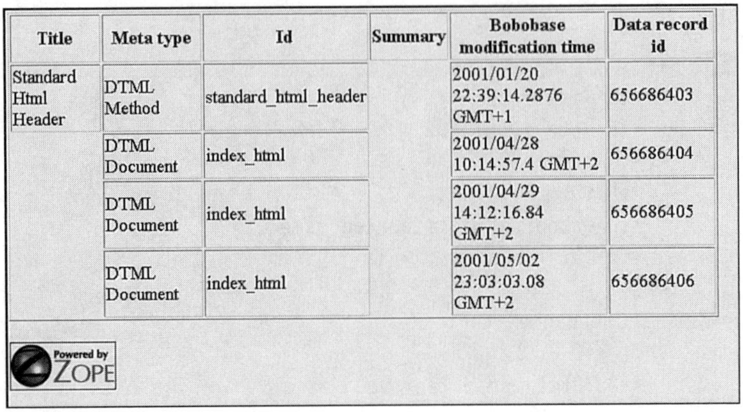

Title	Meta type	Id	Summary	Bobobase modification time	Data record id
Standard Html Header	DTML Method	standard_html_header		2001/01/20 22:39:14.2876 GMT+1	656686403
	DTML Document	index_html		2001/04/28 10:14:57.4 GMT+2	656686404
	DTML Document	index_html		2001/04/29 14:12:16.84 GMT+2	656686405
	DTML Document	index_html		2001/05/02 23:03:03.08 GMT+2	656686406

Powered by ZOPE

Figure 10.16

The standard Results page (Tabular).

Listing 10.7

Standard Results Page (Records)

```
<dtml-var standard_html_header>
<dtml-in MyZCatalog size=50 start=query_start>
   <dtml-if sequence-start>
      <dtml-if previous-sequence>
        <a href="<dtml-var URL><dtml-var sequence-query
                 >query_start=<dtml-var
                 previous-sequence-start-number>">
        (Previous <dtml-var previous-sequence-size> results)
        </a>
      </dtml-if previous-sequence>
   </dtml-if sequence-start>
        <p>
          <dtml-var title>,
          <dtml-var meta_type>,
          <dtml-var id>,
          <dtml-var summary>,
          <dtml-var bobobase_modification_time>,
          <dtml-var data_record_id_>
        </p>
   <dtml-if sequence-end>
      <dtml-if next-sequence>
         <a href="<dtml-var URL><dtml-var sequence-query
            >query_start=<dtml-var
```

Listing 10.7
Continued

```
                 next-sequence-start-number>">
             (Next <dtml-var next-sequence-size> results)
             </a>
         </dtml-if next-sequence>
     </dtml-if sequence-end>
<dtml-else>
  There was no data matching this <dtml-var title_or_id> query.
</dtml-in>
<dtml-var standard_html_footer>
```

Figure 10.17 shows an example of the record layout.

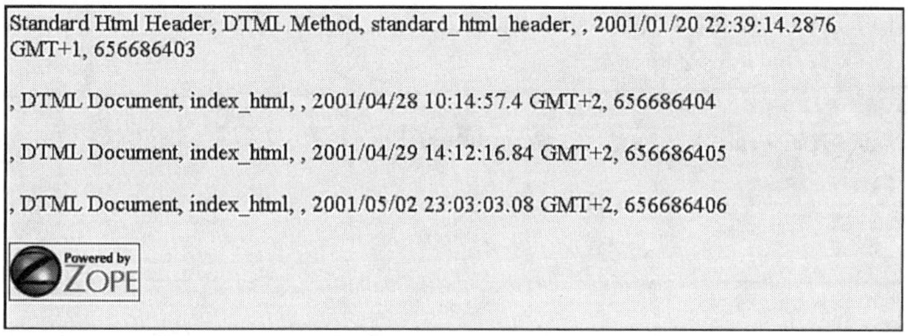

Standard Html Header, DTML Method, standard_html_header, , 2001/01/20 22:39:14.2876 GMT+1, 656686403

, DTML Document, index_html, , 2001/04/28 10:14:57.4 GMT+2, 656686404

, DTML Document, index_html, , 2001/04/29 14:12:16.84 GMT+2, 656686405

, DTML Document, index_html, , 2001/05/02 23:03:03.08 GMT+2, 656686406

Powered by ZOPE

Figure 10.17
The standard Results page (Records).

This layout is harder to read but might be enough for administrative work.

Modifying the Result Page

Although the Z Search Interface is a big help in creating the Result page for a ZCatalog, most of the time you will probably want to add more information on the search or modify the page to meet your needs. This section will give you some examples of how you can do this.

Showing Result Number

A simple but very nice feature for the Results page would be to see the number of results a query produces. For this we "count" the results that are stored in the `searchResults` variable using the `len()` method.

The number of results will be shown in the following manner:

```
130 object(s) found.
```

However, we want a slightly different sentence if there are no results to the query:

```
No objects found.
```

We use the `dtml if` tag to decide whether to use the former or the latter statement. In Listing 10.8, you see how the `if` tag is implemented.

Listing 10.8

Showing the Number of Results

```
1: <p>
2: <dtml-with ZCatalog>
3:    <dtml-if "_.len(_['searchResults']) == 0")>
4:       <b>No</b> objects found.
5:    <dtml-else>
6:       <b><dtml-var "_.len(_['searchResults'])"></b> object(s) found.
7:    </dtml-if>
8: </dtml-with>
9: </p>
```

In lines 3 and 6, you see the use of the `len()` method to get the results number:

```
_.len(_['searchResults'])
```

Now you can add the code in Listing 10.8 at the top of your Results page.

Providing Links to the Objects

In “The Metadata View” section earlier in this chapter, it was mentioned that you can modify the Results page so that objects’ names are displayed as links. The important step for doing this is creating the metadata `absolute_url`. `absolute_url` is a variable that is defined for all objects. It contains the complete path to an object, from the base (`http://localhost:8080/`) to the object ID (`index_html`).

After you have created the metadata `absolute_url` and updated the ZCatalog, replace the line

```
<td><dtml-var id></td>
```

with the following:

```
<td><a href="<dtml-var absolute_url>"><dtml-var id></a></td>
```

Now, every object ID on the Results page is also a link to the respective object.

The Vocabulary

When creating a ZCatalog, you are asked whether a new Vocabulary should be created at the same time or if you want to use an existing one (in case there already is one). So you see, you can also create a Vocabulary independent of a ZCatalog, but, most of the time, it will be in relation with the ZCatalog. It is, after all, part of the ZCatalog product.

In short, a Vocabulary saves words or expressions. These are either entered by you or by the ZCatalog whenever you update it. The words or expressions can contain any characters, and DTML and HTML tags.

> **Note**
> In this chapter, we will use the term *expressions* when we are talking about the words and expressions that are saved in a vocabulary.

Adding a Vocabulary

As previously mentioned, the Vocabulary is part of the ZCatalog product and is, in general, created together with a ZCatalog. But you can also create a Vocabulary on its own. To do this, select the Vocabulary item from the drop-down menu in a folder. As with all Zope objects, the Vocabulary needs an ID and you can define a title.

The Vocabulary-specific part of the Add form is the Globbing? check box. See the next section, "Globbing or Not?," for an explanation of globbing (see Figure 10.18).

After you have decided whether your Vocabulary is to have globbing or not, click the Add button.

Globbing or Not?

You can create a Vocabulary with or without globbing. Technically, a Vocabulary with globbing is a different object from the one without globbing. It derives from a different class.

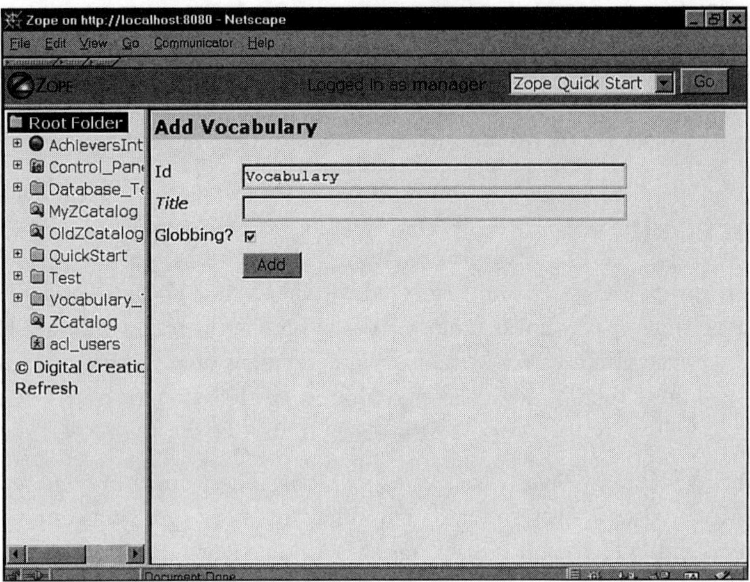

Figure 10.18
Form to add a Vocabulary.

If you create a Vocabulary with globbing, you can use wildcards (*) to search the expressions. For example, if your Vocabulary contains the following expressions

- Hi
- Hello
- How are you?
- Good
- Fine

you can make the query

```
h*
```

and the Vocabulary returns a list of expressions that start with the letter h:

```
['hi', 'hello', 'how are you?']
```

If the Vocabulary was created without globbing, the query would return an empty list:

```
[]
```

> **Note**
> When a Vocabulary is created together with a ZCatalog (when Create One for Me was selected from the Vocabulary select box in the Add form of the ZCatalog), Zope creates a Vocabulary with globbing. Otherwise, wildcard searches of text indexes would not be possible in the ZCatalog.

The Vocabulary View

The main view is called Vocabulary. Here, you can see all the expressions that are currently saved within the vocabulary. The expressions are shown in batches of 20 per page with their word ID (see Figure 10.19).

> **Note**
> DTML and HTML tags are saved without the < and > characters and without hyphens.

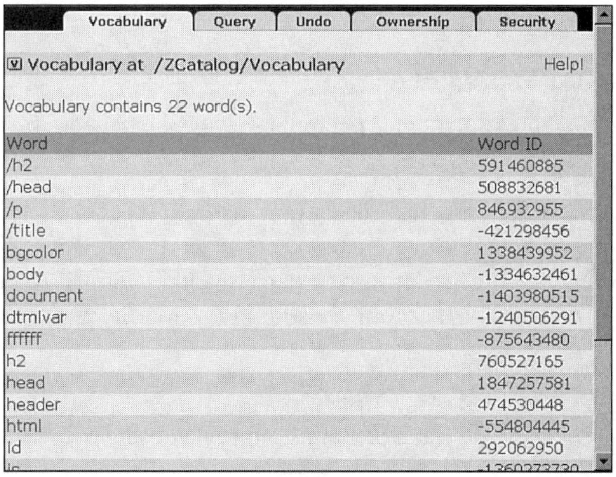

Vocabulary
Query
Undo
Ownership
Security
Vocabulary at /ZCatalog/Vocabulary
Help!
Vocabulary contains 22 word(s).
Word
Word ID
/h2
591460885
/head
508832681
/p
846932955
/title
-421298456
bgcolor
1338439952
body
-1334632461
document
-1403980515
dtmlvar
-1240506291
ffffff
-875643480
h2
760527165
head
1847257581
header
474530448
html
-554804445
id
292062950

Figure 10.19
The Vocabulary view.

The Query View

The Query view (see Figure 10.20) consists of a simple search form. It contains only a text field and a Query (submit) button.

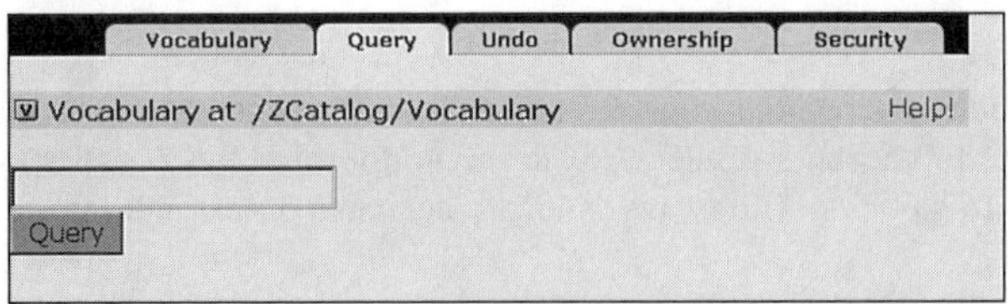

Figure 10.20
The Query view.

Enter a word or expression in the text field and click Query. The results for your query are given as a list:

```
['hello', 'hi', 'how are you?']
```

> **Note**
> Depending on the Vocabulary (globbing or no globbing), you can use wildcards in the query. Remember, Vocabularies that were created together with a ZCatalog are with globbing.

Adding Expressions to a Vocabulary

You can add new expressions to a Vocabulary using the `manage_insert()` method. This method can be called as a URL:

```
http://localhost:8080/ZCatalog/Vocabulary/manage_insert
```

To tell the method what expression you want to add, you need to pass the `word` variable to the method. This is done by adding the following expression to the URL:

```
?word=Expression
```

The complete URL to add the word house to the Vocabulary would be as follows:

```
http://localhost:8080/ZCatalog/Vocabulary/manage_insert?word=house
```

You can also add an expression (a sequence of words). In that case, however, you must use the correct URL equivalents for special characters, such as a `%20` for spaces or `%26` for the ampersand (&). Adding the expression "me & you" would be done as follows:

```
http://localhost:8080/ZCatalog/Vocabulary/manage_insert?word=me%20%26%20you
```

Adding Expressions with DTML

In addition to `manage_insert`, there is a method called `insert()`. With this method, you can create an Add page for new Vocabulary expressions. Listing 10.9 shows an example for such an Add page.

Listing 10.9

`insertExprForm` *DTML Method*

```
 1: <dtml-var standard_html_header>
 2: <h2>Add a new word or description</h2>
 3: <form action="insert_html" method=post>
 4:   <table>
 5:     <tr>
 6:       <th>Word or expression:</th>
 7:       <td><input type=text name=word></td>
 8:     </tr>
 9:     <tr>
10:       <td><input type=submit value="Add"></td>
11:     </tr>
12:   </table>
13: </form>
14: <dtml-var standard_html_footer>
```

Line 3 contains the form's action, `insert_html`, which is a DTML method that will be responsible for inserting the expression. We will come to that DTML method shortly.

In line 7, you see that the name of the text field is word. This name will be used in the `insert_html` DTML method (see Figure 10.21).

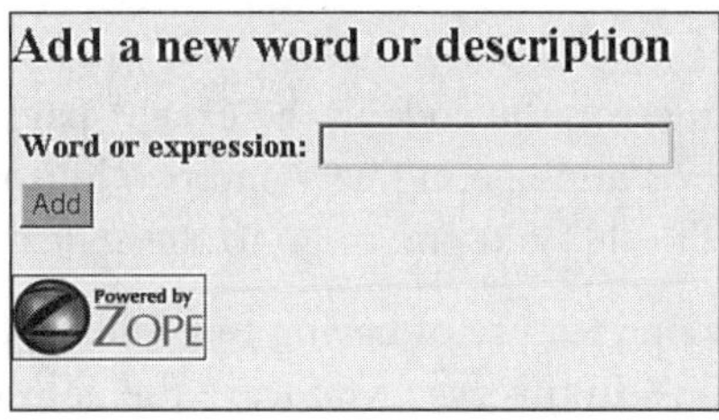

Figure 10.21

The `insertExprForm` *DTML method.*

As was just mentioned, the `insert_html` DTML method is supposed to actually insert the new expression in the Vocabulary. Listing 10.10 shows this DTML method.

Listing 10.10

`insert_html` *DTML Method*

```
 1:  <dtml-var standard_html_header>
 2:  <dtml-try>
 3:    <dtml-call "Vocabulary.insert(_['word'])">
 4:    <b>Word/Expression was succesfully added.</b>
 5:    <form action="index_html" method=post>
 6:      <input type=submit value="OK">
 7:    </form>
 8:  <dtml-except>
 9:    <b>Sorry, there was a problem. The word/expression was NOT added.</b>
10:    <form action="" method=post>
11:      <input type=submit name="insertExprForm:method" value="Try again">
12:      <input type=submit name="index_html:method"
➥value="Go back to index page">
13:    </form>
14:  </dtml-try>
15:  <dtml-var standard_html_footer>
```

We use a `try...except` construct here because, for whatever reason, there might be a problem with inserting the new expression. In line 3, we try to insert the expression we have been given from the form (`insertExprForm`). Here, we use the `insert()` method. Because it is a method that belongs to the Vocabulary object, the method has to be called via that object:

```
Vocabulary.insert(...)
```

If the insertion was successful (see Figure 10.22), the DTML method shows the message in line 4 and an OK button (lines 5–7) that returns the user to the `index_html` page.

If the insertion raises an error, the code in the `except` part (lines 9–13) is executed. This code shows the error message in line 9 and two buttons: one to return to the add form `insertExprForm` (line 11) and one to go to the `index_html page` (line 12).

Here, you can see the Zope feature of having two Submit buttons in one form that have two different actions. In this case, you leave the `actions` attribute empty and add the following expression:

```
:method
```

to the name of the Submit button.

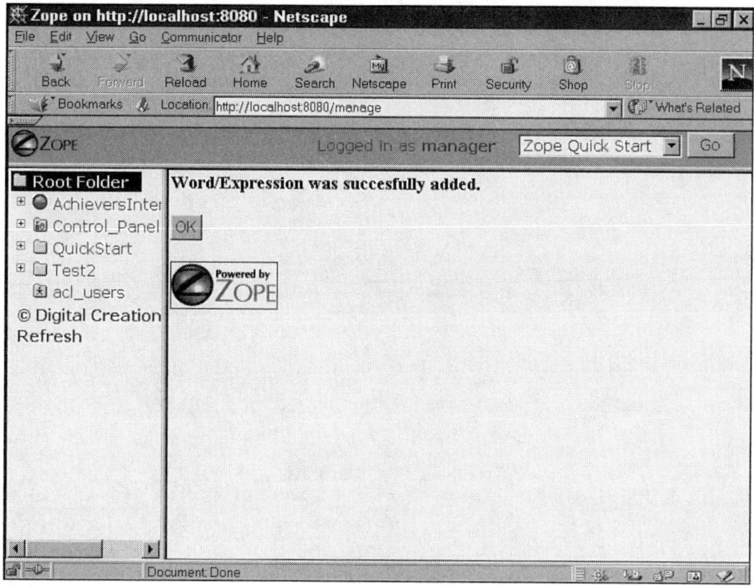

Figure 10.22
The `insert_html` *DTML method (successful insertion).*

Summary

In this chapter, you have learned about the ZCatalog and how to index objects. You have also read about the different types of indexes and seen some examples of each. The Z Search Interface has helped to easily create Search and Results pages for a ZCatalog search.

We have also talked about the Vocabulary, an integral part of the ZCatalog, and how to add new expressions both via the URL and with DTML.

The next chapter deals with Python Imaging Library (PIL) and how to use it in Zope.

CHAPTER 11

CREATING DYNAMIC GRAPHS IN ZOPE

In this chapter, you will learn something about PIL, the Python Imaging Library, which will help you create dynamic graphs in Zope. After the general introduction to PIL, we will come back to the Poll product that was introduced in Chapter 10, "Adding Search Capabilities," and see how PIL is used there to create a pie chart of a poll question's votes. In the last section of this chapter, we will develop a method that will allow us to also create bar graphs for the question's votes.

This chapter will only deal with a small part of PIL. If you want to learn more about it, you can download the PIL Handbook from `http://www.pythonware.com/library/index.htm` or browse it at `http://www.pythonware.com/library/pil/handbook/index.htm`.

The Python Imaging Library—PIL

The Python Imaging Library is a package of Python modules designed for working with images. It provides extensive file format support (bmp, gif, jpeg, pxc, tiff, and so on) and is designed to give fast access to information about the image.

With PIL, images can be easily manipulated (they can, for example, be resized, rotated, or the contrast can be enhanced). PIL also provides a method to create thumbnails that can be used to create a photo album or archive.

The important module for this chapter is the `ImageDraw` module. It contains the methods needed to draw some geometrical forms, such as rectangles or polygons.

We will also use the `Image` module, because first we need an image on which we can then draw.

The Python Imaging Library is very powerful and extensive, and we will only scratch the surface of what can be done with it. In this chapter, we will concentrate on the `ImageDraw` module.

Installing PIL

PIL is a Python library, not a product, so it needs to be installed. PIL should be installed in the bin directory of your Zope installation (mostly Windows) or somewhere on the Python path if you use an external Python version (mostly UNIX).

You can download PIL from `http://www.pythonware.com`. The current version is PIL 1.1.2, which is available only as source. PIL 1.1.1 is available as source and as Zip files for Python versions 1.5.2, 2.0, and 2.1a2.

For our examples, we used PIL 1.1.1 (for Python 1.5.2). This version is easier to install because it does not need to be compiled from C.

After you downloaded the pil-1.1.1-win32-py152.zip file, unzip it to the bin directory or your Python path (see Figure 11.1).

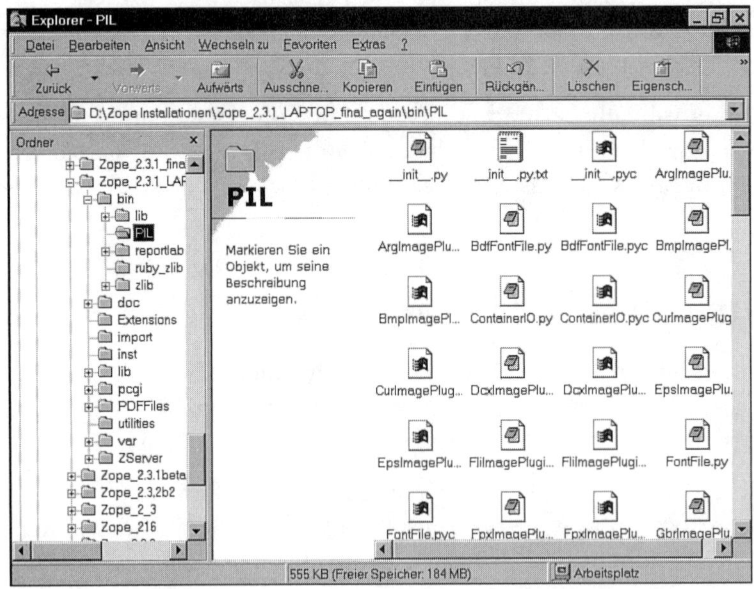

Figure 11.1
The PIL folder in Windows Explorer.

Now you can use the modules provided by the package.

Starting the Python Interpreter

To be able to follow and try the examples given in this chapter, you will need to work in the Python Interpreter. The interpreter allows you to directly enter Python

If you have made some changes to an image and want to know what it looks like now, you can use the `show()` method on the image:

```
>>im.show()
```

This will open the image with a default image viewer (the program Paint on Windows, for example). If necessary, it converts the image beforehand.

The last method we want to introduce here is the `save(outfile [, format [, options]])` method. This method must have at least one argument: `outfile` (the filename that the image is to be saved as). You can also give the format for the image but, if you do not, the format is determined from the filename if possible. Options can be defined to give additional instructions for saving the file.

```
>>im.save('new_image.gif')
```

There are many more methods in the `Image` module, but they are not important for what we are going to do in this chapter. Please read the PIL handbook for further explanations.

The `ImageDraw` Module

As previously mentioned, we will mainly work with the `ImageDraw` module. This section will explain the methods provided by this module and give some examples of how they are used.

The module provides a constructor to initiate an `ImageDraw` object:

```
Draw(im_obj)
```

Before you create an `ImageDraw` object, you need to create an `Image` object:

```
>>import PIL.Image, PIL.ImageDraw
>>im=PIL.Image.new('RGB', (100,100))
>>draw=PIL.ImageDraw.Draw(im)
```

The `Image` object is used by the Draw constructor to create the drawing space on the image. Now you can use the different methods on the Draw object. The methods provided by the `ImageDraw` module are as follows:

- `arc`
- `bitmap`
- `chord`
- `ellipse`

- `line`
- `pieslice`
- `point`
- `polygon`
- `rectangle`
- `text`
- `textsize`

`arc(where, start, end[, fill=color])`
The `arc` method draws an arc within the rectangle given by `where`. This argument is a 4-tupel or a list with two elements containing the x and y coordinates of the upper-left corner and the lower-right corner of the rectangle. The `start` and `end` arguments define at what degrees the arc should start and end. With the `fill` option, you define the color that the arc is to be painted.

Example:

```
>>draw.arc([10,10,90,90], 0, 270, fill=(255,255,255))
```

Output: See Figure 11.2.

Figure 11.2
Output of the `draw.arc()` *example.*

`bitmap(point, bitm[, fill=color])`
This method draws a bitmap at the specified point.

`chord(where, start, end[, fill=color])`
This method only differs from the `arc()` method in that the `end` point and the `start` point are connected.

Example:

```
>>draw.chord([10,10,90,90], 0, 270, fill=(255,255,255))
```

Output: See Figure 11.3.

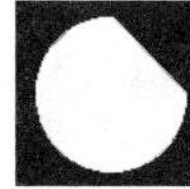

Figure 11.3
Output of the `draw.chord()` *example.*

`ellipse(where[, fill=color[, outline=color2]])`
This method draws an ellipse in the rectangle provided by `where`. The `fill` option defines the color of the ellipse interior, and the `outline` option defines the color of the edge.

Example:

```
>>draw.ellipse((30,40,70,60), fill=(220,220,220), outline=(255,255,255))
```

Output: See Figure 11.4.

Figure 11.4
Output of the `draw.ellipse()` *example.*

`line(from_to[, fill=color])`
The `line` method draws a line between two points. The points are defined by the `from_to` argument. The `fill` option defines the color of the line.

Example:

```
>>draw.line((10,10,90,90), fill=(255,255,255))
```

Output: See Figure 11.5.

Figure 11.5
Output of the `draw.line()` *example.*

`pieslice(where, start, end[, fill=color[, outline=color2]])`
The `pieslice` method works similar to the `arc` method, but it also draws a line between the center of the rectangle defined by `where` and the `start` and `end` point.

Example:

```
>>draw.pieslice((20,20,50,50), 10, 75, outline=(255,255,255))
```

Output: See Figure 11.6.

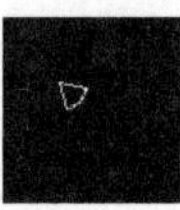

Figure 11.6
Output of the `draw.pieslice()` *example.*

`point(where_list[, fill=color])`
This method draws points at the specified coordinates. The coordinates can either be one point (x,y) or a list of points ((x1,y1),(x2,y2), and so on). The list of points can also be an n-tupel (x1, y1, x2, y2, and so on). The `fill` option sets the color of the point(s).

Example:

```
>>draw.point([(10,10),(12,12),(10,12),(8,8)], fill=(255,255,255))
```

or

```
>>draw.point((10,10,12,12,10,12,8,8), fill=(255,255,255))
```

Output: See Figure 11.7.

Figure 11.7
Output of the `draw.point()` *example.*

`polygon(where_list[, fill=color, outline=outline_color)`

The `polygon` method draws lines between specified points and between the last and the first point. The list of points should contain at least three points. The `fill` option defines the color the image is filled with, and the `outline` option defines the color for the lines.

Example:

```
>>draw.polygon([(10,10),(40,70),(70,40)], fill=(255,255,255), outline=0)
```

or

```
>>draw.polygon((10,10,40,70,70,40), fill=(255,255,255), outline=0)
```

Output: See Figure 11.8.

Figure 11.8
Output of the `draw.polygon()` *example.*

`rectangle(rectcoords[, fill=color1[, outline=color2]])`

The `rectangle` method draws a rectangle between the coordinates given in `rectcoords`. The coordinates are a 4-tupel or a list with two elements naming the x and y coordinates of the upper-left and lower-right corners. The `fill` option defines the color the rectangle is filled with, and the `outline` option defines the color of the surrounding line.

Example:

```
>>draw.rectangle([(10,10),(90,90)], fill=(255,255,255), outline=(0,0,255))
```

Output: See Figure 11.9.

Figure 11.9
Output of the `draw.rectangle()` *example.*

`text(pos, txt[, font[, fill=color]])`

This method writes the text `txt` at the given position `pos`. It uses either the font given or the default font. If given, the font has to be an instance of the `ImageFile` class. The `fill` option defines the text color.

> **Note**
> The `ImageFont` class only recognized BDF and PCF. It does not work with TTF and therefore cannot comprehend Windows font types.

`textsize(txt[, font])`

This method returns the size (width, height) of the given string `txt`. The `font` option specifies the font to be used. The given font should be an `ImageFont` object.

Compatibility with Older Versions

To provide compatibility with programs written with older PIL versions, there is a second constructor as well as some methods defined in the `ImageDraw` class. Those should not be used when writing new code. They are strictly for compatibility purposes.

Constructor:

`ImageDraw(im_obj)`

Methods:

`setink(color)`	Sets the text and fill color.
`setfill(mode)`	If `mode=1`, objects are filled when drawn.
`setfont(font_obj)`	Sets the font for text. `font_obj` is an `ImageFont` object.

Dynamic Graphs of the Poll Product

In Chapter 8, "Creating Polls and Surveys," we worked with the Poll product to get the portal members' opinions about the portal. This product supports dynamic graphs to better represent the Poll votes. Without PIL being correctly installed in your Zope version, the parts of the Poll product that produce the graphs are ignored.

Now that PIL is installed on your machine, the graph should automatically show when you go to either the results page or the Edit view of a Poll instance. However, due to a problem within the Poll product, this is not the case. Instead, you will see a broken image where there should be the graph.

This problem is caused be the `drawGraph()` method. It is located in the `Question` class in the `Poll.py` module. Because at the moment a pie chart is the only supported graph type and there is a `drawPieChart()` method, we can easily work around this problem by exchanging the method name `drawGraph` with `drawPieChart` wherever it appears in the Poll product.

Changes will be necessary in the following files:

- `pollEdit.dtml`
- `questionEdit.dtml`
- `questionView.dtml`
- `results.dtml`

In every existing Poll instance, you need to also change the `results` DTML method in the Documents view of the instance.

Later in the chapter, we will write a new method, `drawBarGraph()`, for the Poll product and will then have to change more than the previously mentioned DTML files. For now, these changes will be enough.

After the changes, the Poll's Properties view will look like Figure 11.10.

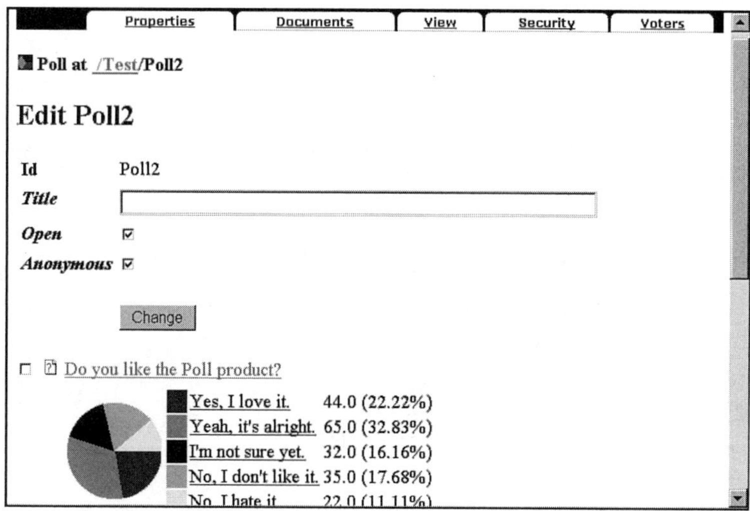

Figure 11.10

The modified Properties view.

Let's see how the `drawPieChart()` method works.

The Pie Chart

The Poll product's main module is `Poll.py`. It contains the `Poll`, `Question`, and `Response` classes. The `drawPieChart()` method that creates the pie chart—if PIL is installed—is located in the `Question` class. The method needs to be in this class because you can have different graph representations for each question within a Poll object and not just one graph type per Poll object.

Listing 11.1 shows the entire code of the method.

Listing 11.1

`drawPieChart()` *Method*

```
def drawPieChart(self, size=500, RESPONSE=None):
        """Draw a pie chart. The sole purpose of counter is
        to keep IMG references unique"""
        import sys
        im = PIL.Image.new('RGB', (size,size))
        draw = PIL.ImageDraw.ImageDraw(im)
        bgcolor = (255, 255, 255)

        draw.rectangle([0, 0, size, size], fill=bgcolor, outline=bgcolor)
        theta = 0.0
        color = 0
        colors = self.getColors()

        for response in self.objectValues(['Poll Response']):

            if response.votes:
                newTheta = theta + (response.votes/self.totalVotes) *
➥360.0

                draw.setink(colors[color])
                draw.setfill(1)
                draw.pieslice( (0,0,size, size), theta, newTheta)
                theta = newTheta

            color = color + 1
            if color == len(colors):
                color = 0

        del draw
```

Listing 11.1
Continued

```
29:
30:         outFile = cStringIO.StringIO()
31:         im.save(outFile, 'GIF')
32:
33:         outFile.seek(0)
34:         RESPONSE.setHeader("Content-type", "image/gif")
35:         RESPONSE.write(outFile.read())
36:         return ''
```

In line 4, the new image is created with the `'RGB'` mode and the width and height as specified by the method's argument size. Now there is an `Image` object, but it is not possible to draw graphics directly on an image. Consequently, an `ImageDraw` object called `draw` is created on the image (line 5). The `draw` object is then "cleaned" by drawing a rectangle of the same size as the `draw` object (line 8) and filling it with the bgcolor color (line 6), which is white.

After some variable initiations (lines 9–11), there is a `for` loop. This loop iterates over the responses to a Poll question (line 13). If there are votes counted for the current response, a pie slice is drawn (lines 16–21). First, the end point is calculated using the votes for the response, the total number of votes as well as the end point of the last pie slice (`theta`). Then the fill color and fill mode are set (lines 18 and 19). The fill color is set according to the color the current response was assigned. As you remember, those two methods only exist for compatibility purposes and should no longer be used. Last, the pie slice is drawn (line 20) and the current end point is set to be the next start point (line 21).

No matter whether a pie slice was drawn for a response or not, the color counter has to be changed so that the color it produces will correspond to the response. The `getColors()` method provides a list of eight colors. This list was given to the variable colors earlier in the method (line 11). If the end of the list is reached, the color is set back to black (lines 24 and 25).

After everything is drawn on the image, the `draw` object can be deleted (line 27).

The last few lines create a filename for the image, save the image, and make the image available by writing it to the `RESPONSE`.

Now let's create our own graph type.

Example: Creating a Bar Graph

In this section, we will program the `drawBarGraph()` method that is in the `Poll.py` module but has not yet been implemented. Figure 11.11 shows you the graph of a question that was created using the `drawBarGraph()` method.

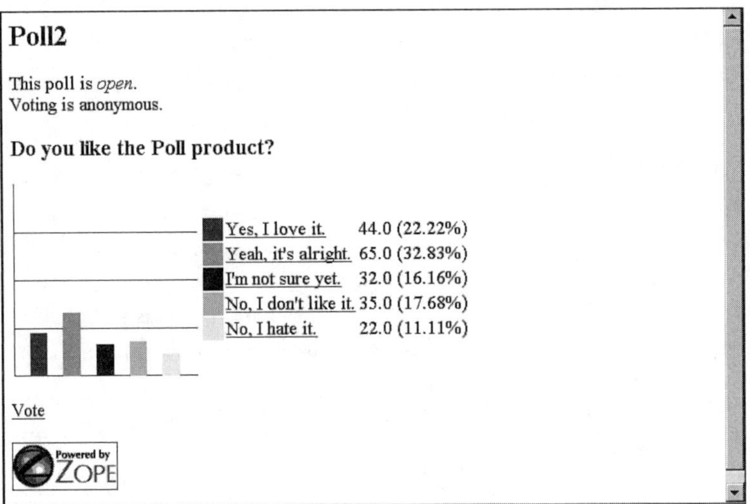

Figure 11.11
A question result with a bar graph.

So, how do we draw the bar graph, and how do we calculate the necessary values?

The look of the graph depends on four things:

- The size of the graph image
- The number of responses
- The amount of votes for each response
- The total number of votes for the question

The bars of the graph are rectangles, so we need two opposite corners to draw the bar. Because the size of the graph and the number of responses are variable, we cannot just define a start value and width for each of the bars. They have to be calculated.

The height of each bar in the graph is also highly variable because it changes with every new vote. Also, we need to consider that each bar is dependent on the total votes for the question. The ratio between the bars has to be correct to represent the number of votes each response got.

Now that we know what has to be calculated, we can start programming the method. We will come back to the actual formulas for the bars during our programming.

To edit the `Poll.py` module, open a text editor and then open the `Poll.py` file in the `lib/python/Products/Poll` directory in your Zope directory. Either scroll down to the method or search for the method to jump there. Listing 11.2 shows the original `drawBarGraph()` method.

Listing 11.2

Original `drawBarGraph()` *Method*

```
    def drawBarGraph(self, size=500, RESPONSE=None):
        """Draw a bar graph. Not implemented yet."""
        return "\n\n"
```

For this method, we will use parts of the `drawPieChart()` method because they are the same for any type of graph you might want to create. We always need to

- Create an `Image` object
- Create a `Draw` object
- Save the image at the end
- Write it to the `RESPONSE`

We can copy the lines 3–8 and 27–35 from the `drawPieChart()` method. Between these two sets of lines, we then program the code for the bar graph.

First, we have to define some variables and constants so that we can use them later to calculate and draw the graph.

```
responses=0
for response in self.objectValues(['Poll Response']):
    responses=responses+1

bar_x1=0.0
bar_y1=size
bar_x2=0.0
bar_y2=0.0

dx=size/(2*responses+1)
dy=size/self.totalVotes
colors=self.getColors()
color=0
```

The responses variable (line 10) is set according to how many responses there are for the question (lines 11 and 12). It is used in line 19 to calculate the difference between an x coordinate and another. But first, we set the start values for rectangle coordinates (lines 14–17). bar_x1 and bar_y1 represent the lower-left corner of the bar, and bar_x2 and bar_y2 represent the upper-right corner.

The width of the bars depends on how many responses there are. The more responses, the smaller the bars, because we only have a certain size for the image. If we have three responses (= three bars), we need to divide the x coordinate of the graph by 7 (= 2*3+1) because two x coordinates are needed for each of the bars, and we have the last x coordinate (which should equal the width of the image) to leave a space between the last bar and the edge of the image. Therefore we get the following formula:

```
dx=size/(2*responses+1)
```

to calculate the difference between the x coordinates so that we can "jump" along the line.

The variable dy represents the number of pixels that will represent one vote for a response. This variable depends on how many total votes there are, because we can then take it times the number of votes there are for one response and calculate the y coordinate for the upper-right corner of each bar.

In line 21, we get the list of colors currently defined in the Poll product. The variable color is the counter for this list, so that we can move through it.

```
24:     lines_dy=size/4
25:
26:     draw.line([0,size-1,size-1,size-1], fill=(0,0,0))
27:     draw.line([0,0,0,size], fill=(0,0,0))
28:     for i in range(3,0,-1):
29:         draw.line([0,i*lines_dy,size-1,i*lines_dy], fill=(0,0,0))
```

Now we draw the grid for our graph (lines 26–29). To draw the lines, we use the line() method of the ImageDraw module. The arguments here are always lists with two points (start and end point) and the fill color, which is black.

```
31:     for response in self.objectValues(['Poll Response']):
32:         bar_x1=bar_x1 + dx
33:         bar_x2=bar_x1 + dx
34:         bar_y2=size-dy*response.votes
35:         bgcolor=colors[color]
36:         draw.rectangle([bar_x1, bar_y1, bar_x2, bar_y2], fill=bgcolor)
37:         bar_x1=bar_x2
38:               color = color + 1
```

```
39:                 if color == len(colors):
40:                     color = 0
```

Now we can create the bars for each of the responses to the question. In lines 32–34, the coordinates for the points of the rectangle are set to the next pixels, according to what we calculated earlier for the `dx` and `dy` variables. The y coordinate of the second point (line 34) is calculated here so that it represents the number of votes for the current response. Remember, `dy` is the number of pixel for one vote. It is multiplied with the number of votes for the response. Then, this needs to be subtracted from the height of the image (size) due to the way the coordinate system is defined in `ImageDraw`. If we don't do this, the graph will be upside down.

In line 35, we set the color for the current response, which we get from the list of colors we defined earlier.

Line 36 finally draws the bar for one response using the coordinates we just calculated and the fill color for this response.

Then we add one to the color counter (line 38) so that we will get the next color in the list when we go through the `for` loop again.

The rest of the method is as was already explained earlier in the chapter when we talked about the `drawPieChart()` method.

Listing 11.3 now shows the complete code of the `drawBarGraph()` method.

Listing 11.3

`drawBarGraph()` *Method*

```
def drawBarGraph(self, size=500, RESPONSE=None):
    """Draw a bar graph."""
    import sys
    im = PIL.Image.new('RGB', (size,size))
    draw = PIL.ImageDraw.ImageDraw(im)
    bgcolor = (255, 255, 255)

    draw.rectangle([0, 0, size, size], fill=bgcolor, outline=bgcolor)

    responses=0
    for response in self.objectValues(['Poll Response']):
        responses=responses+1

    bar_x1=0.0
    bar_y1=size
```

Listing 11.3
Continued

```
bar_x2=0.0
bar_y2=0.0

dx=size/(2*responses+1)
dy=size/self.totalVotes
colors=self.getColors()
color=0

lines_dy=size/4

draw.line([0,size-1,size-1,size-1], fill=(0,0,0))
draw.line([0,0,0,size], fill=(0,0,0))
for i in range(3,0,-1):
    draw.line([0,i*lines_dy,size-1,i*lines_dy], fill=(0,0,0))

for response in self.objectValues(['Poll Response']):
    bar_x1=bar_x1 + dx
    bar_x2=bar_x1 + dx
    bar_y2=size-dy*response.votes
    bgcolor=colors[color]
    draw.rectangle([bar_x1, bar_y1, bar_x2, bar_y2], fill=bgcolor)
    bar_x1=bar_x2
            color = color + 1
            if color == len(colors):
                color = 0

del draw

outFile = cStringIO.StringIO()
im.save(outFile, 'GIF')

outFile.seek(0)
RESPONSE.setHeader("Content-type", "image/gif")
RESPONSE.write(outFile.read())
return ''
```

The new method is finished, but there are still some things that need to be changed. Because the Poll product had only the `drawPieChart()` method before, there is no mechanism to change the graph type of a question. We will build it in now.

Changes in the `Poll` Class

To be able to change the graph type, we need an attribute for the question that tells us which type is currently selected. The first time this attribute is needed is when a question is added to the poll. The `manage_addQuestion()` method in the `Poll` class needs to be changed in accordance with Listing 11.4.

Listing 11.4

New `manage_addQuestion()` Method

```
1:     def manage_addQuestion(self, question = '', responses = [],
➥ grType="Pie chart"):
2:         """Add a question"""
3:         newId = self.makeQuestionId()
4:         newQuestion = Question(newId, question, grType, responses,'bla')
5:         self._setObject(newId, newQuestion)
6:         return MessageDialog(title='Edited',
7:                              message='Entry has been edited.',
8:                              action ='./manage_main',
9:                              )
```

In line 1, we add the `grType` argument and give it a default value of `"Pie chart"`. That way, there is always a graph type selected, even if the user does not enter one when adding the question.

We also need to add the same argument to line 4, because the `Question` class will need this argument as well.

These are the only changes necessary to the `Poll` class. Now we go to the `Question` class.

Changes in the `Question` Class

The constructor method `__init__()` needs the `grType` argument (line 1) because we want to save the graph type within a question. Saving the type is done in line 8, where we define a new `graphType` attribute for the question. Listing 11.5 shows the modified `__init__()` method.

Listing 11.5

New `__init__()` Method

```
1:     def __init__(self, id, question, grType, responses, size = 500):
2:         self.id = id
3:         self.questionId = id
4:         self.question = question
```

Listing 11.5

Continued

```
        self.totalVotes = 0
        self.amPoll = 0
        # for the time being pieChart is the only one
        self.graphType = grType

        for response in responses:
            if len(response):
                newId = self.makeResponseId()
                newResponse = Response( newId, response)
                self._setObject(newId, newResponse)
        self.size = size
```

The next method is `manage_edit()`. Listing 11.6 shows part of this method. The only changes are in lines 1 and 5 where the argument and attribute are added.

Listing 11.6

Beginning of the `manage_edit()` *Method*

```
 1:     def manage_edit(self, question, grType, votes = [], realIds = [],
➥ responses = [], REQUEST=None):
 2:         """Edit the Question"""
 3:         currentObjects =self.objectIds(['Poll Response'])
 4:
 5:         self.graphType=str(grType)
```

Those are all the necessary changes in this class. The biggest change was programming the new method.

But now that we have changed the method declarations within the Python module, we need to adapt the DTML files that produce the forms to manage Poll instances.

Changes in the DTML Files

The DTML files we need to change now are the same as the ones we had to change earlier in the chapter:

- `pollEdit.dtml`
- `questionEdit.dtml`
- `questionView.dtml`
- `results.dtml`

Again, we also need to change the `results` DTML method in the Document view of all existing Poll instances.

The original files contain the following lines:

```
1:        <TABLE BORDER=0>
2:            <TR>
3:                <!--#if fancy_graphics-->
4:                    <TD><IMG src='drawGraph?size:int=200'></TD>
5:                <!--#/if-->
6:                <TD><!--#var pollLegend--></TD>
7:            </TR>
8:        </TABLE>
```

Due to the changes made earlier, line 4 will look like the following in your files:

```
<TD><IMG src='drawPieChart?size:int=200'></TD>
```

These lines have to be replaced by either `pollEdit.dtml` and `results.dtml`:

```
<dtml-if "graphType=='Pie chart'">
    <dtml-call "REQUEST.set('graph', 'drawPieChart')">
<dtml-else>
 <dtml-call "REQUEST.set('graph', 'drawBarGraph')">
</dtml-if>
<TABLE BORDER=0>
    <TR>
        <!--#if fancy_graphics-->
            <TD><IMG src="<!--#var sequence-key-->/<dtml-var graph>?
➥size:int=200&dummy=<dtml-var "ZopeTime().time">"></TD>
        <!--#/if-->
        <TD><!--#var pollLegend--></TD>
    </TR>
</TABLE>
```

or the following code lines (`questionView.dtml` and `questionEdit.dtml`):

```
<dtml-if "graphType=='Pie chart'">
    <dtml-call "REQUEST.set('graph', 'drawPieChart')">
<dtml-else>
    <dtml-call "REQUEST.set('graph', 'drawBarGraph')">
</dtml-if>
<TABLE BORDER=0>
    <TR>
        <!--#if fancy_graphics-->
            <TD><IMG src="<dtml-var graph>?
```

```
➥size:int=200&dummy=<dtml-var "ZopeTime().time">"></TD>
10:             <!--#/if-->
11:             <TD><!--#var pollLegend--></TD>
12:         </TR>
13:     </TABLE>
```

Lines 1–5 set a variable graph according to which graph type is currently selected for the question. If the graph type is `"Pie chart"`, the graph variable is set to `"drawPieChart"`. If not, it is set to `"drawBarChart"`. These strings are the method names of the respective methods in the Poll module. To call the method in the image tag (line 9), we put in the `graph` variable where there was the method call for `drawGraph`, which will call the method necessary for this question.

There are two more changes in the DTML files. There have to be radio buttons in the Poll's Properties and Edit views of a question to be able to choose the graph type.

Listing 11.7 shows the lines that need to be added and changed in the modified `questionEdit.dtml`. The lines have to be added after the row for the question title.

Listing 11.7

Modified Lines of the `questionEdit.dtml` *File*

```
<TR>
  <th align="left" valign="top">Graph Type</th>
  <td align="left" valign="top">
     <input type=radio name=grType value="Pie chart">Pie chart
     <input type=radio name=grType value="Bar graph">Bar graph
  </td>
</TR>
<TR>
     <TH align="LEFT" valign="TOP"><EM><dtml-var
➥"_.str(_['graphType'])"></EM></TH>
```

In the `pollEdit.dtml` file, the following lines have to be added after the row that defines the text area for the questions' answers:

```
<tr>
<th align="left" valign="top">Graph Type</th>
<td>
<input type=radio name=grType checked value="Pie chart">Pie Chart
<input type=radio name=grType value="Bar graph">Bar Graph
</td>
</tr>
```

After you have saved all the changes and restarted the Zope server, you will be able to choose between the bar graph or the pie chart representation for each question in a poll.

Summary

This chapter has given you an introduction to a small part of the Python Imaging Library. You have seen how you can use `PIL` to create and manipulate images and to modify or complement existing Zope products to meet your needs.

The next chapter introduces `PDFGEN` and the `ZpdfDocument` and shows you how to dynamically create PDF files to use on your homepage.

CHAPTER 12

GENERATING DYNAMIC PDFS

In this chapter, we will talk about how you can dynamically create PDF files with Zope. There are two different ways:

- You can use the ZpdfDocument, a Zope product created by Pavlos Christoforou.
- You can use PDFGEN, a Python package from ReportLab, Inc.

While you only need HTML and DTML to use the former, you need at least a rudimentary knowledge of Python to create PDF files with the latter.

> **Note**
> The `pdfgen` package is only a subpackage of `reportlab`. There are also the `graphics`, pdfbase, and `platypus` packages. They provide classes that allow the generation of advanced PDF files (creating page templates and frames).
>
> You will find the methods of the three main modules of the `pdfgen` packages later in this chapter. We recommend you read the Reference Guide, User Guide, and Graphics Guide for a complete overview of `reportLab` that you find in the `reportlab/docs/` directory after installing `reportlab`.

ZpdfDocument

The ZpdfDocument is a Zope product that allows you to create dynamic PDF pages without having to use Python or another programming language. ZpdfDocuments are created and edited just like normal DMTL documents, but you can use either HTML or structured text to compose text.

Installation

You install the ZpdfDocument product like any other Zope product. Download the `ZpdfDocument.tgz` file from `http://www.zope.prg/Members/gaaros/ZpdfDocument` and unzip it in the directory of your Zope installation. Then .restart your Zope server.

Introduction

The ZpdfDocument is used like a DTML document. The user creates an instance in a folder and edits the ZpdfDocument via its Edit view. There are two possible content types in a .ZpdfDocument:

- HTML
- Structured Text

You can choose which format type you want to use by selecting its radio button in the Edit view.

> **Note**
> If you decide to use the HTML format for the ZpdfDocument, all text needs to be contained within HTML tags. Text that is not in a tag is ignored when you call the ZpdfDcoument.

Structured Text

Structured text is a special convention for formatting text. With it, you can structure text into paragraph, headings, lists, and so on without using HTML tags.

Paragraphs in structured text are given a level, depending on how much they are indented. The. following is an example of this level system:

```
This paragraph is on the first level.

    This is the second level.

        And this one is the third level.
```

> **Note**
> A paragraph is defined as a one- or multi-lined text followed by (at least) one single empty line. A carriage return (using the Return key) does not mark the end of a paragraph.

Headings

A heading is a single-line paragraph that is followed by paragraphs of a lower level.

Example:

```
The Road Not Taken

    The Road Not Taken is a poem by Robert Frost. It contains of four stanzas
    with five lines each.
```

Unordered Lists

Unordered list items or bullet items are defined by one of the following characters as the first character of a paragraph:

- - (hyphen)
- * (asterisk)
- o (lowercase O)

Example:

```
-  First list item

-  Second list item

*  Third list item

o  Fourth list item
```

> **Note**
> Normally, bullet items appear with a small dot in front of them. The ZpdfDocument, however, does not create these dots. The items are only slightly indented.

Ordered Lists

Lists can be ordered using either numbers or letters. The lines:

```
1. Subjects

   a. Mathematics

   b. English

   2. Latin

2. Teacher

   1. Mrs. Jones

   b. Mr. Jonson
```

have the following output:

1. Subjects
    1. Mathematics
    2. English
    3. Latin
2. Teacher
    1. Mrs. Jones
    2. Mr. Jonson

As you can see, it doesn't matter whether you mix letters and numbers or whether they are in the correct order. The important part is that there is a sequence of digits or characters that are followed by a period and a whitespace character.

Descriptive List Elements

Descriptive list elements consist of an element title and a description. The elements description is indented. The element title and description are separated by a whitespace, two hyphens (--), and another whitespace. Both title and description are part of one paragraph.

Example:

```
The Road Not Taken — by Robert Frost

The Raven — by Edgar Allen Poe
```

Output:

The Road Not Taken

  by Robert Frost

The Raven

  by Edgar Allen Poe

> **Note**
> Descriptive list elements are not yet supported by ZpdfDocument.

Example Code

You can also show example code that contains, for example, HTML tags. If a paragraph ends with the `::` characters, the following sub-paragraph is treated as code and is output as is.

Example:

```
Here is an example code ::

   <html><title>The Title</title></html>
```

You can also define example code by using single quotes. There has to be whitespace to the left of the beginning quote, and whitespace or punctuation to the right of the ending quote.

Example:

```
The '<title>' tag is used to define the HTML page's title.
```

Output:

The `<title>` tag is used to define the HTML page's title.

Text Formatting: Bold, Italic, and Underlined

Using special characters, you can format text parts making it bold, italicized, or underlined.

To make text parts bold, surround it by asterisks (*):

```
This *word* is bold.
```

Two asterisks (**) are used to italicize text parts:

```
The next sentence is in italics. **This is the next sentence**.
```

If you want to underline text parts, use the underscore (_) in front of and at the end of the text:

```
To _underline_ text parts use the underscore character.
```

> **Note**
> When using the three text formats with the ZpdfDocument, make sure to have either other words or punctuation after the ending format character (*, **, or _).

> **Note**
> Underlining is currently not supported by the ZpdfDocument.

Hyperlinks and Anchors

Links either go to an anchor on the same page, an anchor on a different page, or just a different page. To create a normal hyperlink, write the text for the link in double quotes and then the URL (absolute or relative) separated by a colon:

```
"beehive GmbH":http://www.beehive.de/
```

You can also use the following syntax:

```
"Contact beehive E&P", mailto:zope-ep@beehive.de
```

To create links to anchors within the current page, write the name of the anchor between two brackets:

```
As was discussed at the Python Conference [PyCon_9] ....
```

The following is the code this will create:

```
As was discussed at the Python Conference <a href="#PyCon_9"> ...
```

To be able to use this link, you need to create an according anchor in your document. Each anchor is a new paragraph starting with two periods and whitespace followed by the anchor name. You can use letters, digits, and underscores as anchor names.

Example:

```
.. [PyCon_9] 9th Python Conference, 5-8 March 2001
```

> **Note**
> Hyperlinks are not supported by the ZpdfDocument.

Tables

Tables are created by enclosing blocks of text in double pipes (||). Each block is one cell, while rows are defined by newlines. The cells are center aligned by default. To create colspans of more than one, use the equivalent number of cell separators (||).

Example:

```
|||||| Your shopping cart ||
|| Amount || Description || Total Price ||
|| 2 || Basketball 'Jordan' || $36.70 ||
|| 1 || Basketball shoes 'Air Jordan' || $124.95 ||
```

Output: See Figure 12.1.

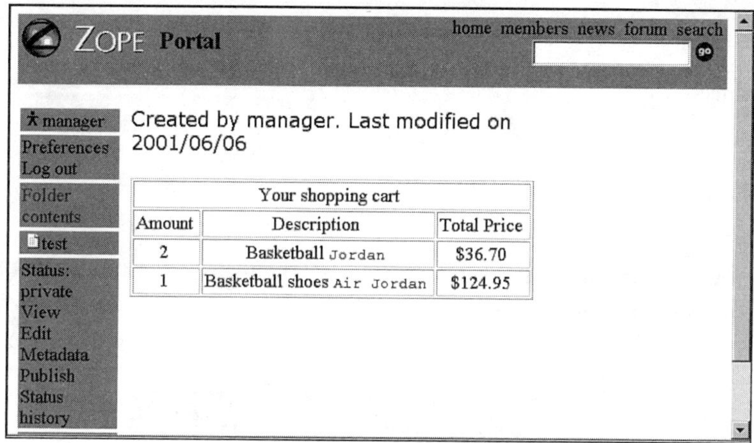

Figure 12.1
The table created by the example code.

> **Note**
> Tables are not supported by the ZpdfDocument.

Creating Dynamic Contracts

In this section, we want to create a dynamic PDF contract—the basic outline of the contract is always the same, but the information about the second person to sign the contract changes.

Of course, you can use a normal PDF file that contains the contract. But then you would either have to create a new PDF file that contains your business partner's information again and again, or you would have to leave blanks. With the ZpdfDocument, you will not need to leave blanks.

Taking data from a form where you enter your partner's information, the ZpdfDocument creates a PDF file that you can save and print.

The Entry Form

Create a new `informationForm` DTML method using the code in Listing 12.1. This code is a simple form with seven text fields and two buttons. The text fields are labeled as follows:

- Name
- First Name
- Title
- Company
- Address
- City
- Phone

and the two buttons are a Reset button to erase the form and a Generate Contract button that submits the data (see Figure 12.2).

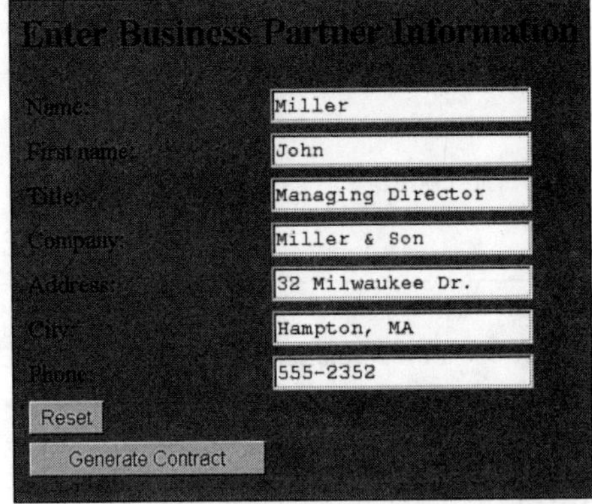

Figure 12.2
The Entry form.

The form's action is `"contract.pdf"`. This will be the ZpdfDocument that contains the contract.

Listing 12.1

informationForm *DTML Method*

```
<html>
<body bgcolor="#0099CC">
<h2>Enter Business Partner Information</h2>
<form action="contract.pdf" method=POST>
<table>
<tr>
<td>Name:</td>
<td><input type="text" name="surname" value="" maxsize=25></td>
</tr>
<tr>
<td>First name:</td>
<td><input type="text" name="first_name" value="" maxsize=25></td>
</tr>
<tr>
<td>Title:</td>
<td><input type="text" name="job" value="" maxsize=25></td>
</tr>
<tr>
<td>Company:</td>
<td><input type="text" name="company" value="" maxsize=25></td>
</tr>
<tr>
<td>Address:</td>
<td><input type="text" name="address" value="" maxsize=25></td>
</tr>
<tr>
<td>City:</td>
<td><input type="text" name="city" value="" maxsize=25></td>
</tr>
<tr>
<td>Phone:</td>
<td><input type="text" name="phone" value="" maxsize=25></td>
</tr>
<tr>
<td><input type="reset" value="Reset"></td>
</tr>
<tr>
<td><input type="submit" value="Generate Contract"></td>
</tr>
</table>
</form>
</html>
```

Now that the form is finished, we can go on to create the ZpdfDocument.

Creating the ZpdfDocument

In the folder where you have created the entry form, add a ZpdfDocument by selecting it from the drop-down menu. Use the ID `"contract.pdf"` that we just used as the form's action.

> **Note**
>
> It is not absolutely necessary to use the extension `.pdf` for a ZpdfDocument. When the ZpdfDocument is called, the browser will know what it is and will start the Adobe Acrobat plug-in. However, using this extension will make it easier to identify links of ZpdfDocuments.
>
> Internet Explorer users might also have a problem if the extension is not `.pdf`. This can be prevented by explicitly marking the content as application/octet-stream.

As previously mentioned, you can use either HTML or structured text for the ZpdfDocument. In our example, we chose to use HTML. Figure 12.3 shows an example of what the ZpdfDocument `"contract.pdf"` will look like.

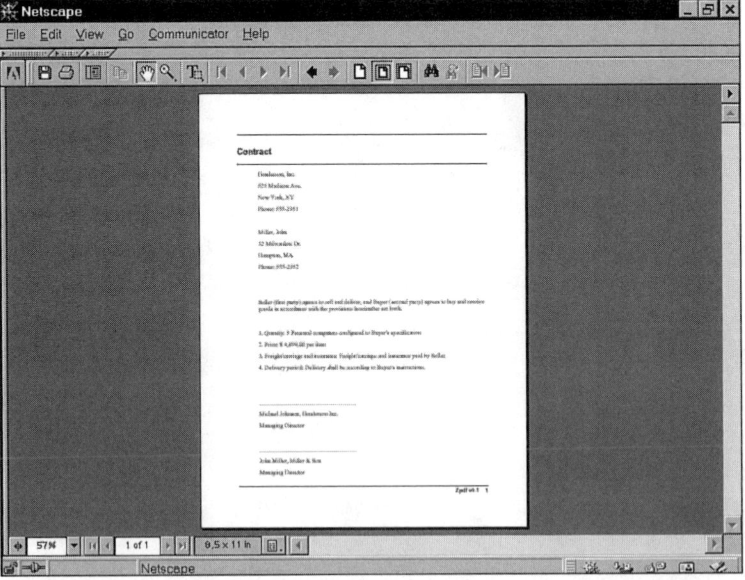

Figure 12.3
Example result of the `ZpdfDocument contract.pdf`.

At the top of the page, between two lines, is the heading Contract. Then there are the two business partners of the contract. The first one is the same for all contracts, but the second one was entered via the form. Next comes the contract body and, at the bottom, are the signature lines for and the names and titles of the two contract partners. Again, one of the signature parts is created dynamically, depending on what was entered in the form.

Listing 12.2 shows the complete code for the `contract.pdf` ZpdfDocument.

Listing 12.2

`contract.pdf` *ZpdfDocument*

```
<html>
<H1>Contract</H1>
<hr>
<p>Henderson, Inc.</p>
<p>523 Madison Ave.</p>
<p>New York, NY</p>
<p>Phone: 555-2951</p>
<p> </p>
<p><dtml-var surname>, <dtml-var first_name></p>
<p><dtml-var address></p>
<p><dtml-var city></p>
<p>Phone: <dtml-var phone></p>
<p> </p>
<p> </p>
<p>Seller (first party) agrees to sell and deliver, and Buyer
➥ (second party) agrees to buy and receive goods in accordance
➥with the provisions hereinafter set forth.</p>
<p> </p>
<p>1. Quantiy: 5 Personal computers configured to Buyer's specification</p>
<p>2. Price: $ 4,899.00 per item</p>
<p>3. Freight/carriage and insurance: Freight/carriage and insurance
➥paid by Seller.</p>
<p>4. Delivery period: Delivery shall be according to Buyer's
➥instructions.</p>
<p> </p>
<p> </p>
<p>______________________________</p>
<p>Michael Johnson, Henderson Inc.</p>
<p>Managing Director</p>
<p> </p>
<p>______________________________</p>
```

Listing 12.2
Continued

```
<p><dtml-var first_name> <dtml-var surname>, <dtml-var company></p>
<p><dtml-var tit></p>
</html>
```

Every (text) part of the ZpdfDocument is enclosed in HTML tags. If you remember, this is necessary because text that is not enclosed in tags is ignored when the ZpdfDocument is called.

Summary

As you can see, using a ZpdfDocument is a simple and a very easy way to create PDFs. However, these PDFs are only temporary. They are not actual files yet. You will need to save them to preserve the contracts. You do this by saving the page you see after you have submitted a completed form.

The ZpdfDocument's Properties

The Properties view of a ZpdfDocument contains a lot of variables needed for formatting the PDF. Figure 12.4 shows some of the properties. As you can see, you can decide, for example, which font size and family is to be used for the different headings (H1 to H6).

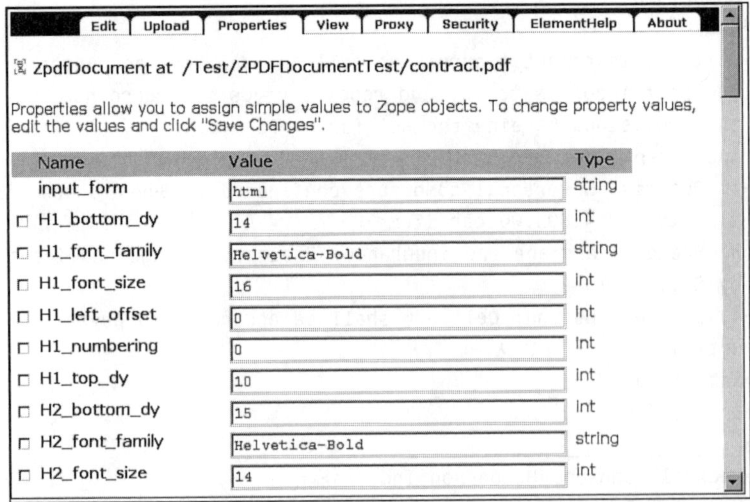

Figure 12.4
The Properties view of a ZpdfDocument.

ReportLab's PDFGEN

ReportLab's PDFGEN subpackage contains classes and methods to create PDF files in Python. They only allow basic design and layout creation but are sufficient for simple PDF pages. With the other subpackages of the ReportLab library, you can create PDF files that are much more advanced—using layers and templates. In this section, however, we only want to give you a short introduction and an example of how to use the PDFGEN subpackage.

Installation

As mentioned before, the `pdfgen` package is a sub-package of the `reportlab` library. To use it, download the `reportlab` library from `http://www.reportlab.com` and unzip the file to either the bin directory of your Zope installation (Windows) or somewhere along the path of your Python (UNIX).

Example: Generating Invoices

In this example, we will create invoices as PDF files. The data for the invoices will come from a database, and there will be a form to choose which customers will be invoiced.

Let's say that you have a database with the following customer information:

- Surname
- First name
- Address
- City
- Zip code
- Type of Contract
- Amount

Figure 12.5 shows a sample invoice.

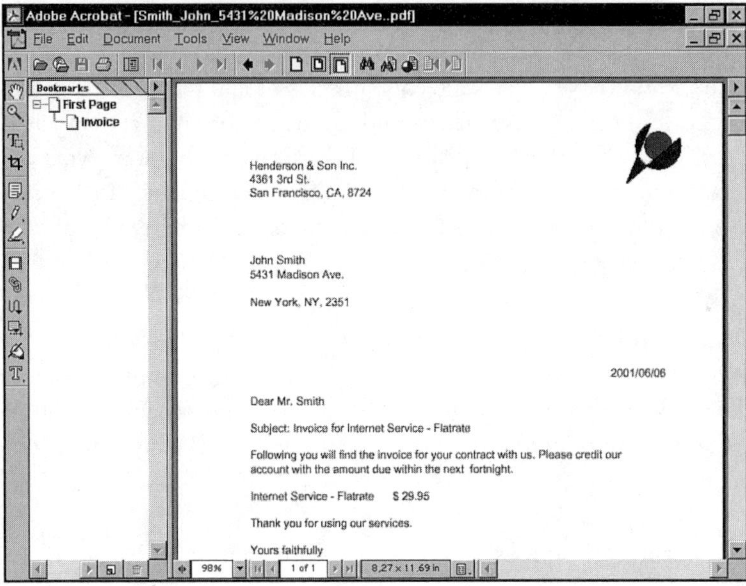
Henderson & Son Inc.
4361 3rd St.
San Francisco, CA, 8724

John Smith
5431 Madison Ave.

New York, NY, 2351

2001/06/06

Dear Mr. Smith

Subject: Invoice for Internet Service - Flatrate

Following you will find the invoice for your contract with us. Please credit our account with the amount due within the next fortnight.

Internet Service - Flatrate $ 29.95

Thank you for using our services.

Yours faithfully

Figure 12.5
Sample invoice.

First Steps

First, start the Zope server, access the Management screen, and create a `Billing` folder in the root folder. To generate the dynamic invoices, we need an established database. For this example, we use the Zope integrated database Z Gadfly. Enter the Billing folder and add a Z Gadfly Database Connection.

Create a `Customers` table with the following attributes:

- `surname`
- `first_name`
- `sex`
- `address`
- `address2`
- `city`
- `zip`
- `ctype`
- `amount`

within the Gadfly database. If you do not remember how to do this, please read Chapter 3, "Connecting Zope to External Relational Databases," again.

Figure 12.6 shows the Browse view of the our database that shows the `Customers` table.

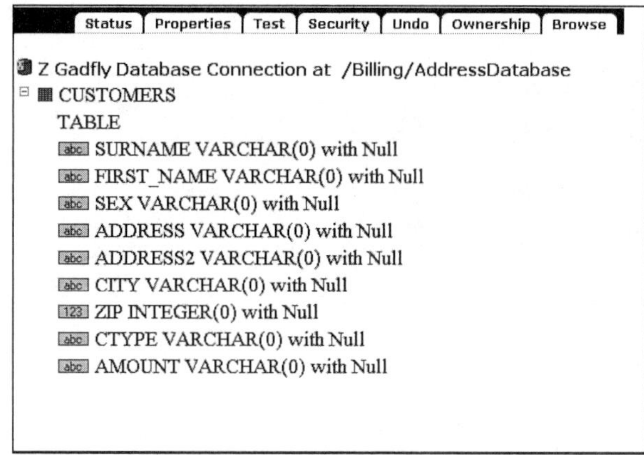

Figure 12.6

The Browse view of the database connection.

Now, enter some data, for example (see Figure 12.7).

Smith; John; m; 5431 Madison Ave.; Appt. 7; New York, NY; 2351; Internet Service—Flatrate; $29.95

Johnson; Sarah; f; 54 5th Ave.; ; Smallville, VA; 1942; Internet Service—min. 30 hrs.; $9.95

Abrahams; Mark; m; 8 Main St.; Appt. 7; Houston, TX; 7693; Internet Service—min. 10 hrs.; $9.95

The Form(s)

Now, let's create the `createInvoiceForm` DTML method that is needed to create the PDFs according to our needs. Figure 12.8 shows what this form will look like.

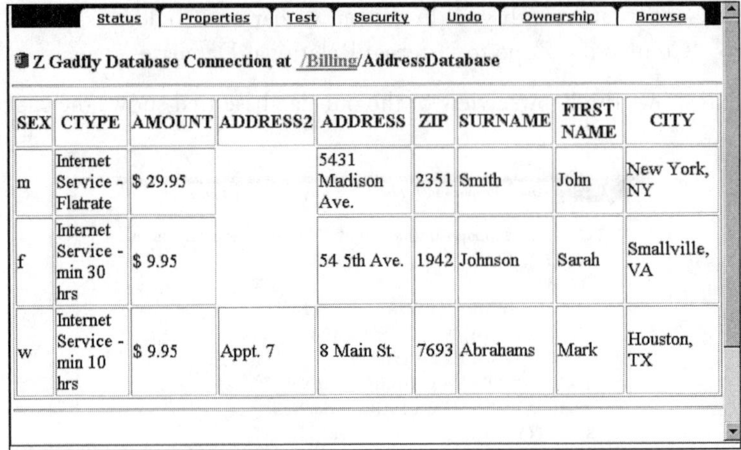
Status | Properties | Test | Security | Undo | Ownership | Browse

Z Gadfly Database Connection at /Billing/AddressDatabase

SEX	CTYPE	AMOUNT	ADDRESS2	ADDRESS	ZIP	SURNAME	FIRST NAME	CITY
m	Internet Service - Flatrate	$ 29.95		5431 Madison Ave.	2351	Smith	John	New York, NY
f	Internet Service - min 30 hrs	$ 9.95		54 5th Ave.	1942	Johnson	Sarah	Smallville, VA
w	Internet Service - min 10 hrs	$ 9.95	Appt. 7	8 Main St.	7693	Abrahams	Mark	Houston, TX

Figure 12.7

The `Customers` table.

Billing: Create Invoice(s)

Create invoice for one customer (new customer):

Name:
First Name:
Sex:
Address:
Address2:
City:
ZIP Code:
Contract Type:
Amount:
Date: 2001/06/06

Or create invoices for customers matching the following criteria:

Name =
Name =
Create invoices

Or all customers:
Create all invoices

Figure 12.8

The form to generate PDFs—`createInvoiceForm` DTML method.

As you can see, there are actually three different forms created by the DTML method.

The first form allows us to enter the name, address, and other data that is not already in the database.

> **Note**
> The data entered in the first form will not be inserted into the database. Of course, that is possible to do but, for our example, we did not program it that way.

The second form enables us to define two criteria that have to be matched. Every entry in the database that matches these criteria will be used to create the PDF invoices.

The third form allows the generating of invoices for all the entries in the database.

Create a `createInvoicesForm` DTML method in the folder where you created the database connection by using the code of Listing 12.3.

Listing 12.3

`createInvoicesForm` *DTML Method*

```
<dtml-var standard_html_header>
<h2><dtml-var title_or_id>: <dtml-var document_title></h2>

<table>
<tr>
<td valign=top>

Create invoice for one customer (new customer):<p>

<form action="createPDFInvoice" method="POST">
<table>
<tr>
<td>Name:</td>
<td><input type="text" name="surname"></td>
</tr>
<tr>
<td>First Name:</td>
<td><input type="text" name="firstname"></td>
</tr>
<tr>
<td>Sex:</td>
<td><input type="text" name="sex"></td>
</tr>
<tr>
<td>Address:</td>
<td><input type="text" name="address"></td>
</tr>
```

Listing 12.3

Continued

```
<td>Address2:</td>
<td><input type="text" name="address2"></td>
</tr>
<tr>
<td>City:</td>
<td><input type="text" name="city"></td>
</tr>
<tr>
<td>ZIP Code:</td>
<td><input type="text" name="zip"></td>
</tr>
<tr>
<td>Contract Type:</td>
<td><input type="text" name="c_type"></td>
</tr>
<tr>
<td>Amount:</td>
<td><input type="text" name="amount"></td>
</tr>
<tr>
<td>Date:</td>
<td><input type="text" name="date" value="<dtml-var "ZopeTime().Date()">"></td>
</tr>
<tr>
<td>
<input type="hidden" name="tmpTime" value="<dtml-var "ZopeTime().timeTime()">">
<input type="submit" value="Create"></td>
</tr>
</table>
</form>
</td>
<td>         
         </td>
<td valign=top>
Or create invoices for customers matching the following criteria:
<form action="doCreateInvoices" method="Post">
```

Listing 12.3

Continued

```
<table>
<tr>
<td>
<select name="attr1">
<option value="surname">Name</option>
<option value="first_name">First name</option>
<option value="sex">Sex</option>
<option value="address">Address</option>
<option value="address2">Address2</option>
<option value="city">City</option>
<option value="zip">Zip code</option>
<option value="ctype">Contract Type</option>
<option value="amount">Amount</option>
</select>
</td>
<td> = <input type="text" name="value1"></td>
</tr>
<tr>
<td>
<select name="attr2">
<option value="surname">Name</option>
<option value="first_name">First name</option>
<option value="sex">Sex</option>
<option value="address">Address</option>
<option value="address2">Address2</option>
<option value="city">City</option>
<option value="zip">Zip code</option>
<option value="ctype">Contract Type</option>
<option value="amount">Amount</option>
</select>
</td>
<td> = <input type="text" name="value2"></td>
</tr>
<tr>
<td><input type="submit" value="Create invoices"></td>
</tr>
</table>
</form>
<p> </p>
```

Listing 12.3

Continued

```
108: <p> </p>
109:
110: <form action="doCreateInvoices" method="Post">
111: <table>
112: <tr>
113: <td>Or all customers:</td>
114: </tr>
115: <tr>
116: <td><input type="submit" value="Create all invoices"></td>
117: </tr>
118: </table>
119: </form>
120:
121: </td>
122: </tr>
123: </table>
124: <dtml-var standard_html_footer>
```

The first form has the `createPDFInvoice` action, while the other two forms have the `doCreateInvoice` action. This is because the first form does not need to access the database to get data from it.

In lines 49 and 53, you see two methods of the ZopeTime module. The `Date()` method calls the current date in the form yyyy/mm/dd. The `timeTime()` method returns a `float` value that represents the current time. We will see later what those two values are used for.

The second form submits four variables: `attr1`, `value1`, `attr2`, and `value2`. `attr1` and `attr2` are select lists with the fields of the database, and `value1` and `value2` are the text fields.

The third form only consists of a button because we will not need any values for the database query.

The Z SQL Methods

Now that we have an established database and a form to enter the data for the PDFs, we can create Z SQL methods to get information from the database. For our example, we will need two Z SQL methods—one to get all data from the table and one to select only the data that matches two criteria.

Create a Z SQL method called `getAllAddresses` without any parameters or arguments and with the simplest of SELECT statements:

```
SELECT * FROM customers
```

Now create another Z SQL method called `getAddresses` with the arguments:

```
attr1 value1 attr2 value2
```

and the SQL statement:

```
select * from customers
where
((<dtml-var attr1>)='<dtml-sqlvar value1 type=string>' OR
 (<dtml-var attr2>)='<dtml-sqlvar value2 type=string>')
```

This SQL statement returns all entries of the table customers where the fields either match the first or the second value.

Calling the Z SQL Methods

The Z SQL methods are necessary for the second and the third forms of the `createInvoicesForm` DTML method. But they are not called directly from those forms. Rather, the data from the form, whichever form was chosen, is sent to another DTML method—`doCreateInvoices`. This DTML method either calls the Z SQL method `getAllAddresses` or the Z SQL method `getAddresses`, depending on which form was chosen and consequently which variables are available. The DTML method then creates some new variables and calls the Python method that actually creates the PDF files. This Python method will be called `createPDFInvoice()`. We will see this method in the next section.

Now, create the `doCreateInvoices` DTML method using the code from Listing 12.4.

Listing 12.4

`doCreateInvoices` *DTML Method*

```
<dtml-var standard_html_header>

<dtml-var try>

<dtml-call "REQUEST.set('tmpFolder', _.str(ZopeTime().timeTime()))">
<dtml-in getAllAddresses>
<dtml-var "_['sequence-index']+1">. <dtml-var "createPDFInvoice(
➥_['surname'],_['first_name'],_['sex'],_['address'],_['address2'],
➥_['city'],_['zip'],_['ctype'],_['amount'], _.str(ZopeTime().Date()),
➥_['tmpFolder'])">
```

Listing 12.4
Continued

```
 8: </dtml-in>
 9:
10: <dtml-var except>
11:
12: <dtml-call "REQUEST.set('tmpFolder', _.str(ZopeTime().timeTime()))">
13: <dtml-in getAddresses>
14: <dtml-var "_['sequence-index']+1">. <dtml-var "createPDFInvoices(
➥_['surname'],_['first_name'],_['sex'],_['address'],_['address2'],
➥_['city'],_['zip'],_['ctype'],_['amount'], _.str(ZopeTime().Date()),
➥_['tmpFolder'])">
15: </dtml-in>
16:
17: <dtml-var standard_html_footer>
```

You see a `try..except` construct with almost identical code blocks. The only difference is the Z SQL method that is called in lines 6 and 13. When this DTML method is called, it tries to call the `getAllAddresses` Z SQL method. Should this fail, it calls the `getAddresses` Z SQL method. Calling `getAllAddresses` will fail if the Create All Invoices button in the form is clicked, because this form does not provide the arguments (`attr1`, `value1`, `attr2`, `value2`) that the Z SQL method needs. Therefore, the DTML method was called by the other form where the user has to enter one or two criteria.

Apart from the `<dtml-in ...>` tag, the two code blocks are the same. The lines 5 and 12 set a new variable, `tmpFolder`, in the `REQUEST` that contains a `float` value provided by the `timeTime()` method. As previously mentioned, this method returns the current time as a `float`. This `float` value will be used later to create a unique folder where the new PDF files will be stored.

With the `<dtml-in ...>` tag, the results of the respective SQL query are iterated and, each time, the `createPDFInvoices()` method is called (lines 7 and 14). Within this call is another method that is called via `ZopeTime()`, again. This method, `Date()`, returns the current date in the form yyyy/mm/dd. This date will be put on the invoice.

The important question now is, what is this `createPDFInvoices()` method?

The `createPDFInvoices` External Method and its Python Module

The Python module/method that creates the PDF files will be an External method. Consequently, it has to be located in the Extensions directory of your Zope installation. Create a new text file in this directory called `PDFInvoices.py`. Listing 12.5 shows the complete code for the Python module.

Listing 12.5

`PDFInvoices.py` *Python Module*

```
def createPDF(surname, firstname, sex, address, address2, city, zip, c_type, amount, date, tmpTime):
        """Generating the dynamic PDF file"""

        ###   Imports   ###

        from reportlab.pdfgen import canvas
        import os
        from urllib import quote

        ###   Creating a new PDF Canvas   ###

        fname=""
        fname=surname+"_"+firstname+"_"+quote(address)+".pdf"
        c = canvas.Canvas(fname)


        ###   Standard Error Message   ###

        ErrorMessage="<html><head><title>ERROR</title></head> \
                        <body><h2>Error</h2> \
                        <p>There was an error while creating the file "+fname+".<p> \
                        <p> </p> \
                        <p>Possible reason:</p> \
                        <ul><li>File already exists</li> \
                        </ul> \
                         <p>Troubleshooting suggestions:</p> \
                        <ul><li>Choose a different name.</li> \
                        </ul> \
                        </body></html>"


        ###   Standard Success Message   ###

        SuccessMessage="<html><head><title>File created</title> \
                <body><h2>Success</h2> \
                <p>The PDF-File "+fname+" was created successfully.</p> \
                </body></html>"


```

Listing 12.5

Continued

```
    ###   Defining the PDF's Settings   ###

    c.bookmarkPage("fst_pge")
    c.bookmarkPage("invoice")
    c.addOutlineEntry("First Page", "fst_pge")
    c.addOutlineEntry("Invoice", "invoice", 1)
    c.showOutline()
    c.setAuthor("Michael Henderson")


    ###   Writing the From Address   ###

    from_address=c.beginText(80,750)
    from_address.textLine("Henderson & Son Inc.")
    from_address.textLine("4361 3rd St.")
    from_address.textLine("San Francisco, CA, 8724")
    c.drawText(from_address)


    ###   Writing the To Address   ###

    to_name=firstname+" "+surname
    to_city_zip=city+", "+zip
    c.drawString(80,650, to_name)
    c.drawString(80,635, address)
    c.drawString(80,620, address2)
    c.drawString(80,605, to_city_zip)

    ###   Writing the Date (right-aligned)   ###

    c.drawCentredString(500,530, date)


    ###   Writing the Body of the Letter   ###

    contents=c.beginText(80,500)
    greeting=""
    if sex=="m":
       greeting="Dear Mr. "+surname
```

Listing 12.5

Continued

```
    else:
        greeting="Dear Mrs. "+surname
    con1="Subject: Invoice for "+c_type
    con2="Following you will find the invoice for your contract
➥ with us. Please credit our "
    con3="account with the amount due within the next  fortnight."
    inv=c_type+"       "+amount
    con4="Thank you for using our services."
    signature1="Yours faithfully"
    signature2="John Camden"
    signature3="Henderson, Inc."
    contents.textLine(greeting)
    contents.textLine('')
    contents.textLine(con1)
    contents.textLine('')
    contents.textLine(con2)
    contents.textLine(con3)
    contents.textLine('')
    contents.textLine(inv)
    contents.textLine('')
    contents.textLine(con4)
    contents.textLine('')
    contents.textLine(signature1)
    contents.textLine('')
    contents.textLine('')
    contents.textLine('')
    contents.textLine(signature2)
    contents.textOut(signature3)
    c.drawText(contents)


    ###   Graphic   ###

    ###### Inner Circle ######
    c.setFillColorRGB(255,0,0)
    c.circle(525,775,15, fill=1)

    ###### Blue Graphic ######
    c.setFillColorRGB(0,0,255)
    pathobj=c.beginPath()
```

Listing 12.5
Continued

```
        pathobj.arc(500, 800, 550, 750, 110, 270)
        pathobj.lineTo(490,735)
        pathobj.close()
        c.drawPath(pathobj, fill=1)
        c.setFillColorRGB(0,0,0)



        c.showPage()
        c.save()
        tmpFolder="PDFFiles\\tmp"+tmpTime+"\\"
        newplace=tmpFolder+fname
        try:
            os.mkdir(tmpFolder)
            os.rename(fname, newplace)
        except:
            try:
                os.rename(fname, newplace)
            except:
                return ErrorMessage

        return SuccessMessage
```

For you to be able to use this Python module and its method, you need to create an External Method object in Zope. Go to the Billing folder and add an External method with the following data:

ID:	**createPDFInvoice**
Title:	
Module name:	**PDFInvoices**
Function name:	**createPDF**

Now, we have a link between Zope and the Python module. Let's go through this module step-by-step and see how a PDF file is created.

You already know what arguments the Python method needs, because you have seen it called in the `doCreateInvoices` DTML method. There, it has eleven arguments that we need to define for this method:

```
1:   def createPDF(surname, firstname, sex, address, address2, city, zip,
➥c_type, amount, date, tmpTime):
2:           """Generating the dynamic PDF file"""
```

After the method declaration, we have to import some modules, classes, and methods.

```
4:       ###    Imports    ###
5:
6:       from reportlab.pdfgen import canvas
7:       import os
8:       from urllib import quote
```

First, we need the canvas class (line 6). This will represent the page of our PDF file. It is part of the pdfgen subpackage and needs to be called via reportlab. Then we need the os module to create new directories and to move files on the file system. The last import (line 8) is needed for creating the PDF filename. To make a filename unique within a folder, we use the surname, the first_name, and the address variable and put them together (line 13). Because the first_name and address variables might contain spaces, we use the quote method from the urllib module to replace all spaces with %20.

In line 14, we create a new Canvas object with the name we just created.

```
10:      ###    Creating a new PDF Canvas    ###
11:
12:      fname=""
13:      fname=surname+"_"+quote(firstname)+"_"+quote(address)+".pdf"
14:      c = canvas.Canvas(fname)
```

Lines 19–34 define an error and a success message. One of the messages will be returned at the end of the method. The messages are strings that contain HTML tags and normal text. When returned, the browser will show this string as an HTML page.

In lines 21 and 36, you see that both messages are created dynamically. Each time, the filename is entered in the string so that the user will know which files were successfully created and which caused problems.

```
17:      ###    Standard Error Message    ###
18:
19:      ErrorMessage="<html><head><title>ERROR</title></head> \
20:               <body><h2>Error</h2> \
21:               <p>There was an error while creating the file "+
➥fname+".<p> \
22:               <p> </p> \
23:               <p>Possible reason:</p> \
```

```
                  <ul><li>File already exists</li> \
                  </ul> \
                  <p>Troubleshooting suggestions:</p> \
                  <ul><li>Choose a different name.</li> \
                  </ul> \
                  </body></html>"


        ###   Standard Success Message   ###

        SuccessMessage="<html><head><title>File created</title> \
                     <body><h2>Success</h2> \
                     <p>The PDF-File "+fname+" was created successfully.</p> \
                     </body></html>"
```

Next, we define some settings for the PDF file. The settings here are two bookmarks and the author. Moreover, we call the `showOutline()` method that defines that the bookmarks frame is visible in the Acrobat Reader when the PDF file is opened.

Bookmarks are set using the `bookmarkPage(bkmk_name)` or `bookmarkHorizontalAbsolute(bkmk_name, horizontal_y)` methods. The former marks the whole page, and the latter marks a defined horizontal position on the page.

> **Note**
> The canvas' origin is in the lower-left corner. The x coordinate goes to the right, and the y coordinate goes up.

Setting the bookmarks will not automatically make them visible in the bookmark frame of the Acrobat Reader. To create the bookmark frame, you use the `addOutlineEntry(title, bkmk_name, level)` method. The title of the outline entry will be visible. The level always refers to the level of the outline entry define last, and must only differ from that level by 1. In our example, the outline will look like the following:

```
- First Page
| - Invoice
```

The author is set using the `setAuthor(author_name)` method. The name will appear in the document's general info.

```
42:        ###    Defining the PDF's Settings    ###
43:
44:        c.bookmarkPage("fst_pge")
45:        c.bookmarkHorizontalAbsolute("invoice", 400)
46:        c.addOutlineEntry("First Page", "fst_pge")
47:        c.addOutlineEntry("Invoice", "invoice", 1)
48:        c.showOutline()
49:        c.setAuthor("Michael Henderson")
```

Now we create the address of the addresser. This should be placed at the top of the page. To write this address, we use a text object. It is initialized in line 54 by the beginTcxt(x, y) method. With this method, you also state where on the page the object is to be placed. Now that we have a text object called from_address, we can enter text using the textLine(txt) method. textLine(txt) writes the text txt and sets the cursor in the next line. After all the text is created, the text object has to be put on the page. This is done with the drawText(txt_obj) method. drawText(txt_obj) has to be called on the canvas (in our case, c) because that is where the object should be placed, and its argument is the text object we created (here, from_address).

```
52:        ###    Writing the From Address    ###
53:
54:        from_address=c.beginText(80,750)
55:        from_address.textLine("Henderson & Son Inc.")
56:        from_address.textLine("4361 3rd St.")
57:        from_address.textLine("San Francisco, CA, 8724")
58:        c.drawText(from_address)
```

With the addressee's address, we use a different way of writing text on the page. If you only have small text parts, you can use the `drawString(x,y, txt)` method to write directly on the canvas. Here, we first create the `to_name` string from the `firstname` and `surname` variables and the `to_city` string from the `city` and `zip` variables. Then the address lines are written on the page.

```
61:        ###    Writing the To Address    ###
62:
63:        to_name=firstname+" "+surname
64:        to_city_zip=city+", "+zip
65:        c.drawString(80,650, to_name)
66:        c.drawString(80,635, address)
67:        c.drawString(80,620, address2)
68:        c.drawString(80,605, to_city_zip)
```

The `drawCentredString(x,y,txt)` method writes a right-aligned string on the page according to the x and y coordinates. Here, we use this method to write the current date to the page.

```
70:        ###   Writing the Date (right-aligned)   ###
71:
72:        c.drawCentredString(500,530, date)
```

Now we write the body of the letter. Again we use a text object. This time it is called `contents`. In lines 79–82, you see that the greeting is created depending on whether the addressee is male or female.

```
75:        ###   Writing the Body of the Letter   ###
76:
77:        contents=c.beginText(80,500)
78:        greeting=""
79:        if sex=="m":
80:             greeting="Dear Mr. "+surname
81:        else:
82:             greeting="Dear Mrs. "+surname
83:        con1="Subject: Invoice for "+c_type
84:        con2="Following you will find the invoice for your contract
➥ with us. Please credit our "
85:        con3="account with the amount due within the next  fortnight."
86:        inv=c_type+"       "+amount
87:        con4="Thank you for using our services."
88:        signature1="Yours faithfully"
89:        signature2="John Camden"
90:        signature3="Henderson, Inc."
91:        contents.textLine(greeting)
92:        contents.textLine('')
93:        contents.textLine(con1)
94:        contents.textLine('')
95:        contents.textLine(con2)
96:        contents.textLine(con3)
97:        contents.textLine('')
98:        contents.textLine(inv)
99:        contents.textLine('')
100:       contents.textLine(con4)
101:       contents.textLine('')
102:       contents.textLine(signature1)
103:       contents.textLine('')
104:       contents.textLine('')
105:       contents.textLine('')
```

```
106:        contents.textLine(signature2)
107:        contents.textOut(signature3)
108:        c.drawText(contents)
```

Next we create the company logo. Some of the logo will be drawn directly on the page and some will be created using a path object.

First we set the color that is to be used for filling figures. We use the `setFillColorRGB(r, g, b)` method and set the color to red (`255,0,0`). Then we draw a circle, at the coordinates x=525 and y=778, which has a radius of 15 pixel and is filled (`fill=1`). The first part of the logo is finished.

For the second part, we want a different fill color—this time blue (`0,0,255`). To draw the blue part of the logo, we create a path object (line 119) using the `beginPath()` method. In line 120, we draw an arc that is placed in the rectangle between the coordinates x1=500, y1=800, x2=550 and y2=750. The arc is started at 110 degrees and goes on for 270 degrees. You can draw circles with the `arc(x1,y1,x2,y2,start,d)` method when you use a degree of 360. Note that the arc's 0 degree is on the right and that it is drawn counter-clockwise.

The next line causes the path to draw a line to the coordinates x=490 and y=735. The line starts where the arc ended. Then we close the path (we return to where it began).

In line 123, we put the path on the canvas and fill it with the currently set color (here, blue, which we set in line 122) using the `drawPath(path_obj)` method.

```
111:        ###    Graphic    ###
112:
113:        ###### Inner Circle ######
114:        c.setFillColorRGB(255,0,0)
115:        c.circle(525,775,15, fill=1)
116:
117:        ###### Blue Graphic ######
118:        c.setFillColorRGB(0,0,255)
119:        pathobj=c.beginPath()
120:        pathobj.arc(500, 800, 550, 750, 110, 270)
121:        pathobj.lineTo(490,735)
122:        pathobj.close()
123:        c.drawPath(pathobj, fill=1)
124:        c.setFillColorRGB(0,0,0)
```

With the `showPage()` method (line 128), we close the current page. Anything we draw on the canvas now is put on the next page. This way, you can create multipage PDF files. With `save()`, we save the file and close it. After this command, the canvas must not be used again.

```
    c.showPage()
    c.save()
```

With the save command, the PDF file is saved in your Zope directory. To move it somewhere else, we try to create a PDFFiles folder, and within this folder we create another folder whose name is created by the variable `tmpTime`. Remember, this variable contains the time at the moment the `doCreateInvoices` DTML method was called. It is a `float` number. This way, every time invoices are created, they are stored in a different folder and the older versions cannot cause problems.

In the `try` clause, we try to create the folder where the PDFs are to be stored (for example, `PDFFiles\tmp991659827.22\`), and then we try to move the PDF file from the Zope directory to this new folder. Should this fail for any reason, the `except` clause is executed. If moving the PDF file fails here, the user gets the error message that we defined at the beginning of the method. If everything worked, the user receives the success message.

```
    tmpFolder="PDFFiles\\tmp"+tmpTime+"\\"
    newplace=tmpFolder+fname
    try:
        os.mkdir(tmpFolder)
        os.rename(fname, newplace)
    except:
        try:
            os.rename(fname, newplace)
        except:
            return ErrorMessage

    return SuccessMessage
```

The `reportlab.pdfgen` Subpackage

The `reportlab.pdfgen` subpackage consists mainly of three modules/classes:

- `Canvas.py`
- `Textobject.py`
- `Pathobject.py`

We have used some of the methods within these modules before in this chapter.

The following method explanations were taken from the ReportLab API Reference that can be downloaded from `http://www.reportlab.com/download.html`. We thank ReportLab, Inc. for letting us use their documentation.

The Canvas Class

```
def addFont(self, fontObj):
```

Adds a new font for subsequent use.

```
def addLiteral(self, s, escaped=1):
```

Introduces the literal text of PDF operations into the current stream. Only use this if you are an expert in the PDF file format.

```
def addOutlineEntry(self, title, key, level=0, closed=None):
```

Adds a new entry to the outline at given level. If `level` not specified, entry goes at the top level. If `level` is specified, it must be no more than 1 greater than the outline level in the last call. The key must be the (unique) name of a bookmark. The title is the (non-unique) name to be displayed for the entry. If `closed` is set, the entry should show no subsections by default when displayed.

Note that you can jump from level 5 to level 3, but not from 3 to 5; instead, you need to provide all intervening levels going down (4 in this case). Note that titles can collide but keys cannot.

```
def arc(self, x1,y1, x2,y2, startAng=0, extent=90):
```

Draws a partial ellipse inscribed within the rectangle `x1,y1,x2,y2` starting at `startAng` degrees and covering `extent` degrees. Angles start with 0 to the right (`+x`) and increase counter-clockwise. These should have `x1<x2` and `y1<y2`. Contributed to `piddlePDF` by Robert Kern, 28/7/99. Trimmed down by AR to remove color stuff for `pdfgen.canvas` and revert to positive coordinates. The algorithm is an elliptical generalization of the formula in Jim Fitzsimmon's TeX tutorial at `http://www.tinaja.com/bezarc1.pdf`.

```
def beginForm(self, name, lowerx=0, lowery=0, upperx=None, uppery=None):
```

Declares the current graphics stream to be a named form. A graphics stream can either be a page or a form, not both. Some operations (like bookmarking) are permitted for pages but not forms. The form will not automatically be shown in the document but must be explicitly referenced using `doForm` in pages that require the form.

```
def beginPath(self):
```

Returns a fresh path object. Paths are used to draw complex figures. The object returned follows the protocol for a `pathobject.PDFPathObject` instance.

```
def beginText(self, x=0, y=0):
```

Returns a fresh text object. Text objects are used to add large amounts of text (see `textobject.PDFTextObject`).

```
def bezier(self, x1, y1, x2, y2, x3, y3, x4, y4):
```

Bezier curve with the four given control points.

```
def bookmarkHorizontalAbsolute(self, key, yhorizontal):
```

Binds a bookmark (destination) to the current page at a horizontal position. Note that the `yhorizontal` of the bookmark is with respect to the default user space (where the origin is at the lower-left corner of the page) and completely ignores any transform (translation, scale, skew, rotation, and so on) in effect for the current graphics state. The programmer is responsible for making sure the bookmark matches an appropriate item on the page.

```
def bookmarkPage(self, key):
```

Binds a bookmark (destination) to the current page.

```
def circle(self, x_cen, y_cen, r, stroke=1, fill=0):
```

Draws a circle centered at (`x_cen,y_cen`) with radius `r` (special case of ellipse).

```
def clipPath(self, aPath, stroke=1, fill=0):
```

Clips as well as draws.

```
def doForm(self, name):
```

Uses a form XObj in current operation stream. The form should have been defined previously using `beginForm...endForm`. The form will be drawn within the context of the current graphics state.

```
def drawCentredString(self, x, y, text):
```

Draws a string centered on the `x` coordinate.

```
def drawInlineImage(self, image, x,y, width=None,height=None):
```

Draws an image into the specified rectangle. If width and height are omitted, they are calculated from the image size. Also allows filenames as well as images. This allows a caching mechanism.

```
def drawPath(self, aPath, stroke=1, fill=0):
```

Draws the path object in the mode indicated.

```
def drawRightString(self, x, y, text):
```

Draws a string right-aligned with the `x` coordinate.

```
def drawString(self, x, y, text):
```

Draws a string in the current text styles.

```
def drawText(self, aTextObject):
```

Draws a text object.

```
def ellipse(self, x1, y1, x2, y2, stroke=1, fill=0):
```

Draws an ellipse defined by an enclosing rectangle. Note that `(x1,y1)` and `(x2,y2)` are the corner points of the enclosing rectangle. Uses `bezierArc`, which conveniently handles 360 degrees. Special thanks to Robert Kern.

```
def endForm(self):
```

Emits the current collection of graphics operations as a Form as declared previously in `beginForm`.

```
def getAvailableFonts(self):
```

Returns the list of PostScript font names available. Standard set now, but might grow in future with font embedding.

```
def getPageNumber(self):
```

Gets the page number for the current page being generated.

```
def grid(self, xlist, ylist):
```

Lays out a grid in current line style. Supply list of `x` and `y` positions.

```
def line(self, x1,y1, x2,y2):
```

Draws a line segment from `(x1,y1)` to `(x2,y2)` (with color, thickness and other attributes determined by the current graphics state).

```
def lines(self, linelist):
```

Like `line()`, permits many lines to be drawn in one call. For example, for the following figure

```
 |

-- --

 |
```

```
crosshairs = [(20,0,20,10), (20,30,20,40), (0,20,10,20), (30,20,40,20)]
canvas.lines(crosshairs)
```

```
def linkAbsolute(self, contents, destinationname, Rect=None, addtopage=1,
name=None, **kw):
```

Rectangular link annotation positioned w.r.t., the default user space. The identified rectangle on the page becomes a "hot link" that, when clicked, will send the viewer to the page and position identified by the destination.

`Rect` identifies (`lowerx`, `lowery`, `upperx`, `uppery`) for lower-left and upper-right points of the rectangle. Translations and other transforms are IGNORED (the rectangular position is given with respect to the default user space).

`destinationname` should be the name of a bookmark (which might be defined later but must be defined before the document is generated).

You might want to use the keyword `argument Border='[0 0 0]'` to suppress the visible rectangle during the viewing link.

```
def linkRect(self, contents, destinationname, Rect=None, addtopage=1,
name=None, **kw):
```

Rectangular link annotation w.r.t the current user transform.

If the transform is skewed/rotated, the absolute rectangle will use the max/min x/y.

```
def pageHasData(self):
```

Information function—an application can call it after `showPage` to see if it needs a save.

```
def rect(self, x, y, width, height, stroke=1, fill=0):
```

Draws a rectangle with lower-left corner at `(x,y)` and width and height as given.

```
def resetTransforms(self):
```

I want to draw something (for example, string underlines) w.r.t. the default user space.

Reset the matrix! This should be used usually as follows:

```
canv.saveState()
canv.resetTransforms()
...draw some stuff in default space coords...
canv.restoreState() # go back!
```

```
def restoreState(self):
```

Restores the graphics state to the matching saved state (see `saveState`).

```
def rotate(self, theta):
```

```
Example: Canvas.rotate(theta)
```

Rotates the canvas by the angle theta (in degrees).

```
def roundRect(self, x, y, width, height, radius, stroke=1, fill=0):
```

Draws a rectangle with rounded corners. The corners are approximately quadrants of a circle with the given radius.

```
def save(self):
```

Saves and close the PDF document in the file. If there is current data a `ShowPage` is executed automatically. After this operation, the canvas must not be used further.

```
def saveState(self):
```

Saves the current graphics state to be restored later by `restoreState`.

For example:

```
canvas.setFont("Helvetica", 20)
canvas.saveState()
...
canvas.setFont("Courier", 9)
...
canvas.restoreState()
# if the save/restore pairs match then font is Helvetica 20 again.
```

```
def scale(self, x, y):
```

Scales the horizontal dimension by x and the vertical by y (with respect to the current graphics state).

For example, `canvas.scale(2.0, 0.5)` will make everything short and fat.

```
def setAuthor(self, author):
```

Identifies the author for invisible embedding inside the PDF document. The author annotation will appear in the text of the file but will not automatically be seen when the document is viewed.

```
def setDash(self, array=[], phase=0):
```

Two notations—pass two numbers or an array and phase.

```
def setFillColor(self, aColor):
```

Takes a color object, allowing colors to be referred to by name.

```
def setFillColorCMYK(self, c, m, y, k):
```

Sets the fill color using negative color values (cyan, magenta, yellow, and darkness value). Takes four arguments between 0.0 and 1.0.

```
def setFillColorRGB(self, r, g, b):
```

Sets the fill color using positive color description (Red, Green, Blue). Takes three arguments between 0.0 and 1.0.

```
def setFillGray(self, gray):
```

Sets the gray level; 0.0=black, 1.0=white

```
def setFont(self, psfontname, size, leading = None):
```

Sets the font. If leading is not specified, defaults to 1.2 x font size. Raises a readable exception if an illegal font is supplied. Font names are case-sensitive! Keeps track of font name and size for metrics.

```
def setLineCap(self, mode):
```

0=butt,1=round,2=square.

```
def setLineJoin(self, mode):
```

0=mitre, 1=round, 2=bevel.

```
def setLineWidth(self, width):
```

(no documentation string)

```
def setMiterLimit(self, limit):
```

(no documentation string)

```
def setPageCompression(self, pageCompression=1):
```

Possible values None, 1, or 0. If None, the value from `rl_config` will be used. If 1, the page data will be compressed, leading to much smaller files, but it takes a little longer to create the files.

This applies to all subsequent pages, or until `setPageCompression()` is next called.

```
def setPageSize(self, size):
```

Accepts a 2-tuple in points for paper size for this and subsequent pages.

```
def setPageTransition(self, effectname=None, duration=1,
direction=0,dimension='H',motion='I'):
```

PDF allows page transition effects for use when giving presentations. There are six possible effects. You can just give the effect name or supply more advanced options to refine the way it works. There are three types of extra argument permitted, and the allowed values are as follows:

```
direction_arg = [0,90,180,270]
dimension_arg = ['H', 'V']
```

```
motion_arg = ['I','O'] (start at inside or outside)
```

The following states which ones take which arguments:

```
PageTransitionEffects = {
    'Split': [direction_arg, motion_arg],
    'Blinds': [dimension_arg],
    'Box': [motion_arg],
    'Wipe' : [direction_arg],
    'Dissolve' : [],
    'Glitter':[direction_arg]
}
```

```
def setStrokeColor(self, aColor):
```

Takes a color object, allowing colors to be referred to by name.

```
def setStrokeColorCMYK(self, c, m, y, k):
```

Sets the stroke color using negative color values (cyan, magenta, yellow, and darkness value). Takes four arguments between 0.0 and 1.0.

```
def setStrokeColorRGB(self, r, g, b):
```

Sets the stroke color using positive color description (Red, Green, Blue). Takes three arguments between 0.0 and 1.0.

```
def setStrokeGray(self, gray):
```

Sets the gray level; 0.0=black, 1.0=white.

```
def setSubject(self, subject):
```

Writes a subject into the PDF file that won't automatically display in the document itself.

```
def setTitle(self, title):
```

Writes a title into the PDF file that won't automatically display in the document itself.

```
def showOutline(self):
```

Specifies that Acrobat Reader should start with the outline tree visible. `showFullScreen()` and `showOutline()` conflict; the one called last wins.

```
def showPage(self):
```

Closes the current page and possibly starts on a new page.

```
def skew(self, alpha, beta):
```

(no documentation string)

```
def stringWidth(self, text, fontName, fontSize, encoding=None):
```

Gets width of a string in the given font and size.

```
def transform(self, a,b,c,d,e,f):
```

Adjoins a mathematical transform to the current graphics state matrix.

Not recommended for beginners.

```
def translate(self, dx, dy):
```

Moves the origin from the current `(0,0)` point to the `(dx,dy)` point (with respect to the current graphics state).

```
def wedge(self, x1,y1, x2,y2, startAng, extent, stroke=1, fill=0):
```

Like `arc`, but connects to the center of the ellipse. Most useful for pie charts and PacMan!

The `PDFTextObject` Class

```
def getCode(self):
```

Packs on one line; used internally.

```
def getCursor(self):
```

Returns current text position relative to the last origin.

```
def getX(self):
```

Returns current `x` position relative to the last origin.

```
def getY(self):
```

Returns current `y` position relative to the last origin.

```
def moveCursor(self, dx, dy):
```

Moves to a point `dx, dy` away from the start of the current line—*not* from the current point! If you call it in mid-sentence, watch out.

```
def setCharSpace(self, charSpace):
```

Adjusts inter-character spacing.

```
def setFillColor(self, aColor):
```

Takes a color object, allowing colors to be referred to by name.

```
def setFillColorCMYK(self, c, m, y, k):
```

Takes four arguments between 0.0 and 1.0.

```
def setFillColorRGB(self, r, g, b):
```

(no documentation string)

```
def setFillGray(self, gray):
```

Sets the gray level; 0.0=black, 1.0=white.

```
def setFont(self, psfontname, size, leading = None):
```

Sets the font. If leading is not specified, defaults to 1.2 x font size. Raises a readable exception if an illegal font is supplied. Font names are case-sensitive! Keeps track of font name and size for metrics.

```
def setHorizScale(self, horizScale):
```

Stretches text out horizontally.

```
def setLeading(self, leading):
```

States how far to move down at the end of a line.

```
def setRise(self, rise):
```

Moves text baseline up or down to allow superscripts/subscripts.

```
def setStrokeColor(self, aColor):
```

Takes a color object, allowing colors to be referred to by name.

```
def setStrokeColorCMYK(self, c, m, y, k):
```

Takes four arguments between 0.0 and 1.0

```
def setStrokeColorRGB(self, r, g, b):
```

(no documentation string)

```
def setStrokeGray(self, gray):
```

Sets the gray level; 0.0=black, 1.0=white

```
def setTextOrigin(self, x, y):
```

(no documentation string)

```
def setTextRenderMode(self, mode):
```

Sets the text rendering mode.

0 = Fill text

1 = Stroke text

2 = Fill then stroke

3 = Invisible

4 = Fill text and add to clipping path

5 = Stroke text and add to clipping path

6 = Fill then stroke and add to clipping path

7 = Add to clipping path

```
def setTextTransform(self, a, b, c, d, e, f):
```

Like `setTextOrigin`, but does rotation, scaling, and so on.

```
def setWordSpace(self, wordSpace):
```

Adjusts inter-word spacing. This can be used to flush-justify text—you get the width of the words, and add some space between them.

```
def setXPos(self, dx):
```

Moves to a point `dx` away from the start of the current line—*not* from the current point! If you call it in mid-sentence, watch out.

```
def textLine(self, text=''):
```

Prints string at current point, text cursor moves down. Can work with no argument to simply move the cursor down.

```
def textLines(self, stuff, trim=1):
```

Prints multi-line or newlined strings, moving down. One common use is to quote a multi-line block in your Python code; because this might be indented, it trims whitespace off each line and from the beginning by default; set trim=0 to preserve whitespace.

```
def textOut(self, text):
```

Prints string at current point, text cursor moves across.

The `PDFPathobject` Class

```
def arc(self, x1,y1, x2,y2, startAng=0, extent=90):
```

Contributed to `piddlePDF` by Robert Kern, 28/7/99. Draws a partial ellipse inscribed within the rectangle `x1,y1,x2,y2`, starting at `startAng` degrees and covering extent degrees. Angles start with 0 to the right (+x) and increase counter-clockwise. These should have `x1<x2` and `y1<y2`.

The algorithm is an elliptical generalization of the formulae in Jim Fitzsimmon's TeX tutorial at `http://www.tinaja.com/bezarc1.pdf`.

```
def arcTo(self, x1,y1, x2,y2, startAng=0, extent=90):
```

Like `arc`, but draws a line from the current point to the start, if the start is not the current point.

```
def circle(self, x_cen, y_cen, r):
```

Adds a circle to the path.

```
def close(self):
```

Draws a line back to where it started.

```
def curveTo(self, x1, y1, x2, y2, x3, y3):
```

(no documentation string)

```
def ellipse(self, x, y, width, height):
```

Adds an ellipse to the path.

```
def getCode(self):
```

Packs to one line; used internally.

```
def lineTo(self, x, y):
```

(no documentation string)

```
def moveTo(self, x, y):
```

(no documentation string)

```
def rect(self, x, y, width, height):
```

Adds a rectangle to the path.

Summary

In this chapter, you learned about two ways to create PDF files in Zope—the ZpdfDocument and the ReportLabs's subpackage PDFGEN. The former is a normal Zope product and needs no special programming knowledge, while for the latter you need to program in Python.

Zope has a vast community, which accounts for new products being developed every day. Consequently, we could only scratch the surface of what is possible with Zope. We hope that this book helped you develop your own Web application and that we have inspired you to continue to look into the different possibilities of Zope.

INDEX

SYMBOLS

A

B

D

I

J - K - L

M

N

O

Q - R

S

T

U

V

W - X

Z

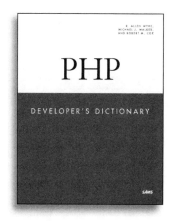

The book's companion CD-ROM contains all the project files used in the book; Zope for Linux, Solaris, and Windows; the Content Management Framework; and MetaPublisher 1.24.

Installation Instructions

Windows

1. Insert the disc into your CD-ROM drive.
2. From the Windows desktop, double-click the My Computer icon.
3. Double-click the icon representing your CD-ROM drive.
4. Double-click `start.html`. All the CD-ROM files can be accessed by the HTML interface.

Linux/Unix

These installation instructions assume that you have a passing familiarity with Unix commands and the basic setup of your machine. As Unix has many flavors, only generic commands are used. If you have any problems with the commands, please consult the appropriate manual page or your system administrator.

Insert the disc into your CD-ROM drive.

If you have a volume manager, mounting of the CD-ROM will be automatic. If you don't have a volume manager, you can mount the CD-ROM by typing

```
mount -tiso9660 /dev/cdrom /mnt/cdrom.
```

NOTE: `/mnt/cdrom` is just a mount point, but it must exist when you issue the mount command. You may also use any empty directory for a mount point if you don't want to use `/mnt/cdrom`.

Open the `start.html` file. All the CD-ROM files can be accessed by the HTML interface.